MAD DOGS, MIDGETS AND SCREW JOBS

MAD DOGS, MIDGETS AND SCREW JOBS

THE UNTOLD STORY OF HOW MONTREAL SHAPED THE WORLD OF WRESTLING

PAT LAPRADE AND BERTRAND HÉBERT

ECW PRESS

Published by ECW Press
2120 Queen Street East, Suite 200, Toronto, Ontario, Canada M4E 1E2
416-694-3348 / info@ecwpress.com

Library and Archives Canada Cataloguing in Publication

Laprade, Pat
Mad dogs, midgets and screw jobs : the untold story
of how Montreal shaped the world of wrestling / Pat Laprade
and Bertrand Hébert.

ISBN 978-1-77041-094-7
ALSO ISSUED AS: 978-1-77090-295-4 (PDF); 978-1-77090-296-1 (ePUB)

1. Wrestling—Québec (Province)—Montréal—History.
2. Wrestlers—Québec (Province)—Montréal—History.
3. Television broadcasting of sports—Québec (Province)—
Montréal—History. I. Hébert, Bertrand, 1971– II. Title.

GV1198.15.Q8L36 2012   796.81209714'27   C2012-902745-6

Editor for the press: Michael Holmes
Translator: Hajer Trabelsi
Image correction: Yan O'Cain
Cover design: Mathew den Boer
Cover images: Mike Lano (Bret Hart), Tony Lanza (Little Beaver), *Wrestling Revue* archives (Mad Dog Vachon)
Back cover image: Bertrand Hébert Collection (Vince McMahon, Jacques Rougeau Jr. and his eldest sons, 1994)
Photo section images: Bertrand Hébert Collection (1, 3 bottom L, 7 bottom, 13), Linda Boucher (2 top, 3 top L, 6 bottom L, 8, 9, 10, 11 bottom, 12 top R, 12 bottom R, 14 top, 16), Paul Leduc Collection (2 bottom, 3 top R, 6 bottom R, 15 bottom), Chris Swisher Collection (3 bottom R, 4), Greg Oliver Collection (5 top), Stéphane Venne Collection (5 bottom L), George Napolitano (5 bottom R), Paul Vachon Collection (6 top), Vanessa Guénette (7 top), Scott Teal Collection (7 center, 12 bottom L), Mike Mastrandea (7 R), JF Leduc (11 top), Carl Ouellet Collection (12 top L), Raymond Rougeau Collection (14 bottom), Gilda Pasquil (15 top)
Printing: United Graphics 5 4 3 2

The publication of *Mad Dogs, Midgets and Screw Jobs* has been generously supported by the Government of Canada through the Canada Book Fund for our publishing activities, and the contribution of the Government of Ontario through the Ontario Book Publishing Tax Credit. The marketing of this book was made possible with the support of the Ontario Media Development Corporation.

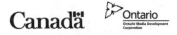

Printed and bound in the United States

In memory of Georges-Simeon Laprade, Jean-Marie Dumouchel, Guy Soucy, Gerry Lefebvre, Robert Fraser, Edmond Bertrand, Gilles Petit, Yvon Robert Jr., Luna Vachon, Jean-Paul Sarault, Édouard Carpentier, Milt Avruskin, Sir Oliver Humperdink and Hans Schmidt.

You would all have unequivocally liked this work.

NOTES AND ACKNOWLEDGEMENTS

When Pat Laprade asked me to take part in this project, I was the happiest person on Earth. I was finally going to share my passion and about 30 years of archiving documents about wrestling with the whole world. I find it sad that my children's heroes are not Quebecers. Consequently, before it's too late and no matter what the future of wrestling may be in the province of Quebec, I am very happy to make this modest contribution and try to give voice to the wrestlers and artists who have made pro wrestling in the Montreal territory a very rich subject.

I would like to thank my wife, Josihanne, and my children, Zakary, Elayna and Jean-Krystophe, for giving me the time to write this book. I also thank my parents, Gerald and Françoise, for giving me and my brother the chance to attend so many wrestling shows. Thanks also to François Poirier and Philippe Belanger for having opened the door of the adventure that was Lutte Lanaudiere, without which my participation in this book would have been impossible. — BH

As I was growing up my dream was to become a journalist — a sports journalist — above all. But destiny had something different in store for me. Even if I have achieved fulfillment at the professional level, I have always tried to nurture the passion that I have always had for journalism. Compiling my almanacs about Quebec wrestling gave me so much joy that I felt the need for an even bigger project. After receiving an email from Dave Meltzer and having some discussions with Michael Ryan, I realized that it was my duty to write the history of professional wrestling in the Montreal territory. I

MAURICE VACHON WITH PAT AND HIS DAD, GUY (GREG OLIVER)

really hope that you will have as much fun reading this book as we had when doing the research, the interviews and the writing. Enjoy!

I would like to thank my father, Guy, who took me to my first wrestling show when I was six, for sharing so many memories with me. I also thank my mother, Monique, for always encouraging me in my projects. This one was, by no means, an exception. My thanks go to Phillipe Leclair and Kim Leduc, who allowed me to embark on the adventure of pro wrestling in the province, without which this book would not exist. I also thank Paul Leduc, Ludger and Serge Proulx, Steve Charette, Patrick Lono and Robert Rancourt, for whom I have worked more than once and who allowed me to get where I am today. Thanks to Michael Ryan for having developed the concept with me and for contributing to some of the texts early on. — PL

BERTRAND WITH HIS CHILDHOOD IDOL RICK MARTEL (PAT LAPRADE)

We'd also like to thank Gino Brito, Raymond Rougeau, Rick Martel, Paul Leduc and Paul Vachon, who were always available to answer any questions. Also, thanks to Denis Archambault for having written the biography of the Weider brothers. A huge thank you to Greg Oliver for his contacts and personal files, as well as Dave Meltzer. Thanks to Nicolas Brouillette, who took the time to read the book and give us some advice. Thanks to everyone we interviewed over the years. Thanks to everyone who gave us information about Montreal wrestling, and thanks to everyone who lent us documents and pictures. You're just too many to be listed, but thank you all for your generosity.

We would like to thank all the journalists for their contributions over the years covering the Montreal wrestling territory. Whether they worked at *La Patrie* newspaper at the beginning of the century, *The Gazette, Montreal Star, Montreal*

Herald, La Presse, le Montréal-Matin, le Soleil, Le Journal de Québec or Le Journal de Montréal, many journalists played a key role in the promotion of professional wrestling, and without them this project would not have been possible. Last, but not least, we thank all our friends and family members who have encouraged us and endured us talking about this book for some years now. You are too numerous to be listed individually, but we know that you'll recognize yourself.

BERTRAND HÉBERT
bertwre@yahoo.ca
quebeclutte.com

PAT LAPRADE
patric_laprade@videotron.ca
quebecwrestling.ca | lutte.com

FOREWORD
BY GINO BRITO

When Patric Laprade and Bertrand Hébert asked me to write a foreword to their book about the history of pro wrestling in the Montreal territory, I was really happy to accept. Since I was a child, I have had the opportunity to mix with the best wrestlers of the golden years of wrestling in the city. When I started, following in the footsteps of my father and uncle (Jack Britton and Lou Kelly), who were both wrestlers, I saw the most renowned Quebec wrestlers, men like Yvon Robert, Larry Moquin, Bob Langevin, the Rougeaus, Johnny and Jacques Sr., Hans Schmidt, the Vachons and many others. Over the years new wrestlers replaced them. Among these gifted wrestlers are Raymond Rougeau and Jacques Jr., Pat Patterson, Ronnie and Terry Garvin, the two strong men Dino Bravo and Jos Leduc — who is backed up by Paul, the exciting Rick Martel and Michel Dubois.

How can I forget the midgets, Sky Low Low and Little Beaver, promoted and managed by my father? Others like Pierre Lefebvre, Tarzan Tyler, Gilles Poisson, Neil Guay, Richard Charland, the Baillargeon brothers and Eddy Auger marked the history of wrestling in their own way. When I had the opportunity of becoming a promoter with the late Frank Valois, new talents were added to the list of famous wrestlers — guys like Armand Rougeau, Sunny War Cloud, Phil Lafon and my own son, Gino Brito Jr. Fortunately, my friends, it's still going on. Since the 1990s we have witnessed the emergence of such athletes as Pierre-Carl Ouellet, El Generico, Kevin Steen and Sylvain Grenier.

Many of these wrestlers are on the list of the top 25 Quebec wrestlers of all time that you'll find at the very end of this book. I took part in the vote, and I think we have come up with an honest list that will stimulate

DINO BRAVO AND GINO BRITO, GRAND PRIX TAG TEAM CHAMPIONS (GINO BRITO COLLECTION)

numerous conversations and generate a lot of interest in wrestling fans. We must not forget that Quebecers have contributed as much as any other party, if not more, to the advancement of professional wrestling. They have wrestled all over the world and filled rings week in, week out.

I really think that this book does justice to our sport. Wrestling is a well-established institution in Quebec and has been loved by Quebecers for more than 100 years. I really hope that fans all over the world will enjoy reading this history. And to Patric and Bertrand, I really wish you both all the success in the world. Thank you!

"Those who live are those who wrestle." — Victor Hugo

Forever passionate,
Gino Brito

INTRODUCTION

Wrestling in the province of Quebec has a rich history, mainly because of its metropolis, Montreal; hence the use of the name of Montreal territory when someone speaks about it. Although wrestling is popular in all the regions of the province, Montreal, with its population, accessibility and position on the Canadian and North American chessboard, has always been a core city when it comes to professional wrestling. Historically Montreal was only behind New York, Tokyo, Mexico and Chicago as far as ranking as one of the biggest cities for the sport. It's right there with cities with a long tradition of wrestling such as St. Louis, Los Angeles, Boston and Toronto. From 1953 to 1957 Montreal dominated the North American wrestling scene as it had the biggest crowd of the year, every year. During that period the Montreal Forum and Delorimier Stadium were the buildings where the fans came to see their heroes. "Lou Thesz, one of the greatest world champions in the history of pro wrestling, has always insisted to make it clear in our conversations that Montreal was the best city for wrestling in North America in the 1950s, but the specialized magazines have never spoken about that because of the linguistic barrier," affirms Dave Meltzer, who has published for 30 years what is considered the *Wall Street Journal* of pro wrestling, the *Wrestling Observer* newsletter.

In 2002 John F. Molinaro published a book providing a list of the top 100 pro wrestlers of all time. Three of them were Quebec wrestlers (Mad Dog Vachon, Yvon Robert and Pat Patterson), and five of them had a major impact on the territory (Hulk Hogan, Andre the Giant, Killer Kowalski, Abdullah the Butcher and Édouard Carpentier). However what strikes one most is that 61of those wrestlers had wrestled in Montreal. Out of the 65 North American wrestlers, 54 had already performed in front of Montreal fans.

In the history of pro wrestling, many championships were considered world championships. Of all the wrestlers who won one of these titles, about 150 wrestled in Montreal. It's impressive: no fewer than eight were Quebecers, namely Yvon Robert (pre-NWA), Don Eagle (pre-NWA), Ronnie Garvin (NWA), Stan Stasiak (WWWF), Chris Benoit (WCW-WWE), Mad Dog Vachon (AWA-IWE), Rick Martel (AWA) and Alexis Smirnoff (IWE).

Five Quebecers have been inducted in the *Wrestling Observer* newsletter's Pro Wrestling Hall of Fame: Pat Patterson, Maurice Vachon, Yvon Robert, Hans Schmidt and Chris Benoit. Out of this hall of fame, four promoters have presented shows in Montreal, namely Paul Bowser, Jack Curley, Vincent J. McMahon and Vincent K. McMahon. Two wrestlers are also part of the WWE Hall of Fame: Pat Patterson and Maurice Vachon. Two of the best midget wrestlers of all time were born here, Sky Low Low and Little Beaver — not to mention the fact that midget wrestling actually started in Montreal.

A National Wrestling Alliance title change took place in Montreal in 1957, when Lou Thesz beat Édouard Carpentier in one of the most controversial episodes in history. On two occasions the WWE title changed hands in Montreal, recently in September 2009, when John Cena beat Randy Orton, and in November 1997, in one of the most eventful matches in pro wrestling's history, when Shawn Michaels beat Bret "The Hitman" Hart in the now-infamous Montreal Screw Job. You will also learn that this wasn't the first wrestling screw job in Montreal's history. Montreal also hosted three WWE pay-per-view events: the Survivor Series 1997, No Way Out (2003) and Breaking Point (2009), which were all presented at the Montreal Canadiens' arena.

These statistics show to what extent Montreal was among the most coveted, prominent territories in which the greatest wrestlers performed and in which the biggest events were held. If you are 70, lots of memories will come back to you while reading. If you are 20, you will learn a lot about the sports entertainment you love, as well as a lot about its history in Montreal. If you live outside the province of Quebec, you will learn about wrestlers you know and, for most of them, how they got started in the business or what they did in the Montreal territory.

So here is the untold story of how the Montreal wrestling territory shaped the world of wrestling . . . with mad dogs, midgets, screw jobs . . . and so much more!

THE ORIGINS OF WRESTLING IN THE TERRITORY

Although wrestling's glory years occurred during the second part of the 20th century, the history of pro wrestling in Montreal goes back to the 19th century. Given that the province has a rich history, spanning more than 400 years, let's leave aside the sport's traditional history, with its Cro-Magnons, Greeks and Romans, and consider its North American roots.

Native Americans had an array of different wrestling styles, probably influenced over the years by contact with other cultures, including the Vikings and other Europeans. Combat has always been an integral part of the Viking mentality; so much so that, in Nordic mythology, Thor is the god of wrestling. Of course wrestling was also very popular in England and France, two countries that would play such a large role in developing North America.

Spanish explorers of the 1500s noted that Native Americans held wrestling contests, very often in the form of tournaments. Later colonizers also said that wrestling was very popular among Native Americans. Focusing on parts of the body, many styles of wrestling were identified, namely Indian Leg, Indian Thumb, Indian Back and Indian Arm wrestling.

The 18th century and the early 1800s witnessed spectacular growth rates for the territory. The population, which numbered just 3,000 in 1666, was 20 times larger by the mid-18th century. The mid-1700s saw the Battle of the Plains of Abraham, probably the most famous battle between Francophones and Anglophones in Quebec history. This battle would pave the way for numerous other linguistic and cultural wars that would be waged in different fields, including professional wrestling.

As the 19th century came along, professional wrestling in North America started not in a stadium or an arena, but in fairgrounds and festivals, carnivals and circuses. A man would challenge all comers. The aspirant had to pay an amount of money, and if he managed to beat the "champion" he would win the jackpot. If he lost, however, he would lose the money he paid. Sometimes the "champion" was facing a plant, someone who was working for the organization and who would beat the champion just to prove to the crowd that he could be beaten. Obviously this is one of the early forms of a worked match. But we are still far away from what pro wrestling is nowadays.

Thanks to Confederation in 1867, Quebec officially became a province of Canada. That was also the year in which the first champion was crowned using a professional wrestling style that would serve as a precursor to what we now know as the collar-and-elbow style. This first style was a mixture of wrestling, judo and gouren, and would be the dominant style of the 1870s. The American collar-and-elbow championship was actually the first official championship of its kind. Its stars were James H. McLaughlin, John McMahon (not related to Vince) and Henry Moses Dufur. Although he was not Canadian, the latter came from Richford, a town in Vermont two miles south of the Quebec border.

THOMAS A. COPELAND AND JOHN MCMAHON, TWO PIONEERS

It's not surprising that the first wrestlers to stand out were Anglophones. After the American Revolution many Anglophone Loyalists sought refuge in what is now the province of Quebec (and, more precisely, in the Eastern Townships), given its proximity to such northeast American states as Vermont.

A man named Thomas A. Copeland took part in a very important wrestling match on July 22, 1873. He lost to John McMahon in Troy, New York. As it was announced, the match saw the U.S. champion facing the Canadian champion, although no title histories exist to prove they had been the champions they were announced to be. Historical records suggest various places of origin for Copeland. While many hold that he came from Peterborough, Ontario, others contend that he came from Montreal. Perhaps it's a mixture of the two, as he may have been born in one town and then lived in another. This was the case of his former opponent, McMahon, who lived in Montreal for the latter part of his life. Although communication technologies were nowhere near as advanced as today, news still travelled throughout North America. The *Boston Globe*, the *Chicago Tribune* and even the *Indianapolis Sentinel* announced the results of wrestling matches held in Montreal or any other city where wrestlers from the territory performed.

In the 1880s wrestling underwent some changes in the way it was performed and, as a result, a new wrestling style emerged, namely catch-as-catch can.

This wrestling style comes closest to what would become modern wrestling. Catch-as-catch can means catch a hold anywhere you can. This distinguishes the catch-as-catch can style from the Greco-Roman wrestling style. The latter allows wrestlers to catch a hold only on the upper part of the opponent's body.

There was also the arrival of William Muldoon, one of the all-time greats, who would become the Greco-Roman wrestling champion during this decade and beyond. This decade was equally marked by the end of the collar-and-elbow title on one hand and the emergence of two other titles on the other hand: catch-as-catch can and the mixed titles. In fact mixed matches, in which two wrestling styles are pitted one against the other, also began to appear. Among the other stars, aside from Muldoon, were Joe Acton, Edwin Bibby, Tom Cannon, Carl Abs, Evan "Strangler" Lewis (not to be confused with Ed Lewis) and the first Quebec-born wrestler to really make a name for himself.

GUS LAMBERT

Born Esdras Lambert in Saint-Guillaume in 1855, Gustave, or Gus, as Americans called him, wrestled principally in the city of New York, but also all over the world. Dan Anderson, wrestling historian, has a list of Lambert matches. Some of the latter matches were held in Cleveland and San Francisco, sometimes even on the same cards as Muldoon, and every one of them happened between 1881 and 1890. Moreover John McMahon, the last collar-and-elbow champion, wrestled Lambert on December 28, 1882, in New York. Almost 20 years after the publication of the first wrestling match results in a Quebec newspaper, *La Patrie*, a newspaper that was published in

Montreal between 1879 and 1978 and that used to cover pro wrestling in an assiduous fashion, announced the results of a match opposing David Michaud and Gustave Lambert in its edition of August 26, 1884. In a double competition Michaud won the feat of strength contest, and Lambert that of wrestling.

LOUIS CYR, NOT ONLY A STRONG MAN BUT A WRESTLER TOO
(CENTRE D'ARCHIVES DE ST-HYACINTHE)

LOUIS CYR AND WRESTLING

Gustave Lambert wasn't just a wrestler; he played a key role in the career of the strongest man in the province, none other than Louis Cyr. According to Cyr's historian and biographer, Paul Ohl, Cyr participated in a number of wrestling matches in Saint-Henri, his own neighborhood, in the mid-1880s. It was not as a wrestler that Cyr made his legendary reputation, but, rather, as someone performing feats of strength. Among the most famous of these are his holding four horses for about a minute, the many weightlifting records performed with only one finger, as well as the back lift, without forgetting the fact that he was the only man to have lifted the Liberty Bell in Philadelphia. Lambert was Louis Cyr's mentor, as well as his first promoter. Louis Cyr influenced many strongmen who, like him, wanted to practise wrestling and have a life similar to that of their hero. Victor Delamarre, the

Baillargeon brothers and Gilles Poisson worshipped Cyr at one moment or another. On the other hand, all of these people had wrestling careers much superior to and longer than that of Cyr.

Undeniably the most important wrestling match of Cyr's career, or at least the one most covered by the media, was held on March 25, 1901. In this match he wrestled "The Giant" Beaupré. Beaupré, whose first name was Édouard, was an almost mythical figure in Quebec, given his exceptional height. Born in Saskatchewan, he stood 8'2"— to this day the tallest pro wrestler of all time. Many Quebec Gen-Xers are surprised to learn that Beaupré really existed and that he was not yet another creation of Quebec folklore. He died of tuberculosis, in 1904, at the age of 23, while he was attending the St. Louis World's Fair. The fair and the games of the third Olympics overlapped in St. Louis and, ironically, freestyle wrestling made its debut there. The match itself was more of a farce than anything else, as Beaupré didn't know how to wrestle, and it was not Cyr's specialty, either. "Beaupré injured his elbow during the match and Cyr beat him," relates Ohl. The match took place at Sohmer Park, where many Quebec and foreign wrestlers performed at the end of the 19th century and at the beginning of the 20th century. Sohmer Park is considered the first mecca of wrestling in Montreal. Sometime before, on January 21 of the same year, Louis Cyr wrestled against a man who would become very famous. In fact at the Montreal National Monument George Little beat Cyr in front of a crowd of more than 2,000 people. Little, well known under the pseudonym Dan McLeod, was a former American heavyweight champion.

In addition to Lambert, Cyr and Little, the end of the 19th century saw Ernest Roeber, one of the best Greco-Roman champions of his time, wrestled several dates in Montreal in July and October of 1898. Roeber's match against Casper Muller on October 18 drew 1,500 people at the Theatre Royal.

1900-1920
THE FIRST TRUE GOLDEN AGE OF WRESTLING IN MONTREAL

Pro wrestling experts regularly say that Montreal wrestling witnessed three golden ages. They refer to the era of Yvon Robert and Eddie Quinn as the first golden age. But the truth of the matter is that the first two decades of the 20th century were very prosperous as far as wrestling was concerned, and this prosperity was mainly due to a former wrestler, who would later become a promoter. He was even able to purchase the Montreal Canadiens!

GEORGE KENNEDY, FROM WRESTLER TO OWNER OF THE MONTREAL CANADIENS

Try to imagine a moment: Hulk Hogan buying the Tampa Bay Lightning or Ric Flair buying the Carolina Hurricanes. Of course these scenarios seem impossible, but something like this actually took place in 1910. In fact on November 12, 1910, George Kennedy, the wrestler-turned-promoter, bought the Montreal Canadiens — a hockey team founded in 1909 by John Ambrose O'Brien — for $7,500 through his company, the Canadian Athletic Club. Kennedy put pressure on the National Hockey Association, claiming that the "Canadien" brand belonged to him, which made the transfer of the hockey team easier.

Kennedy was born George W. Kendall in Montreal on December 29, 1881, and his family focused heavily on religion and, thus, deplored wrestling. So Kendall decided to wrestle under the name George Kennedy, a name he would keep afterward. On October 24, 1902, Kennedy won the lightweight title over the hands of Max Wiley at Sohmer Park in Montreal. He lost it on April 3, 1903, though, in a match against Eugène Tremblay. In this catch-as-catch can match, for which fans had been waiting two years, the victory of Tremblay at Sohmer Park allowed him to become the town's new darling. These two Quebec wrestlers were considered, according to the articles written at the time, the very best lightweights the territory had. After this match Kennedy retired as a wrestler and became both a promoter and trainer to Tremblay, who was now the

new champion. Before he started promoting in Montreal, Kennedy learned his craft with one of the all-time greats. According to D'Arcy Jenish in *The Montreal Canadiens: 100 Years of Glory*, Kennedy worked as a road agent and front man for Martin "Farmer" Burns in Chicago, Des Moines, Kansas City, Omaha and Minneapolis. His job was to rent the venues, schedule the bouts and visit the local newspapers to talk up the matches.

After purchasing the Montreal Canadiens, Kennedy immediately began generating profit with the team. The franchise won the Stanley Cup in 1916, while it was still in the NHA — the league which became the National Hockey League one year later. Kennedy was actively involved in the creation of this new league — essentially created to get rid of

GEORGE KENNEDY [LEFT] WITH BELGIUM'S CONSTANT LE MARIN (BERTRAND HÉBERT COLLECTION)

Eddie Livingstone, owner of the Toronto club. This Stanley Cup was, in fact, the first in the history of the club. The Montreal Canadiens have won 23 other cups since, thus dominating the league's history and being beaten only by the New York Yankees when it comes to the number of championships a North American major sports franchise has won.

He was also the owner of a professional Montreal baseball team in 1911 and a lacrosse team from 1911 to 1914. In addition Kennedy organized soccer matches, had the most modern bowling alley in Montreal and built a gymnasium in the eastern part of the city. It's at this training centre that foreign wrestlers like Raymond Cazeaux and Constant le Marin trained before their matches.

In partnership with Dr. Joseph Pierre Gadbois, Kennedy founded the Canadian Athletic Club in 1905. Gadbois was also a referee and, from time to time, announced the wrestling shows he organized along with Kennedy. This club promoted wrestling, as well as other sports. Thanks to Kennedy, boxing, which had been banned in Montreal since 1887, was legalized in 1916. With New York City wrestling promoter Jack Curley's help, he even succeeded in bringing Georges Carpentier, the famous French champion, to town in 1920.

In spite of his English name, Kennedy spoke French fluently and was able to make connections with many promoters and wrestlers all over the world. One of them was Jack Curley. Curley's real name was Jacques Armand Schuel. He was born in San Francisco to French parents, but spent his childhood in Paris and Strasbourg, France, before coming back to the United States. The first important wrestling match that Curley organized took place in 1907 and showcased Frank Gotch. Then in 1910 he would organize shows in Europe with such wrestlers as Benjamin Roller, Great Gama and Stanislaus Zbyszko. It was during this trip that he convinced the great champion George Hackenschmidt to accept a return match against Frank Gotch, even though the latter had already beaten him three years earlier. A total of 28,757 spectators came to Comiskey Park in Chicago to see Gotch beat, yet again, the Russian Lion. Furthermore, Curley made New York City one of the biggest pro wrestling centres in North America, with the likes of Gotch, Joe Stecher, Wladek Zbyszko and Ed "Strangler" Lewis. In March 1918 Curley, in partnership with the promoters Billy Sandow and Tony Stecher, reached an agreement that allowed promoters to exchange talent. This agreement benefited big centres on the east coast like Boston, Philadelphia, New York and, of course, Montreal.

Curley, nicknamed the Tsar of wrestling, had a working knowledge of French because of his origins. This certainly made the discussion easier and strengthened the trust between the two promoters. It also made it possible for the two men to become friends. It's unquestionably because of this friendship that Kennedy was able to present a championship match between Stanislaus Zbyszko and Constant le Marin on May 24, 1913. This match drew about 12,000 spectators, establishing the largest attendance record in Montreal for more than 20 years. Léon Dumont, the number one promoter in France, also worked with Curley and Kennedy. In 1913 Kennedy managed to send the best American wrestlers to Paris, but World War I put an end to this kind of exchange. On April 22, 1920, in Montreal, Kennedy organized a match between Joe Stecher, the world champion, and Salvatore Chevalier. This was the last important match Kennedy would organize before his death.

In 1919, while the Montreal Canadiens were competing for the Stanley Cup with the Metropolitans in Seattle, Kennedy, like many others, contracted the Spanish flu, in a pandemic that affected tens of thousands. Aside from 2005, 1919 is the only year during which the Stanley Cup was not awarded to any team. Kennedy died on October 19, 1921, after having seen excellent doctors both in Canada and the U.S. Two weeks later, on November 4, 1921, his wife sold the hockey club to Léo Dandurand, Jos Cattarinich and Louis Létourneau for $11,000.

Eighty-eight years later the same hockey club was sold for almost $600 million.

From the beginning of his career as a promoter, Kennedy had been developing big international tournaments that brought together wrestlers from all over the world. It was this kind of strategy that allowed Montreal to become the cream of the crop of the wrestling world.

Under his leadership the Canadian Athletic Club, later known as the Canadian Hockey Club, was the biggest professional sports organization in both Quebec and in Canada. Under his rule Montreal was known as one of the most important cities as far as pro wrestling was concerned. In this regard, one of the best wrestlers of all time, Frank Gotch, wrote to La Patrie. In his letter published in the December 15, 1905, edition, Gotch declared: "I can see from newspapers that Montreal is now one of the biggest pro wrestling centers in America." Upon his death, the New York Times called Kennedy "the best sports promoter in America."

EUGÈNE TREMBLAY, ONE OF THE FIRST LOCAL DRAWS AT THE BEGINNING OF THE 20TH CENTURY

EUGÈNE TREMBLAY, KENNEDY'S HEIR APPARENT

After beating Kennedy, Eugène Tremblay kept going. He wrestled in 1904 in the northeast. In cities as diverse as New York, Philadelphia and Baltimore he wrestled against the likes of George Bothner and the future world champion, Americus. It was actually in his match against Bothner that Tremblay scored one of his most important victories. On September 27, 1907, he defeated Bothner to win the world lightweight championship that Bothner had held since 1903. This was followed by a series of matches between the two, from 1907 to 1909, which were all won by Tremblay. Some of these matches took place in Montreal, Brooklyn and Chicago. Tremblay also had an intense feud with a French wrestler named Jean-Baptiste Paradis. The latter won the title from Tremblay on February 28, 1913, but Tremblay won it back a couple of months later. After having lost and won the title again against Walter Miller, Tremblay lost to Paradis in Montreal on April 1, 1914, but the decision was later reversed, given the fact that Paradis weighed three pounds more than the limit. Paradis wound up staying in Montreal, becoming a wrestling trainer and referee. Tremblay lost the title again, to Milton Harnden on November 15, 1917, in the state of Washington, but continued to defend it in other regions until he eventually lost it in a match against Peter Plourde, on September 22, 1920, in Lowell, Massachusetts. After this fight Tremblay became a promoter, a referee and a trainer.

Ludger Lamothe and Antoine Gonthier, who also wrestled under the name of Carl Pons, were among other notable Quebec wrestlers at the time. Gonthier had a title match against Tom Jenkins in Montreal and also wrestled Gotch in several other places.

FRANK GOTCH AND GEORGE HACKENSCHMIDT, TWO STARS OF THE PIONEERS ERA

(PWHF COLLECTION)

FRANK GOTCH, MONTREAL'S FIRST DRAWING CARD

In addition to having good local talents and good wrestlers from abroad, George Kennedy brought in two of the biggest champions in the history of pro wrestling, namely Frank Gotch and the Russian Lion, George Hackenschmidt.

George Hackenschmidt wrestled three times in Montreal. The first occasion was on May 8, 1905, when he battled Émile Maupas at Sohmer Park. "George Hackenschmidt preferred to wrestle against Émile Maupas in Montreal rather than in New York City in 1905. He knew he would draw a bigger crowd in Montreal because Maupas was French," claims wrestling historian Nathan Hatton. In fact the match drew 5,000 fans at Sohmer Park, at the time a Montreal record. Hack, as he was nicknamed, came back twice — on November 16, 1910, and December 28 of the same year.

Maupas was also the opponent for Frank Gotch's first Montreal visit on December 29, 1904, drawing 4,500 fans. It proved a rare loss for the Iowa athlete. Early in 1905, 4,000 witnessed the match between Gotch and Yankee Rodgers. On April 6, 1906, Gotch tied Hackenschmidt's record, drawing 5,000 fans for his match against KY Karakanoff at Sohmer Park. A year later he would break the record, with 6,000 watching him face Fred Beel. The new record would last for four years until Eugène Tremblay drew 7,000 in 1911. Between 1904 and 1907, Frank Gotch wrestled close to 20 times in Montreal and quickly became a crowd favorite. He was so popular that three of his matches in the U.S. were transmitted via megaphone and many thousands of people stayed until late at night to hear the description. Without a doubt Frank Gotch was the premier local draw in Montreal, ahead of Maupas in the early part of the century. History is not clear regarding the extent to which matches were determined at the time. The journalist Dave Meltzer used to say Frank Gotch was "world champion from 1908 to 1913 in a form that was probably part-shoot part-work"; that is, half real and half scripted. Other historians say that Gotch's matches were very close to real wrestling. "My usual answer is to say that professional wrestling matches were always a work is to oversimplify the situation, but to believe that wrestlers weren't working matches is grossly naive," says Nathan Hatton. Since the 19th century side bets had been a huge part of wrestling and they were clearly a reason to fix matches.

Thanks to his contacts and his flair for business, Kennedy made wrestling in Montreal popular. He organized wrestling cards in more than 20 towns and villages, thus increasing the number of wrestlers and arenas used for wrestling shows. He also gave Montreal fans access to some of the greatest champions of the day and orchestrated the debuts of men like Beck Olsen, Tom Jenkins and Carl Abs — as well as a French wrestler, who was to influence the course of the history of Montreal wrestling.

ÉMILE MAUPAS

Émile Maupas, a grappler of French origin, started wrestling in Montreal at the beginning of the 20th century and faced all the stars of his era. He actually participated in the tournament organized by Kennedy in the fall of 1905. In the 1920s, after having wrestled in Montreal for many years, Maupas decided to establish himself in Val-Morin, north of Montreal. He eventually opened a training centre for athletes, commonly known as the Maupas Camp. Some Montreal Canadiens players went there to refine their training. Athletes from other disciplines went there, too. Obviously, as a former wrestler, it was Maupas who wound up training wrestlers like Frank Valois, Larry Moquin, Tony Lanza, Bob Langevin, Léo Lefebvre and Harry

TEACHER AND STUDENT: ÉMILE MAUPAS AND YVON ROBERT

(ROBERT ST-JEAN COLLECTION)

Madison, but his most famous student was, beyond a shadow of a doubt, Yvon Robert. Even though Robert had spent just 10 months at the Maupas Camp when he made his wrestling debut, the two men maintained a very strong, lifelong relationship. At the Maupas Camp the emphasis was on physical training and cardio endurance, and it was not at all surprising to see Maupas's students going for long walks or skiing in bathing suits.

The 1920s were transitional years for wrestling, both in Montreal and across North America. Kennedy's early death left a big vacuum. A few days before he died, Kennedy asked one of his partners, Lucien Riopel, to contact Jack Curley and ask him if he'd want to take over the Montreal wrestling scene. Alongside Riopel, Curley promoted for a few years. They presented a big tournament in 1924 with the likes of Wladek Zybszko, Renato Gardini, Carl Vogel and Montreal's Georges Deslongchamps.

During the '20s, Deslongchamps became the only wrestler who could move the crowd, even though it wasn't close to the level of Maupas or Gotch. Wrestling just wasn't cool anymore. In 1924 and 1926, no wrestling event took place in Montreal and boxing was clearly the number one combat sport in town. The fans needed another star, someone they could believe in, and they made it clear Deslongchamps wasn't it. That's when another Frenchman came to the rescue.

Henri DeGlane

BEFORE CARPENTIER AND FERRÉ, THERE WAS HENRI DEGLANE (PWHF COLLECTION)

HENRI DEGLANE

Born June 22, 1902, in Limoges, France, Deglane was an Olympic gold medalist, winning Greco-Roman laurels in 1924, in Paris. In December 1927, soon after Deglane turned pro, Curley brought him to New York. Deglane hated New York City however, and so Curley saw a chance to revive the Montreal territory with the French-speaking star-to-be. He sent Deglane to Riopel and he became an instant hit. Using Deglane on top nine shows out of ten, Curley succeeded; wrestling was hot again in Montreal. Shows were now held every week or so at the Mount-Royal arena. On September 17, 1928, Deglane drew 10,000 fans against Stanislaus Zbyszko, the biggest crowd in Montreal during the 1920s.

At war with Boston's promoter Paul Bowser for many years, Curley wound up losing Montreal to his fierce competitor sometime in 1929. Bowser, who aligned himself with Toots Mondt, Billy Sandow and Strangler Lewis, would influence the Montreal territory in many ways.

PAUL BOWSER

Paul Bowser was an influence in Montreal for most of his career. He owned rights to the matches held in the territory, from 1929 right until he sold his share. Yet Quebecers really didn't know him. He usually had someone else in charge of the territory, being busy with his duties in Boston. Lucien Riopel, Jack Ganson and Eddie Quinn were the people Bowser had run Montreal. (Quinn was the most famous and successful.)

Born on May 28, 1886, Bowser started in the business as a wrestler. He started promoting in 1923, having left his native Pennsylvania to establish himself in New England. Boston would become his stomping ground. Although he had already presented wrestling cards, his interest in Montreal became keener when he discovered Yvon Robert after the latter made his Boston debut. By the end of 1929 Bowser had the upper hand on the territory, as the local promoter Lucien Riopel made

BOSTON PROMOTER PAUL BOWSER WAS ALSO IN CHARGE OF THE MONTREAL TERRITORY

(PETER JARVIS COLLECTION)

use of the talents associated with him, including Strangler Lewis, Wladek Zbyszko, Stanley Stasiak, Henri Deglane and Gus Sonnenberg.

VICTOR DELAMARRE

ONE OF THE STRONGEST MEN EVER.
VICTOR DELAMARRE (RONALD CARTER COLLECTION)

The 1930s saw Victor Delamarre, the French-Canadian Samson, follow in the footsteps of Louis Cyr. Born in Hébertville (Lac-St-Jean) in 1888, he was the nephew of Eugène Tremblay. Delamarre performed feats of strength between 1914 and 1931, able to lift weights of more than 300 pounds with only one hand or more than 200 pounds with just one finger. In 1931 he started wrestling, and over the course of his career he would participate in more than 1,500 matches. "My maternal grandfather often spoke to me about his strength. He told me that he was so strong that he could break the ankle of his opponent with only one hand catching it in mid-air, or at least so the legend told," says François Hébert, the former indy wrestler known as Iceman. The November 1952 edition of *Lutte et Boxe* magazine described Yvon Robert as the greatest of all strongmen. His sons, Richard and Victor Jr., would follow in his footsteps, both in wrestling and in strongman competitions.

THE FIRST MONTREAL SCREW JOB

But 1931 was the year of a bigger event. Lucien Riopel and Louis Létourneau were jointly taking care of the promotion in Montreal, still run by Paul Bowser, when Montreal would host one of the most controversial matches in history — nothing less than the very first Montreal Screw Job.

It's almost cliché now: whenever Vince McMahon's WWE is in Montreal, a commentator mentions that Montreal fans are not like others. This is usually followed by a reference to the infamous Montreal Screw Job. It's always implied that the November 1997 incident involving Shawn Michaels and Bret Hart turned the wrestling world upside down. The truth, however, is much more complicated. On one hand, there is the argument saying that Montreal fans know what they like and what they don't like, and it's the promoters' business to adjust their act accordingly and not vice versa. On the other hand, because of the linguistic and cultural distinctiveness of Quebec, the fans in the province simply react differently from others in North America.

Most people know that Bret Hart was robbed of his WWF title in the Molson Centre (now called the Bell Centre) and that this was not the first time something like this occurred in wrestling. What many people do not know, however, is that it also wasn't the first time it happened in Montreal. History really does repeat itself: maybe Vincent K. McMahon remembered a story told by his spiritual grandfather, Toots Mondt, who partnered with Jess McMahon (Vince's grandfather) and Vincent J. McMahon (Vince's father) years before.

Although he and his partners failed to monopolize wrestling, Strangler Lewis was very influential when it came to determining the world champion. After all, Lewis, the best shooter in the world for more than 10 years, lost when he wanted and against whomever he chose. The only way to make sure that Lewis would lose was to pay him. And this is what Paul Bowser did in 1929. According to Marcus Griffin in *Fall Guy: The Barnums Bounce* (published in 1937), when Ed "Strangler" Lewis lost against Gus Sonnenberg on January 4, 1929, at the Boston Gardens, he earned $50,000 of the $70,000 collected at the gate. Lewis and Sandow were also promised an additional $70,000 as a guarantee that Lewis would take his title back when Sonnenberg's value started to diminish. In other words, Sonnenberg was to lose his title to Lewis or pay $70,000 to Lewis and Sandow. (Taking inflation into consideration, it would be more than a $1 million today).

In 1930 Bowser decided to make Olympian Ed Don George the world champ. He beat Gus Sonnenberg on December 10, 1930, at the Olympia in Los Angeles. Sandow and Lewis waited for their payments, but history doesn't tell whether Bowser forgot or refused to pay them. It seems likely he forgot . . . otherwise he would never have accepted to pit his new champion against Ed "Strangler" Lewis at the Wrigley Field in Los Angeles on April 13, 1931. Although some believed the Olympic champion would make mince-meat of Lewis in a real match, they were wrong. "We were supposed to wrestle a three-fall match, and I was going to win, of course," George said, laughing at the memory. "We came out to the centre of the ring for the ref-eree's instructions, and Ed says to me, really casual and friendly, 'Well, Don, tonight's the night.' I knew immediately what he was saying — that he was going to take back the title — and all I could think of to say was, 'Oh no.' Ed smiles and says, 'Oh yes. Now, how do you want to do it? Do we give the fans a great match or do we wrestle?' We were close friends, and we both knew I couldn't beat Ed on my best day, so I just shrugged and said, 'Well, Ed, why don't we just give them a great match, okay?' And that's what we did. The only difference was that Ed was the one whose hand was raised at the end," Ed Don George said in Lou Thesz's autobiography, Hooker.

Paul Bowser could have paid Lewis — but he chose to steal the title, instead. So he organized a match between Lewis and Henri Deglane in Montreal on May 4, 1931. According to Le Devoir, Lewis sent a telegram to Lucien Riopel and Louis Létourneau, telling them that he wanted to bring an American referee along for his match at the Mount Royal arena. They replied that there were competent and impartial referees in Montreal. To resolve the conflict, the Montreal Athletic Commission (MAC) appointed Eugène Tremblay as the official. It's most likely that Lewis's complaint was just a way to increase the interest in the match or an attempt on his part, and that of Sandow, to prevent the appointment of a referee who was not impartial. The conse-quences were very different, frustrating the MAC and causing problems for Sandow during the match and the events that would follow.

The first fall was a duel between Lewis's headlock and Deglane's arm-lock. According to Le Devoir Lewis was wary of Deglane's rolling armlock and tried to counter with his full nelson, but Deglane won the fall with his move in 33 minutes and 15 seconds. Sandow complained in vain that the count had been too fast. Dr. Gaston Demers, the president of the MAC, had to get involved.

As was the custom at the time, both wrestlers returned to their respective dressing rooms for a break. As the story goes, either Deglane bit his own right arm or, as it's suggested by wrestling historian Tim Hornbaker, Deglane's manager and Bowser's policeman, Dan Koloff, was the guilty party. According to *Le Devoir* the two guys came back to the ring for the second fall that lasted nine minutes and 35 seconds. Lewis applied several arm-locks; Deglane's arm became white. Lewis went on top of Deglane for a pinfall and won the second fall of the match. But as Deglane leaned back to his corner, referee Tremblay noticed he held his arm.

ED "STRANGLER" LEWIS LOST HIS TITLE TO DEGLANE IN A HUGE CONTROVERSY (SCOTT TEAL COLLECTION)

Tremblay and Dr. Demers looked at the arm and saw teeth marks. Two rows of teeth marks were perfectly visible on the purple skin of Deglane's arm.

The commissioner told the referee Tremblay to disqualify Lewis and to give the second fall to Deglane. Lewis's manager, Sandow, was furious and kept on arguing. He was then ordered to leave the arena or risk losing his manager's licence. Three officials escorted him out. The next day Sandow protested the match's outcome and gave the Montreal Athletic Commission a $5,000 voucher to overturn the decision, saying that the count was too fast at the first fall and that Deglane mutilated himself during the second fall. The commission's decision to refuse the protest was so commonplace that *Le Devoir* never mentioned it at all. The *Le Devoir* article suggests Sandow's previous schemes made Demers ignore the valid complaint.

This "Battle of the Bite" demonstrates that it was easier for Bowser to execute his plan in Montreal than in any other city because the Francophone fans clearly backed Deglane. The promoters were impartial toward Sandow and Lewis but loyal to Bowser. Offended by Sandow's ways, the Athletic Commission could easily be manipulated. Lewis's complaint was the last straw: demanding an American ref just rubbed them the wrong way. Sandow and Lewis made a political mistake made by countless Anglophones before and after them: they failed to understand that this was not just an insult to the referees, but also to the dominant language and culture of Quebec. Demers and Tremblay certainly knew nothing of the plan, as it was not important to its execution. Demers saw exactly what Bowser wanted him to see: Lewis and Sandow, the evil Americans who were attempting to steal the world championship away from a French wrestler.

According to Lou Thesz, another surprise was awaiting Ed in the locker room. "When he walked in, there was a gloating Paul Bowser, and standing alongside him were five or six hoods armed with baseball bats, just in case Ed decided to give Bowser some trouble. Ed sized up the situation immediately and decided to play it very calm. 'You think you've stolen something from me, but I couldn't care less,' he told Bowser. 'You've actually done me a favour. I'm fed up with this scene, and I'm already booked in Europe, so you can have the belt. I don't need it where I'm going. Besides, I've already proved to you that I can take it back if I decide I want it.'" Still, it's hard to take Lewis's words entirely at face value. He would've been a bigger attraction in Europe with the belt — a world champion drew more spectators than a former champion. At worst, Bowser would've been compelled to give $70,000 to Lewis and Sandow before their departure. Although this story is said to be true, some historians believe it was all a work, and that Bowser was in cahoots with Lewis and Sandow from the get-go. Too many inconsistencies have made some people think that this act served only to establish Deglane even more. Whatever the case may really be, Bowser regained control over the title and solidified his place as Montreal's number one promoter.

1939–1964
THE FIRST GOLDEN AGE OF WRESTLING IN MONTREAL

If the premier era of spectacular success for Montreal wrestling and wrestlers began in 1939, we have to go back seven years to see the emergence of the first major wrestler — the man who would become the sport's principal actor. In the 1930s the nationalist French-Canadian movement led by Henri Bourassa became increasingly a movement of Quebec nationalism. It's no surprise that Quebecers wanted to identify themselves with successful Quebecers. One of the most successful started his career as a wrestler in April 1932. He would ultimately become the most popular wrestler in the history of the province and would be the headliner of the most lucrative era of Montreal wrestling. He was the living god of Quebec wrestling: Yvon Robert.

YVON ROBERT

Many Quebecers have reached the pinnacle of their respective sport. Maurice Richard, Guy Lafleur, Mario Lemieux and Patrick Roy in hockey; Eric Gagne in baseball; Georges St-Pierre in MMA; and Jacques Villeneuve in Formula 1 are all excellent examples.

If Rikidozan is the "God of Puroresu" and El Santo is the "God of Lucha Libre," then Yvon Robert is definitely Quebec's "God of Wrestling."

"Yvon Robert was a god for us all!" confirms Maurice Vachon. "He was a far bigger cultural star than Hulk Hogan or Steve Austin in their wildest dreams . . . and pretty much anyone short of El Santo or Rikidozan," adds Dave Meltzer.

Born on October 8, 1918, in Verdun, Robert was 14 and already a great athlete when he started to train with wrestling veterans. Hating school but

LARRY MOQUIN, BOOM BOOM GEOFFRION, YVON ROBERT JR., ROCKET RICHARD, BUTCH BOUCHARD, YVON ROBERT SR., EDDY AUGER, CLAUDE ST-JEAN AND JOHNNY ROUGEAU (ROBERT ST-JEAN COLLECTION)

studying to become a blacksmith, Robert was looking for something better. In the early '30s Eugène Tremblay sent him to Émile Maupas's camp in the Laurentians. After 10 months with Maupas, Robert continued his training at the Riopel Camp, led by Lucien Riopel.

Finally, on April 4, 1932, Yvon Robert made his debut against John Charette at Montreal's Mount Royal Arena. After two years of proving himself in Montreal, Robert started wrestling well-known wrestlers, like Earl McCready (another Canadian, from Saskatchewan) and eventually made his American debut in Boston.

Boston is where he made a very important acquaintance, both for himself and for wrestling in Montreal, when he met promoter Eddie Quinn. This new friendship allowed Robert to wrestle Danno O'Mahoney, the Boston territory champion. It should be noted that at the time, before the NWA, each territory had its own world champion, with some territories' title being more important than others.

Finally in 1936 Robert became champion for the first time by beating O'Mahoney in Montreal, in what would become the Montreal version of the world title. Robert won this title 16 times during his career. He beat the best wrestlers of his time to become champion. Among these were "Whipper" Billy Watson, Killer Kowalski, Don Leo Jonathan and Buddy Rogers, though it was against Wild Bill Longson that Robert won the National Wrestling Association title in 1942. On January 9, 1939, Yvon Robert conquered France and Europe, winning a match against his idol Henri Deglane. "I was the happiest man on earth. Paris was mine! You all know, I love wrestling a lot, it's my passion. I've never been happier in my career as I was when I pinned the shoulders of the great master, Deglane," confided Robert in the August 1951 edition of Lutte magazine. He would also beat Lou Thesz three times for the Montreal title. Considered by many the best wrestler of all time, Thesz also acknowledged that Robert was a god for the French-Canadian population.

This almost divine popularity is due, in part, to the work of Eddie Quinn. But it was a two-way street because as much as Robert benefited from Quinn, Quinn also benefited from Robert. Red Fisher, writing for The Gazette, had already observed that Quinn created Robert, but also that Robert created Quinn. "Robert and Quinn drew 9,000 spectators to the Montreal Forum every Wednesday night, brought wrestling to television and made it a millionaire industry," reported the CBC, although 9,000 fans is exaggerated. But Robert weighed heavily in the balance. He was not just a wrestler. He had enough influence to make a guy like Larry Moquin the booker, as well as find positions for some of his other buddies in the Montreal office. He also had shares in the territory. "Yvon knew a lot more about wrestling than Eddie Quinn, and Quinn was smart enough to know that without Yvon Robert it would never have been as big," recalls former wrestler and promoter Gino Brito. The union between Robert and Quinn allowed Montreal to be the capital of wrestling in North America during those years. Upon Robert's death, Frank Selke, the Canadiens' general manager from 1946 to 1964 who was in charge of renting the Montreal Forum for wrestling, also stressed in an interview with Le Journal de Montréal the latter's great drawing power: "Yvon Robert allowed Quinn and the Forum to draw exceptional gates."

Robert played a key role in the careers of several wrestlers. In the 1940s he took Larry Moquin under his wing. "Yvon was a spectacular wrestler. He knew all the tricks of the trade. He helped me start my wrestling career," confirmed Moquin upon the death of his mentor. Then in the 1950s he brought in the wrestler who would revolutionize wrestling in Montreal, Édouard Carpentier. "He was the king! It was him who made wrestling what it is here. Women used to cry when he took a beating," admitted Carpentier. Robert also mentored Johnny Rougeau, passing the torch when his own career neared an end. In his last match Robert wrestled in a tag team with Johnny Rougeau, for whom he had served as a manager for some time. "I had differences of opinion with Yvon in the past, but I always give him credit. He's the best French-Canadian wrestler I have ever seen in the ring. He has helped me a lot," said Rougeau. Robert also influenced the career of his son, Yvon Jr., even if the younger grappler was never quite as successful.

After retiring in 1957 Robert served as a referee for some time and promoted shows, especially at the Paul-Sauvé Arena. Yvon Robert died on July 12, 1971, after his eighth heart attack over a period of 10 years, immediately after his admission to Sacré-Cœur hospital. In 1992 he was inducted into the Quebec Sports Hall of Fame and, in 1996, into Dave Meltzer's *Wrestling Observer* Hall of Fame. In 1999 a biography entitled *Yvon Robert: The Lion of French Canada* was published in French by author Pierre Berthelet. Finally, in 2004, he was inducted into the Quebec Wrestling Hall of Fame. "The old wrestling fans who had the opportunity of seeing the hometown boy from Christophe-Colomb Street have never forgotten him!" noted journalist Jacques Beauchamps upon his friend's death.

Eighty years after his debut Yvon Robert still tops the list of the best wrestlers of all time in the province of Quebec. (See the ranking of wrestlers on page 401.) He was a matchless presence in the wrestling world and the first French-Canadian to become a wrestling superstar in his own territory. Decades later no one has surpassed him. He is and will remain (unless nothing short of a revolution takes place in Montreal) the greatest wrestler of all time. His name will be forever etched not only in the memories of those who saw him wrestle, but also in the minds of those who heard their grandparents or parents speak about him. Robert not only left his mark on his sport, but also on a whole generation of countrymen. Like his friend Maurice Richard, he's part of the Quebec sports elite, whose legacy will be passed down from generation to generation.

YVON ROBERT, LARRY MOQUIN AND MAURICE RICHARD ON THEIR WAY TO A WRESTLING SHOW IN AUGUST 1958 (BERTRAND HÉBERT COLLECTION)

Speaking of Maurice Richard, it's important to note to what extent he and Yvon Robert were alike and to what extent they were friends. In the 1940s and 1950s, Yvon Robert's popularity was compared to that of the top scorer of the NHL's Montreal Canadiens. "Yvon Robert was the Maurice Richard of wrestling," said Gino Brito.

In fact the men had many things in common. Richard and Robert were both well-known for their spectacular force. They were also known for their incomparable charisma. Both captivated their audiences, and this is one of the reasons why the fans supported them so much.

Richard and Robert were also the first homegrown sports stars to be featured on TV as Quebecers began to have their own TV sets. On the other hand, one difference separated the two — their salaries. In spite of the fact that Richard played professional hockey in the best league in the world, he clearly didn't earn the kinds of figures we've grown used to.

In the 1940s and '50s the salaries of hockey players rarely became public. Still, it's clear that the maximum Richard earned during a season was $25,000. A document that was exhibited in the Museum of Civilization in Ottawa showed that his salary was $12,000 in 1956. During this period Robert could earn up to $150,000 a year. According to Statistics Canada, at the time $150,000 would be the equivalent of between $1 and $2 million today. "He bought two Cadillacs a year," remembers Brito. To put things into perspective, during that period of time a pair of tickets in the 10th row at the Forum in the middle of the rink for a Canadiens match cost $5.

In order to help Richard top up what he earned with the Canadiens and to help draw more fans to wrestling shows, Robert hired Richard to serve as referee during the summer. Imagine: fans all over the province came to see these two heroes at the same event. A bond so strong grew between the two men that even today their children remain very close. "Maurice made him laugh, and Yvon Robert had considerable interpersonal skills," explains Brito.

Henri Richard, Maurice's brother, remembers: "Once, after having started my career with the Canadiens, Maurice was unable to go, and they asked me to replace him. So I served as a referee for a midget match. They told me to just count until three, but when I was about to do that, they all jumped over me! It was a tag team match. There was Little Beaver and Sky Low Low; they ribbed me pretty good." Other Canadiens members, like "Boom Boom" Geoffrion and Dick Irvin Sr., went to watch the wrestling matches at the Forum when Robert wrestled.

(RICHARD Z. SIROIS COLLECTION)

THE ONLY MONTREAL CANADIEN TURNED WRESTLER, JEAN PUSIE

It's rare to see the paths of two major athletes intersect like Robert's and Richard's. But that kind of thing characterized French Canada at the time; people stood together and helped each other in all spheres of society. Other hockey players, too, were big wrestling fans. Only one Quebec-born player, however, became a full-time wrestler.

JEAN PUSIE

Jean Pusie wasn't an NHL star. He managed only five points in 61 games. But he wasn't really focused on scoring goals. During his pro career he was involved in more than 100 fights. He was a gifted athlete in general, playing 14 different sports. Pusie started wrestling in 1933 in a match against Harvey Blackstone and then came back to wrestling after his hockey career came to an end in 1943. He wrestled in Montreal and for the Northland Wrestling Enterprises in Ontario, owned by Larry Kasaboski, and in many other territories.

JACK GANSON, THE PROMOTER WHO ALMOST KILLED THE TERRITORY

After his wrestling career, Ganson, whose real name was John Karabinas, became a very successful promoter in San Francisco. He also served as a lieutenant for Paul Bowser — until Bowser bought him out in 1935 and replaced him with Joe Malcewicz. After losing power Ganson threatened to break kayfabe (the secrets of wrestling) in an interview with the *San Francisco Chronicle* on December 10, 1935: "I do not want to harm anyone in wrestling, but if the Commission [Californian Athletic Commission] compels me to come and take an oath, I will say everything I know."

Sometime later Bowser tried to make peace by offering Ganson the Montreal territory. At first his new promotion presented solid scientific wrestling, drawing Montreal's biggest crowds ever with Yvon Robert maineventing. Just three years into his run, however, Ganson would find himself involved in the first of many situations that would ultimately cost him his job — and that could have cost a lot more.

On September 14, 1938, Yvon Robert defeated the Masked Marvel to regain his title in front of 13,000 fans. The fans were expecting the hooded wrestler to take off his mask following his defeat and reveal his identity. When he refused, a riot ensued.

In the aftermath the MAC ordered the Masked Marvel to go back to Montreal and reveal his identity. On October 17, 1938, he revealed himself as Ted "King Kong" Cox. Three days later *La Patrie* mentioned that Ganson and the Canadians Arena Co., managed by Tommy Gorman — who had just won the Stanley Cup as the general manager of the Montreal Maroons and who would also become manager of the Montreal Canadiens — were at odds with each other because Gorman wanted Ganson to stop serving as a promoter for territories like Buffalo and Ottawa. Ganson had even closed his office at the Forum. After a month-long stalemate Ganson and Gorman made peace, and wrestling returned to the Forum on November 14, 1938. But things were never the same. The riot would prove to be his last big crowd.

On November 28 Ganson put Yvon Robert against a wrestler making his return to Montreal, Cy Williams. The main event took place in front of a crowd of only 2,000, and the rest of the card was clearly subpar. As if the low attendance and the poor quality of the matches were not enough, the president of the Athletic Commission, Dave Rochon, was struck in the face by a fan who was unhappy with the events that saw Williams win two falls against Robert.

On December 19 Williams defeated Robert in front of 5,000 at the Forum — and at the time sports writers regularly wrote about the dwindling popularity of wrestling. Even Émile Maupas wrote about it in La Patrie. Ganson was blamed for not offering fans an interesting spectacle and bringing the same wrestlers while presenting matches or, rather, match outcomes that people didn't really believe. Worse, Robert left for Europe at the end of December.

The new champion, Williams, became fussy and refused to wrestle against former champions Gus Sonnenberg and Ted Cox. Ganson was forced to cancel a card scheduled for February 13, 1939. After more than two months wrestling returned to the Forum, with Gus Sonnenberg main-eventing against Ted Cox in a show that drew 3,000 people and lasted only 80 minutes. It probably wasn't the return Ganson was hoping for. He made other dubious choices, putting spot guys like the Red Shadow (Leo Numa), Jack Taylor, Jack Washburn and Don Evans in main events. None of them drew more than 4,000 fans. It took the return of Yvon Robert on May 30 to draw 5,000. Ganson promoted that show, stating he wanted to return to a more scientific, less aggressive style and that he was now banning contact with referees, eye-gouging and wrestling outside the ring. Then on June 27 Ganson made things worse, creating an entirely new set of rules that made his wrestling matches more like boxing bouts, forcing his wrestlers to adhere to the so-called Ganson Rules. There were 10-minute rounds with one-minute breaks. Judges would score the rounds and, if need be, decide the winner. The show drew poorly. But it didn't stop Ganson from planning another show with these rules. On July 4, however, the day of the show, the Athletic Commission stepped in and refused to allow the Ganson Rules to stand. The show didn't draw 1,000 — even with Ed Don George facing Gus Sonnenberg in the main event. After this the Forum was booked for a full three weeks of roller derby — and Ganson would never hold a show there again. He left for Europe and then promoted in Buffalo, until Bowser finally bought him out in 1941.

EDDIE QUINN

Eddie Quinn was the logical choice to replace Jack Ganson. He had been a boxer and a taxi driver before promoting in his hometown (Waltham, Massachusetts) for Bowser starting in the mid-1930s. He had also been Yvon Robert's manager for a number of years. Eddie Quinn knew that Yvon Robert would make Montreal successful again. He got his licence on July 27, 1939, and his first card was presented at the Forum on August 8. Stuck with a champion (Cy Williams) who didn't want to come to Montreal to defend the title, Quinn held a tournament to name an interim champ. Ernie Dusek, part of the infamous Dusek Riot Squad, won. "Ernie was the best of the Dusek brothers," confirms Gino Brito, comparing him to Emil, Rudy and Joe.

La Patrie praised Quinn's first show, explaining that it had a good mix of scientific and rough matches. Business was about to pick up, they maintained, if Quinn could present more cards like this. And that's just what Quinn did.

Dusek was awarded the actual title by the Athletic Commission on August 10, but he was just a transitional champion. Less than two months later Yvon Robert won the first of his six-title reign under Quinn's guidance. Quinn managed the Montreal territory with a master's hand. And he had a full house for many of the matches held at the Montreal Forum. Even during World War II Quinn managed to draw decent crowds and, more importantly, presented good wrestling cards. The feuds between Robert and Bill Longson and Robert and Bobby Managoff were box-office hits. Although the NWA almost always only recognized one champion, Quinn received a special waiver in 1952 for his operations in Quebec — a rare accomodation.

EDDIE QUINN SITTING BETWEEN TWO ALL-TIME GREATS, DON LEO JONATHAN [LEFT] AND YVON ROBERT [RIGHT] (TONY LANZA)

In addition he started presenting wrestling cards at Delorimier Stadium. Although he drew his biggest crowds at the stadium, Quinn never really liked the venue that also hosted the Brooklyn Dodgers' farm team, the Montreal Royals, for which Jackie Robinson used to play. When rain cancelled the second show in a row at the stadium, with a main event that was to oppose Yvon Robert and Buddy Rogers, Quinn told *La Patrie* that he would present his next card at the Forum on August 22, 1951. "It never rains at the Forum," he said. "He managed the promotion there in an extraordinary way because he had the showbiz sense," said Yvon Robert Jr. in *Les Saltimbanques du Ring* (*The Entertainers of the Ring*), a documentary about the history of the Montreal territory.

On July 18, 1956, Quinn presented his biggest show ever, with 23,227 spectators in Delorimier Stadium to watch Édouard Carpentier battle Argentina Rocca. It was the biggest crowd ever drawn in Montreal, the biggest crowd of the year in North America for a wrestling match and a record that would not be broken in Montreal for 16 years. Today it's still the third-biggest crowd in the history of the province.

History will show that Quinn drew 10 out of the best 20 wrestling crowds in Quebec, and in this regard he's not outmatched by any other promoter, Vince McMahon included. "Eddie Quinn is the greatest promoter of all time in Montreal," Maurice Vachon says, even though Vachon was never a star with Quinn's promotion.

If Quinn started as a simple promoter in the Montreal territory, he ended his career as its primary shareholder, having bought out Paul Bowser. Quinn also made Yvon Robert a partner, thus guaranteeing his presence. Bobby Managoff, as well as the lawyer Louis Dezwirek, also had a stake in the promotion. Quinn had shares in the St. Louis wrestling office, partnering with Lou Thesz, Bill Longson, Managoff and Frank Tunney, as well as money invested in the Boston territory.

From June 1959 to August 1960 he tried in vain to put Chicago promoter Fred Kohler out of business in a promotional war. Quinn even presented a program on the local CBS affiliate, but after 19 shows in Chicago, many of which were presented at the Chicago Stadium (host of the Blackhawks hockey team), Quinn closed his promotion there.

In 1961 and 1962, Quinn brought over a young Japanese wrestler who would become one of the all-time best and a great promoter himself — Shohei "Giant" Baba. In Montreal, Baba wrestled the likes of Édouard Carpentier, Argentina Rocca and Bruno Sammartino.

Quinn had been involved in the National Wrestling Alliance from 1950 to 1957 and then from 1959 to 1963, after which he quit the world of professional wrestling and returned to New England. TV no longer covered wrestling events, and attendance rates dropped drastically in Montreal. He also had a licence to promote boxing, but after having cancelled the match opposing Archie Moore and Robert Cleroux at the last minute he was admonished by Mayor Jean Drapeau, and the commission took away his licence in December 1961. Although he was never to get a boxing promoter licence again, he was given another wrestling promoter licence in February 1962.

Edmund Regan Quinn died of a cerebral hemorrhage on December 14, 1964; he was 58. In 2009 he was inducted into the Quebec Wrestling Hall of Fame, the first promoter to achieve this honour, thus cementing his status as the best wrestling promoter in the history of the territory.

Quinn's golden age saw the debut of many Quebec wrestlers. One of the first to become successful was the most courageous globetrotter in the history of Montreal wrestling.

BOB LANGEVIN

Few wrestlers at the world level had a career and life as eventful as that of Bob Langevin. Born Florian Langevin in 1913, he was orphaned at the age of four, became a professional wrestler at the age of 21 and wrestled in Canada, the U.S., Europe and even Cuba. He also worked as a bodyguard, an actor and a policeman; he beat cancer; his two legs were paralyzed; he was a promoter and he received more honours and honorary titles than anyone else in the history of professional wrestling. "He's the most decorated wrestler," says one of his closest friends, Paul Leduc. As if this were not enough, he wrestled in the world's first match broadcast on TV against Léo Lefebvre. "It was a request by the Canadians Arena Co., for which he worked as a promoter. It took place on March 18, 1939, for the BBC in England," Leduc says.

After pursuing an amateur career, Langevin went to the Maupas Camp at the age of 19, where he had the opportunity to train with Yvon Robert, Léo Lefebvre, Lou Gagnon and Arthur Legrand, under the supervision of Émile Maupas. Frank Sexton continued his training over at the YMCA. In 1934 he started his professional career at the Exchange Stadium in Montreal, but quickly after that he went to Ontario and the U.S. Then, one night in Toronto, he was nicknamed Legs. "There used to be a champion wrestler. He used the airplane scissors for his finish. It was Jim Browning. I had strong legs because, in the United States, I used to split a bag of flour by squeezing with my legs. He thought that I had good legs to make his hold. So, he showed me how to do it. The first time he showed it to me, I did it perfectly," relates Langevin in an interview for SLAM! Wrestling. This nickname was to stick to him throughout his life. "Bob was a force of nature," says Leduc. He performed feats of strength. He would apply leg scissors to his opponent's waist and then twirl him a little bit like a Japanese armlock,"

BOXING CHAMPION JOE LOUIS ABOUT TO WRESTLE BOB LANGEVIN IN CUBA (PAUL LEDUC COLLECTION)

adds Leduc. Langevin was also part of the wrestling cards presented at the Mount Royal Arena, which was the venue that was used the most for wrestling at the time, before being replaced by the Forum.

In 1934 a terrible incident occurred. A reckless fan hit Langevin's genitals with an electric cord. The mishap occurred in Saint-Jérôme near Montreal and left Langevin impotent at the age of 21. The tragedy would not stop Langevin. He actually played a key role in Yvon Robert's success, as he travelled a lot with Robert. "He was Yvon Robert's sidekick," explains Leduc. "When Yvon went to Boston, he wrestled against Bob. Yvon's first match in Europe was also against Bob. He was familiar with Yvon's style and knew that Yvon was the guy that the promotions wanted to get over. Guys like Bob, Eddy Auger, Ovila Asselin and Frank Valois all played the role of a sidekick at some time or other. Thus, they had a preference in the promotion's roster." We must not look at the work accomplished by these guys with disdain because you had to be a very good wrestler and a very humble one above all to perform this role. "Bob was a guy on whom you could count, a guy you could trust," relates Leduc. It was probably for this reason that the Canadians Arena Co. hired him as promoter when he was only 26.

Bob Langevin was also very involved in the security business. In the mid-1930s he was part of the commandos in Ethiopia in its war with Italy. He also participated in the Spanish Revolution. Langevin then worked for the provincial police upon his return from England. This led him to serving as a bodyguard for many politicians, like former prime ministers of Canada Mackenzie King and Louis St. Laurent, as well as Iran's Princess Soraya. Some Hollywood stars like Richard Burton and Elizabeth Taylor also benefited from his services while in Montreal. The many years he had spent in Europe also gave him the opportunity to act in films with such stars as Marlene Dietrich and Douglas Fairbanks Jr.

His wrestling career also took Langevin around the globe. "I think that he wrestled in 60 countries," says Leduc. He wrestled in Cuba many times. One of his matches held there in 1956 was a tag team match with him and Billy Two Rivers against Don Eagle and Eddie Perez. "We were in Florida and had the opportunity to go wrestle in Cuba through Don Eagle," remembers Billy Two Rivers. "They put us in the same team because we both came from Quebec. It drew a good crowd and they wanted to hold another match the following week. I was the only one of the threesome who stayed there. It was at the time when Fidel Castro was to stage a coup against the dictator Batista. The show never took place, and they got me out fairly quickly. Castro was the most dangerous of all heels there!"

But Langevin also wrestled against a famous boxer in Cuba. "He wrestled against Joe Louis three times. Two of the three matches were held in Cuba," remembers Leduc.

"Bob was also called upon to wrestle against those who had some technical difficulties so that he may guide them in the ring," adds Leduc. Such a role not only demands a lot of talent, but also, and more importantly, a lot of humility. "Édouard Carpentier would never have accepted this," says Leduc in comparison. Other big names wrestled Langevin. "I wrestled Lou Thesz in Hawaii," says Langevin in an interview with SLAM! Wrestling. "Then I wrestled Jim Londos. I even wrestled Strangler Lewis in New York." In the 1950s and '60s he did for Carpentier what he had first done for Yvon

BOB LANGEVIN VERSUS LÉO LEFEBVRE WAS THE FIRST WRESTLING MATCH TELEVISED ON THE BBC
(PAUL LEDUC COLLECTION)

Robert, following Carpentier from city to city and serving both as his interpreter and his foil. "At the beginning, I couldn't speak English very well. So he travelled and wrestled everywhere with me. He wasn't just anybody, and I regret having lost him every day," explains Carpentier.

When Johnny Rougeau relaunched Montreal wrestling in 1965, he made Bob Langevin his promoter, a role that Langevin had also played for Eddie Quinn in the early 1960s. Obviously Rougeau could not wrestle and have his name on a promoter's licence at the same time as this was prohibited by the MAC. So Langevin played the role for the 10-year existence of Johnny Rougeau's All Star Wrestling (as de la Lutte).

In 1966 misfortune struck again. Langevin underwent colon cancer surgery. As a result of complications, his legs were partially paralyzed. It would take him seven months to walk again. Due to the psychological problems ensuing from his paralysis, he tried to commit suicide twice during that period. "Johnny Rougeau and I spent three days and three nights watching over him so that he didn't commit the fatal act," relates Leduc, sadly. "Dreadful is probably the right word because you don't really accept the situation," said Langevin in an interview with Le Journal de Montréal. "But thanks to friends who kept on encouraging me, I was able to continue with my life."

When Paul Leduc says of his friend that he's the most decorated wrestler in the history, he's not exaggerating. Among his honours are that in 1973 he was invited by professor Pellerin from the Neker Hospital in Paris to a symposium on the colon and rectal surgery. On May 6, 1988, he was invested as a member of the Order of Canada by the Right Honourable Jeanne Sauvé, the first female governor general of Canada, and in January 1994 Pope Jean Paul II bestowed his papal blessings on Langevin for 25 years of volunteering for patients who underwent enterostomal therapy.

On October 8, 2005, sometime after having been interviewed for the Les Saltimbanques du Ring documentary, Bob Langevin died at the venerable age of 91. He had wrestled for 38 years, participating in 5,672 matches. "The number of messages he had delivered to patients who underwent enterostomal therapy was as large as the number of matches in which he participated during his career," says Leduc. "He was Johnny Rougeau's most faithful friend and companion, and he was a very much appreciated speaker at the conferences organized by the Canadian Cancer Society and the Montreal Ileostomy and Colostomy Association."

The WWF recognized Bob Langevin in 1995. During the last wrestling show to be held at the Montreal Forum, they offered him and Omer Marchessault a commemorative plate for their six decades in the wrestling world. Indeed, up until the 1990s, we could still see Langevin at the wrestlers' and media entrance at the Forum working for the WWF. In 2006 he was inducted into the Quebec Wrestling Hall of Fame.

HARRY MADISON, THE FORGOTTEN OLYMPIAN

Harry Madison was part of Canada's wrestling team in the 1932 Olympic Games in Los Angeles. He beat Yvon Robert in the Canadian try-out to secure his spot and finished fourth in freestyle at 87 kilos, losing his second match to the eventual gold medalist, American Pete Mahringer.

Madison was born Henry Maddison on October 7, 1909, in Verdun. After the Olympics, he trained at Maupas Camp before starting a professional career that lasted 20 years. Madison, who wrestled barefoot, was a big star in Montreal for smaller promoters like Lucien Grégoire and Gerry Legault. He was lightweight champion in the city many times. "He was a tough guy; the real deal," says Maurice Vachon.

FRANK VALOIS, WRESTLER, PROMOTER, ACTOR AND FAMILY MAN

Fans remember Frank Valois primarily as the promoter of International Wrestling in the 1980s, but his wrestling career should not be underestimated. In fact he was very successful in Europe and, in addition to discovering Édouard Carpentier and Jean Ferré, he became world champion, winning the title in a match against his hero and teacher Yvon Robert. "In 1949, the French wrestler Felix Miquet invited me to come for a tour of France. I was supposed to stay there for three months, but I ended up living there for three years, from 1949 to 1952," explained Valois in an interview with Le Journal de Montréal. "My mother always said that he wasn't able to even simply walk on the street. Even as a heel, everybody loved him," insists his daughter Françoise, who worked with her father in the wrestling office in the '80s. "He was a big star in France. People don't know this, but he was very well known there," confirms Guy Hauray, who came to Quebec from France. To put his popularity in Europe into perspective, it's important to realize that his wrestling career led him to a career in acting both in the movies and in the theatre.

"He acted on screen in a film entitled La Promesse de L'Aube, with Melina Mercouri. His film that I loved most is The Brain, with Belmondo, Bourville and David Niven. He also played Brother Tucker in Rabelais. He went on tours both in France and the United States," says his daughter, thus summing up his acting career. In France he would also serve as the bodyguard for two former presidents, Georges Pompidou and General Charles de Gaulle.

Born Fernand Levis Valois on December 17, 1921, in Montreal, his path crossed that of Yvon Robert at an early age, while playing basketball at the Kent Academy in Outremont. "Now that you're going to grow up, a man your size should practise a man's sport," the Lion of French Canada had told him. At 15 he already stood six feet tall and weighed 200 pounds. He started training with Robert, but he also continued his training in amateur wrestling under the supervision of Eugène Tremblay. "Yvon Robert trained my father at the Maupas camp," confirms his daughter. In 1939 Valois made his debut at La Tour de Québec, a famous building for wrestling in Quebec City. After having wrestled at the Forum for six months, Eddie Quinn sent him to Boston for promoter Paul Bowser. "You are not Fernand anymore, you're Frank," Bowser told him. "We moved to the United States when I was five. I came back at the age of 13. We went first to Texas, then to North Carolina, Florida and Ontario, and we finally came back in 1967, just before my father returned to Europe," explains Françoise.

His wrestling career continued after his time in Europe, even though he would never be world champion outside of the old world. He was very well respected by his fellow wrestlers. "In Quebec I loved working with Frank Valois," said Édouard Carpentier, who owes his career, to a large extent, to Valois.

The irony is that Frank's career came practically to an end almost before it started.

In 1945 he was in a serious car accident. A tanker ran a red light and hit his car. "He told the doctor to save his career, saying that wrestling was the only thing he knew how to do," explains Françoise. He was left with a scar on his face that distinctly marked the two phases of his career.

In the early 1980s Frank Valois put an end to his career travelling the world with Andre the Giant and returned to Montreal to become partners with both Gino Brito and his protégé André in the Varoussac promotion. "My father had a very good reputation; he was a very good businessman. He was honest and straight to the point. He had always done his best to keep his boys working. Moreover he never had a cheque bounced back when he was at the head of Varoussac," relates Françoise, proudly. Like any other promoter he had his difficult moments, as well as moments of glory. "The departure of the Giant was his worst moment when International Wrestling was still Varoussac. His best moment, on the other hand, was when we first had a full house at the Forum. He smoked the cigar that Serge Savard, the Montreal Canadiens' GM also in charge of renting the Forum, had offered him. He told my father that he was his wrestling promoter for the Forum," says his daughter with pride.

But the years he spent as the head of International Wrestling would certainly affect him negatively, as well. "It seems my father got 10 years older during his first year running Varoussac," says Françoise. After his success in Europe, both as a wrestler and an actor, after putting an end to his wrestling career in 1978 and his promoting career in 1986, Frank Valois died on December 31, 1998, at the age of 77. In 2010 he was finally elected to his rightful place in the Quebec Wrestling Hall of Fame.

FRANK VALOIS BECAME A MOVIE STAR IN FRANCE AS WELL AS A WRESTLING CHAMPION

Not only were Quebecers like Langevin and Valois wrestling in France, but Frenchmen were also coming into Montreal. Felix Miquet, who drew the biggest crowd of the year twice in Montreal, once against Yvon Robert in 1937 and once against Bobby Managoff in 1945, was one. His brother François, better known as Corsica Joe, not only came to Montreal, but also teamed with a Quebecer throughout his career.

CORSICA JEAN

Corsica Jean, whose real name was Jean-Louis Roy Sr., met François Miquet when the Frenchman arrived in Quebec in 1948. They teamed for the first time a couple of years later in Tampa, Florida. The two men would become

CORSICA JOE AND CORSICA JEAN, PIRATES OF THE SEVEN RINGS (SCOTT TEAL COLLECTION)

one of the most hated duos of all time in Memphis in the 1950s and 1960s. They would develop the characters of corsairs or, if you prefer, pirates. "I was a kid watching them beat up all the babyfaces at the Hippodrome in Nashville. I thought they were the toughest guys around. Later, as a promoter, I was happy to book them. Jean and Joe were tremendous heels who knew how to get heat and make their opponents look good in their comeback. They had a lot of charisma and spoke with disdain of Americans with their French accents," revealed promoter Jerry Jarrett to journalist Scott Bowden upon the death of Joe in 2010. Jean-Louis Roy Sr. lived until 1992, when he was assassinated in a bar he owned in Florida. In 2008 the two men were inducted into the National Wrestling Alliance (NWA) Hall of Fame.

All those who remember the time of Yvon Robert also remember the first wrestler to be presented as the next Yvon Robert, not only a fantastic wrestler, but also a real comedian.

Wrestling in California, Larry Moquin got an unheard-of opportunity. Many newspaper articles noted the resemblance between Moquin and Bud Abbott, part of the famous comedic duo Abbott and Costello, the creators of the stand-up classic "Who's on First?" In addition to staging their comedy in cabarets, the very creative duo also produced films — no fewer than nine movies during the second half of the 1940s. Moquin decided to capitalize on the resemblance. "My father acted as a stunt double for Bud Abbott in some of his movies when he worked in California," proudly relates Laurent Jr., his son.

Acting as the stunt double for one of the greatest comics in history is in total harmony with the kind of person Larry Moquin was. "Always happy, always telling a funny story," is how Jean Paul Sarault describes him in his book entitled *Fais-le Saigner*. During an interview broadcast on Radio-Canada, Moquin said, "I never laugh, see; that's my only flaw!" bursting into laughter.

During a match in Chicoutimi, Larry was teaming with Bobby Managoff against the Togo Brothers. He suggested that Managoff soak his armpits in cheese to gross out their opponents. "The trick worked to perfection," continued Sarault in his book.

This anecdote gives a very good idea of the kind of man Laurent "Larry" Moquin was.

"That guy was a comedian outside the ring," adds Maurice Vachon. To support his comment, Vachon says that Moquin used to show his butt to other cars when he was travelling. Eddie Quinn heard about it and asked him to stop, believing it wasn't acceptable behaviour for a professional wrestler. Sometime later, however, on his way to Ottawa, Moquin saw a car coming toward him and decided to show his butt yet again. But to his big surprise, the driver of that car was . . . Eddie Quinn himself!

Stories about Moquin's pranks and gags are as numerous and notorious as Andre the Giant's beer and wine stories. Yet, in the world of professional wrestling, Moquin wasn't just a mere prankster; he was actually hand-picked for a bright future. But unlike his mentor, Yvon Robert, Moquin was never to become the world champion in the Montreal territory.

On Radio-Canada Moquin talked about the origins of his career. "When I was a kid, Yvon Robert was the hero . . . We didn't have a lot of money,

LARRY MOQUIN LEARNING HIS CRAFT AT THE WELL-KNOWN MAUPAS CAMP

(LAURENT MOQUIN JR. COLLECTION)

and everyone in my school wanted to be like Yvon Robert, who was a rich star. There was wrestling five nights a week in Montreal, and I often saw Mr. Robert and I asked him how I could become a wrestler, too." When Moquin was playing junior football, Eddie Quinn finally asked him if he was interested in a wrestling career. "I trained for wrestling under the tutelage of Émile Maupas in the Laurentians. He was an extraordinary teacher."

He would actually make his debut at the Montreal Forum on February 26, 1942, at the age of 19. Right from the get-go he was promoted with Robert in his corner, and Horace Lavigne described Moquin as Robert and Émile Maupas's protégé in *La Patrie*. He won his first match against Jack Miller and even used some of the holds that Robert himself used.

Consequently Moquin was considered by many as Robert's heir apparent

LARRY MOQUIN WAS A STUNT DOUBLE FOR SOME ABBOTT AND COSTELLO MOVIES

(LAURENT MOQUIN JR. COLLECTION)

— the wrestler who would succeed the champion once the latter's career came to an end. Unfortunately that was not to be. Greg Oliver, in his book *The Pro Wrestling Hall of Fame: The Canadians*, compares the Robert and Moquin relationship to that of Batman and Robin. Moquin was never to replace Robert — not in the ring, nor in the hearts of the fans. Still, he was a highly respected and much-loved wrestler.

"As a talent in the ring, he was one of the best French-Canadian wrestlers," says Gino Brito. "I have always loved the sport; it was my life. The dropkick was my favourite hold and speed was my greatest asset," Moquin explained to Radio-Canada. His skillfulness in the ring didn't surprise his widow, Marthe. "My husband was very intelligent. He spoke and wrote both French and English. He learned very easily in many different fields."

So, it's not surprising to know that Moquin used to play handball, racquetball and golf, not to mention rugby and football. "He was more of an athlete than an intellectual, but was very educated at the same time. It's a side of his personality that many people are unaware of," she adds.

Eddie Quinn also recognized Moquin's talents, using him to main-event some shows and in many semifinals over the years. In 1945 Moquin was involved in the very first tag team match in Montreal with Yvon Robert at the Forum. In the late 1940s it was common to see Moquin and Robert teaming against the Duseks or even against a team formed by Lou Thesz and "Whipper" Billy Watson.

But Moquin was never able to draw like Robert. In the summer of 1951 Yvon Robert drew 10,000 people twice against Buddy Rogers. Moquin, against the same opponent, drew 7,000.

In spite of everything, Moquin continued his merry ways in the wrestling world. "My best year was 1950. I earned $40,000 that year," Moquin says in an interview with Jean-Paul Sarault. We have to bear in mind that $40,000 in 1950 was a large amount of money, approximately the equivalent of $350,000 today.

Moquin continued wrestling in the Montreal territory during the 1940s and 1950s, but what history leaves out is that he also wrestled outside the territory, in the United States and Europe.

Marthe Moquin says, "We got married in 1954 and spent our honeymoon in Hawaii. We spent six months there. Larry had contacts with the wrestling office in Hawaii and he wrestled there once a week during our stay." It was during this period that Moquin won the most important title in his career, the NWA Hawaii heavyweight title. Then, after Hawaii, they moved on to Europe. "We came back to Quebec. I spent some time with my parents and then we went to France to continue our honeymoon," she remembers.

The year to which his wife refers is, more precisely, 1955, when Moquin wrestled at the famous Palais des Sports in Paris. But his travels as a wrestler go back to the early days of his career. In 1943, barely one year after his first match, he wrestled in Texas, not as Larry Moquin, but under the name Larry Robert. He was announced as being either the cousin or the brother of Yvon Robert.

Moquin also wrestled in California at the famous Los Angeles Grand

Olympic Auditorium in 1947–48 and in the Atlanta territory. Later in his career, in 1959, he wrestled against The Sheik in the mecca of pro wrestling, Madison Square Garden (MSG) in New York City.

"He could not take wrestling seriously enough," relates Gino Brito. "It's actually a sad story," he adds referring to Moquin's potential. But Larry was Larry. He did things his own way for himself and to please the crowd. During a charity hockey game, Moquin wore a Toronto Maple Leafs jersey, and to caricature their more physical and rough style he went to Léo Lamoureux, who played for the Montreal Canadiens, pinned him on the ice and applied a leg lock, much to the joy of the crowd.

Moquin stopped wrestling in the early 1960s. Like Yvon Robert, Moquin opened a hotel, Hotel Canada, in Saint-Anne-de-Bellevue on October 9, 1951. He also worked as a promoter and cabaret artist during this period. After his hotel burned down, Moquin returned to wrestling. "The last years he only wrestled on weekends," remembers his son. He continued wrestling until the 1970s with Grand Prix Wrestling.

He contracted Meniere's disease — an illness that affects hearing and equilibrium — in the late '70s. It deprived him of quality of life for 10 years. Larry Moquin's name will always be associated with Yvon Robert. "He made me. I owe everything to Yvon," said Moquin at the end of his career. He succumbed to cancer on December 12, 1988. In 2011, he was inducted in the Quebec Wrestling Hall of Fame.

The first golden age wasn't just good for Quebecers. Some outsiders became almost as popular as the wrestlers born and raised in Quebec.

BOBBY MANAGOFF

Yvon Robert won a 1955 popularity contest organized by Lutte et Boxe magazine. An American from Chicago came second. He was clearly the most popular American wrestler in Montreal in the 1940s and 1950s. "When Dino Bravo and Jimmy Snuka started to inspire my dreams to become a wrestler, my father told me about the Roberts, Moquin and Vachon. But he kept on remembering Bobby Managoff, in addition to the Quebec wrestlers," says François Hébert.

BOBBY MANAGOFF'S GOOD LOOKS ALWAYS MADE HIM
POPULAR IN MONTREAL (TONY LANZA)

Managoff, whose real name was Robert Manoogian Jr., was trained by his father, Bob Sr., and made his debut in 1936 at the age of 18. His career spanned 30 years and he participated in 4,000 matches. "Bobby was a fantastic wrestler and a man of class. In addition, his father travelled with Frank Gotch and knew him well," said Lou Thesz, when giving him the first Frank Gotch Prize, awarded to a wrestler who was an athlete in the ring and also made wrestling popular through his actions outside the ring. In 1941, in Texas, he defeated Yvon Robert to become the National Wrestling Association champion. He would subsequently have a big rivalry with the Lion of French Canada. The biggest crowd he drew in Montreal was with Robert on August 5, 1943, when 15,000 people showed up at the Forum. The biggest non-Robert crowd he drew was 14,000 on October 17, 1945, against Felix Miquet. Besides working in a lot of main events, he also tagged with Robert on some occasions. Managoff lived in Montreal for a long time and helped young wrestlers train at the Tony Lanza Wrestling Club. He would end up winning the Montreal title four times before his final match in 1966. He died of heart failure on April 3, 2002.

LOU THESZ

Almost every wrestling fan knows something about the storied career of Lou Thesz. What most are not aware of is that Thesz was a very close friend of Eddie Quinn — so much so that upon his return to the ring in 1958, Quinn and Toronto's Frank Tunney would serve as his agents when pro-

moters wanted to obtain his services. "Lou would've done anything for Eddie." confirms Lou's widow, Charlie. Thesz even asked Quinn to invest in a promotion in St. Louis, when he was trying to oppose Sam Muchnick. "Eddie was one of wrestling's great success stories," affirms Thesz in his biography. And even if he hadn't been a friend of the Montreal promoter, the fans would've seen Thesz one way or another; he had been touring the North American

MONTREAL'S LOVER LOU THESZ WITH HIS FRIEND TONY LANZA (TONY LANZA)

territories from top to bottom. What is surprising is that in spite of the fact that Thesz was one of the biggest attractions in the history of wrestling, Montreal was not his best city, as he didn't draw well on a regular basis there; it's further evidence of the territory's uniqueness. He wrestled Yvon Robert, Bobby Managoff and eventually Édouard Carpentier, with whom he would have a feud that would go beyond the frontier of the province.

Aloysius Martin "Lou" Thesz was born in 1916 in Michigan. Along with Ric Flair, he's probably the wrestler most associated with the National Wrestling Alliance. For years a debate has raged about who was the better wrestler.

The last of the great shooters, or hookers, as Thesz was known, just like his mentor Ed "Strangler" Lewis, he was able to defeat his opponent against his will if the latter wanted to stray away from the original plan of the match. In fact Thesz was more like a mixed martial arts fighter than the professional wrestlers we know today. Even though his full-time wrestling career came to an end in 1979, he continued to make appearances in the ring until 1994, when he wrestled against his own protégé, Masa Chono, in Japan at the venerable age of 78. "The two best wrestlers in history were Yvon Robert and Lou Thesz," affirms Robert's protégé, Larry Moquin. He died on April 9, 2002, following complications during surgery, and he was elected into the Quebec Wrestling Hall of Fame in 2007.

BUDDY ROGERS

Born Herman Rohde, "Nature Boy" Buddy Rogers is, without a doubt, the American wrestler who had the most drawing power in the Montreal territory, before the arrival of Hulk Hogan. "Buddy Rogers drew thousands of people at Delorimier Stadium in Montreal. You didn't need a local to draw fans with Rogers. When you added a Quebec-born wrestler like Yvon Robert, you would just draw even more people," says Gino Brito. "We were never what you would describe as friends, but I respected Rogers as an attraction, so I called Eddie Quinn in Montreal and arranged some bookings for him there. I owed Eddie, and I figured Rogers would be good for him. I was right, too, because Rogers was, as usual, an immediate hit," relates Lou Thesz in his biography. He would become one of the biggest stars in the history of wrestling — and not just in Montreal. With his electric personality, he was one of the first stars of wrestling on the DuMont Television Network. On October 7, 1959, he took part in one of the best-ever matches opposing a wrestler to a boxer, facing former champion Jersey Joe Walcott at the Forum.

His spectacular popularity was at the origin of the creation of the WWWF (now WWE) in 1963. In fact, when he was unable to convince the NWA to keep him as a world champion, promoter Vince McMahon Sr. made him his first champion. Rogers was an innovator whose name, style, movements, clothing and whole personality were copied many times and still influence wrestling today. "Buddy Rogers, he was the best wrestler of all time for me. He was so good, he made anyone look like a great champion," Gino Brito recalls. His wrestling career came to an end in the late 1970s. In the early 1980s he was the host of "Rogers' Corner" on the WWF television show. On June 26, 1992, when he was about make a comeback for one more match, he died of a massive heart attack. In 2007 he was inducted into the Quebec Wrestling Hall of Fame, ironically at the same time as the wrestler who made it possible for him to wrestle in Montreal, Lou Thesz.

BUDDY ROGERS AND EDDIE QUINN WITH THE MONTREAL TERRITORY TITLE (TONY LANZA)

PAT O'CONNOR

Pat O'Connor was already successful in Montreal in the mid-1950s, when a feud opposing him to Killer Kowalski made him one of the top babyfaces in the territory. A match against Yvon Robert on August 18, 1954, drew 21,616 people to Delorimier Stadium, the biggest crowd in the history of the Montreal territory at the time. "O'Connor was a good technical wrestler, a real hard worker," remembers Gino Brito. It was common for main events featuring O'Connor to draw more than 10,000 fans. He would wrestle against the biggest names in the world, like Bobby Managoff, Argentina Rocca, Buddy Rogers, Lou Thesz and Don Leo Jonathan, just to name a few. During these years, he got the MAC title twice, beating Kowalski each time.

Born on August 22, 1924, in New Zealand, O'Connor was one of the greatest NWA champions of his era. His match against Buddy Rogers at Comiskey Park in Chicago in 1961 drew 38,622 and held the U.S. attendance record until *WrestleMania* III in 1987. His last visit to Montreal occurred in March 1984, when he served as referee in the final match between Dino Bravo and Rick Martel at the Forum. He died of cancer in 1990.

GENE KINISKI

Born in 1928, Eugene Nicholas "Gene" Kiniski was to become known in wrestling circles as Canada's greatest athlete. He became AWA champion in 1960, defeating Vern Gagne, and NWA world champion in 1966, beating Lou Thesz.

Before winning those laurels Kiniski won his only Montreal territory championship title on June 12, 1957, against Carpentier. Two weeks after, on July 17, 1957, he lost it to Killer Kowalski in front of a crowd of 21,851 fans. At the time it was the second-biggest crowd in Montreal's history. The match was also the biggest draw in North America for the entire year. Kiniski would later trigger a riot during a match between Kowalski and Carpentier. On August 7, 1957, he intervened in favour of Kowalski, and after Kiniski threw a chair in the direction of Carpentier thousands among the 14,789 fans did the same thing. The incident became known as the flying chairs riot. Kiniski's last match in Montreal took place on August 18, 1959, against Yukon Eric. Gene Kiniski died of a cancer on April 14, 2010.

GORGEOUS GEORGE

Before Hulk Hogan, Gorgeous George was arguably the most well-known wrestler of all time. Many credit George with being the first to have transcended his sport. It was television that allowed him to do so. Some even speculate that the character was actually created for television or that, rather, television was created for him! In the end he arguably influenced the biggest names in sports and the world of show business, from Muhammad Ali and Prince to Bob Dylan and James Brown.

Although he was not as active in Montreal as some of his contemporaries, his match against Yvon Robert on November 1948 at the Forum drew one of the biggest crowds that year, not only in Montreal, but throughout North America, with an attendance of 15,233 people. "His presentation took nothing away from him as a wrestler," said Larry Moquin. "He smelled so good that Yvon Robert always said he didn't know whether he should hit him or kiss him!" he added, laughing, as usual.

Notable in his Montreal history is a match against Lou Thesz in 1953 for the NWA world title. Inducted into the WWE Hall of Fame in 2010 at the same time as Maurice Vachon, he's considered an inventor of American pop culture. Born George Wagner, he died in 1963 and was buried in his ring robe in a coffin the colour of an orchid. He sold his gimmick even in death, an image that still influences wrestling today.

HANS SCHMIDT, FROM GERMANY BY WAY OF QUEBEC

"The world needs heroes, and it's better they be harmless men like me than villains like Hitler," is what the recipient of the Nobel Prize, Albert Einstein, said about the Nazi movement. In 1939, when World War II broke out, Germans became the enemies of all westerners.

Four years after the end of the war, a 24-year-old named Guy Larose made his pro wrestling debut. Under the name Guy Ross, he fought mainly in the state of Michigan and the rest of Canada against wrestlers like Stu Hart, Bob Lortie and Pierre Lasalle (Eddy Auger). Near the end of the year 1949 and during the next he was to wrestle mainly in New England under his real name. He finally made his Montreal debut on February 21, 1951, against Manuel Cortez. After having wrestled in some preliminaries in Montreal he returned to the United States. In 1952 he adopted the persona who would make him known around the world. From then on he would be known as Hans Schmidt.

"It was hard with a French name like that," he said, referring to his real name. "When you got to the States, people were making jokes. I met a promoter in Boston, Paul Bowser. He was German and he told me I looked like a German. That's when he gave me that name, Hans Schmidt," explains Larose in an interview with *SLAM! Wrestling*.

"We are responsible for his becoming a wrestler," affirms Billy Two Rivers, speaking about the Native American community. "Guy Larose was 18 years old and he aspired to become part of the RCMP. He was training then. At the time, it was prohibited to drink alcohol in the Kahnawake reservation. There was an RCMP station near our frontier, and they decided to

A BLOODY HANS SCHMIDT WITH KILLER KOWALSKI AT HIS SIDE (HANS SCHMIDT COLLECTION)

go to a wedding in order to arrest people drinking alcohol. This was not the best way of proceeding, as the owner of the place switched off the lights, and the RCMP agents were beaten. So they called upon the RCMP school nearby for help. Everyone came here. I do not know whether Guy was in the second or third truck, but the wheels of the trucks got punctured. Some guys were hitting the trucks with baseball bats. It was Guy who told me this story; I was too young. He said: 'We never left the truck. Everyone was losing their cool. We went back to the station, and on the following day I resigned! So I decided to become a pro wrestler.' This is a real story. I knew the story about that night, but I didn't know that he was personally involved until he told me himself."

Without knowing it, those he was jokingly blaming for his adventure in the world of professional wrestling certainly did him a huge favour. "Hans Schmidt was one of the major stars in the DuMont Network with Gorgeous George when wrestling began to be broadcast on TV," says Gino Brito. "He was one of the best heels in the early 1950s during the period following World War II with his Nazi persona." According to Dave Meltzer, he was one of the best-paid wrestlers at the time.

It must be said that he embodied a persona that was very much needed. "The history of wrestling is based on social circumstances," explains Paul Leduc. The aftermath of World War II actually witnessed the appearance of many "Nazi" characters like Kurt Von Hess, Fritz and Waldo Von Erich, not to mention the first wrestler to have embodied this kind of persona, Kurt Von Poppenheim. Even if Larose impersonated a German, he would never adhere completely to the role; he would leave the swastika and the Hitler salute to others. Obviously the mere act of impersonating a German was enough to incite people's hatred in the 1950s, as the Americans and the Canadians were barely recovering from the war. This gimmick still plays tricks on Schmidt today, as many historians believe that his success stems only from the character he played, not from his abilities as a wrestler.

Born on February 7, 1925, in Joliette, Schmidt drew big crowds and quickly became one of the major attractions in wrestling. Promoters fought over who would book him. "I only got two words to describe Schmidt: a heat machine!" said Sir Oliver Humperdink. It was actually Jim Barnett, the man who recommended John Cena to WWE just before he died, who launched Hans Schmidt's career. During the 20 years that followed, Schmidt wrestled in almost all the North American territories, from east to west, north to south, with some tours to Japan (where he teamed a couple of times with Bruno Sammartino, Waldo Von Erich and Lou Thesz against Giant Baba, among others). Even if he never won the title, he participated in many NWA championship matches. As a matter of fact, according to Meltzer's *Wrestling Observer* newsletter, the big names aside, Schmidt participated in the largest number of championship matches in the most territories, which certainly shows that he was over everywhere.

His official return to Montreal as Hans Schmidt took place on May 19, 1954. If more often than not the man behind a gimmick remains unknown, such was not the case for Larose. In fact, in its May 1954 edition, *La Patrie* states: "We can't wait to attend the debut of Montreal's own Guy Larose, better known as Hans Schmidt." It was common for Larose to speak French in his interviews or in the ring while fans insulted him. So it was easier for Larose to go incognito in the United States than in Quebec, where his accent and his interviews betrayed him.

In the 1960s, and more precisely starting from the mid-1960s, when Johnny Rougeau took over the territory, Schmidt wrestled more regularly in Quebec. He actually won the MAC title many times. It's also during these years spent in Quebec that he teamed with another German: Baron von Raschke.

Some years before Schmidt had been part of the last wrestling program presented by the man who suggested this persona to him, Paul Bowser. On July 15, 1960, he teamed with Killer Kowalski against Édouard Carpentier and Lou Thesz at the Boston Garden.

He returned to the United States in the 1970s, mainly performing in Ohio, Detroit and Buffalo, and made a couple of stops in Toronto before coming back to Montreal in 1974. More and more inactive due to the decline of wrestling in Montreal, Schmidt participated in his last regular matches in 1976 and 1977. In 1983 he returned once more for promoter Denis Lauzon. Among his peers he was considered a stiff worker. "I remember in Hull in 1965 he strangled me with a cord so tightly, I started to think I'd lose consciousness. When we discussed it in the back, Hans told me that it looked good and the crowd believed it. For Christ's sake, even I believed it!" Brito says.

On May 26, 2012, Schmidt, 87, passed away peacefully in his sleep at the Joliette hospital. He had water in his lungs and had been suffering from arthritis for a number of years.

Schmidt is historically ranked fifth as far as being in the top ten of those drawing the biggest crowds year after year. The period between 1953 and 1959 was very profitable for him, as he main-evented many shows. In Montreal he participated in the main event of the show that drew the biggest crowds in 1959 and 1961. On both occasions he wrestled against Édouard Carpentier. It's no accident that the 1998 documentary entitled *The Unreal Story of Professional Wrestling* describes Schmidt as the classic foreign villain. In 2012 he finally received his well-deserved place in the *Wrestling Observer*'s Hall of Fame.

If for the United States and the rest of the world he was Hans Schmidt, the terrifying enemy, for Quebecers he was, and will forever be, Guy Larose, one of our own and one of the best wrestlers the Montreal territory has ever had.

Native Americans may have helped create Hans Schmidt, but many actually became professional wrestlers themselves over the years. The Montreal territory witnessed the emergence of three of the most successful.

CHIEF WAR EAGLE

"There were many wrestlers in the Kahnawake Mohawk reservation in the 1920s. They launched a small organization and performed in the local arena. Chief War Eagle had already been a professional wrestler and spent the time he could spare between two trips helping the youths of the reservation improve. He was a light heavyweight wrestler. He weighed about 175 pounds. He wrestled in Michigan, Illinois and Ohio. He wrestled in the 1920s and 1930s. He won a light heavyweight title in the regions of Michigan and Ohio." This is how Billy Two Rivers described the career of his trainer's father.

Some people say that Chief Joseph War Eagle was actually Don Eagle's uncle and that he was promoted as his father only for wrestling, which is completely false. John Joseph Bell was born on March 21, 1899, in Kahnawake, near Montreal (also called Caughnawaga at the time). Besides working in the U.S., he also wrestled in Montreal on occasion. After his career as a wrestler he worked in construction, building bridges. He had only one son, Carl Donald, whom he helped train as a wrestler. Once his son's professional career took off he became his manager, both in the ring and behind the scenes. In his book about the NWA, Tim Hornbaker quotes Fred Kohler, saying that he "had to consult with Chief War Eagle, Paul Bowser and Al Haft before bringing Don Eagle to his territory." Managing his son's career was the last thing War Eagle did in wrestling. He died on August 27, 1979, but through his offspring he allowed two generations of Native American wrestlers to leave an important legacy in wrestling.

FATHER AND SON: CHIEF WAR EAGLE AND DON EAGLE, BOTH FROM KAHNAWAKE (PWHF COLLECTION)

DON EAGLE

On May 26, 1950, Don Eagle was defeated by Gorgeous George in Chicago, losing his AWA title. If title switches in wrestling are common, this one was different. In fact Don Eagle was scheduled to win, but was screwed out of it. This match is one of a very short list of championship matches that had an outcome different from the original scenario. While Eagle had only one shoulder pinned to the mat, referee Earl Mollohan counted to three quickly and declared Gorgeous George the winner. The crowd, who noticed that Eagle had only one shoulder pinned, started throwing things and began to riot. Furious at what had just happened, Eagle chased Mollohan down the hall after he left the ring and hit him hard, between the shoulders. As if being screwed out of his title wasn't bad enough, the Illinois Athletic Commission suspended Eagle for attacking the referee. It's probably the screw job that was the closest to the one that took place in Montreal between Michaels and Hart, especially with the involvement of the referee. Ironically, in both cases, the ref's name was Earl.

It was Fred Kohler who was behind the outcome. Following the incursion of promoters Leonard Schwartz and Al Haft into Chicago, a town he considered his territory, and following the silence of the National Wrestling Alliance, Kohler decided to take the law into his own hands and avenge himself. He had used Don Eagle for more than a year and did good business with him on top. Eagle was the first wrestler to distinguish himself with Native American costumes, in addition to the dances he performed. "In the United States, Don Eagle was quickly becoming popular with his spectacular style and gimmick. The arrival of television contributed a lot to his popularity," adds his student Billy Two Rivers.

On November 18, 1949, Eagle defeated Cyclone Anaya in Chicago and became Illinois' heavyweight champion, the last local champion before Kohler recognized the NWA champion as his champion. But what really bothered Kohler was that his competitors also used Eagle. It must be noted that Eagle was also AWA champion, having won the title three days prior to his match against George, defeating Frank Sexton in Cleveland, a city that belonged to Haft. Kohler decided that if Haft wanted to use Eagle, he would make sure to diminish his value, even if that meant throwing away a year's worth of work and promotion of his star. So he asked George to do what had to be done to win the match and also informed referee Mollohan. Kohler didn't care about the AWA title, contrary to what normally happens in a screw job. What he wanted was to simply harm his opposition's star. The match was actually never promoted as a championship match, and no belt was ever given to the winner.

Obviously Haft and Schwartz, as well as Paul Bowser in Boston, continued to recognize Eagle as champion. Eagle defeated George in Columbus on August 31, 1950, to re-establish the title's lineage. Even if Kohler didn't act in the name of the NWA, the latter must not have been too dissatisfied with the situation, since the AWA title claimed a lineage as far back as Ed "Strangler" Lewis in 1928 and, ultimately, George Hackenschmidt in 1905.

Carl Donald Bell was born on August 25, 1925, in Kahnawake. His father began training him after he'd played football and done some boxing. "He started his career in New York and the east coast of the United States," relates Billy Two Rivers. His first match in Montreal took place on August 15, 1945, against Jacques Trudeau at the Forum. Although he was more successful in the United States, mainly in Ohio and Illinois, Eagle participated in some main events in Montreal during his career. His first main event was held in October 1949 against Lou Thesz for the NWA championship, a match that drew 11,000 people at the Forum, one of the biggest crowds that year. After his match against George he continued to wrestle in the United States, having a classic against Argentina Rocca in 1951. Eagle, who was known for driving his Cadillac with a 20-foot canoe on top of it for promotion, returned to wrestling in 1953 after recovering from a back injury. He continued until 1963, wrestling more than ever in the province of his birth. When his back began to give him a hard time again, he decided to retire once and for all. On March 17, 1966, he was found dead after having, according to media reports, shot himself. However the people who were closest to him don't believe it. "I am convinced that he didn't kill himself, that he didn't commit suicide," asserts Two Rivers with authority. Either way the expert of the Indian deathlock died at the very young age of 40.

He's recognized historically as one of the best, if not the best, Native American wrestlers of all time and is part of the 20 best Canadian wrestlers in history, according to wrestling historian and journalist Greg Oliver. One of his sons, Flint Eagle, is a well-known Hollywood stuntman.

BILLY TWO RIVERS

In 1959 luck decided the fate of Billy Two Rivers. "I had the choice of going either to Calgary or England. I made my decision on a coin toss, and England won," says Two Rivers, candidly. Allowing chance to dictate one's life often brings the unexpected and so, thanks in part to television, Billy became a star in England from 1959 to 1965. "As a Native American, with the Commonwealth agreement, I could stay there as long as I wanted, so I lived there for six years. From England I travelled everywhere in Africa and Europe. Like Don Eagle in the United States, I became a TV star when this medium was starting." Former WWE wrestler William Regal remembers Two Rivers well. "It was very common at the time that Billy Two Rivers was a big star in Britain [for people] to have a Mohawk [haircut] because he was hugely popular."

Born on May 5, 1935, in Kahnawake, Two Rivers made the acquaintance of Don Eagle after Eagle returned to Kahnawake to heal a back injury. Being only 15, Two Rivers played lacrosse like many other youths on the reservation. That's when Don Eagle made his offer. "Don and his father drove us to different lacrosse competitions. One day he suddenly offered to train me as a wrestler," remembers Two Rivers. Sometime later, when Eagle was ready to go back on the circuit, he asked young Billy to follow him. In 1953, in Detroit, Billy Two Rivers started a 25-year career that was to take him everywhere around the

(PAUL LEDUC COLLECTION)

BILLY TWO RIVERS HAD A TON OF SUCCESS IN ENGLAND BEFORE RETURNING TO QUEBEC

world. From Ohio to Florida, passing through Boston, Charlotte, Japan and even Cuba, he wrestled in both singles matches or in tag teams, mainly with Don Eagle. "When I had enough experience, Don Eagle proposed that I become his partner."

The wrestler, who had never had the opportunity to perform in front of his home fans, was eventually invited to the Montreal territory. "It was Paul Vachon who called me and asked me to come back and wrestle for Grand Prix," he remembers. "I had met Paul in England upon his return from India, and we wrestled together at Royal Albert Hall." He was paired with Johnny War Eagle, who wasn't a Native American, but with whom Two Rivers got along. "At the beginning the fact that there were fake Indians bothered me. When I matured I understood the importance of using gimmicks to make money for promoters. They were ambassadors, as we were for our people, and they respected our culture when they presented the gimmick," he explains.

After the end of the Grand Prix adventure he went back to England and also Germany before returning to finish his career in Montreal, where he won the Athletic Commission title at a time when wrestling in the territory was not what it used to be. Later he got involved in politics, having been an important member of the Native American community during the Oka Crisis in 1990. "Immediately after Grand Prix I was offered the opportunity to be part of the tribal council, and I was to hold that position for 20 years," he says, proudly. Two Rivers is also very proud of a role he played during the last couple of years. "I inducted 10 Native Americans all at once into the Pro Wrestling Hall of Fame in Amsterdam, New York. It was an injustice that no other hall of fame had Native American wrestlers among its members," he says.

The 1950s also witnessed the debut of the two brothers from Ville-Émard, now a part of Montreal. If the first was a fierce wrestler, the second had a vision and an understanding of the industry like few others before and after him.

MAURICE VACHON

In an interview with the *Wrestling Observer* radio program, former British wrestler Billy Robinson, who now trains and coaches MMA fighters, had this to say about Maurice Vachon: "Mad Dog is a street fighter. If Mad Dog was coming up today, he would be MMA world champion." Former wrestling and boxing promoter Régis Lévesque also feels he would have the edge, even on MMA champion Georges St-Pierre.

Maurice Vachon's reputation for being a fierce wrestler is such that many who have written their autobiographies include an anecdote about the strength of the little guy from Ville-Émard (as he likes to call himself).

Born on September 1, 1929, he was strong, even as a child. In fact he was able to beat the father of one of his classmates at the tender age of 13.

In order to allow his sons to concentrate their energies in the right place,

MAD DOG BEING INDUCTED IN THE QUEBEC SPORTS HALL OF FAME WITH NICOLAS FONTAINE,
MÉLANIE TURGEON, MARC TARDIF, EDGAR THÉORET [PRESIDENT] AND CLAUDE MOUTON'S WIDOW

(PAT LAPRADE)

Ferdinand Vachon — Maurice's father — took his three sons to the YMCA in downtown Montreal for them to learn wrestling. The YMCA teacher was none other than Frank Saxton, the former coach of the Canadian amateur wrestling team, who coached former professional wrestlers Earl McCready and Harry Madison for the 1928 and 1932 Olympic Games.

In 1948 Maurice left his native Quebec to represent Canada in Greco-Roman wrestling at the Olympic Games in London, England. Barely 18, he wrestled in the first round against the champion of India, Keshav P. Roy, and defeated him in less than a minute — even though Vachon was three years younger. Although he would finish seventh, it should be noted that the three opponents he faced were all older and much more experienced. The man who was to shatter Vachon's dream of winning the medal, Turkish wrestler Adil Candemir, was 12 years his senior. (Candemir was awarded the silver medal.)

Maurice's gold medal dreams didn't come to an end with his return from London. Two years later, during the British Empire Games in Auckland, Maurice Vachon represented Canada one more time. And this time destiny was in his favour. Maurice came back to Montreal with gold. The little guy from Ville-Émard, who used to fight every day after school, was now a world champion.

The high of his success was short-lived. He had a reputation, but that was not synonymous with money, and that aspect of Vachon's life hadn't yet changed.

Upon returning from New Zealand he took a job as a club bouncer. In a very short time Maurice earned a reputation. He'd fight anyone, anytime, whenever necessary. People knew of Maurice's international exploits, and nearly every day one the clients wanted to test himself, but Vachon won each and every fight. His reputation was becoming dangerous.

Armand Courville, a former professional wrestler who later became Vic Cotroni's (Montreal's Mafia boss) right-hand man, also worked as a bouncer. Vachon explained: "Courville told me once that if the guys weren't able to defeat me with their fists, they would do it with a weapon. It was getting dangerous for me to work at the clubs. That was when he introduced me to professional wrestling."

Vachon broke into the business in 1951, working for promoter Gerry Legault alongside his best friend Fernand Payette, who had also participated in the '48 Olympics, finishing fourth in the light-heavyweight division.

But, once again, success wasn't immediate. At the beginning of his career Maurice wore a simple jacket and trunks to the ring. He had no beard at the time and had dark hair. Vachon's look was a far cry from that of the mad dog with the thick beard, for which he would become famous. In the 1950s very few Quebecers were able to succeed as babyfaces. Yvon Robert, who had a say in the office managed by Eddie Quinn, didn't allow just anyone to share in his spotlight. Moquin enjoyed some success, and the only other man chosen to get a share of that spotlight was Johnny Rougeau, years later. Others like Vachon, Pat Patterson and the Garvins had to exile themselves to become successful or, if you prefer, make money.

Although this might seem unfair, what was going on at the time shouldn't be underestimated. Quebecers, or rather French-Canadians, as they were called at the time, had not yet fully recovered from the conquest of the province by the Anglophones 200 years before. Vachon knew this reality very well, after having to fight young Anglophones when he was in school. His experiences fighting against the English establishment proved similar to battles Maurice Richard faced — and this may be one of the reasons why Robert and Richard got along so well, too.

Clearly when a French-Canadian reached the top he had to do everything in his power to remain there. In Robert's case, this meant that he had to choose the other French-Canadian he was to rub shoulders with, and hand-pick the one to eventually succeed him. They could only repeat what they had learned from their battle with the English establishment. Maurice would, on the other hand, help countless Quebecers get a start in pro wrestling in different territories.

After having wrestled here and there in Quebec for small promoters, Vachon left to wrestle across the United States and the rest of Canada, including in Calgary, where he performed for the legendary Stampede promotion for Stu Hart. There he was able to have one of his own by his side — and not just any Quebecer. Maurice's younger brother, Paul, who also practised amateur wrestling, went to Calgary to follow in the footsteps of his famous brother.

After his second stint in Texas and a tournament in Hawaii, Maurice finally settled in Portland, Oregon. The promoter there, Don Owen, was to have a crucial influence on his career.

"During a match I went outside the ring and started to turn everything upside down," remembers Vachon. "A policeman tried to stop me, and I hit him, too." When he got backstage, Owen had two words for him that changed not only his career, but also his life: "You just looked like a real mad dog out there," he told Maurice. From that day forward, Maurice Vachon, a real French-Canadian athlete, became Mad Dog Vachon, a dangerous man from Algeria.

It was in the Midwest that Mad Dog was the most successful, especially in Minnesota for promoters Verne Gagne and Wally Karbo. Vachon became one of the greatest stars that the territory ever knew. For the fans

BEFORE THE MAD DOG, MAURICE VACHON HAD A TOTALLY DIFFERENT IMAGE (TONY LANZA)

in Minnesota, Nebraska and many other surrounding states, Mad Dog Vachon was not a wrestler from Montreal or Ville-Émard, but from a country about which the West knew very few things, aside from its Islamic religion and its war with the French. It was, however, enough to bestow mystery upon his persona, and to this day people there still believe that Vachon is from Algeria.

Maurice is a five-time AWA world heavyweight champion. Teaming with his brother, he won the AWA tag team title and together they became one of the biggest drawing acts in the business. He had a long-lasting feud with Verne Gagne, who was worshipped in the American Midwest.

The 1970s had something new in store for Maurice, as he decided to come back to Quebec to invest in a new promotion that was to run opposition against All Star wrestling, which was managed by Johnny Rougeau. So it was with Yvon Robert Jr., Édouard Carpentier, his brother Paul and some other partners that Grand Prix made its debut in 1971. The contacts of the Vachon brothers helped Grand Prix in the beginning, as their friends were to make numerous appearances on the early shows.

It was during that time that Maurice wrestled, unquestionably, his most important match in a Montreal ring. In fact on July 14, 1973, at Jarry Park Stadium, home at the time of the Montreal Expos, Vachon defeated his nemesis, Killer Kowalski. In order to boost the event, Vachon had stated that he would commit suicide if he didn't beat his rival, a declaration that would create a lot more commotion if it had been made today. But Vachon's out-rageousness paid off, as 29,127 people were on hand that night, a record that has not yet been broken 39 years later. The day after his victory the lead story of the newspaper read, "Vachon triumphs in front of 30,000 people and gives up on suicide!"

When the Grand Prix promotion shut down, wrestling in the province took a major hit, which led, among other things, to Maurice returning to his first love: the AWA. After having wrestled his last match for Grand Prix in November 1973 against Toru Tanaka, he wrestled in tag team mainly with The Crusher, in a feud with Nick Bockwinkel and Ray Stevens. Then in 1975 he became IWE champion in Japan, upon defeating Mighty Inoue. The same year he formed a tag team in the AWA with his enemy in Montreal, Jos Leduc, against the Valiant brothers. In 1976 he forged a new tag team with Baron von Raschke. Vachon came back to Montreal from time to time, having a bloody feud with Gypsy Joe, but wrestling in Quebec was still in a relatively comatose state at the time.

At the end of 1978 longtime AWA fans would witness something that they had never expected, the reunion of not only two legends, but also two sworn enemies: Maurice Vachon and Verne Gagne. Wanting to treat his fans to something new, Gagne decided to team with Maurice against the villains coming from the West, Pat Patterson and Ray Stevens. In the early 1980s Vachon was almost exclusively wrestling in the AWA and most of the time he worked tag teams, as he tagged with different partners like Dick the Bruiser, Tito Santana, Jim Brunzell, Andre the Giant, Rick Martel and Dino Bravo, as well as a young grappler named . . . Hulk Hogan.

Then in 1984 and 1985 Maurice divided his time between the AWA, the WWF and, from time to time, International Wrestling in Montreal. Vachon finally announced a retirement tour in the summer of 1986. He travelled everywhere in Quebec, thanking the fans who had supported him one last time. Finally, on October 13, 1986, at the Paul-Sauvé Arena, teaming with his arch-enemy in the Montreal territory, Jos Leduc, he had his last match against Man Mountain Moore and Gilles Poisson.

But the 1980s were far from over for Maurice. A series of happy and sad events would fill not only his career, but also his life. Maurice was working on television shows in Quebec, making commercials, recording a rap song, doing the traffic report on the radio and starring in a children's morning show entitled *Mad Dog the Pirate!* But it was as if each good moment was counterbalanced by tragedy: Maurice was struck by a hit-and-run driver while he was jogging early one morning when vacationing in Iowa. He lost a leg, which tragically put an end to his second career. His wife revealed to *Le Journal de Montréal* the strength of her champion: "He accepts what happened a lot better than I do. Even if his heart is broken, he has accepted his fate; I was so impressed with him. He insisted on declaring that he had always wrestled to succeed in life and that he would go on with one leg." More than ever Quebecers supported their hero. He received more than 40,000 letters of sympathy. "There were so many that I could easily have covered my hospital room with them. Even Canada's Prime Minister Brian Mulroney called me," he related to *Le Journal de Montréal* upon his glorious return to Montreal. In fact the government of Canada sent a plane to bring him back.

After many interviews and appearances for the WWF (where his wooden leg was actually used as a prop), after moving to Nebraska and being inducted into the *Wrestling Observer*'s Wrestling Hall of Fame and the Quebec Wrestling Hall of Fame and after losing the use of his remaining leg (and having to use a wheelchair), he had bestowed upon him an honour that had been bestowed upon just one professional wrestler before him: he was inducted into the Quebec Sports Hall of Fame, taking his play with athletes like Maurice Richard, Guy Lafleur, and of course, Maurice's hero, Yvon Robert!

And if this was not enough, less than six months later WWE decided to induct the 80-year-old legend into their hall of fame during *WrestleMania XXVI*. "It's a great honour for me. I am really proud of that," said Maurice, commenting on this nomination.

Throughout his life and career, Maurice had to fight. Whether it was against a bully, the champion of India, a nightclub thug who thought he was stronger than he really was, a wrestler who wanted his spot or a promoter who wanted to cheat him out of a payday, Vachon never let anything defeat him.

Maurice "Mad Dog" Vachon had been, without a shadow of a doubt, the most hated wrestler in the history of professional wrestling in Montreal. However, near the end of his career and around his retirement in 1986, he

AWA WORLD TAG TEAM CHAMPIONS PAUL AND MAURICE VACHON (PAUL VACHON COLLECTION)

became the people's hero. "Throughout my career, I tried to make myself hated. But, I certainly failed there!" he said.

"At the Colisée de Québec, I wrestled along with Jos against Maurice and Paul. They had injured Jos before. So we were both against him, and at some point the crowd changed sides and was supporting Maurice. The crowd empathized with him," relates Paul Leduc. "Jos said to Maurice: 'Shit, you're turning us heels!'"

Maurice worked 50 years for his popularity. He sweated blood to achieve it.

PAUL VACHON

"Paul Vachon was ahead of his time." This is according to one of his most fierce opponents Paul Leduc. And although Leduc and Vachon wrestled against one another on many occasions, it wasn't regarding Vachon's talent as a wrestler that Leduc made this nice statement.

In fact the biggest achievements in Paul Vachon's career were probably made outside of the ring. In spite of his height and build, he had never been the world champion for a big wrestling promotion like the AWA or the NWA. He often wrestled in tag team with his brother Maurice and almost always wrestled in his shadow. But he was not going to allow his status as the youngest in the family to prevent him from making a lasting impression. What so few people knew was that Paul Vachon had an unheard-of flair for the professional wrestling business, and this flair was revealed in the early 1970s in the Montreal territory.

After having bought Gerry Legault's share in the wrestling promotion that would become Grand Prix Wrestling, Vachon was put in charge of rescuing the young company from the abyss after only a couple of months of doing business. But even before becoming partner in the adventure, Vachon realized that having a successful promotion in Montreal depended on three things: a TV show, a licence from the Athletic Commission and being able to hold shows at the Montreal Forum. However Vachon had no promotional experience or even business experience. Paul was famous for being "a bon vivant," with whom it was always nice to spend time. "I adore The Dog, but I had more fun with Butcher!" confirms "Cowboy" Bill Watts. Verne Gagne told the company shareholders one time that they needed three things to succeed and he actually talked about the three same things Paul understood. He had an incredible instinct that almost never failed him. When it came time to choose whether Carpentier or Maurice were to be the head of the company, Gagne told them that neither was to be considered for that position, as they were the stars of the promotion and suggested Paul instead. Even though this choice was not unanimously adopted, Paul was put in charge of the promotion, which had debts of thousands of dollars. At the same time Yvon Robert died, leaving his shares to his son, Yvon Jr. Paul Vachon, who had been a professional wrestler for 15 years and who had no business experience, had to get the burgeoning promotion back on its feet and make it compete with a promotion that had been established for five years, namely Johnny Rougeau's All Star. It was then that Paul Vachon's genius was put to work.

Making daring and sometimes risky decisions, Vachon set in motion a plan to turn his promotion into the number one wrestling show in Montreal. In a short time he succeeded in reaching an agreement with one of the biggest radio stations in town, CKVL. Its offices were a stone's throw away from the Verdun Auditorium, where shows were held each week. He succeeded in getting the tape of the show that CFCF, a Montreal English station, had filmed during the early days of the company in order to sell it to other stations. CFCF was not interested at the time. He also finally struck a deal to get one hour of airtime on TV each week on Télé 7 from Sherbrooke. Of greater importance was the time slot. Paul Vachon changed wrestling's habits on TV in Montreal forever. Up until that time wrestling used to be presented on Wednesday evenings or Saturday afternoons, but Sunday at 11 a.m. would become the new tradition that International Wrestling and the WWF would follow in the 1980s. Suddenly CFCF, which had not been interested early on, wanted in on the adventure and, in a short time, Vachon's first objective was achieved: he had a wrestling program that was seen in Montreal, Quebec City, Sherbrooke and even as far away as Ottawa.

His other objectives would soon be met. Having always been self-confident, talking as if he had been in control of his business (although that was far from the truth on many occasions) and making use of all the contacts he could, Paul Vachon achieved everything by January 1972. He had a weekly TV program, both in English and in French, a licence from the Athletic Commission and dates at the Montreal Forum. Giving CKVL a share of the profits, he managed to reach an agreement with the station, too, a first at the time in the territory. "People didn't understand why I spent so much money on radio ads, but what they didn't know was that the radio station was simply a partner," explains Vachon. He paid for his production, which made him owner of whatever was filmed. Thus he didn't depend on a TV station. This is actually a concept that Vince McMahon Jr. would make use of years later. In fact no promoter in Montreal had ever done things this way before. "Eddie Quinn didn't pay production costs," remembers Vachon. "Johnny wasn't able to sell his tape, as he didn't pay for the production," adds Paul Leduc. "I don't know if I was the first in North America to do that, but I remember that Verne Gagne and

PAUL VACHON WITH HIS YOUNGER LOOK-ALIKE "STONE COLD" STEVE AUSTIN AT THE CAULIFLOWER ALLEY CLUB 2012

(PAUL VACHON COLLECTION)

Wally Karbo in Minneapolis told me that I was crazy," says Vachon. Moreover the English version of his program was presented from St. John's, Newfoundland, to Edmonton, thus covering most of the Canadian territories. His programming could have easily become a national promotion or at least it was national so far as the broadcasting of its TV show was concerned. "I gave my tapes to all the stations; I didn't sell it to them," explains Vachon. In return I asked them to grant me two minutes of advertising when I needed it. Our program was, thus, broadcast everywhere without additional costs. It made the Grand Prix brand known throughout Canada . . . I am proud of being compared to Vince McMahon and Jim Barnett, who made WWE what is today," he says. "But at the same time, I didn't think about that . . . And I still don't see it in that light. I simply did my best to make Grand Prix the best wrestling promotion possible."

Born on October 7, 1937, Paul Vachon was 14 when he started amateur wrestling training. Although he never participated in the Olympics or in the Commonwealth Games, he deserves credit for having finished second in Canada in the 191-pound category. He was only 17 at the time, and the Canadian championships took place in Regina. Paul went to Chicago after these competitions to train in a YMCA and called his brother Maurice to tell him about his silver medal. Maurice told Paul that during the summer he should start with the professionals and that he had done enough amateur wrestling. During the following summer Paul was touring with Maurice all over northern Ontario and Quebec, as well as Texas. Sometime later he was wrestling under the name of Nicolai Zolotoff. "It was promoter Bert Ruby in Detroit who came up with this persona because Jack Britton found that

I looked too young with hair and no beard," explains Vachon. Then near the end of the 1950s he worked for Stampede Wrestling with Maurice, this time under his real name. It was the beginning of a career that would take him around the globe. Vachon was successful everywhere he went, mainly in tag teams, and he won many titles with many different partners like Louie Tillet, Chavo Guerrero Sr., Stan Vachon and Hard Boiled Haggerty.

Until 1969 Paul and Maurice really hadn't formed a full-time tag team. Yet, in spite of this, they'd already captured the tag titles in Texas, the Carolinas and Georgia. Calgary, Minneapolis and Montreal were, without a doubt, the three territories where the Vachon brothers were the most successful. The year 1969 marked the return of the Vachon brothers to wrestling on a regular basis, this time with Verne Gagne's AWA. From August 30, 1969, to May 15, 1971, the Vachons were AWA tag team champions for one of the three biggest wrestling promotions in North America. In 1969 Paul and Maurice were so popular that they were part of the 10 top wrestlers and teams who drew the biggest crowds in the world. Their consecutive reign of 623 days ended in a loss against Red Bastien and Hercules Cortez, only to be outmatched in AWA history by The High Flyers, Greg Gagne and Jim Brunzell in the early 1980s. "We had no choice; we had to let the title go if we wanted to concentrate on the wrestling promotion that we were starting in Montreal," explains Paul. In 1970, their cage match against The Crusher and Dick the Bruiser at Comiskey Park in Chicago drew 21,000, the biggest crowd in the world that year. In Quebec their feud with the Leduc brothers is legendary. From 1969 to 1973 the Vachons were one of the teams who drew the biggest crowds in the wrestling world. When the shows were held in Montreal, Paul, who had his name on the promoter's licence, was not allowed to wrestle. He would hang up his wrestling boots for the night and become the promoter; he could deliver the goods in that role, as well. The arrival of Andre the Giant, his feud with Don Leo Jonathan, the arrival of the Hollywood Blonds, the switch of the Leducs and the match at Jarry Park Stadium between Maurice and Killer Kowalski, a very strong tag team division that included the Kiwis (young Bushwackers), Brito and Dino Bravo, and Johnny War Eagle and Billy Two Rivers, among others, are some of the Vachon-inspired things that made Grand Prix a success. "I liked making stars out of local talents," he says, referring to Zarinoff Leboeuf and Gilles Poisson, among others. "In addition our contacts allowed us to bring whomever we wanted." In fact Grand Prix also distinguished itself from All Star Wrestling by the sheer number of foreign wrestlers.

Once the Grand Prix adventure came to an end for the Vachons, Paul started to work for his good friend Vince McMahon Sr. Then he headed west to work in Los Angeles and Portland. After having gone to Florida he returned to New York, where he would wrestle until his retirement in 1985. However what people remember most is Paul Vachon's wedding that aired on the WWF show *Tuesday Night Titans*. Vachon got married in the ring, with his brother Maurice as a witness. A number of twists and turns would follow, including David Schultz's sabotage of the reception, not to mention a food fight between all the wrestler guests. Sky Low Low, "Captain" Lou Albano, Fred Blassie and Fabulous Moolah, as well as Vince McMahon Jr., among others, were part of it. "I was really going to get married, and Vince wanted me to do that in the ring. I agreed, but a couple of weeks before our wedding I broke up with the bride-to-be. Vince wanted to go ahead, none-theless, and hired an actress to play the role of my wife for the program!" reveals Vachon. (The whole episode can be seen on YouTube today.)

Paul Vachon is clearly one of Quebec's true wrestling geniuses, in the same vein as Jack Britton and Pat Patterson. When Grand Prix closed for good, Paul Vachon, who had sold his shares earlier, got involved in another promo-tion, Celebrity Wrestling. "Paul Vachon was a great salesman. After All Star Wrestling and Grand Prix, he succeeded in airing Celebrity on TV, from Halifax to Vancouver. CFCF, the main English television station in Montreal, started presenting Celebrity. We were on our way to presenting shows at the Forum. It lasted about a year, but it had the potential to go further," says Paul Leduc.

Paul Vachon enjoyed a 30-year wrestling career that allowed him to travel the globe. He's been inducted, along with his brother Maurice, into the Wrestling Hall of Fame in Amsterdam, New York, the Quebec Wrestling Hall of Fame and also the George Tragos/Lou Thesz Hall of Fame, which recognizes those who had a wrestling career both as an amateur and a pro-fessional. The years he spent as a promoter, however, really showed that he understood the wrestling industry like no other. Simply put, he was a visionary. Paul Leduc concludes: "When Paul Vachon was involved in a project that had to do with wrestling, people wanted to get involved in it, as they knew that it was going to work."

One mustn't be surprised at the help Maurice and Paul got from the likes of Gagne, Bruno Sammartino and others. Maurice, for example, was celebrated as someone who fearlessly helped others.

Jim Raschke's wrestling persona, Baron von Raschke, for example, was Maurice's idea. "If it wasn't for Montreal and Mad Dog, the little Jim Raschke that I was would not have had the career I had," confirms Raschke, whose daughter was born on the south shore of Montreal. The Butcher nickname for his brother Paul came from a discussion between the two. In fact Maurice found that he benefited a lot from the nickname Mad Dog and wanted his brother to have a similar opportunity. "My brother wanted to dub me The Pig, says Paul, laughing. I finally opted for The Butcher and it really did help me a lot." Among his countryman he gave without reservation. One who benefited was Rick Martel. After he had been under his brother Michel's tutelage, providence put Rick in Maurice's path. "I respect him. He was leaving the territory, and the booker Red Bastien asked Maurice to lose by DQ against me. Maurice answered back: 'I'm going to do a job for him!' I got to know him better in Minneapolis, but I was very impressed," says Martel, reminiscing about his stint in Texas. Besides Martel, two other Quebecers would also benefit from Vachon's help.

RENE GOULET

"I wrestled in Montreal against Maurice Vachon, and he asked me why I didn't give it a try in the United States. Then I told him that I didn't speak English. He told me that he would call Wally Karbo in Minneapolis, and that there would be no problem," Rene Goulet relates. "I finally called in 1963, and Maurice kept his promise. I told my wife that if it didn't work after six months, we would come back and I would find some other career. I have lived in the United States ever since!"

Born Robert Bédard on July 12, 1932, in Quebec City, he played hockey and practised boxing and amateur wrestling. After his first pro wrestling match against Gérard Dugas in 1956, he went on to tour the Montreal territory, even though he didn't make a lot of money. "Once in Rivière-du-Loup for Lucien Grégoire I made $100 for the match, but after all the expenses

RENÉ GOULET AS SGT. JACQUES GOULET

(CHRIS SWISHER COLLECTION)

I only had $3 left," remembers Goulet. Yet he also had the chance to wrestle in some big matches in Montreal, against Killer Kowalski and the NWA champion Buddy Rogers, among others. Although he had started his career under the name Bob Bedard, he would become Rene Goulet upon his arrival in the AWA. "There was a very popular singer called Robert Goulet. It was because of him that Verne Gagne gave me that name." He wrestled for the AWA for 10 years. "It was the best territory in the United States," affirms Goulet.

After the AWA he wrestled across the United States, in territories like Omaha, Nebraska, Amarillo, Texas, and San Francisco. From San Francisco he left for Portland and promoter Don Owen, having been recommended by Pat Patterson. It was then that he would become an American citizen and afterward he travelled to Florida, Dallas and New York.

On December 6, 1971, in New York, he won the most important title of his career. Teaming with the legendary Karl Gotch, they became the second WWWF tag team champions, after defeating Luke Graham and Quebecer Tarzan Tyler. But their reign was short-lived. "Gotch went to Japan, where he would work as a booker, and Vince Sr. didn't like the fact that he didn't ask him before going," explains Goulet. But before leaving the WWWF he also wrestled for Grand Prix, when the Vachons needed him to push Don Leo Jonathan at the beginning of his feud with Andre the Giant. Goulet had just made the acquaintance of André in Japan and remained friends with him. "Johnny Rougeau called Vince McMahon Sr. to complain that he was sending guys to his opposition," relates Goulet. "McMahon replied that he wasn't in the know."

Having lost his partner he moved on to Nashville, Los Angeles, Australia, Hawaii, Japan and Oklahoma. "He was a real professional and a guy with whom I had a lot of fun," says Oklahoma territory promoter Bill Watts, who first met him in Minneapolis. It was also in the early 1970s that he worked in Germany. "The promoter thought I looked so much like Buddy Rogers with my blond hair that he decided to call me Buddy Rogers Jr.," he explains. Then in 1974 he became Sgt. Jacques Goulet, playing the role of a Frenchman from the foreign legion. "It was the idea of Dick the Bruiser in Indianapolis," Goulet says. "I then teamed with Don Fargo and Zarinoff Leboeuf, who became a soldier for the occasion. Our team was called Les Legionnaires." Then he wrestled in Charlotte, North Carolina, at the request of George Scott. He also wrestled in California with Quebecer-turned-Russian Alexis Smirnoff, in Atlanta and finally called Andre the Giant, returning to New York in the late 1970s. In the early '80s, he hosted "Café René" during *Tuesday Night Titans* before putting an end to his full-time wrestling career and becoming an agent. It was actually common in the 1980s and 1990s to see Goulet on WWF TV, breaking up brawls. He stayed as an agent from 1982 until 1997, when he retired in his new home, North Carolina.

BRUTE BERNARD

Jim Prud'homme made his debut in the Montreal territory in 1957 for promoter Jack Britton. "Brute's character was that of a big, brutish simpleton," explains his manager and friend Gary Hart in his autobiography. In fact magazines of the time often called the punch or kick his favourite holds. He became famous in the United States as part of a team with Skull Murphy. They were actually U.S. tag team champions for the WWWF before the transformation of this title into the world tag team championship they use today.

SKULL MURPHY AND BRUTE BERNARD MADE A
NAME FOR THEMSELVES AS A TAG TEAM

He was a star in Australia, the Carolinas, Florida and Texas, thanks to Maurice Vachon's recommendation. Still actively wrestling, he accidentally killed himself with a firearm on July 14, 1984, thinking it was empty or loaded with blanks. "Brute took his family very seriously. He grew up an orphan in Montreal on the street of Montreal, and he loved his teenaged son more than anything. His love for Tommy, combined with my knowledge of how he felt about Skull Murphy's suicide and the fact that I had spent a day with him a week before his death and had seen no sign of any kind of depression, made me truly believe Brute Bernard didn't intend to kill himself; it was an unfortunate accident," says Gary Hart. He left his son Tommy and his wife, wrestler Betty Jo Hawkins, in mourning.

PAUL LEDUC, FROM GLADIATOR TO LUMBERJACK

"We have joined Grand Prix because I believe that it's very important for a wrestler to progress. That is what happens with Grand Prix; we have better conditions and opportunities as far as the evolution of our career is concerned." This is what Paul Leduc had to say on February 1, 1972, when he and his "brother" Jos left All Star Wrestling for its competitor. "With Grand Prix we earned $1,500 a week in addition to a $5,000 bonus each upon signing the contract," remembers Paul, still proud of that deal 40 years after the fact. If, at the end of the 1990s, it was common to see wrestlers switching from the WWF to the WCW and vice versa, in the early 1970s it was unheard of, and the arrival of the Leduc brothers was certainly a great acquisition for Grand Prix.

It's this controversial side that allowed Paul Leduc to have such a good career in wrestling, because it goes without saying this wasn't the first controversy for Paul Leduc. Right from his debut as a professional wrestler up until the years he spent as promoter, Paul Leduc has always generated controversy and he still invokes that proudly today.

Whether it was early in his career, when he was one of the few who wrestled with different promotions in Montreal, or in Mexico, where he basically insulted Salvador Lutteroth, or in his match against Hans Schmidt, or when he decided to launch his own wrestling federation at the beginning of the 21st century, he has always known how to attract attention. It's no surprise that for almost two decades after his wrestling career ended he worked for Quebecor — a company that owns Sun Media and *Le Journal de Montréal*, the most widely read daily newspaper in Quebec that does not hesitate to engage in sensationalism and polemics in order to sell papers.

Born on November 10, 1936, and originally from Mont-Louis, Gaspésie, a town seven hours from Montreal, Léodard Mimeault was a big wrestling fan, even though his hometown was not really in the middle of the action. "Back then, in Gaspésie, we used to receive a newspaper once a month, and I always wanted to read wrestling results to see if Yvon Robert or Paul Baillargeon won their matches. These were two heroes who were always on

BEFORE BEING A LUMBERJACK, PAUL LEDUC WAS A GLADIATOR! (PAUL LEDUC COLLECTION)

my mind when I went to bed," relates Leduc. Like many wrestlers, Mimeault legally changed his name to Paul Leduc in the late 1970s, because people had been calling him that since the late 1960s.

Long before he became Paul Leduc, he learned amateur wrestling at the Palestre Nationale and the craft of professional wrestling at the locally famous Loisirs St-Jean-Baptiste in 1952. "Our coach, Mr. Beaulieu, prohibited us from seeing the 'clowns' at the Loisirs," remembers Leduc. After having seen pro wrestling at the Loisirs once, the coach gave Paul an ultimatum. "If you return, I don't want to see you here again," he told Leduc. "Already a guy ready for controversies, I left the Palestre for the Loisirs." The Loisirs St-Jean-Baptiste was a one-man show, and that man was Pat Girard. Many Quebec wrestlers started there over the years.

During these years Girard didn't let his wrestlers battle anywhere else

EARLY PROMOTIONAL SHOT OF THE LEDUC BROTHERS

(PAUL LEDUC COLLECTION)

— the promotion at the Plessis Center or the Mile-End Stadium, for example, were off limits. But Paul Leduc was not the kind of guy who would be satisfied with wrestling just twice a week. "Pat only allowed War Eagle and me to wrestle elsewhere," says Leduc. Having a fairly developed sense of show business, Leduc developed a colourful character. "When I moved to Montreal at the age of 11, I had the opportunity of living one floor down from Oliver Guimond (one of Quebec's greatest comedians of all time). When I heard him rehearse his lines I realized that theatre had many things in common with pro wrestling," remembers Leduc. "I was wearing a Roman gladiator costume, with a helmet with a big ball of incense on top. I was also accompanied by a St. Bernard dog," explains Leduc about his first character, Del Mimo El Gladiator.

Then at the age of 18, after having spent a few years moving from one small promotion to the next, he went to Mexico. "It was thanks to Raymond Couture and Chin Lee's (Claude Johnson's) help that I went to Mexico," remembers Leduc. "Couture wrestled under the name Roy Landru in Mexico, and Chin Lee wrestled under the name Algeria. Chin gave me the address and wrote something to the promoter in Spanish." Leduc would spend three years in Mexico, wrestling for the biggest promotion there and managed by Salvador Lutteroth. Today the promotion is known as CMLL. "The first time I met Lutteroth I made a huge mistake — so big that my booker, who was accompanying me to introduce him to me, was very unhappy. I told him that Lutteroth didn't sound Mexican to me but, rather, Jewish. He turned berserk, saying that he was Mexican and that he was born in Mexico and grew up in Mexico! I thought I was speaking to a Bob Langevin or something . . . Lutteroth controlled wrestling and boxing in 187 cities! I had to apologize!" remembers Leduc, laughing. So he was part of the same wrestling shows as Mexican legends Blue Demon, Black Shadow and El Santo. "I travelled in the same bus as El Santo," remembers Leduc. "He liked to practise his English with me. I often saw him without his mask."

Leduc came back to Quebec in 1957. For a decade he balanced wrestling and regular work, always with his Roman character. One day Bob Langevin called Pat Girard, because he needed a guy in Trois-Rivières. This was his entry into the big wrestling office of Montreal, owned by Johnny Rougeau. He would develop a special relationship with Rougeau over the years. He travelled with Gino Brito, who told him to leave his "lucha libre" style in the dressing room when working with Hans Schmidt. Seeing another opportunity to draw controversy, he went between Schmidt's legs and moved rapidly in the ring to start off the match. "I knew that when Schmidt was to get a hold of me . . . that would be it. After the match, Schmidt was so pissed off he was screaming, 'Now I have to wrestle the midgets!'"

Gino Brito liked what Paul showed during the match with Schmidt, and they called him back. But Paul was an opportunist. "I spent my days off with Johnny at the office. He liked that I always came up with new ideas. He could also call me at night if he came up with an idea and he wanted to discuss it," relates Leduc. This is how he made his way into the promotion. After having brought Michel Pigeon (who became Jos Leduc) to the persons in charge at All Star Wrestling, Jack Britton came up with an idea that was new at the time in Quebec: a team of lumberjacks. The Vachon brothers had used this gimmick in Calgary in 1959, but never in Quebec. "We were trying to come up with a name. We thought of Leblanc, but I finally proposed Leduc. It's pronounced easily in both in French and English," relates Paul. So they first went on a tour of the province in 1967 to continue Jos's training. "The guys who put us over throughout the province were Larry Moquin and Eddy Auger," says Paul, proudly.

It was time to make their big entrance into Montreal. Back then the Leducs were babyfaces, and before a match between Johnny Rougeau and

PAUL LEDUC MARRIED HIS WIFE, PIERRETTE, AT THE MONTREAL FORUM WITH JOS AS HIS WITNESS (PAUL LEDUC COLLECTION)

Waldo Von Erich they were introduced to the crowd and they sat at ringside. Von Erich won the first fall, and with the help of the Leducs Johnny won the second. Between the second and third falls, Jos and Paul were called out by Von Erich, who was trying to convince them to become his allies. Obviously the Leducs declined and returned to their seats. Then, during the third fall, at the moment when the fans expected it the least, they attacked Rougeau and helped Von Erich. The crowd was furious. "We had to get out of the Paul-Sauvé Arena in the trunk of a car," relates Paul.

One of the greatest moments in Paul's career could not have happened if he had stayed heel. Lucky for him fans turned the Leducs into babyfaces quickly enough. On December 27, 1971, Paul married Pierrette Brault, not in a church but in a wrestling ring. It was not a work, but a real wedding. Paul Leduc can now explain why it happened that way.

"I had convinced Johnny to lose his championship title against Jos earlier in the year. He was hesitant but I managed to convince him," explains Paul, who, by spending a lot of time in the office, had easy access to Johnny's ear. So he owed the boss a favour. "That's why I agreed to get married in the ring!" To everyone's surprise, one month after the wedding Paul and Jos were to sign a contract with Grand Prix. They were very successful, winning the promotion's tag team title twice. It was also during the Grand Prix years that the best feud in the history of the province was born; it featured the Leducs and the Vachons. "We must've wrestled each other at least 200 times," he adds, with fire in eyes. "The Leducs versus the Vachons broke attendance records at the Colisée de Québec," Gino Brito remembers.

But some months before the Grand Prix show at Jarry Park Stadium, the Leducs, then in Florida, made it known that they were to return to All Star Wrestling. In fact the Leducs advised promoter Dick Marshall that they weren't going to be present at the show he was going to hold on May 14, 1973. Marshall announced the sad news to the fans and as a result drew a very poor house. Newspapers at the time also noted that All Star Wrestling took some considerable losses after the departure of the Leducs a year before, while, on the other hand, Grand Prix had increased its crowds with the lumberjack duo, which is exactly what Paul wanted to happen when they made the decision.

While in Florida they defeated Dick Slater and Dusty Rhodes to win the Florida NWA tag team titles, one of the biggest titles Paul won with Jos. The Leduc brothers wrestled all over the United States, including Florida, Texas and Boston, before Paul had a heart attack in 1978 and had to retire.

His post-wrestling career was very busy. He was also involved in the early stages of his son Carl's career, when the latter was making his debut for Jacques Rougeau's promotion and ultimately the WWF.

In 2000, after writing columns on the Internet, he launched his own wrestling promotion in Quebec. Having a penchant for controversy, Paul called his wrestling promotion the FLQ, making a reference to the Front de libération du Québec (Quebec Liberation Front), a nationalist, leftist movement that emerged in the 1970s and was directly involved in the incidents of the October Crisis.

When controversy didn't follow Paul Leduc, he managed to create it himself. "I was very nosy in those days!" he admits, proudly. Paul Vachon, in his autobiography, nicknames him The Weasel, referring to the fact that nobody saw him coming and that he knew how to turn things to his advantage. "I don't know whether he has read it, but I'm sure that he would be proud of and happy with this nickname!" says Vachon. In fact Paul Leduc has always managed to carve a place for himself and has succeeded in doing that, no matter what means he took to achieve his goals. Former WCW president Eric Bischoff called his autobiography *Controversy Creates Cash*, but it could easily be the title of Paul Leduc's!

ÉDOUARD CARPENTIER,
WHEN A FEW WEEKS BECOME A LIFETIME

In the award-winning 1961 documentary *La Lutte* (*Wrestling*), the star is a French wrestler who has been in Quebec for five years. The crowd was chanting his name as if he were one of them. "The people loved him a lot," admits Frenchy Martin.

Born on July 17, 1926, in Roanne (Loire), France, Édouard Carpentier is certainly the most "Quebecois" of the foreign wrestlers who wrestled in Quebec. "I came to Quebec for a six-week contract and I have never left," explained Carpentier in an article published in *Le Lundi* magazine in the early 1980s. Few wrestlers can claim their own performances have changed the way wrestling is practised. Carpentier is one of them. "My biggest victory consists in having revolutionized wrestling and having turned it into a sport entertainment," he revealed to *La Presse*.

Today few are the wrestlers who do not use the third rope as part of their game, but in the 1950s Édouard Carpentier became one of the very few who did. He also had a unique physical shape. "I was very muscular compared to the other wrestlers who were flabby. They thought that a layer of flab could protect them from the impact of blows," said the former champion. In retrospect his style and physical condition put him 40 years ahead of his time. "Do some physical training, run, eat a lot and register at a wrestling school. The human body is like a machine — a strong machine . . . Take care of it and it will follow you." This was Édouard Carpentier's answer to a young Sunny War Cloud's question about how to become a wrestler. Édouard's build made him stand out as a wrestler, as Gino Brito, Paul Leduc and Raymond Rougeau affirmed upon his death. "He was the Maurice Richard of wrestling. He was always ready to train," says Jacques Rougeau Jr., upon hearing about the death of one of his sources of inspiration. "When I was the coach of the national boxing team, I saw Édouard Carpentier often at the Claude-Robillard Sports Complex. By the time we arrived at the centre at 7 a.m. we would find that he had already started training, and when we left at 9 p.m. he would still be training. That good build of his was really hard-earned," says the owner of the important boxing organization (GYM), Yvon Michel. Édouard Carpentier proudly tells the interviewer of *La Presse*, "I was the first wrestler to stand on the third rope and perform high-risk manoeuvres." Even today fans who saw Édouard Carpentier in action talk about him with tearful eyes.

"Anyone can hit hard and give a good shot," says Carpentier. But in order to give the fans a good show, you need a large selection of holds." It's obvious that he felt nostalgic when watching WWE on TV. Wrestlers who adopted his style became international stars, making thousands of dollars. "Rey Mysterio is great! Unfortunately wrestlers today do not need to know how to wrestle," he said.

Contrary to the legend woven around his involvement in the resistance during World War II, his nephew, Jacques Magnin, also known as Jackie Wiecz, set the record

GRAND PRIX CHAMPION ÉDOUARD CARPENTIER
(TONY LANZA)

straight. "My father was involved in the resistance, Édouard's father, too, but never Édouard himself. That was simply part of the story they invented upon his arrival in Canada." Before coming to Quebec, Carpentier, whose real name was Édouard Wieczorkiewicz, had a hard time in France. The other children laughed at him. "I was fighting all the time, because the other children called me a 'dirty Polak.'" This led the young man of Polish origins to find a refuge in combat sports. "It was Lino Ventura, the actor, who launched my career," he explained to Le Journal de Montréal upon the death of the actor. "Lino was looking for talent and he approached me on a number of occasions, as he knew that I was an Olympic wrestler and member of the French gymnastic team in 1948. After I had rejected his offer, I changed my mind when the social climate got worse." Before accepting Ventura's offer, Carpentier had time to participate in the 1950 World Gymnastics Championship. "I wanted to become an acrobat but we didn't have money, so I went under the tent to watch the spectacle at the circus. I was caught but the guard was Polish and told me to come the following day for the training of the acrobats. It's actually one of these acrobats who told me to go to a gymnastic club." However his talent was to be revealed mainly through wrestling and combat sports. "Lino took all of 1951 to train me. From 1952 until I moved in Montreal in 1956, I went on so many tours for him," says Carpentier, continuing his story in *Le Journal de Montréal*. "I owe my career to Lino Ventura." Wrestling helped him make his dreams come true. "I started my wrestling career in 1952. I was 27. I was really happy to have this experience, as it allowed me to visit many countries," said Carpentier, this time to the interviewer of *Sport Hebdo*.

Despite his bodybuilder's physique and his spectacular style, he was relegated to the Cirque d'Hiver, a famous wrestling venue in Paris still in use today, which featured light heavyweights. "Frank Valois challenged me after having insisted that the promoter should make me wrestle with the heavyweight wrestlers at the Palais des Sports," he says, when talking about his first wrestling experience with Quebec wrestlers. Frank Valois was one of his favourite opponents, and the latter saw him as a potential star for the Montreal territory. Although it's widely believed that Yvon Robert brought Carpentier to Quebec, this isn't what actually occurred. "While we were in Paris, Larry met Édouard Carpentier. He told him that he was a good wrestler and that he could help him come to Canada. Frank Valois was in Paris at the same time as my husband. We even had dinner together. Yvon Robert has never been involved in bringing Carpentier to Montreal," says Marthe Moquin. This was confirmed by Gino Brito, who says, "Frank Valois and Larry Moquin brought Carpentier to the territory, because they saw him wrestle in France."

Before bringing him into his territory, Eddie Quinn wanted to know what Carpentier could do, so he sent Valois, Moquin and Yvon Robert to see him to get a better idea about Carpentier's potential. Carpentier, who became a Canadian citizen in 1977, said in his last interview: "Quinn asked me to come to Canada. He first sent Moquin and Yvon Robert. Robert and I wrestled Moquin and Valois. Then Robert told me that I had to come to Canada and that my wrestling style would make me a star." However, before moving to Canada, he had to come up with a name that was more easily pronounced. "I asked George Carpentier, the former boxing world champion with whom I trained, whether I could use his family name. He agreed and encouraged me to do so, as his name was well known in America," Carpentier revealed.

Eddie Quinn was not impressed when Yvon Robert showed him his new acquisition. "Quinn said that he didn't need a midget," Gino Brito says. "Larry Moquin and Yvon Robert told Quinn to wait and see how Carpentier worked out." Quinn's attitude inflamed Carpentier's passion. "I'm gonna show him what a fucking midget can do," reminisced Carpentier. And he kept his promise. After making his Montreal debut against Angelo Savoldi on April 18, 1956, Carpentier participated in his first main event and wrestled against Ernie Dusek at the Montreal Forum only two weeks later, on May 2, 1956. Three months later, on July 18, Carpentier was again in the main event against Argentina Rocca at Delorimier Stadium. They drew the biggest crowd yet in the history of the territory, 23,227. Before the end of the summer Carpentier had headlined two other big houses of more than 20,000 fans. On both occasions he faced Killer Kowalski. "That level of consistent business was unheard of in North America at that time, outside of the hottest periods of wrestling in New York," explains Dave Meltzer, to show how Carpentier became the number one attraction in the wrestling world. "The crowd adored me immediately, and Quebec became my favourite place to wrestle," admitted Carpentier in his last interview.

In 1957, however, Carpentier was unwillingly involved in a situation that is still debated among historians. The question? What really happened the night Carpentier became NWA world champion?

THE CONTROVERSY BEHIND THE NWA TITLE: THE TRUTH AT LAST

In the autumn of 1957 Lou Thesz, then champion of the NWA, was planning a tour of Australia, Japan, Hawaii and Europe. In order to guarantee better gates, the NWA board of directors wanted to continue promoting a champion in North America. They were also scared that Thesz would drop the belt in Japan. The NWA decided that Carpentier would be the one defending the title while Thesz was away. On June 14, 1957, in Chicago, Carpentier scored a victory in the third fall over Thesz, as the latter could no longer continue wrestling. Although it was in reality the referee who put an end to the match, the media, probably influenced by the promoters, used the term "disqualification" to describe the outcome of the match. The crucial role of the promoters is to be noted here. It was therefore announced that the NWA would have to analyze the result, but, meanwhile, Carpentier was recognized as the champion in many territories. Immediately after this match, Eddie Quinn, the promoter who was also Carpentier's manager, put a spoke in the wheel of the NWA. In fact, at this time, the champion of the NWA had to regularly visit many territories covered by the organization. If Carpentier had done that he would not have been in Montreal very often.

In an interview with Dave Meltzer, former promoter Jim Barnett — also assistant of the Chicago promoter Fred Kohler — says that Quinn wanted Carpentier to spend three days a week in his territory, thus considerably limiting the champion's travelling schedule. If we look at the situation from Quinn's perspective, the money Quinn earned when Carpentier wrestled outside of Montreal was nothing compared to the money he earned when the star of the biggest North American territory wrestled at home. Quinn quickly regretted allowing Carpentier to become NWA champion and was looking for a way out. On July 24, in a return match in Montreal, Carpentier was disqualified against Thesz for having hit the special referee, Yvon Robert. This was a golden opportunity for Quinn. The following day *La Patrie* announced, in bold letters, Carpentier's loss of his NWA title. Since the promoters controlled what was published in newspapers at the time, we can safely suppose that this was the story Quinn wanted printed. The situation became even more crazy when Sam Muchnick, the St. Louis promoter who was also president of the NWA, announced that Carpentier could not lose his NWA title because of a disqualification and that Carpentier was, accordingly, still the champion — even though he himself did not recognize the French wrestler as a champion in his territory!

On August 23 Sam Muchnick invited Jack Pfefer, a controversial promoter considered by some as a sort of cancer in the business, to the annual NWA convention in St. Louis. It was the final piece of the puzzle for Quinn, who saw in this invitation the perfect reason to quit the NWA. Quinn sent a letter to Muchnick, stating his anger at the presence of Pfefer during the convention and asking him to return the $10,000 bond he had put on Carpentier's title, thus ending his involvement with the NWA. But the die was already cast. While Thesz and Carpentier wrestled, Thesz was announced as champion and Carpentier as the challenger for the title. Two days later the NWA announced that the wrestling match that took place in Chicago was ruled a disqualification. This meant that Thesz was still the champion! Consequently Carpentier's championship was erased from the history books.

"I didn't know that the NWA wanted two champions," said Carpentier in the only interview he ever did about this issue. "They gave me a belt for the match that I had won. I was, however, aware of the letter that Quinn sent to Muchnick."

This title switch has been contested by historians for decades, and this version of the story is the closest to what really happened in 1957. But the story does not stop there. Three territories, namely Boston, Los Angeles and Omaha, decided to continue acknowledging Carpentier's championship.

Following Carpentier's win over Thesz in Chicago, the former would be recognized as the first champion in the Los Angeles territory. It would become the WWA, one of the most important organizations in the 1960s. Moreover Carpentier is always mistakenly considered the first champion of the AWA, because of his victory over Thesz. In fact this is not quite true.

The Omaha territory continued to recognize Carpentier as its champion. He lost the title in 1958 to Verne Gagne. Gagne, who was not able to become NWA champion, decided to found his own wrestling company, the American Wrestling Association, in the American midwest in 1959. Gagne won the Omaha title on three occasions before taking it one last time on September 7, 1963. In 1963 he held both the Omaha title and the new AWA championship and unified them. Since then some historians have gone back to Carpentier in their outline of the history of the AWA titles, which is far from the truth. On the other hand, it is fair to argue that Carpentier's championship influenced Gagne's career, as well as the history of wrestling itself.

The match that took place in June 1957 between Thesz and Carpentier was certainly one of the most important in professional wrestling history. This is not because of the number of fans who came to see the contest, but because it ultimately led to many of the territories associated with the NWA breaking with the organization. In fact Thesz wound up going to Australia, Hawaii and Japan before returning to the United States to lose the belt to

Dick Hutton, a belt he was not supposed to have. Then he left the NWA again and went on a European tour. Many promoters didn't want Hutton to be a champion and decided to simply resign from the organization.

This match left many in the NWA bitter. Years later Thesz and Muchnick remained vague about the issue and made it clear they preferred this chapter of their history to never have happened.

Although we may never know for sure what actually occurred, it's highly probable that if Quinn had not acted the way he did, then a match opposing Thesz and Carpentier to unify both titles before Thesz's departure for Europe would have occurred. Who knows what would have happened to the NWA and other promotions had this been the case.

One thing is certain. After the event Carpentier's relationship with Eddie Quinn deteriorated. "In September 1957, I wrestled for Vince McMahon Sr. Eddie Quinn received the cheque and gave me my share, $1,000. The second time, for the return match, McMahon himself gave me the cheque. The cheque was for $6,500. I told him that there must be a mistake. The first time I only got $1,000. He said no, the first time it was $6,500, as well." Upon his return to Montreal, Quinn asked Carpentier to give him the $5,500. Carpentier refused to do so and left Quinn's wrestling promotion.

"Yvon Robert came to see me and told me that he was a shareholder in the territory and that he needed me. I went back, but I considered myself as working for Yvon Robert and not for Quinn," explained The Flying Frenchman, adding that from there Quinn was no longer his manager.

This situation led him to wrestle Thesz many times over the years. "Lou Thesz is my favourite opponent. He was a specialist in old-school wrestling. He told me that I was going to have a wonderful career and that he would take me to Los Angeles with him," remembers Carpentier with nostalgia. He spent a considerable part of his career in California, where, in addition to wrestling, he also worked as Elvis Presley's bodyguard during some of his trips to California in the late 1950s. "At the end of the 1950s my salary ranged between $75,000 and $100,000 a year," he told La Presse.

In the early 1960s, while he was working in New York, he wrestled a young Giant Baba, one of the biggest Japanese stars of all times. After a very serious car accident in 1963, which would've led many wrestlers to an early retirement, he came back. But the sport was not what it used to be. At the time he was more of a commentator than a wrestler for All Star Wrestling and he was probably looking to tie his boots more often. He would become a huge star in the territory again, this time with Grand Prix Wrestling, through two strong programs, first with Maurice Vachon and then with Don Leo Jonathan.

In the early 1980s his wrestling career came to an end, as he started working full time as a commentator for the Varoussac promotion. He was working side by side with Guy Hauray. "Despite our differences, when I saw him a year ago, we spoke as if nothing had happened. I really enjoyed working with him all those years," explains Hauray. When Hauray transferred the airtime of Varoussac to the WWF, Carpentier, who was basically retired as a wrestler, followed him. Their presentation of WWF matches would go on to influence a whole generation of fans all over the world in French markets. These shows were broadcast in France and other Francophone countries, as well as in Quebec. Carpentier would also become the promoter of the WWF in Quebec, when the promotion took over the territory in 1985. Unfortunately the WWE would not mention his passing, thus confirming what Carpentier said before his death: "Vince McMahon Jr., you know he never liked me."

After leaving the WWF, until 2000, he remained involved in wrestling as a trainer; it was something he had been doing for a long time. In fact, near the end of the 1960s and in the early 1970s, he trained Michel "Justice" Dubois, as well as Yvon Robert Jr. In the 1980s he was in charge of the wrestling school managed by Gino Brito and Dino Bravo at the Paul-Sauvé Arena. Carpentier was known for focusing on cardiovascular training even before his students got in the ring. "You could bend your leg 100 times, do 100 push-ups, you had to run 10 times around the Paul-Sauvé Arena and you still had to climb up the stairs running after that and you had not yet hit the ring yet," says Nelson Veilleux, one of Carpentier's former students. Another alumnus of Carpentier's schooling, Serge Jodoin, remembers the technical side of Carpentier's training. "After this he had us work a lot on the sequence. Carpentier was someone who paid a lot of attention to this. He showed us how to get free from any hold." His students at the time were pegged to wrestle for International Wrestling. Aside from Veilleux and Jodoin, Denis Goulet, Raymond Coutu, Reynald Dube, Richard "Dick"

Tessier, Yvon Laverdure, André Malo, Luc Poirier and Sylvain "Le Tigre" are the best known of Carpentier's students. "Having been trained by Édouard earned the respect of other WWF wrestlers without having to prove anything to them. Édouard simply said, 'He's okay,'" explains Veilleux, proudly. In the mid-1990s Carpentier opened another wrestling school, this time in the Claude-Robillard Sports Complex. "What I remember most from my training with Édouard are the basics. Édouard mainly showed us the basics," remembers Charles Savoie, who is also known as MTH. Like many other Carpentier students of the time, Savoie wrestled on the independent scene in Montreal.

Carpentier is still synonymous with spectacular wrestling, and he's remembered as the person who made "high flying" popular. "He came with a new style," says Paul Leduc in the documentary *Les Saltimbanques du Ring*. "Many wished that he would break his neck." He's one of the rare wrestlers in the 1950s and 1960s with whom we would like to see the stars of today wrestle. "In 1982 I saw him wrestling Greg Valentine in Paul-Sauvé and he was still the most spectacular wrestler on the card," remembers François Hébert. The narrator of the *Saltimbanques du Ring* succinctly and eloquently sums up the importance of Édouard Carpentier in Quebec: "At the time when René Lévesque [who would become premier of Quebec] explained the world through his television show, Édouard Carpentier was noted both for his excellent communication skills and his prowess on the wrestling mat. Quebecers, even before the Quiet Revolution, opened up little by little to the world. Charles Aznavour, Charles Trenet and Édouard Carpentier were models of a new genre to be followed. In this whirlwind characteristic of the Quiet Revolution, Édouard Carpentier stands out from his fellow wrestlers."

Édouard Carpentier was not meant to stay in Montreal more than a few weeks. He wound up spending 54 years. On October 30, 2010, he died after a heart attack. He called 911 himself, but it was too late. Feeling nostalgic for the good old days and realizing Quebec's historical loss, every media outlet jumped all over the story. He had made his last public appearance at the ToW wrestling show on March 5, 2010, where he was honoured to the great joy of the fans in attendance. If the old remember the wrestler and the young remember the commentator, he's certainly one of the most popular athletes in the history of Quebec. And it's now an opportunity for Carpentier's fans to repeat a catchphrase he made famous, "À la semaine prochaine, si Dieu le veut!" ("See you next week, God willing!")

WLADEK KOWALSKI, THE HEEL VERSION OF CARPENTIER

Killer Kowalski had an impressive body, as he did a lot of physical training, unusual then in the wrestling business. It was a physique he would later give up in favour of a vegetarian diet. "It was 1953. I was reading a lot of books, studying the effects of food on the body. At first, I wasn't too sure about becoming a vegetarian . . . In the beginning it was for athletic reasons, but later I became more concerned about life itself," he revealed to Barry Harris of the website vegetarianusa.com. This new way of thinking about food also took his matches in a new direction. "I was one of the first people to increase the speed of a match, because I had tremendous endurance. I had wrestlers throw up on me in the ring; I'd rubbed their face in it and stomp them," said Kowalski, laughing in an interview that aired on an American TV channel. Champion Lou Thesz agreed with him in his own biography. "He was one of the top brawling villains of all time, an absolutely tireless worker, always in motion, and a top card wherever he appeared."

But when he made his debut in 1947 he was wrestling under the name of Wladek or Tarzan Kowalski. "The night I tore away Yukon Eric's ear was when I got the nickname Killer," he confided proudly to Jean-Paul Sarault of Le Journal de Montréal in 1986. Of course everyone knows about that event. On October 15, 1952, at the Montreal Forum in front of 10,000 people, Kowalski did his kneedrop from the top rope and tore away a piece of his opponent's ear. "Yukon Eric was a big, big guy, all upper body, huge barrel chest and big head, but no ear," remembered Kowalski, joking. Eric Holmback was born in Monroe in the state of Washington, near Seattle. He was described as a simple man, who had the personality of a lumberjack and wrestled barefoot. This allowed him to connect with the average fan of the time and he became very popular everywhere, including Montreal. In fact in 1950 he even became the champion recognized by the MAC, winning the title in a match against the very popular Bobby Managoff. Sadly, in 1965, following

KILLER KOWALSKI IN ALL OF HIS GLORY

his divorce and probably suffering from depression, he committed suicide. His name and career are still an integral part of folklore in the province of Quebec today.

Some described the incident as an accident, but no one explained exactly why it was an accident and even less why this was so important. It was one of the most important moments in the history of wrestling and still it could never be duplicated today. It was a moment typical of this era, Kowalski's era, and the era of kayfabe. His finishing move at the time was, and still is, considered a work of art, a kneedrop from the top rope to his opponent's throat. The move looked so vicious that it was banned in all promotions in which Kowalski worked, as it was very often demanded by the fans in order to protect their heroes or by the promoters who wanted to draw even bigger crowds on that stipulation.

During this famous night at the Montreal Forum, Kowalski landed perfectly. Unfortunately, while he jumped, Yukon Eric's body betrayed him and he moved slightly. "He moved, and my chin bone brushed his cheek . . . ripping his cauliflower ear. His ear just rolled across the ring. All that was left was the lobe," related Kowalski for the 1,000th time to an American TV channel. Blood gushed in a way never seen before. "I didn't see it, but that's how it was told to me. Referee Sammy Mack collected the ear from the ground and put it in his pocket, thinking at first that it was part of some trash that had just been thrown in the ring. Kowalski seized the opportunity and punched him right on the ear. Blood was flowing everywhere and even reached the crowds in the first rows. Women were losing consciousness, and the police had to intervene to stop the match," relates Gino Brito, who was then a young man.

A couple of days after, Kowalski visited Eric at the West General Hospital, but started laughing at the bandages covering his entire head. Journalists, probably present at the request of the promoter, saw him laughing and called him sadistic, although Eric himself found it funny. "The match took place on a Wednesday;

VACHON TRIES TO HELP HIS PARTNER, KOWALSKI, AT THE HANDS OF LEDUC (PAUL LEDUC COLLECTION)

when I went to get my pay on Friday, the promoter Eddie Quinn compelled me to apologize to Eric," explained Kowalski about his visit.

This goes against the rules of kayfabe protecting wrestling at the time, doesn't it? Kowalski was visiting his victim? Some could interpret this gesture as showing concern . . . Eric's head was enveloped like a mummy in a Boris Karloff movie. He looked so ridiculous that Kowalski and Eric simply started laughing. Many interpretations of this exchange could have been reported. To the great joy of wrestling promoters, the interpretation that stood out was the one giving birth to the nickname Killer for Kowalski. "Killer Kowalski visited Yukon Eric at the hospital to laugh at him!" the newspapers alleged the next day.

At the next show a full house at the Forum was chanting, "Killer! Killer! Killer!" And Wladek Kowalski became Killer Kowalski for the rest of his days. What a stroke of luck for wrestling promoters that the journalists in the room chose this interpretation over the facts . . . maybe.

Probably each journalist in the room knew, or was pretty sure, that wrestling was based on scenarios and that the cooperation of the participants was needed. Perhaps they were simply in Eddie Quinn's pocket? In fact the day after the accident, the newspapers didn't put more heat on the story. All journalists understood that what had just happened to Eric was an unfortunate accident. Before this visit, newspapers insisted on the accidental nature of the injury that led to a "no contest" in the first fall of the match. The journalists were probably laughing with Eric and Kowalski, and one could argue that all journalists in the room conspired in order to keep the myth of wrestling alive. From there the heat was on.

The return match, which took place on January 14, 1953, was the first wrestling contest from the Forum to be broadcast on live television. The incident would help Kowalski draw bigger crowds than any other victory or defeat of his career.

As mentioned earlier Kowalski's 1973 Jarry Park Stadium battle with Vachon broke records, and history shows he drew seven of the 20 biggest crowds in the history of the territory. Matches against Kiniski, Carpentier and Robert all drew more than 20,000.

In Australia he was a six-time champ. In Montreal he would win the MAC title seven times during the years 1953 to 1962. Only Yvon Robert and Édouard Carpentier won more single titles in the Montreal territory. In 1962 he scored a victory in Montreal against NWA world champion Buddy Rogers, when the latter broke his ankle. The NWA never officially recognized him as champion, but he met Rogers's obligations and was announced as champion in many territories. In the 1970s he was twice singles champion and a four-time tag team champ with Grand Prix.

Born Edward Walter Spulnik on October 13, 1926, in Windsor, Ontario, and of Polish origin, like Carpentier, he was almost peerless in the art of drawing crowds. His 52 NWA title matches up until 1983 show that he was highly regarded by promoters. Before he retired he won the WWWF tag team championship wrestling under a mask and partnered with one of his first protégés, "Big" John Studd, as the Masked Executioners. Today a new generation of fans know him perhaps as the wrestling trainer of Triple H, Chyna, Perry Saturn, A-Train, Kazarian and Eddie Edwards. Kowalski sums up his career simply and logically, saying that what made him a big success in wrestling was that people used to come to the arena in order to watch his matches.

After dealing with some health issues, Kowalski died in his hometown of Boston, on August 30, 2008, at the age of 81. "He had a huge influence on me," said Triple H, his most well-known student, in a Fox Sports Radio interview. "Walter was really big on making things spectacular and making you realize that wrestling is larger than life and to make anything you do larger than life to draw attention to yourself . . . Then you stand out, then you're a star."

Still, even in the 1950s, a wrestler could distinguish himself with the gear he used or with his charisma. This was certainly the case with "The Boot" Tyler.

TARZAN TYLER

"A classy gentleman, he was a walking encyclopaedia on pro wrestling."

This is how Elise Boucher, editor of *Revue Lutte* magazine, described Tarzan Tyler after his tragic death in 1985. However this is exactly the opposite of how Camille Tourville presented himself on television as Tarzan "The Boot" Tyler in the International Wrestling promotion of the mid-1980s. He probably was a great comedian who took the path of the extreme theatre — wrestling. He was featured on many TV shows, not to mention some commercials, the most famous of which was an Oh! Henry chocolate bar spot with Gino Brito and Jos Leduc that can be found today on YouTube. "He was a comedian, but a very good wrestler, as well," explained Édouard Carpentier.

Born on April 6, 1927, he made his Montreal debut under the name Tarzan Tourville, without the multi-coloured trunks and platinum blond hair that were to be his hallmark later on. "My friends started calling me Tarzan when I was 10 or 11 years old. Many thought that it was a ring name, but it's simply a story that goes back to my childhood and that stayed with me. Today, even my friends call me Tarzan," he revealed in a 1983 interview with *Revue Lutte* magazine.

"I had first practised amateur wrestling at the Palestre Nationale; then one morning I received a call from promoter Sylvio Samson and I got started in professional wrestling. I had my first match at the old Tour de Quebec in Quebec City against the brothers Butch and Paul Neron," he remembered in the same interview. Strangely enough the wrestler who would become one of the

TARZAN "THE BOOT" TYLER AND HIS PROTÉGÉ SUPERSTAR
(LINDA BOUCHER)

greatest heels in the history of Montreal started off his career as a fan favourite. "I started out on the side of the good guys, but at a certain point I realized that heels like Kowalski earned a very good living. I was way too tall and big to gain the sympathy of the fans." Like many talented go-getters in Montreal, but without the right contacts in the office, it was in the United States that he made a name for himself. "When I noticed that French-Canadians were not given a chance in Montreal, I decided to go wrestle in the United States. I built a good reputation for myself there before coming back to Montreal. I left in 1959 and came back in 1973. I had not wrestled in the province for 14 years!" said Tyler. It's actually in the United States that his name was changed — it was too difficult for most Americans to pronounce and remember. "I started under the name Tarzan Tourville, but the St. Louis promoter told me one day that Tourville was finished. It's going to be Tarzan Tyler from now on." The pieces of the puzzle were falling into place, and he was to be very successful in the United States and Japan.

During the 1960s Tyler would end up working on top wherever he wrestled, whether it was in Texas, Atlanta or Florida. In 1962 he fought Verne

Gagne for the AWA world championship. In 1963 he wrestled Lou Thesz for the NWA world title at least six times. The NWA and Lou Thesz protected the championship fiercely at the time, and only the best wrestlers would find themselves in the same ring as Thesz. The Atlanta promotion, in fact, created a world championship that was won by Tyler against Eddie Graham, the promoter from Florida, but the title ceased to be recognized as a world championship when the promotion joined the NWA. Tyler and Thesz were to meet again in 1964 and 1965. From 1964 to 1971 Tyler would dominate his home base Florida territory. The fans who followed Tyler in the 1980s in Montreal remember a chubby man who was in his late 50s, but that was certainly not the physique he had when he reigned supreme in Florida. "I had never seen anyone as muscular as he was. He was cut from head to toe. Tarzan and I had a good program going, trading the Florida heavyweight championship back and forth," remembers one of his most fierce opponents in Florida and former NWA world champion, Jack Brisco. In 1967 he would win the NWA International tag team championship in Japan with Bill Watts, a title he would subsequently lose against the dream team composed of Giant Baba and Antonio Inoki, the most popular Japanese wrestling duo of all time. "Tyler was a very good guy. I have a deep respect for him. He was a guy on whom you could count. He was very professional and also a damn good wrestler. A very good heel, with his own style," remembers Watts. In Australia, Tyler made a very strong impression on a young Gerald Brisco: "Tyler took me aside and really taught me a lot about the business. He took time with a young man and shared his knowledge with me and taught me things I didn't know how to do." Brisco, who was a friend of Yvon Robert Jr., was even more impressed with how Tyler could influence the promoter. "In Australia we had a very strict dress code — coat and tie — but you couldn't get Tarzan in a coat and tie. He would always wear a t-shirt, a pair of Bermuda shorts and flip-flops. The promoter Jim Barnett was scared to death of Tarzan so he wouldn't tell him to wear his coat and tie . . . the dress code went from being strict to casual! We didn't want Tarzan to leave!" he adds.

He also teamed with Fred Blassie and Pat Patterson in Japan. "He was a very big star in New Zealand, Florida and Georgia," adds Luke Williams.

In 1971 he came to New York for Vince McMahon Sr.'s WWWF and wrestled against world champion Pedro Morales. Before working there as a regular, he drew the biggest crowd of the year against Bruno Sammartino at MSG in 1965. Then he teamed with "Crazy" Luke Graham, and they would become the first WWWF world tag team champions. It's the championship that WWE wrestlers still compete for today. It must also be noted that this team was the second championship team to be managed by the late "Captain" Lou Albano, who left his mark as a world tag team champion's manager and who actually made his debut as a wrestler in Montreal in 1953. On July 24, 1971, Tyler and Graham wrestled Morales and Gorilla Monsoon in front of 21,912 fans at MSG, the first gate surpassing $100,000 in New York City. After achieving glory in New York, Florida and pretty much everywhere else in the world of wrestling, Tyler decided to go home to Montreal. "In 1972 I told my wife, 'Heck, we're gonna go work in Montreal and see.'"

His nickname The Boot became part of Montreal slang, but its origin has been, until now, unclear. "I got that nickname here in Quebec. In the days of Grand Prix, Édouard Carpentier and Fernand Ste-Marie were the commentators on television and each time they saw me go into the ring they'd scream: 'Here is La Bottine again!' The name stayed with me, as the fans also started using it. I've got nothing against it," said Tyler. Fernand Ste-Marie remembers this story differently. "Dave Singer, my English counterpart, prepared me, explaining that his nickname was The Boot and that he came from the United States. I naturally translated the expression, calling him La Bottine, and it stuck." Either way Tyler built his reputation with a gimmick that would become a wrestling classic: the loaded wrestling boot. He'd lightly tap the tip of his foot three times to load the hidden object into position and then effortlessly knock his opponent senseless. It was, in a sense, an early version of what The Iron Sheik did in the WWF.

While he wrestled for Grand Prix he suffered an injury that would almost put an end to his career. "Andre the Giant lost hold of me in the Verdun Auditorium, and I injured my neck. I wasn't able to wrestle for nine months," he explained to Revue Lutte. In the late 1970s, after the end of both Grand Prix and All Star Wrestling, while George Cannon continued to present shows with his Superstars of Wrestling from Montreal rather than Toronto, Tarzan was to become one of his stars, always on the heel side.

In 1980 he wrestled for Varoussac, then in its first year in business, feuding with Gino Brito and with his former partner, Sailor White. It was one of the rare occasions when Tyler became a babyface. In February 1981, once again a heel, he lost to Dino Bravo, the new god of the territory, in 26 seconds and then left the promotion. He finished his in-ring career for promoter Denis Lauzon, who was competing with Varoussac in 1983. Tarzan was also his booker. "It's Tarzan who told Lauzon, a businessman who sold furniture, to hire me when he got TV in Trois-Rivières," remembers Fernand Ste-Marie. In 1984 Eddy and Floyd Creatchman stopped working for Varoussac, which was transformed into International Wrestling, and Tarzan Tyler became the manager of King Tonga, Rick Valentine (Kerry Brown), Sailor White, Pierre Lefebvre, Richard Charland and Frenchy Martin. He had a spectacular year as the leader of the heels when the territory was in its heyday. "He was my tag team partner first and then he became my manager after that. Tyler was excellent working with the younger guys," the late Sailor White told SLAM! Wrestling. Listening now to interviews first broadcast on Télé 7, you can hear the influence of "Captain" Lou Albano on Tyler. Albano disowned Italy when his men wrestled against Bruno Sammartino; similarly, Tyler disowned his Quebec origins and sang the praises of his foreign wrestlers when the latter wrestled other Quebecers.

Tyler died tragically in a car accident in December 1985. Rick Martel had actually spoken to him about his plans for 1986 on the day of his death. "Tarzan, I loved him so much professionally and personally. As a booker, I was seeing him everywhere in my stories."

In 2005, more than 20 years after his death, Tarzan "The Boot" Tyler was inducted into the Quebec Wrestling Hall of Fame, confirming what he'd already said in an interview from 1983: he had nothing to prove anymore. "If I were to go back in time, I would make the same choices," he explained. "I can walk with my head held high."

There are some hugely talented wrestlers who never became world champions, while others were treated differently by fate.

STAN STASIAK

Official: "Pedro makes the big comeback and gives you a belly-to-back."
Stan (bored): "Uh-huh."

Official: "The referee will go down to make the count."

Stan (paying about half attention while he tied his boots): "Right."

Official: "The referee will count, "One, two . . ."

Stan (matter-of-factly): "Of course . . ."

Official: "At two, you roll your right shoulder . . ."

Stan now looks up to pay attention, realizing this must be a false finish leading to another spot after which Morales would hit the top rope splash for the win.

Official (matter-of-factly): "Pedro's shoulders will still be down and the referee will hit three."

Stan stopped what he was doing and took a long look at the official.

After a pause that seemed like it took several minutes, Stan spoke.

Stan (somewhat confused): "You mean I win?"

Official (matter-of-factly): "Yes."

Stan: "Is this a title match?"

Official (matter-of-factly): "Uh-huh."

Stan was really confused now, as the official just stared at him blankly.

Stan (in disbelief): "You mean I win the title?"

Official (somewhat impatiently): "Yes."

In everyday life we meet people who seem born to become champions. Others have to work hard for the opportunity. Still others win, and we can't seem to figure out how or why.

The story of Stan Stasiak fits into the last category.

The conversation above took place on December 1, 1973, backstage at the Philadelphia Arena. At least that's how Stan Stasiak remembered it to Frank Dusek.

History shows that on that day in Philadelphia Stan Stasiak won the WWWF heavyweight title by defeating Pedro Morales. Nine days later, on December 10, Stasiak was defeated by a former champion, Bruno Sammartino. Stan Stasiak had the strong quality of making his opponent look good while staying credible in the process. No one was surprised to see him win matches and, yet, his credibility didn't suffer when he lost. But no one expected this victory against Morales. "To everybody's surprise, Stan Stasiak became heavyweight's champion. Contrary to what would be expected today, no one told him that he was gonna win before he prepared his match in the locker room," relates Frank Dusek. If Stasiak knew the outcome of the match only a couple of minutes before it started, the crowd in Philadelphia left the arena thinking their favourite wrestler had kept his championship title.

"Stasiak held Morales in a full nelson, but Morales was able to reach the ropes and managed to fall with his opponent on the mat in a situation in which the two wrestlers had their shoulders pinned. It's the same finish used by Morales when he won the title against Ivan Koloff three years earlier in Madison Square Garden. After the referee counted to three, the only announcement made by announcer Buddy Wagner was 'Let's applaud Pedro Morales!' which made the fans think that the champion prevailed," Dave Meltzer explains, adding they probably wanted to avoid a riot.

Stasiak later defeated El Olympico, which was broadcasted on TV on December 4, lost a tag team match on December 6, then defeated Chief Jay Strongbow on December 7. He already had a match scheduled against Bruno Sammartino for December 10 at Madison Square Garden, a match now for the WWWF title. Sammartino won the match and became champion one last time.

George Stipich was born on April 13, 1937, in Arvida, a small village five hours north of Montreal. His father worked for Alcan, a company that made aluminum, and Stipich made use of his origins early in his career, adopting the nickname the Assassin of Arvida. Stipich became a fan of wrestling as a youngster and was known for making trouble during the wrestling shows held in Chicoutimi. Don Leo Jonathan relates in the book *Pain and Passion* that Stipich and his friends would take cheap shots at the wrestlers. According to Jonathan, Stipich was big but fast. One night he trapped him, ducked a shot Stipich threw and hit an uppercut that knocked Stipich out. "I'd never see him back at the matches after that," remembers Jonathan.

The altercation with Jonathan probably discouraged him; he changed interest and became a hockey player, like so many other Quebec youths. He played in the Quebec Amateur Hockey Association, where he was known for his lack of discipline. "The last hockey coach I had told me one evening that I had so many penalties that it looked as if there were problems each time I was on the ice. So, he told me: 'You know what you should do? Become a professional wrestler. You can then let go of all of your frustrations.' And that's what I did!" remembered Stipich during an interview with Roberta Morgan for

STAN STASIAK WAS ONCE THE WWWF WORLD CHAMPION
(LINDA BOUCHER COLLECTION)

Main Event: *The World of Professional Wrestling*.

Stipich made his debut in 1958 after training in Montreal. "He made his debut for a promotion that competed with Quinn," relates Rene Goulet. "After having wrestled a couple of times in Montreal he was discouraged by Billy Red Lyons, who suggested that he take the bus, go back home and find himself a job." He went to Ontario, where he picked up the name Stan Stasiak, a name used by a heel who main-evented shows in Toronto before dying of blood poisoning on September 13, 1931, 10 days after having broken his leg in a match against Ed Don George. *The Ring Wrestling* magazine related this story in its July 1963 edition: "Stan Stasiak, a heavyweight Canadian, who is Yvon Robert's protégé, abandoned a possible professional hockey career for the glory and fortune that come with a wrestling career. Established in the east coast of the country, the journalists and commentators nicknamed him 'the Assassin of Arvida.'" He saw Lyons again in Toronto and told him, 'You know, I've never took that bus!' says Goulet today.

In his early days Stasiak was also known as Crusher, because he used a bear hug as his finisher. But it was another finishing move that would make Stasiak famous. Portland promoter Don Owen, the one who gave the nickname Mad Dog to Maurice Vachon, greatly influenced Stasiak's career. In fact on June 18, 1965, Stan "The Man" Stasiak had the upper hand in a match that opposed him to Vachon, and he won the NWA Pacific Northwest title with the finisher that was to follow him to the end of his career — the heart-punch. Wrestling fans in Montreal who got riled up when someone used this manoeuvre probably didn't realize that it was invented by one of their own at a time when finishing moves were much simpler than they are now.

The heart-punch was simple in and of itself, but selling it was complicated. At the time punching with a fist was against the rules and could even possibly lead to disqualification, and Stasiak became known as a dangerous man. When his fist was aimed at an opponent's heart, he would become diabolic. Over time Stasiak mastered the move and performed it in a way that allowed the crowd to see what he was doing, but not the referee. "He'd get you in a position where he'd put your left arm over your head, sort of holding it. Then he'd turn you around from the referee and give you a heart-punch. He'd just use it once," explains Moose Morowski in ProWrestling Hall of Fame:The Heels. To add to the move's mystique, Stasiak explained in interviews how his punch affected an opponent's organs using medical jargon everyone believed. "He never hurt you with this punch," remembered Buddy Rose. Stasiak went to Texas after Portland, where he won the Brass Knuckles championship, usually held by the toughest wrestler in the territory. He also won the first world title of his career, winning the IWA title in Australia, before joining the WWWF. "Stan was able to have a good match with anyone," remembers Gino Brito. "He could have a good match with Gorilla Monsoon, which was not easily done. He could also have a good match with Bruno Sammartino or Pedro Morales, and if you were to make him wrestle against a smaller guy he would also have a good match."

Right from the start it was clear that Stasiak was to be a transitional champion; he was credible enough as a heel to defeat Morales and still vulnerable enough to lose the title the first time he faced Sammartino. According to the WWWF, another reason explaining Stasiak's short reign was a problem with alcohol. "He was good enough to [be champion], but everybody, including Vince, knew they couldn't put the belt on him because they knew he was not dependable sometimes, but only because of alcohol, not because he was a bad guy or anything," relates Dominic Denucci. This being said, he wasn't a no-show guy. "He was a guy who never missed a booking. If he had to be in a city, oh my God, he was going to make the town," says former promoter Don Owen.

After his brief title reign Stasiak returned to Ontario as a babyface, wrestling against many world champions from 1975 to 1978. Then he returned to Portland, where he won the territory title for the sixth time, on June 30, 1979, this time against another Canadian, "Rowdy" Roddy Piper. He also returned to Texas in 1980, before finishing his career back where he was the most successful, Portland.

After his career came to an end Stasiak became a commentator and car dealer in Portland, before moving to Toronto in 1984, where he worked as a security guard for 10 years. When his health began to deteriorate he returned to Oregon in 1994. He died there at the age of 60.

Ironically, the master of the heart-punch died of a heart attack.

His son, Shawn Stasiak, followed in his footsteps. The family name opened doors in the WWF and WCW in 1999, but injuries, combined with some bad backstage political moves and being saddled with dubious gimmicks, sabotaged his career even before it really got going. "I promised my father that I would win the WWE world title and that we would be the first father and son combination to be champions," relates Shawn in an interview with Club WWI. Winning the WCW tag team titles with Chuck Palombo was the closest he'd ever come.

In spite of his demons and the fact that he wasn't rich at the beginning or at the end, Stan "The Man" Stasiak is still highly regarded by his peers. "Stan gave us a lot of his time," remembers Paul Leduc, explaining that the only way of having a career in this industry was to go on the road and wrestle for as many promotions as possible. For his son Shawn, the WWWF title was the apex of his career. "It doesn't matter if he held it for nine days, nine seconds or nine years. He held it and was one of the original WWE champions. His reign will always be cemented in WWE history. I'll always remember him referring to it as the happiest nine days of his life," he says in The WWE Championship: A Look Back at the Rich History of the WWE Championship. For Montreal fans Stasiak is known, after more than 40 years, as the only Quebecer to hold the WWE world title.

Canada's vast size has meant, historically, that different wrestlers were revered in different parts of the country. If Yvon Robert was the "chosen one" to Quebecers, "Whipper" Billy Watson occupied the same place in the hearts of their neighbours from Ontario.

QUI GAGNERA LE CONCOURS DU PLUS POPULAIRE LUTTEUR

| Buddy Rogers | Bobby Managoff | Lou Thesz | Yvon Robert | Billy Watson | Yukon Eric |

Au moment d'écrire ces lignes, nous n'acceptions plus aucun vote pour le concours du LUTTEUR LE PLUS PO-PULAIRE de l'Amérique du Nord. Cependant, à cause d'un recomptage final des bulletins, nous ne pouvons encore vous donner le nom du vainqueur. Cependant, nous pouvons vous dire qu'il sera choisi entre Yvon Robrt, 8 fois champion du monde, Yukon Eric, le co-lossse de l'Alaska, Lou Thesz, la merveille de St-Louis, Bobby Managoff, l'as de la savate et du marteau, Buddy "Nature Boy" Rogers et ses multiples talents de gladiateur et Whipper Billy Watson et sa prise de l'avalanche.

Nous avons reçu des milliers et des milliers de lettres de nos lecteurs qui ont voté et qui nous ont tenu si occupés de même que le facteur. Nous avons cru bon de demander aux juges de ce concours de recompter tous les votes

afin qu'il n'y ait pas de critique possible, afin de donner justice à tous les lutteurs.

Comme nous savons que nos lecteurs ont hâte de connaître le vainqueur de ce concours, nous leur réservons une surprise en leur disant qu'ils sauront le nom du gagnant au concours "M. CANA-DA", au Monument National, 1182 rue St-Laurent, le 26 octobre. Tous nos lecteurs qui ont suivi ce concours de près, seront heureux d'apprendre qu'ils pourront voir le gagnant en personne le 26 octobre. Ils peuvent obtenir des billets pour le gala de "M. CANADA" en écrivant à Ben Weider, 4466 Colonial. Les prix des billets sont de $2.50, $2.00 et $1.50. Il s'agit là d'une soirée culturiste, avec concours des athlètes les plus musclés, vaudeville, tours de force, etc., soit un spectacle où personne ne s'embête.

Ajoutons que nous avons décidé de poursuivre notre concours jusqu'en janvier pour nos lecteurs d'Europe qui pourront aussi voter encore pour leurs gladiateurs favoris. A ce sujet, disons que nous avons réellement été étonné de recevoir tant de votes de cette partie du monde, où les fervents de la lutte peuvent encore aider à déterminer qui recevra un superbe trophée par avion en janvier.

LE CONCOURS D'EUROPE

Voici les meneurs du concours d'Europe qui se continue jusqu'au 1er janvier 1952:

1-	Félix Miquet	2894
2-	Henri Deglane	2292
3-	Charles Rigoulot	1889
4-	Bert Assiratti	1580
5-	Yvan Martinson	1112
6-	Frank Valois	824

THE MOST POPULAR WRESTLERS IN MONTREAL ACCORDING TO *LUTTE ET BOXE*

(BERTRAND HÉBERT COLLECTION)

"WHIPPER" BILLY WATSON

"Yvon Robert was the Billy Watson of Quebec," says Phil Watson, Billy's son. Television made Watson, like Robert, a national star. Born William John Potts in 1915 in East York, Toronto, Watson was supported by the local promoter, Frank Tunney, the way Robert was supported by Quinn. His exploits are still remembered fondly by old-school Ontario wrestling fans.

In the 1940s and the early 1950s Robert and Watson wrestled against each other many times; it was a natural feud between English- and French-Canadians. They exchanged the British Empire championship recognized by the Toronto territory a couple of times. Then they became partners in the logical progress of a feud between two of the greatest heroes in Canada. "They wrestled against each other quite often, they often teamed, but, above all, they were united because they were both Canadians," explains his son. Actually both Robert and Watson ensured that promoters made a lot of money. From 1940 to 1960, while he was starting his career in Ontario after having made a name for himself in England, Watson would commute between Montreal and Ottawa, wrestling from one city to the next against the major wrestlers of the time. A former NWA champion, Watson made his last appearance in Montreal in 1970 at the Forum for All Star Wrestling. His career suddenly came to an end due to a car accident in 1971. He died on February 4, 1990, struck down by a heart attack during a trip to Florida. "Yvon Robert and my father are, in my opinion, the two greatest Canadian wrestlers," concludes Phil Watson.

In the late 1950s the son of a great Montreal wrestling promoter made his debut as a wrestler. Later he, too, would become a promoter and the leader of what would become known as Montreal's Italian Connection.

GINO BRITO

Gino Brito was born Luigi Acocella in Montreal on May 18, 1941. He started his professional wrestling career with his father, Jack Britton, in Detroit. "My father sent me with four midgets throughout the United States, to the East for Vince McMahon Sr., to Texas for the Funks, to California for Roy Shire and to Portland for Don Owen," remembers Brito, nostalgically. With his partners he would later become the last promoter to make the Montreal territory his own. His Varoussac Promotions would metamorphose into International Wrestling, the last local outfit to run on Montreal TV. "I only have good memories of him. A very good person who was always ready to listen to his wrestlers," remembers Guy Hauray, who produced Varoussac's TV programs early on.

Many other promoters built their operation around themselves, without paying attention to all the other talent on the roster. But this wasn't like Gino Brito at all. "I respect Gino as a person, wrestler and businessman. He's a man of his word," explains Rick Martel, who was an International Wrestling partner.

His father's contacts opened doors for him, but the promoters and wrestlers who gave him a chance could feel his passion for the profession. "In next to no time Gino Brito will be a heavyweight world champion. He's so gifted that much ink will be spilled to talk about him," affirmed one member of the Italian Connection in the early 1960s, photographer Tony Lanza. Even today Brito speaks of wrestling with a remarkable passion, and many consider him to be the authority on the history of wrestling in Montreal. "Ask Gino, he certainly knows that!" is something commonly heard from former wrestlers when they are asked a question to which they do not have the answer. The most amazing thing about him is that he can talk as easily about Yvon Robert and the1950s as he can about Ring of Honor (ROH) star Kevin Steen.

Even though his father was a promoter, that doesn't mean things were easy for Brito. "When I started to wrestle my father sent me to work television in Moline, Illinois, 700 miles away from

THE YOUNG TEAM OF GINO BRITO AND TONY PARISI

(GINO BRITO COLLECTION)

Detroit, and I was paid $25," Gino says. The young man wasn't too happy but he was to learn quickly a very important lesson about the power of TV on wrestling. "I was booked on the card featuring the main event between Johnny Valentine and Buddy Rogers at Comiskey Park," Brito remembers. "I earned $200, and my food and transport were paid for, as well. My father told me: 'See, it's because you've worked on television.'"

He carried in the Detroit territory, where his father was promoter with Bert Ruby. It's there that he would make the acquaintance of a young man who was to be an integral part not only of his career, but also of the Montreal

THE COMPLETE ITALIAN CONNECTION: BRITO, DENUCCI, LANZA, SAMMARTINO AND BRAVO

(TONY LANZA)

territory in the early 1980s. "You're gonna wrestle against Antonio Pugliese, a real amateur wrestler, my father told me one night in 1959," Brito recalls. "We quickly became friends," he explains, referring to the wrestler who would become Tony Parisi. He would be Gino Brito's primary partner. "We travelled together. The promoters often teamed us with one another, and we were acquiring experience," explains Brito.

Finally the two men were to get their break. "We were going to Tennessee for two weeks to put guys over. During our first match against the Fargos (a star team in the territory), we worked so well that the Fargos told promoter Nick Gulas to keep us. Three weeks later we became champions and stayed there seven months," says Brito. The two men, however, had to turn into brothers. "They called us Gino and Tony Calza. It was a big name from the 1940s in that territory."

The two men were to light up the territory and wrestle against two former NWA world champions in a program that would draw a full house. "We filled the arena together in Memphis when we worked against Pat O'Connor and Lou Thesz on three occasions," he says. In a territory that was known for paying its wrestlers badly, the two men earned $1,200 per week. "In another territory we would've made twice that amount for the same program, but still it was $1,200! But it was thanks to our wrestling there that promoter Eddie Graham from Florida wanted to bring us in," explains Brito.

In the 1970s he would work in the Montreal territory for Johnny Rougeau's All Star Wrestling and would become tag team champion with his good friend Jacques Rougeau Sr. He would jump to Grand Prix in order to team with his protégé, Dino Bravo, with whom he would also become champion. Dino Bravo would become a star on whom Gino Brito would count to build his own company a few years later. In 1975 Gino adopted the name of Louis Cerdan (after boxer Marcel Cerdan) in the WWWF, as the territory was full of Italians like Bruno Sammartino, Dominic Denucci and his partner, Tony Parisi. Teaming with Parisi, they would become world champions after defeating the Blackjacks. About six months later, in 1976, they would lose the belt against the Masked Executioners, composed of Killer Kowalski and "Big" John Studd. "It was a period during which I made the most money as a wrestler. In fact after that I took a six-month vacation . . . I thought I was a millionaire!" Brito remembers.

In 1980 he cut back on his wrestling schedule and embarked on a promoter's career after the death of his father. Montreal didn't have a major promotion at the time, and Gino Brito, with Frank Valois and Andre the Giant as partners, would become the promoter of the last golden age of this sport. He would call upon Tony Parisi, and the two men would have a fantastic feud with Pierre Lefebvre and Pat Patterson, then with Lefebvre and Frenchy Martin. He was also the wrestler whom any new heel challenger invading the territory would vanquish before reaching Dino Bravo and the title match. In 1982 he wrestled in a last match for Vince McMahon Sr. and he was recognized as the WWF international champion. He lost his title against an individual who would become a legend in Japan, Tatsumi Fujinami, the inventor of the Dragon Sleeper and the Dragon Supplex. In 1984 Brito faced Ric Flair for Flair's first ever Montreal match. It was a battle of the figure-four leglock. Brito used it for his finishing move, just like the man who would go on to be a 16-time world champ.

Martin and Lefebvre would be the wrestlers to have the honour of "retiring" Gino from wrestling once and for all. He wanted to put an end to his activities in the ring to concentrate 100 percent on his role as promoter. "At one time or another, one has to make the decision to call it quits. Retirement means working six days a week to coordinate and promote everything," explained Brito to *Revue Lutte* magazine in 1984. He was very well regarded as a promoter: Jacques and Raymond Rougeau, for instance, were very tactful when the time came for them to leave Gino for the WWF in 1986. "I've got deep respect for Gino," says Raymond.

In 1987, trying in vain to save International Wrestling and his investment in the face of WWF expansion, Gino put his boots back on to wrestle against Abdullah the Butcher in the last days of the promotion. "I was probably the person who wrestled the most often against Abdullah," says Gino, who never shied away from a physical match. After his own promotional doors closed he remained involved in the business, as he became the WWF contact in Montreal. "Vince McMahon told me that he needed me for six months, and the salary was good so I said yes," Brito remembers. In the 1990s he would referee here and there, keeping in touch with the new generation of wresters.

Coming from a cultural heritage that puts great value on family and friends, it wasn't surprising to see Gino Brito teaming with Tony Parisi, Dino Bravo, Dominic Denucci, Bruno Sammartino, his own son, Gino Jr., and Luigi Mascera and Tony Lanza, who were both very close to Brito. These people will always be of great importance to both his career and life, and it was rare to find Gino in a promotion without at least one of his friends by his side. If the Italian Connection in Montreal was mainly Brito and Bravo in the 1970s and Brito and Parisi in the 1980s, it could also have been Brito and Denucci or Brito and Sammartino. In fact Gino Brito was the cornerstone of this connection.

While Brito was running the big office in Montreal, Pat Girard was making sure that new stars were being created by running the biggest wrestling training facilities in Montreal's history.

PAT GIRARD

Near the end of the 1950s someone by the name of Fernand Girard took control over the sports centre at the corner of Berri and Rachel in the heart of Montreal. The centre actually didn't belong to him, but he was in charge

PAT GIRARD REFEREEING A MATCH AT "HIS" LOISIRS ST-JEAN-BAPTISTE (PAUL LEDUC COLLECTION)

of the wrestling school. It would become the most important training centre in the history of Montreal wrestling, the Loisirs St-Jean-Baptiste.

The name Pat Girard and Loisirs St-Jean-Baptiste are practically inseparable. Girard, himself a wrestler, had an international career under the name Pat Curry. "He had wrestled 10 to 15 years in Europe before coming back here in the late 1950s," remembers his nephew, Robert Girard. "When he came back he kept the first name he used in Europe." He wrestled in front of the Queen of England, and his agent in Europe was the actor Lino Ventura. "He booked him in England, Germany, Spain, everywhere in Europe," says one of Girard's favourite students, Ludger Proulx.

As a trainer Girard was known to be tough. "Pat Girard was someone very serious. He was famous for doing things his own way. It was either his way or the highway. He had a very good reputation and he was very impressive when you first met him," remembers Ronnie Garvin, who was a Girard student.

"Some fat guys wanted to become wrestlers, but once they trained with Pat you didn't see them again," explains "The Hangman" Neil Guay. "He would pay particular attention to those who weren't scared of training and took it seriously."

The Loisirs, as it was so often called, closed down in 1990. The list of wrestlers who have gone through the school is long and prestigious: Pat Patterson, Terry Garvin, Ronnie Garvin, Raymond Rougeau, Pierre-Carl Ouellet, Paul Leduc, Neil Guay, Sunny War Cloud, Ludger Proulx, Serge Proulx, Louis Laurence, Johnny War Eagle, Andy Ellison, Guy Ranger, Chin Lee, Fernand Frechette, Georges Guimond, Bertrand Proulx and many others all went there to learn wrestling, either as rookies or to polish their careers later. "Most of these guys worked on television, for Johnny Rougeau's office or the one of Brito and Valois," notes one of Girard's students, Serge Proulx.

Pat Girard, who was born in the town of St-Gabriel-de-Brandon, died on March 5, 2002, at the age of 83.

In the early 1960s three of Girard's friends and trainees decided to go to Boston. It wound up being the best decision of their careers.

PAT PATTERSON

It was as the first Intercontinental champion that Pat Patterson was introduced to the crowd at the Bell Centre in Montreal in September 2009, during the presentation of the WWE Breaking Point PPV. In fact Patterson was the right-hand man of Vince McMahon Jr. during the expansion of WWE in the 1980s. Many people agree that he was, by far, the number two in the organization for many years. "There was McMahon, and right after him it was Patterson," Gino Brito remembers. "For a Quebecer, that's an incredible position to reach." Raymond Rougeau, who worked for the WWF for a long time, thinks the same way. "As far as creative is concerned, Pat was a key player. Today there's a whole team, but then the team was just Pat and Vince, that's it. They could sit for 16 hours straight together, preparing the booking; two people, sharing the same passion for wrestling."

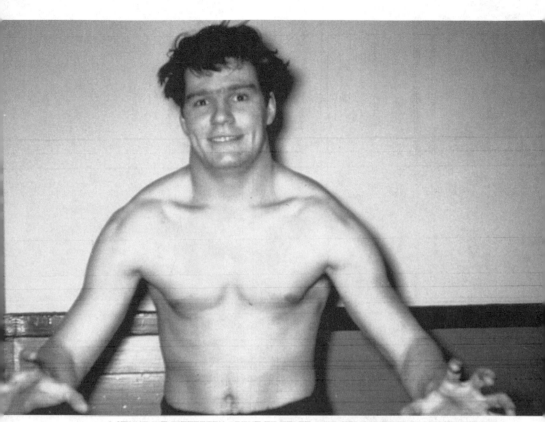

A YOUNG PAT PATTERSON ABOUT TO START A 55-YEAR CAREER IN PRO WRESTLING
(SYLVAIN SAMSON COLLECTION)

Others even contend that without him the WWF might not have enjoyed the same success. "Much of the credit for the success of the WWF should go to Pat Patterson," explains J.J. Dillon in his biography. Dillon worked side by side with him for the WWF in the late 1980s and early 1990s. Patterson is actually the originator of the Royal Rumble, the second most important event in the WWE calendar after *WrestleMania*. Patterson remembers: "We had this meeting with Dick Ebersol, president of NBC Sports with whom we worked on *Saturday Night's Main Event*, who was looking at doing a three-hour special for the USA network. We needed an idea so Vince told me, 'Pat, pitch him that fucking idea of yours!' Ebersol went crazy for it so Vince told me to write it. I put everything together by myself that first night. I didn't come up with the name though, we had people in the office for that. We didn't want it to be battle royal; they came up with Royal Rumble and it was perfect!"

PAT PATTERSON HAD A TALK-SHOW SEGMENT CALLED "LE BRUNCH DU RÊVE DU QUÉBEC" (LINDA BOUCHER)

The role Patterson played was thankless and yet it was of the utmost importance as Vince's voice on the floor and on the road with the boys and the other staff members. "Guys like 'Macho Man' Randy Savage and Hulk Hogan were working hard at television tapings with all the matches and interviews that were to be conducted. I had a match against Macho Man and we had to be at the gorilla position five minutes before the beginning of the match. Randy came in late, and Pat admonished him openly in front of everyone. Savage, who was a big star, apologized for being late with his tail between his legs," relates Nelson Veilleux, thus explaining the authority that Patterson had in the WWF. "He was straight and direct with everyone and made positive as well as negative comments," he adds. It's obvious that you can't just force people to respect you this way. This respect was gained by winning the trust of the boys with programs and ideas that were conceived to help boost their career. "What's interesting about Pat is that you and I may think of something for tonight, but in addition to doing that, Pat would also come up with six months' worth of ideas for the program," Gino Brito adds. "He's a wrestling Jedi and the smartest man I've ever met in wrestling. He taught me 90 percent of the things I know about how to put together a match, and when I first approached him I had no idea how little I really knew about the psychology of the business," affirms Chris Jericho, WWE multiple world champion, in his second biography, Undisputed.

Patterson's success most certainly paved the way for other Quebecers in the organization. "Pat Patterson never forgot about his roots. Be it Rick Martel, Dino Bravo, Pierre-Carl Ouellet or Jacques Rougeau, we should all thank him for having put his trust in us," explained Jacques Rougeau to Le Journal de Montréal in 1995. In fact 10 years later Patterson would also play an equally, if not more, important role in the career of the last Quebec wrestler to have made the WWE roster, Sylvain Grenier. Singing from the same hymn sheet, Marc Blondin, who was the WWF interviewer for the Montreal market for a long time, adds: "I used to work with him, as he was the agent in Montreal. He was the one who told me what to do and what to say. It was thanks to him that I got promoted in the WWF."

What's perhaps less well known is that from 1984 up until the early 1990s, in addition to Pat Patterson and many Quebec wrestlers, two other members of the WWF staff were also Quebecers, namely Rene Goulet and Terry Garvin (Terry Joyal). "Rene was like Pat's right-hand man. When it came to smaller shows, he was the boss. He had all the responsibilities of a booker, and at the end of the night he would report to Vince," explains Veilleux. "We made the shows work. We produced the matches. I could wrestle in the first match, change, watch the rest of the show and then take the box-office report," he says. "We helped build the company."

"As for Terry, he had Steve Lombardi as an assistant, as he was a little bit older, but he and Rene shared the small cities and had the same responsibilities, like making sure matches went smoothly and collecting the gates while Pat took care of the big shows," remembers Veilleux. "Terry was George Scott's assistant at the beginning," says Goulet. Scott was the head booker from 1983 to 1986. "George Scott got fired and then Vince wanted me in the office," recalls Patterson. In his autobiography J.J. Dillon adds: "As a wrestling promoter, Terry Garvin was an asset to every promotion he ever worked for."

In spite of all this, the scope of Patterson's influence is barely known in his native Montreal. Montrealers were given a rare glimpse behind the scenes, however, in 1994, on the night of Jacques Rougeau's first retirement. On that occasion Patterson explained his place in the WWF to La Presse in detail. "I'm the one who writes the shows, comes up with scenarios for our television programs and finds ideas for our characters. You must be creative, have a fruitful imagination, create characters that allow spectators and TV audiences to have fun and react for the show the way you would react for a good movie." Even today he's still recognized as one of the best in the world at coming up with a finish and he still works for WWE part time. "Pat Patterson is the most creative person in the history of wrestling in putting a finish together," Bret Hart said in one radio interview. "This is precisely why he was put in charge of the main event of *WrestleMania XV*," adds The Rock, speaking of his match against Stone Cold Steve Austin. Still, before getting this prominent role as a creative backstage force, Patterson was a fantastic wrestler and worker.

Born in Montreal on January 19, 1941, and one of nine children, he learned the basics of the profession at the locally famous Loisirs St-Jean-Baptiste, under the tutelage of Pat Girard. He got his first real opportunity in 1958. "It was the promoter Sylvio Samson who gave me a break at the Palais des Sports on Poupart Street," he revealed to *Le Journal de Montréal* in 1987. "At the age of 20 I went to Boston. It was 1962, and I didn't speak a word of English. I had a hard time but I survived," he adds. Then at the ceremony honouring Maurice Vachon at the WWE Hall of Fame in March 2010, he added: "Maurice brought me to Portland when I was starving in Boston."

He had already started making use of his creative side back then, wearing a pink shirt and lipstick, and bringing a poodle to the ring with him to anger the spectators. He most probably drew his inspiration from Gorgeous George, who made use of similar antics in the 1940s. He would also make use of evocative names like Pretty Boy Patterson and Lord Patrick Patterson. Besides a few dates here and there he would not set foot in a Montreal ring for 20 years. "If I had decided to work mainly in the United States it was because I could make more money there. I came back in 1980 to the Paul-Sauvé Arena in order to please the promoters," says Patterson. Although he was very successful in Portland, it was in California that he would make the biggest splash, wrestling for promoter Roy Shire, who greatly influenced Patterson as far as his creative side is concerned. It's actually Shire who asked Patterson to dye his hair blond in order to put him in a team with his former partner, Ray Stevens. "After Ray Stevens, he was the second most popular wrestler in the history of northern California," affirms Gino Brito. But he isn't the only one to think so — Patterson's considered one of the greatest heels in history. "He was a flawless heel, vicious and aggressive, and did everything with precise timing," says "Superstar" Billy Graham.

As the Blond Bombers, he and Ray Stevens would dominate the tag team division and their territory in the 1960s. According to former NWA champion Dory Funk, Stevens and Patterson were the best tag team in the 1960s and they proved that through the number of world cham-

PAT PATTERSON, THE RIGHT-HAND MAN OF VINCE MCMAHON (BERTRAND HÉBERT)

pionship titles they won." From one side of the United States to the other, for the NWA or Verne Gagne's AWA, they were not only champions, but also the team upon which the territory was built. According to Dave Meltzer, their team was much copied and clearly influenced Greg Valentine and Ric Flair in the Carolinas and also Steve Austin and Brian Pillman in WCW. "He had started helping Roy Shire with booking," remembers Brito, explaining Patterson's emergence behind the scenes. He was both a heel and a babyface in San Francisco and was the biggest star in the territory in the 1970s. His match against Don Muraco is considered one of the best matches held at the Cow Palace, the main arena of the territory. He also starred in a legendary feud with Ray Stevens, once they were no longer a team. In 1968, in Japan, he would wrestle many matches against the legendary Antonio Inoki, and he formed a tag team with another Quebecer, Tarzan Tyler.

In 1973 he befriended the Maiva family, forming a team with both Peter

Maiva and his son-in-law Rocky Johnson, on one of the rare occasions in which he wasn't a heel in California. This relationship would allow a certain Dwayne Johnson 20 years later to become one of the biggest stars in the history of the business. According to The Rock's autobiography, Johnson invited Patterson to one of his training sessions and afterward asked Pat to give him his honest opinion about whether he could succeed in the business or not. Patterson simply smiled and answered: "You're going to be okay." This is what Pat Patterson relates on the DVD entitled *The Most Powerful Families in Wrestling*, produced by WWE: "I called Vince and told Vince, 'You don't want him tomorrow, you want him yesterday!'" Coming from Pat Patterson, that was all that needed to be said.

In 1978 he wrestled principally for the AWA, and though he ultimately joined the WWF in 1979 he still continued to work for the Minneapolis promotion. Indeed he wrestled for the two territories until 1983. In New York he would have many chances to win the WWF world championship title held by Bob Backlund. He even became the North American champion, after defeating Ted DiBiase Sr., a title that was morphed into the Intercontinental championship. One of his highlights of this era was a big money feud with Sgt. Slaughter, and their boot camp match held on April 21, 1981, at MSG was voted match of the year by *Wrestling Observer*.

It was around this time that Patterson finally came home. He would leave an indelible mark on the memories of fans while wrestling for Varoussac in matches that mainly involved the Rougeau family. "He's such a good wrestler. Along with Raymond, I had an intense feud with him and Pierre Lefebvre," remembers Jacques Rougeau during an interview with RF Video. "Pat Patterson, he's a great wrestler with an exceptional psychology. He's a general in the ring. I have wrestled with him for a whole summer in one-hour draws and, in spite of my considerable experience, I still learned a lot from him. He's a professional guy, with whom it's very easy to work. He's a credible guy, with whom you don't run the risk of getting injured," says Raymond Rougeau about his biggest single feud. For the WWF he conducted a "Piper's Pit"–type segment on French television, in which he laughed at the guests he didn't like and glorified those he loved. "The Dream of Quebec's Brunch" is still one of the segments most remembered by fans. "He called the Rougeaus 'hot-dog eaters,'" remembers former *AttitudeQc* journalist Claude

Tousignant. "I was coming back to Quebec under the name Pat Patterson, and I'm a Quebecer. Pat Patterson doesn't really sound like a Quebecer . . . I wanted something different so if Dusty Rhodes was The American Dream, I would become the Dream of Quebec or in French le Rêve du Québec," reveals Patterson. Patterson won many tag team championship titles with International Wrestling, principally with Lefebvre and Raymond.

He later would become a commentator for the WWF before definitively retiring in 1984 and slowly becoming Vince McMahon's right-hand man. "He made me quit wrestling and work in an office, something I had never liked. I didn't like working in an office — I mean, I quit school so I wouldn't have to work in an office. I became senior vice president and I had no idea what that meant. The only thing I knew was pro wrestling," Patterson candidly recalled. "My vision of wrestling impressed him. He learned with me how wrestling should work, how to put a match together and how to create a finish," he adds. He made a brief return in 1987, in a feud against Brutus "The Barber" Beefcake in Montreal that would cost him part of his blond hair. In the late 1990s and early 2000s, the fans of the Attitude Era would discover him playing a more comedic role with Gerald Brisco, as one of Mr. McMahon's "yes men." He would actually feud with Brisco for the Hardcore title. "Since Patterson is 61, he probably can't go long, but for a one-minute match he's just about the best worker in the company at knowing how to work a crowd," said Meltzer, after a tag match between Patterson and Brisco against Pete Gas and Rodney in 1999.

Although he no longer has the influence he had 20 years ago, he's still active as a consultant for WWE. "I choose my own schedule now. I take time to travel, instead," said Patterson in September 2009. Rey Mysterio Jr., in his autobiography, credits Patterson for the world title he won in 2006, saying that Pat was the one who pushed the most for this idea. "There are two guys who were geniuses in this business, Eddie Graham and Pat Patterson. Pat lives for the business. Pat Patterson is more than a friend to me, he is family," Gerald Brisco adds.

Along with Yvon Robert, Maurice Vachon, Hans Schmidt and Chris Benoit, he's the only other member of the *Wrestling Observer*'s Hall of Fame born in Quebec, and with Maurice Vachon, the only Quebec wrestlers in the WWE Hall of Fame. He's also been recognized in his native province, with his induction into the Quebec Wrestling Hall of Fame in 2004, proving his nickname of 25 years ago to be right, le Rêve du Québec!

"He's the one who helped me start my career as a referee. He was and still is very important for the WWE," relates Jimmy Korderas, former WWE referee. Ever since he got his American citizenship he changed his name from Pierre Clermont to Pat Patterson, the name that made him famous worldwide for more than 50 years.

RONNIE GARVIN

Becoming NWA World champion was the ultimate recognition for a professional wrestler for more than 40 years. Ronnie Garvin is the only Quebecer who has had this honour and, strangely enough, he's also the only wrestler amongst the best 25 wrestlers (see ranking on page 401) who was never really a star in the Montreal territory — except for the summer of '85. Ironically the only time that the NWA was on the air in Montreal on a French network was during the period that he became world champion. Yet his origins were never revealed during these programs. Like all good stories in the world of wrestling, his world championship reign is still the subject of controversy more than 25 years later. "In Detroit, Michigan, Ronnie Garvin became world heavyweight champion and he deserved it," explains Dusty Rhodes in the DVD *Secrets of the Ring*. "Flair and Garvin did $40,000 in Chattanooga, Tennessee. Jesus, that's pretty good for there," he adds, to help explain the decision.

"Dusty didn't really agree with the idea that I should win the belt. It's Jim Crockett who wanted me to be champion," Garvin says today. "I had four towns a night. Four towns! What I was thinking? I had 100 guys working these nights. 100 guys. I was responsible for 100 guys! Sure, some of them were going to be pissed off. I don't blame them," continues Rhodes in the same DVD interview. According to other observers, it's obvious that Garvin had credibility, but he wasn't the ideal choice for a national promotion. "He was not always flamboyant, but what he did was believable. I never would have second-guessed Dusty's decision to have Ronnie Garvin as world champion," explains J.J. Dillon, who was Dusty's assistant at the time. "See, Garvin was popular in Greensboro and places like that . . . my high-living persona . . . was ready-made for a city like Chicago," explains Ric Flair in his autobiography, speaking about the reaction of the crowd to Garvin during their return match, when he won the belt back at *Starrcade 1987*. Flair became involved in a long program with Garvin after making advances on the wife of Garvin's "brother" Jimmy. Their rivalry would later introduce the battle of the chops to a national audience as blood would flow from both men's chest by the pure power of their bare hands.

In addition to nicknames like One Man Gang and Rugged, Garvin is mainly

RONNIE GARVIN: NWA WORLD CHAMPION IN 1987
(PRO WRESTLING ILLUSTRATED)

known as Hands of Stone. Remembers Ric Flair: "I wouldn't characterize this as a great match, but I definitely enjoyed myself. Ronnie and I grounded the life out of each other. He beat my chest raw. I was rubbing Neosporin into my skin for a year. It's amazing I didn't get a staph infection."

Dave Meltzer draws a parallel between Garvin's reign and that of John Cena in WWE in 2006, saying that Garvin had to face a similar problem. The fans supported Garvin as he chased Ric Flair for the title, but as soon as he became champion they turned, believing Flair deserved the title more. Unfortunately for Garvin the NWA didn't have as much patience as WWE had for Cena. Less than a year later, while Crockett was selling his interest to Ted Turner, Ronnie Garvin left the NWA. "It all started when I had to lose the title to Flair and have a series of return matches against him. But Rhodes changed plans, as he didn't want to give me a push," explains Garvin. "That night also saw Ronnie Garvin make his big heel turn, with J.J. Dillon and me seen paying him off backstage. That was done because Dusty wanted to work a program with him, but Ronnie was, like Johnny Valentine, a very methodical worker who had no problem not getting a response for 20 minutes. Therefore Dusty asked me to manage Ronnie, so I could add some excitement to their matches. I was happy to do it, but before their series could even get off the ground Ronnie up and left for the AWA," explains Gary Hart, who also worked in the office at the time. "Dusty didn't want another wrestler to be popular. In my case, I also had blond hair. I was a warrior coming from the southern States, exactly like him. And his ego was much bigger than the United States," Garvin says about The American Dream.

To understand someone as strong-willed and hard-headed as Garvin, you need to consider his early career. Born in Montreal on March 30, 1945, Roger Barnes was trained at the Loisirs St-Jean-Baptiste by Pat Girard. He went to school with Pat Patterson (Garvin dated his sister) and the man who would become his first brother, Terry Garvin. "I was 15 when I went there the first time to learn boxing. In 1962 we went to the United States, the three of us, and started in Boston." But it was in the south of the United States that he was to become a star and settle down. "It was really difficult to succeed in Montreal. I was not part of the clique. Without being part of that, you couldn't make good money. In the south, the cost of living was lower, and people were much more relaxed. That's why I've always liked that part of the country," he explains. For 20 years he would travel from one territory to the next in North America. He'd also wrestle for Larry Kasaboski's territory in Ontario, but returned to Montreal only a handful of times in 1966 and 1967, teaming with Terry.

It's interesting to note that Garvin was Jack Brisco's first opponent in Oklahoma City, Oklahoma, on May 15, 1965. Brisco had just put an end to a prestigious career in amateur wrestling, while Garvin counted only three years of experience as a pro. Garvin was at his last stretch in the territory and when the promoter asked him to put Brisco over he accepted without any fuss. In his biography Brisco addressed the following message to Garvin: "Thank you for helping me out in Oklahoma, Ronnie; a lot of guys would balk at doing a job for a 'green' kid in his first match." Brisco went on to become one of the best wrestlers of all time and an NWA champion.

Garvin also had a memorable feud with Jake "The Snake" Roberts in the Mid-Atlantic territory, not to mention his successful time in Tennessee. "I am the original Stone Cold," Garvin explains, talking about his time in Kentucky in the 1970s. "I broke a car windshield, I threw food in the faces of fans and I even stole a belt and threw it the river!" He would also have an intense feud with Randy Savage in Tennessee from 1979 to 1983 for the promotion owned by the Poffo family. He even became a minor shareholder there. Later Garvin would ply his trade all over, and it was in Georgia that he was to win the first of his five NWA TV championships.

In 1985 Ronnie came back to Montreal with Jimmy Garvin to battle the Rougeau brothers. It's this program, combined with his NWA world championship run, that was responsible for Garvin's induction into the first class of the Quebec Wrestling Hall of Fame in 2004. In fact Garvin is the only wrestler to have wrestled against the whole Rougeau family; over the course of his career he faced Jacques Sr., Johnny, Raymond, Armand and Jacques Jr. After a short stint with the AWA, where he became TV champion, he joined the WWF at the end of 1988. "It was Pat Patterson who called me. I didn't think I was a good fit, but I went anyway. My friend Raymond Rougeau was there, so I stayed two years instead of one," he explains. He started feuding with Greg Valentine, which would lead to Garvin "leaving" wrestling to become a referee. "It was my idea to be a referee. I knew that to make money I needed to be on PPV and for that you need to be in a good story and a hot feud."

"His matches with Valentine were really hard; neither of them held anything back," remembers Jimmy Korderas. He wrestled in many events and at *WrestleMania V* he worked against another Quebecer, Dino Bravo. It was actually during this period that fans in the province would learn about his origins, as he expressed himself well in French during the WWF Francophone programs. During the summer of '85 the Garvin brothers had been presented as Americans by International Wrestling. "He had his yellow tights and threw his towel in the crowd. But his character was old-fashioned compared to most WWF characters," remembers Marc Blondin. For many observers the time he spent in the WWF remains perplexing; he really didn't fit with their philosophy. Many believe that they simply wanted to showcase a former NWA world champion as a mid-carder in the WWF, just as they did or would do with Harley Race, Ron Simmons and, ironically, Dusty Rhodes.

In fact many think that he would've been a much more important element in the federation had he worked during the days of the WWWF, at a time when Bruno Sammartino was the champion, and his style would've clicked in perfectly with that of other wrestlers like Pedro Morales and Pat Patterson.

After leaving the WWF at the end of 1990, Ronnie Garvin was to slowly put an end to his activities as a full-time wrestler. He would principally work a reduced schedule in Puerto Rico for the WWC and for Jim Cornette's SMW. He would occasionally wrestle a couple of matches in Montreal for Jacques Rougeau Jr., in addition to making a number of appearances in the south of the United States. He had prepared for himself a second career as a pilot, which allowed him to leave wrestling with dignity and with an untarnished legacy. "If I had been flying when I was 17, I would have never wrestled," he told *SLAM! Wrestling*, as his wrestling career was drawing to an end. Garvin is happy that he no longer wrestles, especially for the WWE, because, as he puts it: "I can't sing, I can't dance and I can't rock 'n' roll!" What he always was, instead, was credible "You always felt the blows he gave you. When you left the ring after wrestling against him, you could still feel his blow all over your body," explained former AWA world champion Rick Martel, laughing.

TERRY GARVIN

Born in Montreal, Terry Joyal worked in northern Ontario in 1958, often teaming with promoter Larry Kasaboski under the name of Terry Dobec. It was at the Loisirs St-Jean-Baptiste, under the tutelage of Pat Girard, that he was to meet the wrestler who would become his "brother" a few years later, Ronnie Garvin. His career would last 20 years. "Terry came up with the name Garvin," explains Ronnie. "Jimmy and I took it from him." In fact Terry had already used the name "Fabulous" Terry Garvin when he was wrestling in Ontario. Terry and Ronnie were very successful, winning many tag team championships in many territories.

Having formed a team that would last from 1964 to 1974, they worked mainly in Louisiana, Florida, Carolina, Tennessee and Georgia. Early on Percy Pringle, better known as Paul Bearer, was their manager, a role that would also be undertaken by Jimmy Williams in the early 1970s. "I managed Terry and Ronnie in Tennessee in 1973 and in Atlanta in 1974," relates the man who would become the third brother, Jimmy Garvin. "Terry was a very good wrestler, very old school," he adds.

In addition to the United States, Terry and Ronnie wrestled for Larry Kasaboski's territory in northern Ontario from 1965 to 1969. "Larry had a hard time finding new talent. So he gave Terry and me 25 percent of the gate each, so that we may work at bringing new blood to his promotion," remembers Ronnie. Terry effec-

THE FIRST GARVIN BROTHERS, TERRY AND RONNIE
(CHRIS SWISHER COLLECTION)

tively ran the business until their departure in 1969. Wherever they went they were tag team champions, as they were a very coveted team. "We were always too busy to accept offers from Minneapolis and Portland," adds Ronnie.

During the second half of the 1970s, Terry wrestled mainly in San Francisco and Amarillo, where he also worked in the office for promoters Dick Murdock and Blackjack Mulligan. During these years he also toured New Zealand. "Terry was a heel. He drew considerable crowds in New Zealand. They hated seeing him cheat," remembers Luke Williams. After having done and seen it all as a full-time wrestler, Terry became Bob Geigel's assistant in the early 1980s and the booker of his promotion Central States, which mainly covered the Kansas City area. In addition to being an agent he was also Pat Patterson's assistant from 1985 to 1992. He left the WWF in disgrace after allegations of sexual misconduct with members of the ring crew emerged. Terry Garvin died on August 17, 1998, at the age of 60.

BEN AND JOE WEIDER, WHEN BODYBUILDING MEETS WITH WRESTLING

Few people know that at one point Ben and Joe Weider were a boxer and wrestler, respectively. The two world-famous brothers quickly grasped the importance of bodybuilding as a source of strength in their sports. They also understood that there was a void in the physical fitness market and it was going to make them successful well beyond the expectations of the business world, as they became the fathers of bodybuilding. Weider Health & Fitness was founded in 1939. Ben and Joe, both born in Montreal, were passionate about physical strength. Wrestlers, hockey players, football players and athletes of amateur sport formed the original core of their customers of this burgeoning company. These customers were to make Weider Health & Fitness one of the most important private companies in the world of sports. The growth of the company eventually lead to the foundation of the International Federation of Bodybuilding and Fitness (IFBB), as well as the famous magazine *Muscle & Fitness*.

Back in the world of wrestling, from 1950 up until

ONE OF THE FATHERS OF BODYBUILDING, BEN WEIDER [RIGHT] NEXT TO LOUIS CYR'S DUMBBELLS

(DENIS ARCHAMBAULT COLLECTION)

pretty much the end of the decade, Ben was the editor of a magazine first called *Lutte* and then *Lutte & Boxe*. It was the first French magazine of its kind in the province and it was also distributed in France, Belgium and many other French-speaking nations. The magazine also had an English version called *Boxing and Wrestling* and influenced the Mexican magazine *box y lucha*. Stanley Weston worked for Weider at the time and would go on to launch *ProWrestling Illustrated* years later. Ben died on October 17, 2008, at the age of 85, while his brother Joe celebrated his 90th birthday in November 2012.

Many wrestlers were bodybuilders before starting their careers, and Montreal has known its share. Ovila Asselin, a former Mr. Canada, wrestled from the '50s to the '70s and was part of the first North American tour in Japan at the end of 1951. Another former Mr. Canada, Sammy Berg, wrestled in the '50s and the '60s. Pierre Gagne, Michel Payette, Lionel Robert, Denis Gauthier and Guy Gagne were all bodybuilders before becoming wrestlers. All of them, at one point or another in their bodybuilding or wrestling career, were influenced by the same individual.

TONY LANZA

The Montreal wrestler most often associated with bodybuilding is Tony Lanza. In the late 1940s he worked with the Weider brothers to create the IFBB. Being close with the Weiders also made him one of the main editors of the brothers' pro wrestling magazines. In 1950 he was named Mr. Healthy Quebec at a bodybuilding competition. It was during the same period that he started his career as a photographer. "He was

(LINDA BOUCHER)

THE GREATEST PROMOTER AND THE GREATEST PHOTOGRAPHER, VINCE MCMAHON AND TONY LANZA

ONE OF LANZA'S TRAINEES AND THE SECOND
TO WRESTLE RIKIDOZAN, OVILA ASSELIN

the best photographer in the world," Ben Weider would say upon Lanza's death. He was actually recognized as the number-one photographer in the world, as far as wrestling and body-building were concerned, for many years. The biggest names in both sports passed through the studio in his converted basement. The likes of Steeve Reeves and former Mr. Universe–turned-actor-and former governor of California Arnold Schwarzenegger all posed for him. In order to protect his photography career he'd often wrestle under a mask and he portrayed numerous characters over the years. In the mid-20th century Lanza started a wrestling school in the basement of his home on Bordeaux street in Montreal.

"The biggest name he trained is, without a doubt, Dominic Denucci," says Gino Brito, who lived a couple of houses away. Brute Bernard, Sammy Berg and Ovila Asselin were some of the others he trained.

Like bodybuilding, football is another sport closely linked to wrestling. Only one Quebecer, however, excelled in both sports.

GEORGE CANNON

Born George McArthur, George Cannon was a Montreal native. Unlike other football players–turn-wrestlers like Herb Trawick, Angelo Mosca, Mike Webster and Glen Kulka, Cannon didn't play for the Alouettes but for the Saskatchewan Roughriders in the CFL. He made his debut as a wrestler in Japan in 1953, but after two lean years he left the business. He would return to wrestling in 1959, when Texas promoter Morris Siegel dubbed him Cry

Baby, a nickname he was to keep for the rest of his career. He wrestled in the American Mid-West, as well as in Toronto and in Montreal for All Star Wrestling. Then in 1968 he went to Los Angeles, where he wrestled and hosted a variety show on KTLA Channel 5 for two years.

GEORGE CANNON AND GINO BRITO WORKED TOGETHER FOR A SHORT PERIOD IN THE EARLY 1980S (LINDA BOUCHER)

In the early 1970s he was to become even more famous, as the manager of the Fabulous Kangaroos, Al Costello and Don Kent, one of the best tag teams of all time. In 1975 former NWF promoter Pedro Martinez (who wrestled in Montreal in 1940 as Ignacio Martinez) and Chicago White Sox shareholder Eddie Einhorn (who helped turn Major League Baseball into a billion-dollar industry and who helped make college basketball popular on television) founded the IWA. They chose Cannon as their booker; this prepared him to run his own wrestling promotion in partnership with Milt Avruskin a few years later. From 1976 to the early 1980s he was able to get his shows broadcast throughout Canada, including the Montreal area (where he was also running house shows at the Verdun Auditorium), but the venture wasn't really successful. After having sold his television contract to the WWF, he became their local promoter for two years before falling ill. On July 1, 1994, Cannon died at the age of 62.

During the Eddie Quinn period, fans at Montreal matches frequently saw former boxers as referees. Jack Sharkey, Jack Dempsey, Rocky Marciano and Joe Louis were all used as special enforcers for a hot feud or when a "normal" referee wasn't enough. Generally, though, it was important to have referees who commanded the respect of the wrestlers. Fortunately for the territory, the first golden era of wrestling supplied it with men of quality.

GUY SOUCY, GINO BRITO, OMER MARCHESSAULT, A WRESTLING FAN, HANS SCHMIDT, BOB LANGEVIN AND STEVE PARADIS (PAUL LEDUC COLLECTION)

OMER MARCHESSAULT

After having tried in vain to be part of the Olympic wrestling team in 1936, Omer Marchessault launched his professional wrestling career. It was in 1942 that he adopted the identity of the Green Mask. Then in 1949 he created his most well-known character, la Merveille Masquée or the Masked Marvel. It was in order to protect his livelihood as a fireman that Marchessault worked under a hood. "My bosses didn't think too highly of wrestling, especially of playing the role of a heel, as it was a bad example for young people. I solved the problem by covering my face," he explains. After having won the junior heavyweight championship in 1950, he became a referee for the MAC. "When I realized that I didn't earn more than $40 in most matches and that I risked my career as a firefighter each time, I chose security," he said.

He would occupy this position until 1975 and serve as a referee in the biggest matches of the time, including the last victory of Yvon Robert in 1955, the match of the century between Andre the Giant and Don Leo Jonathan for Grand Prix and Johnny Rougeau's battle with Abdullah the Butcher at Jarry Park Stadium. "Those were the best 25 years of my life. I commanded the respect of the public and the wrestling world who regarded me with esteem," he explained to the *Revue Lutte* magazine in 1988. In 1973 he was a trainer at the Grand Prix wrestling school and Richard Charland was one of his students. In 1983 he became a timekeeper for the Athletic Commission, a position that he would occupy for more than 10 years in wrestling, boxing and kickboxing. After the arrival of the WWF, he was the only recognizable figure of the glorious era of wrestling in Montreal at ringside, and it stayed that way up until the mid-1990s. Always in love with the sport, he attended and played the role at some indy shows as well. "I had a busy and eventful life. I don't regret anything. If I had to live my life all over again, La Merveille Masquée would be as over and would certainly make more money!" he told the late journalist Jean-Paul Sarault. Omer Marchessault died on December 26, 1996, at the venerable age of 83. One year earlier the WWF honoured him, along with Bob Langevin, at the Montreal Forum for his 60 years of service to wrestling. Many still consider him the best wrestling referee that the territory has ever had.

DAN MURRAY AND SAMMY MACK

REFEREE SAMMY MACK HOLDS THE BLOODY EAR OF YUKON ERIC (TONY LANZA)

In the 1940s and 1950s Dan Murray and Sammy Mack were the two most influential referees in the Montreal territory. A Montreal native, Murray was often used for main events or the more important matches. He was also the referee most often used for ref bumps at the time. "Dan Murray was as popular as Yvon Robert for Eddie Quinn's promotion," Paul Leduc contends. "Omer Marchessault actually learned from him." Sammy Mack is famous for having picked up the bloody ear of Yukon Eric and he even took some pictures with it in the dressing room.

In the end the golden era witnessed the emergence of a very important player in the territory, the man who was considered Yvon Robert's heir apparent and who earned the nickname The Gentleman.

JOHNNY ROUGEAU

The name Rougeau has been synonymous with the Montreal territory for many years, to the point that some people call it the Rougeau territory. Young people today know Jacques Jr. and his sons Jean-Jacques and Cédric through his wrestling promotion. Others remember The Quebecers, a team consisting of Jacques and Pierre-Carl Ouellet, or the Fabulous Rougeau brothers, Jacques Jr. and Raymond. The older fans remember the brute strength of Jacques Rougeau Sr. But the one who started this dynasty was none other than Jean "Johnny" Rougeau.

Born on June 9, 1929, Johnny Rougeau started his wrestling career in 1951. Rougeau was proud of his convictions, and when he was given convincing arguments he could get involved in multiple projects, as demonstrated by the numerous careers he juggled. It's no surprise, therefore, that he decided to help create the first trade union at Coca-Cola in the 1950s. The move ultimately cost him his job. His uncle, Eddy Auger, wrestled in the Detroit territory at that time. When someone was injured, Auger called his nephew. Out of work, Johnny decided to accept his uncle's invitation. It was the beginning of an incredible career.

At the time it was difficult to break into the Montreal territory, so Rougeau continued to wrestle in the United States. Performing as Handsome Johnny Rougeau, or the Ladies' Man, he became a star. Where's Montreal in all of this? Eddie Quinn found Rougeau, like many local boys, to be too small. This offended Johnny. Being a man of integrity, when Quinn finally approached him to wrestle, Rougeau thought about it, then made Quinn wait many months for an answer. But since his wife had given birth to their first daughter, Rougeau wanted to be closer to his family and finally decided to settle down in Montreal.

In 1957 Yvon Robert took Rougeau under his wing. Rougeau commanded respect and was easy to work with. That's probably why so many people wanted to partner with him or help him out. Johnny Rougeau would say that Yvon Robert polished his style and that he improved when he was under the tutelage of the former champion. Robert taught him the tricks of the trade, even the Japanese armlock, the famous submission hold he used to win so many matches. It was actually during that year, teaming with Rougeau, that Robert wrestled his last match. "People said Rougeau was the next Yvon Robert," says Gino Brito. Then in 1960 Robert officially became his manager. It was in 1961, under Robert's management, that Rougeau won the Montreal title for the first time,

INTERNATIONAL CHAMPION "GENTLEMAN" JOHNNY ROUGEAU (TONY LANZA)

defeating Hans Schmidt. After having been successful in the United States, Rougeau finally sat on top of the Montreal territory.

But being a man driven by projects, Rougeau started to open up to other businesses. In the early 1960s he became friends with René Lévesque, who was still in the Liberal Party at the time, long before he became associated with the Parti Québécois. From 1960 to 1980 Lévesque had occupied a very important place in Rougeau's life, as Johnny was sometimes his bodyguard, his confident and his most fervent militant. "Jean Rougeau, idol of real wrestling fans, was one of the most fundamentally honest men I've ever met," Lévesque wrote in his autobiography. Former wrestler Édouard Carpentier also bears witness to his honesty. "Johnny Rougeau is the most honest person I've ever known," he once said, making a reference to a show in which Rougeau paid him his guarantee despite a poor turnout.

After winning the title Rougeau bought the Mocambo, a downtown Montreal night club that wasn't doing well. Rougeau's perseverance eventually made it the most successful club in Montreal. Artists from all over

REFEREE YVON ROBERT AND BOB LANGEVIN RAISE
THE ARMS OF JOHNNY ROUGEAU (PAUL LEDUC COLLECTION)

the world came to perform, including the likes of Chubby Checker and Liberace, as well as the who's who of Montreal local performers. Even Ronnie Garvin went there to hang out when he was a young man. In spite of the club's success, being keenly aware that the approaching Expo 1967 might take people away from his establishment, he decided to sell it in 1965.

With his involvement in politics and entertainment, Rougeau somewhat neglected wrestling. However after selling the Mocambo he decided to launch a wrestling promotion and All Star Wrestling was born. His first show was held at the Paul-Sauvé Arena on May 6, 1965. But wrestling wasn't the only sport that enthralled Rougeau. In the 1950s he'd taken part in the training camp of the CFL's Montreal Alouettes. "I left the team one week before the Alouettes' season started. Michel Normandin had convinced me to do the camp. I was okay with the team, but I didn't get along with the coach, Peahead Walker," Rougeau explained on Radio-Canada TV in 1971.

Rougeau was to be more successful with junior hockey. In 1969 he bought the Rosemont Bombardiers of the Metropolitan League. This team, renamed the Rosemont National, participated in the first season of the Quebec Major Junior Hockey League (QMJHL). The team subsequently moved to Laval, was sold and then bought back by Rougeau after he retired and had sold All Star Wrestling. Two of his players went on to very successful

NHL careers. Robert "Bob" Sauve played goalie for the Buffalo Sabres and is now one of the most influential player agents, while Mike Bossy won four Stanley Cups with the New York Islanders and is considered one of the greatest NHL snipers of all time. Rougeau was both coach and general manager of the team, which has since moved to Bathurst, New Brunswick.

In hockey, as in wrestling, Rougeau commanded respect. Journalists, players and the management on other teams all appreciated his frankness and well-defined ideas. It was his initiative, for example, that sent the league's young players back to school. In 1981 he was named president of the QMJHL, a title he would keep until his death. A trophy is now awarded in his honour to the team that finishes first in the regular season.

On May 25, 1983, Johnny Rougeau, 54, died after battling cancer. More than 7,000 attended his funeral, one of the biggest in pro wrestling history. Only icons like El Santo, Giant Baba and Mitsuhara Misawa were honoured by more. The former captain of the Montreal Canadiens, Jean Béliveau, was nicknamed Gentleman Jean. Says Raymond Rougeau about Béliveau and his uncle: "They were two respectable men who respected each other." For many Gentleman Jean was also Jean Rougeau.

1965-1976
THE SECOND GOLDEN AGE

It was with the full-time return of Johnny Rougeau to wrestling that the province witnessed its second golden age. But it wasn't only the return of Rougeau that made this era successful.

ALL STAR WRESTLING VERSUS GRAND PRIX

Promotional wars are nothing new to wrestling fans. In Mexico AAA and CMLL have been at war since the 1990s. In Japan, during the 1970s, '80s and '90s, Giant Baba's All Japan and Antonio Inoki's New Japan battled over the same talent. In the United States Vince McMahon's WWF and Ted Turner's WCW crossed swords in the '90s in what was probably the most important promotional war in the history of wrestling.

The Montreal territory was no different. And in the early 1970s the province saw its first and only true territorial war. At the time All Star Wrestling and Grand Prix ran head to head. Forty years later Raymond Rougeau, one of the All Star Wrestling shareholders, had this to say: "Grand Prix was only a flash in the pan — it disappeared after two years." Paul Vachon, promoter and shareholder in Grand Prix, saw things differently: "All Star Wrestling wasn't really an opposition; we were so much stronger than them." These very different takes, decades after the fact, indicate the kind of rivalry the companies had.

All Star Wrestling, under the control of Les Entreprises Sportives de l'Est, began running shows in 1965. They were the ones who had the right to present cards at the Montreal Forum and they were the only ones to have a licence from the MAC on Montreal Island. On paper the promoter was Bob

THE LEDUC BROTHERS JUMPED TO GRAND PRIX FOR A MORE LUCRATIVE CONTRACT

(PAUL LEDUC COLLECTION)

Langevin, but it was actually Johnny Rougeau who pulled all the strings. In the 1960s, according to the rules of the MAC, a promoter was not allowed to wrestle. Fans of All Star Wrestling were treated to the TV program *Sur le Matelas* (*On the Mat*), featuring the Leduc brothers, Abdullah the Butcher, the rookie years of Raymond Rougeau and Gino Brito; they were also drawn to shows at Jarry Park Stadium and the Paul-Sauvé Arena. Ultimately they tuned in to appreciate the prowess of Johnny and his brother Jacques.

In 1971 a group consisting of Édouard Carpentier and Maurice Vachon, former wrestler Yvon Robert Sr., promoters Lucien Grégoire and Gerry Legault and lawyer Michel Awada started their own wrestling promotion under the banner Les Entreprises Sportives Transcanada. It would later become Les Entreprises Sportives Grand Prix. They put on a few occasional shows, notably the one at the Maurice Richard arena, but it wasn't until June 5, 1971, that the new federation made its debut at the Verdun Auditorium. It would turn into a weekly feature.

When Yvon Robert Sr. died in July 1971, Yvon Jr. took over his father's shares. At the same time Gerry Legault decided to sell his stake, and Paul Vachon, who was involved in the promotion but was not shareholder yet, bought them. Vachon quickly managed to get TV contracts with Télé 7 Sherbrooke and CFCF 12. In 1972 they presented their first show at the Forum, with Paul Vachon as promoter, leaving the spotlight to his brother Maurice and Carpentier. During their few years of existence, fans were able to discover and enjoy such wrestlers as Jean Ferré, Gilles "The Fish" Poisson, The Kiwis and John Studd. "I was surprised by the quantity and the quality of the talents," commented Luke Williams, one of the Kiwis tag team, who would later be better known as The Sheepherders and finally as The Bushwhackers.

All the ingredients for the most important feud in the history of Quebec wrestling were in place. But to better understand the feud, one must first know the reasons that drove the four major Grand Prix shareholders to launch their own promotion.

When Radio-Canada decided to drop wrestling, Eddie Quinn approached channel 10, which began broadcasting in March 1961, and by September of that year he was back on TV. This time, however, he wasn't presenting new matches or live events. He gave the station a master tape of something like 20 to 25 hours of wrestling. This new program was broadcast in the same time slot that Radio-Canada used to present wrestling, on Wednesday night. But what's even more surprising is that this show was called *Sur le Matelas*, more than four years before Johnny Rougeau made a success out of it. Quinn's program ran from September 1961 to September 1962, when it was cancelled. Then, in September 1963, after a full year without wrestling on TV, *Sur le Matelas* came back, this time on Saturday afternoons. From September 1963 up until Rougeau started his version of the program in early 1966, the show was a mix of Quinn's taped wrestling and some Maple Leaf Wrestling footage. Johnny Rougeau was one of the wrestlers most often featured in this early version of *Sur le Matelas*.

Yvon Robert also started his promotion at this time, running a few shows at the Montreal Forum beginning in July 1963, but mainly using the Paul-Sauvé Arena. History has always told fans that Johnny Rougeau had quit the business in 1962 to take care of his nightclub and other business endeavours and that he only returned to wrestling when he opened All Star. But history had been misleading fans, historians and even former wrestlers for decades. The truth is, Rougeau was wrestling on a semi-regular basis for Robert, until Robert later closed down his promotion in November 1964. When Rougeau started his wrestling company, his first move was to get on TV. To do so he took Quinn's master tape, which Robert inherited at Quinn's death in December 1964, without either asking Robert's permission or offering him a partnership, and went to channel 10 to pitch his new show. In his biography Rougeau credits Roland Giguere, who was a director on *La Lutte* at Radio-Canada and who was then in charge of programming at channel 10, with the resurrection of Montreal wrestling. "This is what allowed me to make things work again," he says.

LUKE WILLIAMS AND BUTCH MILLER LATER BECAME KNOWN AS THE BUSHWACKERS (BERTRAND HÉBERT COLLECTION)

At this point the relationship between Robert and Rougeau fell into disarray, with Robert angry that Rougeau had not included him in this new venture, even though he'd helped him when he started and booked him on his shows in the past years. On the other hand, some speculate that Robert owed him money from the shows he wrestled on. Whatever the case may really be, the animosity lasted for many years. Robert didn't want to work for Rougeau afterward; he refereed matches, occasionally, because the fans were asking for him and he didn't want to disappoint them. But it's clearly

TOP ROW: RAYMOND ROUGEAU, HANS SCHMIDT, JOS BÉLANGER, DENIS GAUTHIER, JP PARADIS, LEN SHELLEY, JOHNNY ROUGEAU, TONY MULE, GINO BRITO, JOHNNY WAR EAGLE, EDDY CREATCHMAN AND MICHEL DUBOIS. BOTTOM ROW: ANDRÉ PROULX, PIERRE LEFEBVRE, LUIGI MASCERA, ROSEMONT NATIONAL'S GOALIE, BULL GREGORY, BUTCH MORGAN, MASKED #1, MASKED #2, RICH COUTU (TONY LANZA)

the main reason why he went to meet with the Vachons about starting Grand Prix Wrestling. Also he didn't want his son to wrestle for Rougeau.

For Édouard Carpentier, Johnny Rougeau's other responsibilities were the key reasons. "Johnny Rougeau started taking care of his junior hockey team more and more seriously, and when I noticed that I asked him whether I could start something else and he told me to do what I wanted," explained Carpentier. As for Yvon Robert Sr., he saw an opportunity to have his son wrestle regularly and get a real push. For their part the Vachon brothers had always wanted to be their own bosses.

The new group's first big acquisition was, without a doubt, Jean Ferré. The arrival of Ferré, or Andre the Giant as American fans know him, gave Grand Prix the number one draw in Montreal for years. The battle between André and Don Leo Jonathan in Grand Prix became known as the match of the century. It was broadcast on CKVL radio station. "It's one of the best matches I've ever seen," remembers Williams.

The war wasn't only waged through the opposing house shows, but also through television. In his book Paul Vachon explains that he offered his show to CFTM, showing the people there what CFCF 12 had filmed at the Maurice Richard arena. Grand Prix was shot in colour, while, at the same time, Sur le Matelas was still in black and white. After having viewed and refused Vachon's offer, one week later Sur le Matelas was now suddenly in colour!

Both sides tried anything and everything to try to achieve victory. In the beginning Grand Prix's biggest sponsor was the CKVL radio station. Johnny Rougeau, however, managed to get himself interviewed by the star host of the station. Paul Vachon was furious.

To really be number one in Montreal, however, you had to book the Forum. All Star Wrestling had exclusive access to the venue, but Grand Prix also had its eyes set on the home of the Canadiens. The Montreal Athletic Commission clearly favoured Johnny Rougeau. So they put up road blocks in front of Grand Prix, refusing to give them a licence to promote wrestling on the Montreal island. Further in order to get a licence for the island Grand Prix had to have confirmed dates at the Forum, while the Forum demanded a licence before giving Grand Prix any dates. The catch-22 clearly privileged All Star Wrestling.

A couple of years earlier a false rumour about Johnny Rougeau and Jean Béliveau's wife had made headlines. Although everyone agrees today that there was no truth to the story, the "news" left the Montreal Canadiens captain with a bitter taste in his mouth. Knowing that Béliveau was a fan of wrestling, Paul Vachon decided to pay him a visit — in the Forum where Béliveau now had an office. In next to no time Grand Prix had its dates confirmed! The arrival of a new player in the Forum was a pivotal event: the two promotions were playing on an even field for the first time.

The dishonestly of the Athletic Commission also added fuel to the war. Paul Vachon has an interesting anecdote about how far the Athletic Commission would go. One day, while he was visiting boxing promoter Régis Lévesque to get tickets for a boxing match, Jean Laroche, the president of the commission, came over to talk. Vachon was wearing an old hunting shirt. Confusing him with Jos Leduc, Laroche told Vachon to pass on the word to Johnny Rougeau and tell him to book his dates at the Forum as quickly as possible because Vachon had his set, so the commission was no longer able to block his request for a licence. Needless to say Laroche regretted his candour when he discovered that he wasn't talking to Leduc.

The media also helped fuel the war. According to Gino Brito, Johnny Rougeau was a good friend of Pierre Peladeau and Jacques Beauchamps, the owner and the star sports journalist of *Le Journal de Montréal*. These relationships helped Rougeau get better coverage. *Le Journal de Montréal* devoted half a page to the first show held by All Star Wrestling at Jarry Park Stadium the day after it took place, as well as a whole page of photos two days after the event. One year later, when Grand Prix organized a show at Jarry Park Stadium and drew an even bigger crowd than Rougeau, the event was covered on just a quarter of a page and with only one photo.

After the Jarry Park Stadium All Star Wrestling show riot that took place in July '72, the Athletic Commission accused Grand Prix of deliberately giving its wrestlers the night off, so they could start the ruckus and damage their competitors' reputation. Once again the Athletic Commission was adding oil to the fire.

As for the wrestlers, as in any promotional war, some decided to switch camps. This was the case of Dale Roberts and Jerry Brown, the Hollywood Blonds, Jos and Paul Leduc, Gino Brito, Dino Bravo and many others. Each of them had his own reasons. "It was obvious to me that Dino was to remain a wrestler stuck in preliminaries with All Star Wrestling. So I sent him to Grand Prix," explains Gino Brito. As for Paul Leduc, he saw a gold mine for him and Jos in joining Grand Prix and working against the Vachons. In fact the Leducs were involved in another very interesting story that helped fuel the fire of the rivalry. For the big show at Jarry Park Stadium, Grand Prix had the idea of putting Mad Dog Vachon against Jos Leduc in the main event. But a few months before the show, Jos made it known that he wasn't going to be participating. Why? The Leducs were switching back to Rougeau's All Star! "We heard ahead of time that Grand Prix' days were numbered, so we left before it was too late," recalls Paul Leduc, who handled the team's business. On the other hand, Paul Vachon states in his book that the Leducs left because Jos was making more money than Paul.

OMER MARCHESSAULT IS THE REFEREE OF A BATTLE BETWEEN ALL STAR AND GRAND PRIX AT THE FORUM

(BERTRAND HÉBERT COLLECTION)

Gino Brito was another who benefited from these battles over talent. "After having sent Bravo to Grand Prix, I wanted to go there myself, but I wanted them to make me an offer to have the upper hand in the negotiations. A couple of months later Lucien Grégoire, who never stops asking me to sign a contract with them, finally made me an offer I could not refuse and that would allow me to make twice as much money as I was making with All Star Wrestling," he says. "I went to see Johnny and I told him that if he would increase my salary by 25 percent I would stay. But he wouldn't. So, I gave him my two weeks' notice and told him to do whatever he wanted to do with me as far as booking was concerned. He got angry, telling me that my father was a partner and that it was just unacceptable. I looked at him and told him: 'You did the same thing in the 1950s, when Quinn asked you to wrestle at the Forum. You were supposed to main-event at the Exchange Stadium and you didn't even bother to go. I wasn't there, but I know the story.' He told me that I was right and I added that I wasn't like the Leducs and that at least I gave him advance notice. When Grand Prix shut down, he took me back," Brito explains.

Depending on who you're talking to, there were different high points in the war. As far as Raymond Rougeau is concerned, the rivalry started when wrestlers from All Star Wrestling jumped to Grand Prix. "In 1972 the rivalry reached its highest point. The Leducs, Gino Brito, Dino Bravo and the Hollywood Blonds all changed sides," he remembered. According to Gilles "The Fish" Poisson, however, something else was more important: "The popularity of Jean Ferré was the event that made this feud." For Paul Vachon it was all about taking control of the Forum in 1972 and 1973, when Grand Prix held about twice as many shows there. "Suddenly Grand Prix had the upper hand, and All Star Wrestling didn't even realize it," Jackie Wiecz, nephew of Édouard Carpentier, explains.

Near the end of 1973 the Vachons sold their Grand Prix shares to Tony Mule, and after their departure things started to go sour. In the hope of generating interest among the dwindling number of fans of both promotions, All Star Wrestling and Grand Prix presented joint shows between January and April 1974. These shows featured programs between, among others, Michel Dubois and Johnny War Eagle, Carpentier and The Sheik and Raymond Rougeau in tag team action with Denis Gauthier against The Kiwis. After drawing only 6,200 people at the Colisée de Québec on January 31, 1974, with Carpentier main-eventing against Dubois, their first joint show at the Forum drew 18,184 on February 12 and featured Don Leo Jonathan against Jacques Rougeau. Both companies' champions were facing off in the ultimate dream match. The third joint show took place in Hull and opposed Rougeau to Tarzan Tyler. The fourth drew 12,711 on March 11 at the Forum for the return match between Jonathan and Rougeau. The fifth and final show, also at the Forum, drew 12,000 fans on April 8, with Jonathan main-eventing against The Sheik. Although these crowds were the biggest of 1974, the shows didn't have the desired effect. "The golden goose had been sacrificed again to protect everybody's ego during the joint shows, and the two companies weren't able to recover from it," François Poirier says. Poirier was right, and soon after, the beautiful story that was Grand Prix came to an end.

There are divergent opinions about whether the rivalry had a positive or negative impact on wrestling in general. Traditionally such a war compelled the two parties to outmatch one another in order to be acknowledged as the best. Raymond Rougeau and his father saw it like this, however: "It opens up room for wrestlers . . . but there were seven hours of wrestling a week on television; it got saturated." Sir Oliver Humperdink, who managed the Hollywood Blonds in those days, thought "it was good for the guys, as it gave them an alternative." Édouard Carpentier agrees: "It helped breathe new life into wrestling in the Montreal territory, and we were a solid promotion." Paul Leduc says, "The objective of Grand Prix was to operate at a national level, to present shows across Canada, instead of remaining a territorial promotion, as it was the case of all promotions at the time." Paul Vachon, he further insists, had come up with this idea well before Vince McMahon managed to realize the dream with his WWF.

With the feud wrestling witnessed another golden age in the province. All Star Wrestling was to go on for almost two more years. The group, managed principally by the Rougeaus, returned to the top of Quebec wrestling. But two groups emerged from the ashes of Grand Prix to compete with them nonetheless.

CELEBRITY WRESTLING, GRAND CIRCUIT WRESTLING AND THE END OF ALL STAR WRESTLING

In TV terms a spinoff is a program revolving around one or many characters from another show. A good example of this is the comedy *Frasier*, which was a spinoff of the popular program *Cheers*. It's also pretty much what happened with Grand Prix.

When the Vachon brothers left the promotion they helped create, it took them just a couple of months to start a new one, called Celebrity Wrestling. In fact in April 1974, a few months after leaving Grand Prix, the Vachons announced that they had signed with All Star Wrestling, their competitors over the past few years. One month later, when they officially announced their new wrestling promotion, they also announced they had an agreement with All Star Wrestling that would allow them to have some of their wrestlers. The truth of the matter was that the Vachons created this new entity one month before signing with All Star Wrestling. Being good businessmen the Vachons knew that it would be much easier to reach an agreement with All Star Wrestling if they had a contract with them.

"I had bought a production company before I left Grand Prix named Mirabelle Productions. So I wanted to make the best of my investment. I was producing the matches of the WHA's Nordiques, roller derby and wrestling was something I knew very well — it was more than normal for me to produce it, as well," Paul Vachon says. Many rumours of the time suggested the Leduc brothers, the Hollywood Blonds and others were shareholders in Celebrity Wrestling. Paul Leduc sets the records straight: "The only two people who invested money in the promotion were Paul and Maurice. I only worked in the office."

Celebrity Wrestling had the assets to succeed. Paul Vachon used the same methods that worked so well in the early days of Grand Prix. It was no big surprise, then, when Celebrity Wrestling made its TV debut on June 1, 1974, on Cablevision, channel 9, at noon. Before the end of the month, they were also on Global in Ottawa. "The difference between Paul and Johnny was that the tape belonged to Paul. He owned it. Thus he could sell his show anywhere he wanted. This is precisely why Grand Prix was broadcast across Canada, and the same thing happened with Celebrity Wrestling. As for Johnny, the tape belonged to CFTM; he had no voice at this level," explains Paul Leduc. Indeed almost no video footage of All Star Wrestling exists today, while collectors still find episodes of Grand Prix.

While Celebrity Wrestling exploited the south shore of Montreal and Ottawa, nothing seemed to work for Grand Prix. Talent began to leave that promotion, either for All Star Wrestling, like Eddy Creatchman, or for Celebrity Wrestling. As if this weren't enough, a strike of Verdun city workers made their favourite arena unavailable to them. In fact in the summer of 1974, there was so little talk about Grand Prix in the newspapers that one had to wonder whether it still existed.

As far as Celebrity Wrestling was concerned, things seemed to progress smoothly. They presented the match that could not be booked the previous year between Jos Leduc and Mad Dog Vachon in Longueuil, Quebec, and Cornwall, Ontario, among others cities. The Cornwall match was actually a big hit. "It was the most savage match, the bloodiest match that I've ever seen in my life," said journalist Guy Émond. Celebrity Wrestling also featured new wrestlers, like the young "Rowdy" Roddy Piper, who made his first appearance in Montreal on July 23, 1974. The Vachons had even brought their sister Vivian to the province during that summer, but after a few weeks she returned to the United States, where she could make more money. Female wrestling wasn't very popular in Quebec at the time. And, unfortunately, it wasn't just female wrestling that wasn't very popular.

The popularity of wrestling itself was in a downward spiral. All Star Wrestling wasn't even able to draw 10,000 people to the Forum and Celebrity Wrestling, in spite of its good start, wasn't fully established. Wrestlers could no longer make the money they used to just a couple of years earlier. Times were so tough, and competition so fierce, that the idea of wrestling exclusively for one promoter was becoming more and more unpopular. The wrestler who would make the most of this new situation was Mad Dog Vachon. In fact in July and August 1974, Vachon would wrestle for All Star Wrestling, Celebrity Wrestling and the return show of Grand Prix in Verdun. "Wrestling is ultimately a business, and Maurice, like everybody else, wanted to make money," his brother Paul explains.

But Grand Prix's return was relatively brief, as the company no longer knew what to do to draw more than 2,000 fans. On September 29, 1974, the last episode of Grand Prix aired on CFCF 12; on October 18 it was CJOH's turn to cancel the program. With Grand Prix out of the picture, Celebrity Wrestling had a golden opportunity. They took the time slot left by their predecessors on CFCF 12 in October 1974 and began to run house shows at the Verdun Auditorium. Celebrity Wrestling built up the brutal rivalry between Mad Dog Vachon and Gypsy Joe. Don Leo Jonathan made his comeback, and former enemies even teamed up when Mad Dog Vachon and Paul Leduc joined forces. Ultimately it wasn't enough.

According to Paul Leduc, another factor has to be taken into account. "Paul Vachon's wife, Van, was pushing a lot for the roller derby. They lost a lot of money on that, and Celebrity Wrestling suffered the consequences."

In the same weekend, the first of 1975, Celebrity Wrestling lost its two last time slots, CFCF 12 and WEZF 22 in Burlington, a Vermont station Quebecers could get with an antenna. Johnny Rougeau made no mistake this time and jumped on the opportunity to broadcast his shows on more than one station. He took over the TV contracts that Celebrity Wrestling had in Montreal, Ottawa and Vermont, including the important contract with CFCF 12, Montreal's English station.

But the spinoff from Grand Prix wasn't limited to Celebrity Wrestling. Don Leo Jonathan, in partnership with his friend Fred Major, the man behind the fishing equipment line of the same name, started Grand Circuit Wrestling. Rougeau had more competition. Taking the same group of wrestlers used by Celebrity Wrestling, as well as the same cities, Grand Circuit made its debut in the Montreal territory in January 1975. On June 14, 1975, Grand Circuit started broadcasting a program on WCAX 3, another Vermont station Quebecers could access. The show was short-lived — three months later the program was cancelled. Major, Jonathan and their third partner, Killer Kowalski, can't be accused of not trying whatever it took to make things work.

A contest between Jonathan and Kowalski was held at the Municipal Stadium in Verdun. Grand Circuit brought back Andre the Giant and Pat Patterson and even Lou Thesz to referee a match, but it wasn't enough. "Major called me to talk about the wrestling industry in Montreal, and I gave him a piece of advice — quit wrestling very quickly!" Paul Vachon remembers. Grand Circuit shut its doors in the spring of 1976.

All Star Wrestling also had its share of problems. Clearly wrestling wasn't as popular as it used to be, and three promotions running shows at the same time didn't make things any better. Desperate, too, Johnny Rougeau even made a comeback. He wrestled against champion Tarzan Tyler at the Forum on September 3, 1975, and won the title for the first time since 1970. In spite of this, the crowd was considered a disappointment. It was a definite sign. When one of the most popular wrestlers in the history of the territory makes a comeback and isn't able to draw a considerable crowd, it means that it's high time to do something else. Jean Rougeau became even more involved in junior hockey and with the fast-approaching Olympic Games, he decided to sell the promotion.

The three companies are easily mixed up. Within 24 months, but with almost the same wrestlers and the same arenas, the fans would see Grand Prix, Celebrity and Grand Circuit, one after the other. Even the names are kind of similar. The journalists of the day also had a hard time distinguishing between the promotions, which speaks volumes about the situation that creates confusion to this day.

If the full-time return to wrestling of Johnny Rougeau was great for professional wrestling in the '60s and '70s, the return of his brother Jacques was almost as good.

JACQUES ROUGEAU SR.

When Jacques Rougeau Sr. learned that he was ranked as the eighth-best Quebec wrestler of all time (see ranking on page 401) his first reaction was brutally honest: "I didn't really know how to wrestle!" Although Mr. Rougeau was a wrestling star in the territory, he was considered a better boxer than a wrestler. "Raymond should have been ahead of me," he said, having also heard that his son ranked ninth. So how do we explain the committee's ranking, when he wouldn't have ranked himself that high? Raymond Rougeau has an answer: "My father was credible. He looked like a real wrestler. I would have paid to see my father wrestle."

This is what characterized wrestling from the 1950s until the 1970s: everything was a matter of perception. Unless they were exceptionally talented, the height, size and stature of the wrestler played a crucial role in how fans perceived them. This is actually one of the reasons why Eddie Quinn wasn't that impressed with Édouard Carpentier. "Who's the fucking midget?" are what Carpentier remembers as the first words Quinn spoke to him. It wasn't quite like it is today; they didn't necessarily look for a muscular, sun-tanned guy standing 6'5". On the contrary, Jacques Rougeau looked like a man, a real one, very much like many of the wrestlers did back then. "Sailor White wouldn't make it in wrestling these days," Sunny War Cloud says. However, Sailor White looked like a wrestler, with his build and his attitude. Like Jacques Rougeau, people looked at him and said that he could legitimately harm someone. "People believed in me," Rougeau recalls.

Rougeau also had credibility in a ring. He never competed as an amateur

THE FIRST VERSION OF THE FABULOUS ROUGEAU BROTHERS, JACQUES AND JOHNNY (SYLVAIN SAMSON COLLECTION)

wrestler, like so many of his generation. Instead, he trained to be a boxer. As a matter of fact he was a legitimate Golden Gloves champion. "I fought 36 amateur matches and won 35 of them," Rougeau says.

With a brother and an uncle in the business, a wrestling career was in his blood. Uncle Eddy Auger convinced him to lace up the boots at some point in early 1956. Born on May 27, 1930, Rougeau was already 25. It was in Tony Lanza's basement that Jacques Sr. started his training, under the supervision of Auger. He made his debut for promoter Lucien Grégoire, for whom he wrestled a couple of matches.

At the time Eddie Quinn organized shows in smaller markets, and Grégoire took care of promoting them. "I was paid $15 to wrestle in Rivière-du-Loup, but transportation cost me $12," Jacques explains. As he wasn't well paid, Rougeau decided to reorient himself and quit wrestling.

He became a bouncer at Mocambo, the legendary club in Montreal owned by his brother Jean. Rougeau had a reputation among the Montreal night-life crowd and is said to have knocked out a lot of troublemakers. When his brother sold the Mocambo and decided to reinvest himself in wrestling, Jacques started to wrestle regularly again, too, until 1976.

He wrestled on many occasions with Johnny. For wrestling fans in the 1980s, the Rougeau brothers were Raymond and Jacques, but for those who followed the sport in the 1960s and 1970s, the Rougeau brothers

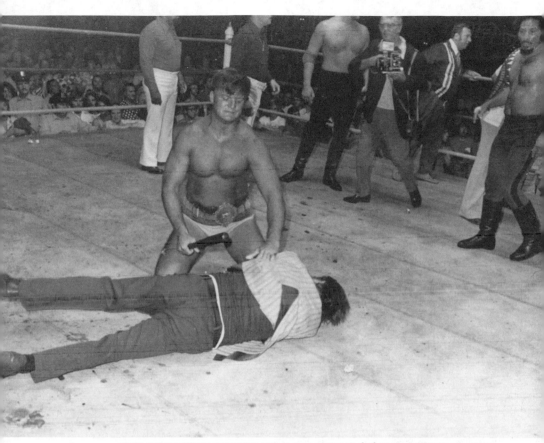

EDDY CREATCHMAN PAYS THE PRICE FOR HIS PROTÉGÉ DICK TAYLOR'S NO SHOW

(PAUL LEDUC COLLECTION)

were Johnny and Jacques Sr.! Jacques Sr. was called upon to work with such guys as Maurice Vachon, Hans Schmidt, Baron von Raschke, Abdullah the Butcher and The Sheik, just to name a few.

As we've mentioned, one of the biggest shows ever held in Montreal took place at Jarry Park Stadium on July 17, 1972, and Rougeau is proud to say that he, his brother and his son were all on top on that card. In fact Raymond Rougeau beat Don Serrano in the first semifinal. In the other semifinal Jacques Rougeau beat The Sheik, while in the main event Johnny Rougeau wrestled Abdullah the Butcher to a co-contest. The show earned the biggest gate in the history of the Montreal territory, $101,650.

During these years, Rougeau won the Montreal territory heavyweight title five times. During one of his reigns, an incident occurred with Dick Taylor, a journeyman wrestler from Detroit. Taylor and Rougeau were supposed to

JACQUES ROUGEAU

JACQUES ROUGEAU SR. WOULD BECOME INTERNATIONAL CHAMPION LIKE HIS BROTHER JOHNNY

wrestle in the main event of a show in Quebec City in 1973. To everybody's surprise, Taylor didn't show. Someone told Rougeau that Taylor was selling drugs to young people in a bar in downtown Montreal. Rougeau went there with Jos and Paul Leduc. Because he knew the bouncer he made arrangements to wait for Taylor in the stockroom. "Dick Taylor showed, and he was given a damn good beating. He needed 118 stitches in his face," Rougeau remembers. (He was accused of assault but the trial never took place.) A return match was eventually announced six months later, but Taylor never returned. "We've never set eyes on him again. I had to beat up Creatchman to satisfy the crowd," Rougeau concludes, laughing.

It wasn't actually the first time that Rougeau had to face the justice system. During his brother's electoral campaign in 1966, he was accused of beating up Paul Martin Jr. — yes, the same man who would become prime minister of Canada in 2003.

Rougeau also wrestled for the NWF in the Buffalo and Cleveland areas for promoter Pedro Martinez. He eventually became the promotion's champion and also held the tag team titles with Johnny Powers. Having worked with, among others, The Sheik, The Love Brothers, Waldo Von Erich and Sweet Daddy Siki, Rougeau compared this territory to Montreal in terms of talent.

Jacques Rougeau also travelled to Japan three times, twice during the period between 1967 and 1969, and on a final occasion, in 1975, with Raymond. He only wrestled for Antonio Inoki's promotion and worked with Kenta Kobayashi and Seiji Sakaguchi. He also wrestled in tag team matches with Inoki himself. "Jacques was my manager once in Japan," recalls Toronto wrestler Tiger Jeet Singh. When his brother Johnny sold the wrestling office in Montreal in 1976, it was the end of Jacques Rougeau's career. But in the 1980s Jacques came back from retirement when he was given the chance to team with his sons. One of those matches took place on July 23, 1984, at the Forum in front of 15,562 fans. The four Rougeaus, Jacques Sr., Jacques Jr., Raymond and Armand wrestled against and beat Tarzan Tyler, Masked Superstar, Mad Dog Lefebvre and Richard Charland.

One of the last programs in which Rougeau participated occurred a year later. It was the infamous St-Jean-Baptiste Massacre, when the Rougeaus were involved in a war with the Garvins, as well as their valet Precious. The crowd became enraged when the Garvins attacked Jacques Rougeau Sr., kicking him until he was forced to leave the ring on a stretcher.

In 2004, after a solid career, Rougeau was inducted in the Quebec Wrestling Hall of Fame. Despite all his success, some still remember him as Jean's brother. As Gino Brito explains, "He has always wrestled in the shadow of his brother Johnny." To others, he's the father of Jacques Jr. and Raymond. The true history of Montreal wrestling remembers him as the link between generations. He teamed with his uncle, his brother and his three sons.

The wrestler who made his debut as Paul Leduc's brother, like Jacques Rougeau Sr., was successful on both sides of the border. He was known everywhere as a lumberjack. While Montreal fans would get to know his more noble side, south of the border he was seen more as a psychopath.

JOS LEDUC

Jos Leduc left his mark on the Montreal territory, and with his "brother" Paul he reached the apex of popularity, drawing record-breaking crowds that will probably never be matched by other Quebec wrestlers in their own territory. "Jos Leduc against Maurice Vachon broke all attendance records

JOS AND PAUL LEDUC WITH JOURNALIST AND BASEBALL COMMENTATOR RODGER BRULOTTE

(PAUL LEDUC COLLECTION)

in cities like Quebec City and Sherbrooke. They managed to jam-pack these arenas four or five times," explains Gino Brito. But his career in singles competition in the United States was based on a totally different image than the one projected in Montreal. "He was similar to Abdullah. He used to cut his own arm with his axe and lick his blood," Brito remembers, while explaining that in Montreal he never had to do such things to rile a crowd. "He was way too popular," he justifies. But the buzz about his lumberjack blood oath, performed in Memphis (where he did, indeed, cut his own arm with an axe), would precede him in every territory, thanks to the magic of videotape. "I've seen interviews of Jos Leduc where he was so intense that he started to get crazy," says Jerry Jarrett in the documentary *Memphis Heat*.

One thing that did not change from one territory to the next was the spectacular natural power he possessed. "He was a real strong man," says Édouard Carpentier. When he started he frequently displayed this strength, asking five members of the audience to come to the ring and try to break his bear hug by pulling his arms on each side with a rope and a harness. In Memphis, where he was managed by Jimmy Hart, his name is still legendary because of his feud with Jerry "The King" Lawler. "Jos helped Lawler make so much money," maintains Paul. "Jos and I drew a lot of money," Lawler remembered in an interview with Dave Meltzer upon the death of his former foe. "We drew as much money with him as with any big-name heel who ever came through here." In a world as close-knit as wrestling it's easy to understand why his reputation opened doors.

"Johnny Rougeau asked me if I knew a guy bigger than myself who was passionate and who wanted to become a wrestler. I told him, yes, there was a guy who worked with me at the 1967 International Expo at Terre des Hommes and that he had a black belt in judo," Paul Leduc explains, adding that Johnny gave him the green light to talk with Jos.

The man he knew was Michel Pigeon. Born on August 31, 1944, he was an officer for Expo 67, just like Paul. "He had been screwed over by Bob Lortie, who had charged him $3,000 for wrestling school," Paul remembers. "He knew the basics, he took good bumps, but he was green as grass. Johnny, Jack Britton, Bob Langevin and I took him to a cultural centre, and in six days we made a professional wrestler out of him. We had to be fast. Johnny wanted us to start on a tour that was to take place precisely in a week's time." Jos Leduc's first match was in a tag team with Paul at the agricultural exhibition in Saint-Hyacinthe, 30 minutes east of Montreal. "We wrestled against Roy and Don McLarty," says Paul.

In 1968 Jos and Paul would go to Calgary for Stu Hart in order to gain experience. After having won the tag team titles there they came back to Montreal, attacking Johnny Rougeau in a money-drawing way. Three years later, in 1971, Jos Leduc became the only other Quebecer besides Maurice Vachon to take the International championship out of Johnny Rougeau's hands. In 1972 the Leducs were so popular and had such draw that they left Johnny Rougeau's All Star Wrestling to accept an offer from Grand Prix. It was literally the event of the season. "We made the move because what counts is our career and we see more possibilities with Grand Prix," Jos Leduc explains in wrestling programs at the time. From this move would be born the rivalry between the Vachons and the Leducs that would end up sending Maurice and Jos in opposite directions. They would cross paths one last time in 1986, as partners for Maurice's retirement match. "It was an honour to tag with you," said Jos to Maurice after the match. "It was the first time and unfortunately the last!" Maurice replied to this, saying, "We should have been a team a long time ago!"

In the mid-1970s, when wrestling wasn't doing that well in Montreal, Jos teamed with Larry "The Ax" Hennig in the AWA. The team was called The Ax and the Double Ax and they had a good feud with the Valiant brothers. After Paul's retirement in 1978, Jos Leduc went on to have a fine singles career in the United States. The highlight of his success occurred in Florida, where he won the Florida Southern championship, recognized by the NWA, many times. He would later also become very successful in Memphis for promoter Jerry Jarrett, both in singles competition and in tag teams. "Jos told me we should be teaming. We worked with Bill Dundee and a number of partners and we drew full houses," remembers "The Hangman" Neil Guay from his often-forgotten partnership with Jos.

In the early 1980s the Canadian Freight Train travelled around the world, from New Zealand to Japan and ultimately to the south of the United States. He also went to the Mid-Atlantic territory, managed by the Crockett family. He was assigned to Sir Oliver Humperdink, who he knew from Grand Prix as the manager of the Hollywood Blonds. "Oh my god, when he got those eyes bulging, he was fearsome-looking! Jos was totally different outside of the ring," the late Sir Humperdink explained.

But outside the ring, he was just one of the boys. "When I first got into Charlotte, I didn't have a car. Jos let me use his Lincoln Continental for about a month. That's the kind of guy Jos was," reveals Road Warrior Animal. In July 1984 Jos Leduc came back to Quebec to work for International Wrestling. Back then he'd cut interviews that were ahead of their time. In fact, to explain his absence, he confided to the fans that he had many hardships with alcohol after the accidental death of his wife, but now, people in Montreal were to see the real Jos Leduc. Paul Leduc would make a brief appearance, the last time the two guys would be seen together in wrestling. During this last appearance he was attacked by Tarzan Tyler's stable, including Masked Superstar and King Tonga. Jos would seek justice against all the perpetrators all over the province. He got over to a certain extent and even starred in both the English and French versions of an Oh Henry! chocolate bar commercial.

As over as he was, he was behind Bravo, Martel and the Rougeaus in the heart of wrestling fans. In 1985, probably hoping to create the kind of heat he enjoyed against Maurice Vachon, he betrayed his friend and partner Dino Bravo and joined the stable of Tarzan Tyler. While Bravo was wrestling against Masked Superstar at the Forum, Leduc, under a hood, came to give a hand to Masked Superstar in order to beat up the International champion. "Even to my young mind, at the age of 13, the fact that Jos Leduc joined Tyler and Masked Superstar didn't make sense. They had so savagely brutalized his brother Paul on television!" François Hébert remembers.

This was probably the reason the feud never really got off the ground. It should be noted, however, that immediately afterward International Wrestling struck up

JOS LEDUC DIDN'T ONLY HAVE SUCCESS IN TAG TEAMS, BUT IN SINGLES TOO

a partnership with the WWF. Dino Bravo was on the front lines of this, leaving very little room for such a feud. Leduc, therefore, became partners with Abdullah the Butcher and started a feud with the Rougeau brothers. In December 1985 a dramatic turn of events took place. Leduc turned his back on the promotion just before the big main event of the Christmas show, refusing to lose against Raymond Rougeau. *Le Journal de Montréal* announced that Leduc had been suspended for refusing to wrestle.

One year later with the departures of Bravo, Martel and the Rougeaus for the WWF, the situation changed considerably for International Wrestling. Jos Leduc came back as if nothing had happened. "During the previous year, I have travelled here and there between Georgia and Tennessee. It's

JOS AND PAUL LEDUC, TAG TEAM CHAMPIONS IN THE FLORIDA TERRITORY (PAUL LEDUC COLLECTION)

terribly exhausting to travel like that. That's why I came back to wrestle in Montreal," Jos explained in the December 1986 edition of the *Revue Lutte* magazine. Unfortunately Leduc could not revitalize a promotion on his own that was looking for a new identity. In 1987, when the links between Puerto Rico and Montreal were very strong, he continued with his career in the WWC, adding the North American title to his impressive resume.

Leduc was also part of the first film produced by the WWF for New Line Cinema, *No Holds Barred*. It starred Hulk Hogan and came out in 1989. In fact in 1988 the WWF gave him a chance, seeing in him an opponent who could very well play the role of the heel against the Hulkster. He was assigned Frenchy Martin as a manager and he was asked to try many different gimmicks, but none of them brought him success. In fact he would never work a full-time schedule and he was barely seen on TV. This was not Jos' first stint with the WWF as he wrestled then-WWWF champion Bruno Sammartino in 1970.

Finally in 1993, after 25 years in the profession and more than 4,800 matches, he announced his retirement. "I now want to settle down in my new home with Jeannot, this childhood friend who I've married recently," he explained to local papers. Two years later, however, the Memphis territory organized a reunion event, and he stole the show. Unable to completely walk away, he participated in a few more matches in the Montreal territory, occasionally teaming with Dangerous Dan against Guy Sauriol and Gino Brito.

Sadly, and practically anonymously, Jos Leduc died on May 1, 1999, after respiratory complications following a bad fall that punctured one of his lungs. His exploits earned him entry into the Quebec Wrestling Hall of Fame in its first year of existence. "Wherever we went, we got belts. We had it easy. We had a role to play, we worked hard and gained the trust of promoters," his long-standing partner Paul Leduc says. During an interview with *Echos-Vedettes* magazine in 1996, Jos summarized his own career. "In 1968, after having served on the team in charge of the security of dignitaries who came to visit the Expo, I met Paul . . . We became the Leduc brothers. Promoter Bob Langevin came to see us at the gym and he was immediately conquered. A new life started for me. I discovered the world . . . and discovered myself as well."

In this era too, foreign wrestlers enjoyed spectacular careers in Montreal. Some became so well known that they are now part of Quebec popular culture.

JEAN FERRÉ

When André Roussimoff died on January 27, 1993, the legend of Géant Ferré took over from the reality of his personal life. Because he'd lived this character day in and day out, every day, in hotels and airports and whenever he was anywhere in public, there was little room left for the real Roussimoff. "André hated it when people came to him and asked him to show them his hands and fingers. He hated talking to people so much that he didn't even go to his room, and we got him from the hotel bar in the morning," says Rene Goulet, sadly, in an interview with RF Video. Goulet used to travel and work with him for years.

But he wasn't always like that. He was "super nice, a man with a vast knowledge on different subjects with a taste for refined things . . . but he was suffering. Unfortunately by the time Vince paid for his back surgery, it was too late," fellow Frenchman Guy Hauray adds. It must be said that his relationship with his fellow wrestlers was totally different from the one he had with fans. "For us, the Giant was just one of the boys and he appreciated that a lot. We didn't consider him a phenomenon in the locker room," explains Raymond Rougeau. Stories about travelling, playing cards and drinking late into the night with André are legendary among his peers.

"The only ones who could keep up with André were Arnold Skaaland and Pedro Morales. One time he kept me 10 days in his apartment. I like having a drink, but after three days, I started to get restless. After four days, someone call the police! After six days, have another cognac. After nine days, I started to tell myself that I had to get out; he was getting harder and

THE EIGHTH WONDER OF THE WORLD ANDRE THE GIANT WITH THE "GREATEST," MUHAMMAD ALI

(PAUL LEDUC COLLECTION)

harder to keep up with," relates Frenchy Martin, laughing. "He was a good guy, but people didn't really understand him. You go to the washroom like everybody else, even when you're a giant. But everyone wanted to talk to him and touch him . . . never one minute of peace," adds Martin.

"It's a real disability. I would give a lot to spend one day a week in the skin of an ordinary man," the Giant told the Reader's Digest in the early 1980s. This was probably why he lived his life without worrying about the future. "He often said: 'Why deprive myself? I will die before the age of 50, anyways,'" Édouard Carpentier told the press after André's tragic death following a heart attack, as he had predicted, before the age of 50. André suffered from acromegaly, a syndrome that occurs when the anterior pituitary gland produces excess growth hormone after epiphyseal plate closure at puberty. Those with the condition never stop growing.

André was born on May 19, 1946, in Grenoble, France. "I was born and raised in the Alps, but my father was Bulgarian and my mother Polish. They weren't surprised with my size, as my grandfather was seven feet and eight inches," Ferré explained in an interview with Le Lundi magazine. "I, who came from the home country of Louis Cyr and the six Baillargeon brothers, have never seen a person with as much brute strength as André," Frank Valois explained to Reader's Digest, talking about his discovery. "My father saw him in France and was sure that we could do something special with him. 'He's strong and impressive,' he said. My father wanted to bring him to the Montreal territory, but he wanted to continue wrestling in Europe and elsewhere. It was finally Carpentier who took care of Jean Ferré upon his arrival here," Françoise Valois explains. "I met the Giant for the first time in Paris in 1964. He's the strongest wrestler I've ever known," Carpentier said to Le Journal de Montréal. Upon his arrival here in Montreal in 1971 he was still full of life and always in a good mood. "At the beginning he wanted to show that he knew how to wrestle. I told him that his role was to demolish his opponents," Carpentier, who encouraged him to immigrate and come to work for him at Grand Prix, said. "I've always been the protector and guardian angel of the Giant," Frank Valois said to Le Journal de Montréal. It must be said that the man who came from France to Grand Prix was an athlete who was nothing like the shaky Andre the Giant at the end of his career with the WWF. "I remember that I was surprised to see a guy of his stature doing dropkicks with such ease," Killer Kowalski remembers. After having made his debut in North America in Verdun on June 1, 1971, he was to become a big star here because of his involvement in a feud with Don Leo Jonathan. "The arrival of the Giant was the catalyst for our promotion," Paul Vachon would affirm years later.

It's actually Vachon who was behind the Giant's name change. "Dick the Bruiser called to ask me about the Giant. He wanted to bring him to Chicago, and after we managed the financial side of things he asked me about his name. I told him that it was the Géant Ferré. He seemed surprised and asked me 'What do you really call him?' I told him that it was the name le Géant Ferré. He asked me what it meant, and I told him that it simply meant Giant Ferré." It's important to mention here that Ferré, once said in English, can really sound like "fairy" instead of "ferray," as it sounds in French! "Bruiser laughed, saying we can't call him the giant fairy. He asked me about his first name, and I told him it was André. He then said that he would call him Andre the Giant. As it happened, I went with the Giant to Chicago, and his very first match under the name Andre the Giant took place on January 9, 1972, in a handicap contest against Larry Hennig and me."

Many urban legends revolve around the Giant. Upon his arrival in Quebec, he was announced as 7'4" inches, and that's the height everyone remembers. But the truth of the matter was that André measured, at best, 6'10", maybe 6'11". In 1984, in a photo taken with basketball player Wilt Chamberlain, André was about three inches shorter than Chamberlain, who measured 7'2". However, the latter was barefoot, while the Giant wore shoes with lifts. In 1976, in Japan, the journalists there estimated that his height was 6'9". Vince McMahon Sr. reprimanded him each time he took a photo with an athlete taller than him, as he wanted to protect him and protect the legend that André was the tallest athlete in the world. "It would probably be fair to say his size was his gimmick, the reason for his popularity and his drawing power," Dave Meltzer explains. Indeed, aside from

André's height, the fact that he let himself get body-slammed in an early Montreal match was another headache he gave his promoter. Seeing that it could take away the myth behind the man, Paul Vachon made sure that it never happened again.

"Why did you let him pick you up and body-slam you?" Vachon asked.

"I wanted to make him look good because I'm so tired of wrestling against jabbronies."

"Don't ever do that again."

"Okay, boss," Ferré said with a big smile.

After Grand Prix it became obvious that the Giant was much more efficient as a draw who would feature periodically in the territory, rather than as a permanent star. Frank Valois, who spoke English, would go on the road with his protégé; they'd make stops in each wrestling territory of the time. "My father was the real manager of the Giant during those years," Françoise Valois says. "He travelled all over the world with the Giant for five years. He managed the Giant's bank account and took care of paying his bills. He kept on being his manager until his departure from Varoussac in 1982. Vince McMahon Sr. contacted my father when he wanted to send the Giant all over the world, even after Varoussac started its operations in 1980. The Giant was like his own son," she adds. The Giant's involvement as a partner with Varoussac came to a natural end, but his association with Valois sadly also came to an end when the Giant chose to sign a full-time contract with Vince Jr. and the WWF. The two men, as close as a father and son, would never speak again.

André became a big star in Japan and wrestled there until just before his death. Although he also became Andre the Giant there, he worked as Monster Roussimoff, Butcher Roussimoff and Giant Machine, as well as Monster Eiffel Tower in Japan. "In Japan, for instance, when I go for a walk, everyone wants to touch me because touching a giant is said to bring good luck over there," he told Le Journal de Montréal. "As a team, André and I beat Inoki and Fujinami in a tournament," Rene Goulet told RF Video. "This was something special, because Inoki and Fujinami never lost to foreign wrestlers in those days." With guys like Fred Blassie, Abdullah the Butcher and Hulk Hogan, the Giant was part of a select group of gaijin who became legends wrestling in Japan. He became legendary in North America, as well. You only have to type his name and a territory into a YouTube search to discover him working everywhere in his youth: in California with Pat Patterson; in Memphis with Jerry Lawler; in Detroit against The Sheik; in Florida with Dusty Rhodes; in New York with Bruno Sammartino — all the big names of the sport either wrestled with or against the Giant.

This widespread success made Andre the Giant one of the first wrestlers since Gorgeous George to become a full-fledged pop culture icon, even if he never quite became as big as Hulk Hogan. In Montreal viewers watched him appearing on many sitcoms. In the United States he sat on the couch beside Johnny Carson and David Letterman. He starred as Bigfoot in *The Six-Million Dollar Man* with Lee Majors, one of the most popular programs in the 1970s. "André likes to travel, wrestle, drink beer and live the good life. He couldn't stand waiting around a back lot all day in a big ape suit. The producers of the show made sure that they didn't kill off the Bigfoot creature André played. The show with André as the Sasquatch was such a success that they wanted him to do it again. They asked me if he would work cheaper. I asked André and he said that he wouldn't do it for fifty thousand. They actually offered him fifty thousand, but André was unmoved. 'I won't do it,' he said, 'I just won't do it. I don't need the money and I don't like it,'" says Gene Lebell, who was a wrestler, actor and stuntman in California. His performance in the acclaimed hit film *The Princess Bride* was lauded by critics just as he was coming to terms with the fact that his wrestling career was drawing to an end. "I made my debut in the movies in 1967 in *Casse-tête chinois pour le judoka*. It was usually not very difficult for me, I just play my own role," he confided to *Le Journal de Montréal*. In spite of this success, wrestling was always his first love.

After undergoing back surgery that allowed him to continue as a wrestler, the Giant wrestled in the last and perhaps most important program in his career. He was feuding with Hulk Hogan, in the role of the heel. In the late 1970s, when Hogan was just starting, the two had a feud that culminated in a match in August 1980 at Shea Stadium. At the time André was the babyface, while Hogan was the heel. After having chosen Bobby Heenan as a manager, he was to challenge Hulk Hogan just prior to *WrestleMania III* at the Pontiac Silverdome in a very famous "Piper's Pit" segment.

For Bobby Heenan it was a historical moment and a great sign of respect from the Giant. "It was quite the honour. No one had ever managed him before, and he never wanted to be associated with anybody else. André

JEAN FERRÉ WITH SOME MONTREAL EXPOS
PLAYERS AT JARRY PARK STADIUM IN 1973

(ROSAIRE FONTAINE COLLECTION)

always talked for himself. I think he just felt I was over and he could trust me." But, according to Édouard Carpentier, the wrestler who was nicknamed the Eighth Wonder of the World by the WWF had also seen that the future of wrestling was named Hogan. If André was to leave his mark for posterity, he had to be a part of the history of Hulkamania. "People will remember me much more in defeat than if I had beaten him," he explained to his fellow Frenchman after the match.

"André was so pleased with himself . . . he was so proud of that," Vince McMahon Jr. reveals in *The True Story of WrestleMania*. The feud would go on, as the Giant finally won the WWF title before selling it to Ted DiBiase during *The Main Event* on NBC, which was witnessed by 33 million TV viewers in February 1988.

The whole Hulk/André angle is still one the most vivid memories for wrestling fans of the time. Not only did the Hebner twins make their appearance as referees, but it was also the first time since 1984 that Hulk Hogan wasn't the WWF champion. Their match was actually voted match of the year by *Pro Wrestling Illustrated* in 1988.

During this period André was the undisputed king of the locker room. The wrestler who called everyone "Boss" was considered the boss by everyone else, and his role then was comparable to that of The Undertaker today. He commanded respect and he would bring the new guys down a peg, when needed. "One night, in the ring at Madison Square Garden, André got his hands on Bam Bam Bigelow and practically killed him for real. That was all the attitude adjustment Bigelow needed, and he changed his ways," Bret Hart says in his biography. Bobby Heenan tells a story about The Ultimate Warrior not understanding that hitting someone with a clothesline didn't have to be stiff to appear real. One night, when the Warrior dashed forward with his clothesline, André waited for him with his hand made into a fist and knocked him out. The following match, Warrior's clothesline was very soft, and André made it appear like it was devastating. André looked at Heenan and said: "He's learning!"

He continued to wrestle for the WWF with memorable feuds against both Ultimate Warrior and Jake Roberts. He also won the tag team titles with another well-known wrestler in the Montreal territory, King Tonga, who wrestled under the name Haku in the WWF. The team was called Colossal Connection. After having lost the titles to Demolition at *WrestleMania VI*, he turned babyface once again. His career, however, was essentially over and he left the WWF and only appeared in tag matches in Japan and Mexico. On September 2, 1992, he would make his last appearance on television, surprisingly enough with the WCW, in order to celebrate the 20th anniversary of wrestling on TBS. "When André showed up on Ted Turner's broadcast it was just such a shock," Shane McMahon said in André's biography. "I remember my dad called André and said, 'Boss, I've just gotta say that you really hurt my feelings. After everything, to see you with a competitor really hurt.' I think André apologized."

In the end the only question that remains about his wrestling career is, was he, in spite of everything, happy? In his interview with *Reader's Digest* André gave this answer: "I was lucky and I'm grateful to life for everything it brought me. If I were to die tomorrow, I would have at least eaten more good food, drank more beer and fine wine, made more friendships and travelled more around the world than most men."

ABDULLAH THE BUTCHER

For almost 50 years, Abdullah the Butcher has terrorized the planet. Out of control and capable of anything, no wrestling fan can manage not to quiver after seeing Abdullah covered in blood and brandishing his fork. Like a magician, Abdullah was wrapped in secrecy. Be it his origin, real name or even date of birth, he's one of the few wrestlers who managed to keep

(ALYSSA SILVER COLLECTION)

THE TWO OF THEM COULD CREATE RIOTS IN AN INSTANT: ABDULLAH AND EDDY CREATCHMAN

fans guessing. Even today the most fervent historians of wrestling debate his age. In the Montreal territory Abdullah the Butcher became a name that's part of Quebec's pop culture, the subject of rumour and legend that has been handed down from one generation to the next. Whether you're a wrestling fan or not, almost everyone has heard of the madman born Lawrence Shreeve in Windsor, Ontario. No, he wasn't from the Sudan, as announcers all over the world have said. In Montreal he's more famous than Ric Flair, something that most Americans just can't understand. In April 2009 more than 500 people gathered in Montreal to watch what was announced as his last match. The general sports press covered the event — a rarity since the end of wrestling's golden years. It was then that journalist Ronald King helped shed light on the true story of the Madman from the Sudan.

Abdullah actually showed the reporter his passport and green card. Both documents shared the same date of birth, January 11, 1941. He wasn't quite 73, as some people estimated. "It surprised me to read that he was more than 70, because I've always thought he was my age, and I only turned 70 in 2011," Gino Brito says. He was known everywhere for his bloody matches and ability to cause riots and as a wrestler who drew big crowds. "Blood is how he establishes himself, blood is how he stays over and blood is what the fans want from him," Gary Hart says in his autobiography. With the forks, chairs, tables and whatever else he could find around the ring, Abdullah was hardcore before this style of wrestling was even a style.

Yet his beginnings as a wrestler were very different — and he actually started out under his real name. He made his debut in Detroit, the territory managed by Bert Ruby and Jack Britton, but he was never formally trained. "He was a born wrestler," says Gino Brito, who knew him since his debut for his father's territory and who, even today, is one of Abdullah's good friends. "Dick Garza, who wrestled under the name Mighty Igor, worked with him in Indiana and told me that it was as if Abdullah has been wrestling for 10 years." At the time Abdullah wrestled under the name Zelis Amara. Then, when he was wrestling in Vancouver, the promoter Rod Fenton decided to call him The Butcher. "He told me I wrestled like a butcher in a match I did in Seattle. The match was fairly violent, and the video was shown around the world," Abdullah says. "Fenton told me, 'But you need another name. There's a lot of Indians here, we're going to call you Abdullah.' And I became Abdullah the Butcher." Probably influenced by "The Sheik" Ed Farhat, who came from Detroit, he added a costume that was very much like the one of The Sheik. It wasn't his costume that drew people, but, rather, his dangerous character and the fact that he wasn't scared of spilling blood or seeing his own blood flow. He was not only to distinguish himself and draw crowds, but also to become a legend. "I watched this monster, unlike any I'd ever seen in wrestling, sell out week after week, telling violent, bloody stories. Around the house, we called him Abby," Bret Hart recalls.

Tony Angelo, Deepak Singh and Eddy Creatchman successively managed The Butcher in the Montreal territory. It's actually difficult for fans in Montreal to dissociate him from his mouthpiece. The manager in his corner played a key role in his success in each territory where he worked. Abby chose never to speak, which made him even more mythological. "Once I needed stitches after one of my matches and I adhered so much to my character that the doctor never wanted to touch me!" says Abdullah today. Fans today remain shocked when Japanese video shows him speaking a couple of words. "The mysterious person you see is who he was, and almost like The Sheik, he lived the gimmick. The only time I saw him out of character was down at the Underground nightclub one night," says Dusty Rhodes in his book. In fact he would only allow himself to speak with fans during autograph sessions in the late 1990s.

Respected by his peers, he drew crowds wherever he went. "Abby, he was always main-eventing shows," explains Gino Brito, who used him a lot for International Wrestling. "I loved working with him because I like to work stiff. He broke some of my ribs, but never broke my teeth! I knew that we would get a lot of heat for my comeback," he relates.

In spite of his success Abdullah was no picnic for a promoter. "I love Abdullah to death, but booking him was never easy. For starters, he didn't like to lose. One time I had to get pretty creative and sneaky to get him to do the right thing. I told Abby I was booking him and Mark Lewin in a two-out-of-three falls match. He noticed that Mark had gone back to the dressing room. Confused, he looked at me and asked: 'Where's Mark?' You're the mark,' I said. 'He's gone back to the dressing room.' It was a one-fall match," Gary Hart says. "When he made his debut in Detroit, Bert Ruby told him that wrestlers were paid less when their matches were broadcast on TV because it gave them exposure in return. He also told him that he would get 10 if he won and 15 if he lost. Abby wrestled three matches, so he got three envelopes and each of them contained $15. He came to see me to find out what was going on; he thought it would be $10,000 or $15,000," Brito remembers, smiling.

"The years when we worked the Paul-Sauvé Arena was such a good time. We earned a lot of money. We didn't make the money wrestlers make today, but at the time a Cadillac cost $15,000, a good house, $20,000. We were privileged. Johnny Rougeau and Jack Britton were promoters. It was Britton who brought me to Montreal. I spent many summers here. We used to live at the Ritz Motel in Saint-Léonard. There was a bar on the first floor, and we used to get together in the evening with André the Giant and the others who lived there. In the winter I went to South Africa, Australia, New Zealand, Japan and Korea," Abdullah told Ronald King about his career in the province of Quebec. In fact Abdullah main-evented the second-biggest crowd in the history of Montreal on July 17, 1972, against Johnny Rougeau. The end of the '60s and early '70s were really when Abdullah was at his peak, and he drew big crowds against the likes of Jacques Rougeau Sr. and Carlos Rocha. But no one can approach the money he drew with Johnny. During that period he won the International title four times, but he never

A RARE BATTLE BETWEEN ABDULLAH THE BUTCHER AND ANDRE THE GIANT (LINDA BOUCHER)

kept it long because he would travel a lot from territory to territory. Even though Abby didn't need a belt to draw, his gimmick being enough, he was often used as a transitional champion to pass the belt from one babyface to another. He's among the 10 best draws in the history of the territory, second to Killer Kowalski if you only consider the heels. But as big as he was in Montreal, in Japan he was even bigger. In fact even today he's still a big draw there. In Japan he's considered a living legend and one of the most hated and successful outsiders in the history of Japanese wrestling. He was also a big star in Puerto Rico, until the murder of his friend Bruiser Brody, with whom he toured all over North America in the late 1980s, including performing a few matches in Montreal in 1987.

Much like Andre the Giant, Abdullah never worked in the same place for a long time. In the early 1990s he even went to WCW and enjoyed some success with a new generation of wrestlers. "Abdullah and I were getting over like a million bucks on TV. Our interviews were becoming a much-anticipated enjoyed part of the shows. Abby didn't talk, but his mannerisms and facials expressions were tremendous," Mick Foley says in his first biography.

As big as he got, he never worked for Vince McMahon. His character was probably too violent and he had the reputation of being too unpredictable, even though he might have been the perfect heel for Hulk Hogan. Nonetheless he wrestled Hogan in Japan before Hulkamania dominated wrestling in North America. "I saw Abdullah the Butcher in Tampa in January 2005. We hadn't seen each other for years, and the first thing he said to me was that I made a big mistake by not bringing him into the WWF when I worked for Vince. After all those years, Abby still doesn't get it," J.J Dillon said in his book. Ironically, in 2011, out of respect for his spectacular career, WWE inducted him into its Hall of Fame during *WrestleMania XXVII* in Atlanta, where Abdullah now lives. "I made so much money with him, I'd marry him if I could!" said Terry Funk, while inducting him. He's currently the owner of a restaurant called Abdullah the Butcher's House of Ribs and Chinese Food, a highly profitable business and a place that wrestling fans like visiting because they just might get to meet the owner. In 2012, he was scheduled to tour Japan, but a hip injury prevented him from travelling. He's been in a wheelchair ever since, waiting for surgery.

Abdullah has wrestled in the Montreal territory during each decade since the 1960s, and this fact just reinforces why he was inducted into the Quebec Wrestling Hall of Fame in 2005.

When will he stop? As he explained it to Sylvain St-Laurent from *Le Droit* newspaper: "Maybe I'll stop when I die in the ring. That could very well be my exit!"

There was more going on in Montreal than Giants and Butchers; however, the second golden age would also witness the rise of a third generation of Rougeaus.

RAYMOND ROUGEAU

Raymond Rougeau is stubborn, and the man who can change the way he thinks or acts has yet to be born.

In the ring he earned the respect of his peers many times over. Whether it's Zarinoff Leboeuf, Jos Leduc, Bob Orton or Dynamite Kid — they all knew Rougeau as a man who knew how to defend himself when necessary. In a world where ego and physical strength held sway, Rougeau knew how to navigate. He also commanded the respect of promoters like Steve Paradis, Gino Brito, Eric Bischoff, Ole Anderson and Vince McMahon. Along the way he managed to be honest and faithful to himself. It's probably because, more than anything else, he was able to put together such a storied career.

Raymond was 13 when his father Jacques Rougeau asked him if he wanted a wrestling career. To his father's delight, he said, "Yes." Even at such a young age he was remarkable. He began training, but not like everybody else. The story goes that he trained 364 days in his first year. The one night he took off, his father read him the riot act! If he followed instructions, his father said, he would let him step into the ring at 16.

So, it was in the basement of Lionel Robert's gym, with the help of two Mexican wrestlers, that Raymond learned the basics, always under the supervision of his father. The training paid off. He made his debut on May 3, 1971, in Joliette, against Butch Morgan. The place was packed. At the time his uncle Johnny's office managed two cities each night. Johnny was present for Raymond's debut, but his father had to wrestle the same night at the Paul-Sauvé Arena. Raymond explains why it was important for Johnny to watch him starting out: "My uncle Jean had two daughters and wanted to have a son so much. In a sense I think that I was that son he never had."

The years 1971 and 1972 were great years for young wrestlers in the territory. Rick Martel, Dino Bravo and Pierre Lefebvre also made their debuts. Unfortunately for the others, their uncle wasn't the promoter. "I had an advantage compared to other wrestlers. If you have three good wrestlers and one of them was a family member, you just favour your family member over the others," Rougeau explains.

But Raymond didn't have it all easy. "The burden I had on my shoulders was to be up to the task at hand — a lot was expected from me," he says. In the early days of his career Rougeau mainly worked with Morgan, Chin Lee, Don Serrano, Denis Gauthier and the Castillo brothers. In 1975 he went to Japan with his father for Inoki's New Japan. At the time Raymond was co-owner of All Star Wrestling. In fact Raymond, his uncle Jean and his father Jacques each had 25 percent of the shares, while Hans Schmidt and family friend Guy Soucy had 12.5 percent each.

By '76 the Rougeaus and their partners had sold the promotion. Wrestling wasn't drawing as it had, and Pedro Martinez, a promoter in the Buffalo and Cleveland region, took over — but not for long. "He was involved in many other businesses," Johnny Powers remembers. "Not to mention the fact that the territory was so dysfunctional . . . the elements that held things together were gone." Eventually Steve Paradis bought 100 percent of the shares on the condition that Raymond, the only Rougeau still wrestling, stayed with the promotion. At the time Paradis had a reputation of not always paying his workers well. Rougeau agreed to stay on, with this caveat: he would quit once a single cheque bounced.

"It lasted about two months and then one of my cheques bounced," Rougeau remembers. Raymond told Paradis to pay him before the next show — but Paradis didn't. Next Rougeau went to the brother of then Quebec Premier René Lévesque, lawyer Fernand Lévesque. They had the gate of Paradis's show seized until Raymond was paid. Once that was done Raymond, being a man of his word, quit.

Promoter Jim Barnett had been trying to get Raymond to work for him in Atlanta for some time. With the Montreal territory no longer open to him, he decided to accept Barnett's offer. He would stay there for three years, returning to Montreal to wrestle only in the summers. While in Atlanta he worked primarily with Randy Savage, Rick Steamboat and Ole Anderson, who eventually became the booker.

Many Quebecers were to meet in Georgia Championship Wrestling in those years. Jos Leduc was already there when Raymond arrived; Rick Martel wound up there, as well, as did Pierre Lefebvre, who had just gotten back into wrestling.

In 1980 Varoussac, later known as International Wrestling, opened its doors. Naturally Quebecers working internationally found their way home. Rougeau wrestled in tag team with none other than Pat Patterson, winning the promotion's titles twice. Like any team worth its salt, they eventually parted ways and became involved in a feud of their own. Rougeau only has good memories of this program with Patterson. "In spite of the fact that I had 10 years of experience, I was able to learn a lot from him." Then Raymond started teaming with his brother Jacques. Many years after their father and uncle dominated, the Rougeau brothers were back! Along the way they won the tag team titles many times, in addition to having taken part in one of the biggest feuds in the 1980s, a war that pitted them against the Garvin brothers.

Raymond began working in 1971 and Jacques Jr. in 1977. In 1982 another Rougeau was to make his debut, their brother Armand. In one of his first matches Armand wrestled against Zarinoff Leboeuf, a hard-boiled wrestler in the ring as well as in real life. Dissatisfied with his booking Leboeuf mistreated Armand who, still being quite new to the business, didn't know how to defend himself. When his brother came back to the locker room in a sorry state, Raymond vowed to exact revenge — for real. He managed to get a match scheduled with Leboeuf. Raymond gave Leboeuf, who was a noted street fighter, a beating he'd remember for a long time. Today, listening to others talk about the match, you're likely to think it was a UFC contest, well before MMA became popular. "No one has seen Leboeuf close to a wrestling ring ever since," Raymond Rougeau comments. Gino Brito confirms it: "I've never seen Leboeuf after that! His wife came in to pick up his last cheque!"

Similarly, in an International Wrestling main event with Jos Leduc, Raymond was to go over. But, for whatever reason, Leduc didn't want to lose. Upon learning this Raymond told referee Adrien Desbois to pass on a

ALMOST WWF TAG TEAM CHAMPIONS: THE ROUGEAU BROTHERS (BERTRAND HÉBERT COLLECTION)

message to Leduc — that in the end he'd be staring up at the lights, one way or another. Remember, at the time, heels and babyfaces didn't share the same locker rooms. In fact they were still usually segregated on completely opposite sides of a venue. Once Desbois's message was delivered, Leduc, who was at first glance a much more impressive physical specimen, decided to leave without competing.

In January 1986 Édouard Carpentier let Raymond know that an offer from Vince McMahon and the WWF had come in for his services. "I was not looking for a new job. I didn't need the money. I was financially independent already," Rougeau explains. Rougeau was always a good businessman and he saw in the offer a good opportunity. He imposed some conditions before accepting the deal. He wanted to wrestle as a tag team with his brother Jacques, he would not relocate to the New York area, and finally he wanted a guarantee that he would not be used as a jobber.

A meeting between McMahon and the Rougeau brothers was organized. Once the deal was accepted by both sides, McMahon wanted the Rougeaus to start wrestling immediately. Raymond — being an honest man — said that wasn't possible. "I have always had a good relationship with Gino. I respect him a lot. I was going to give him respectable notice and finish my booking. Vince appreciated that; he appreciated loyalty."

In the WWF the Rougeaus started out as babyfaces, as they had always been. About a year after their debut, in February 1987, they beat WWF tag team champions the Hart Foundation in Quebec City, in a match where the titles weren't at stake. "Doing so, a promoter increases the credibility of the local talents to the level of the champions, because they just beat the champions," explains Patrick Lono, former NWA Quebec booker. "The goal of professional wrestling being to draw the biggest crowd possible, the key was, thus, to have a return match in which titles would be at stake, because the fans were to come in bigger numbers, hoping to see their local team become champions," says Lono.

A championship match between the two teams was arranged at the Montreal Forum on August 10, 1987, as an example of this philosophy in action. Near the end of the match, in an effort to help his buddies, Jimmy Hart, the manager of the Hart Foundation, dropped his megaphone in the ring. Unfortunately for the Mouth of the South, the Rougeaus took possession of it . . . and then, because the referee wasn't looking . . . they used it to win the match. The referee, having seen nothing, declared the Rougeaus winners and the new WWF tag team champions. Footage of their victory ran that night during TVA's sports news. In reality the Rougeaus knew they weren't really the champions. The fans would soon learn through Jack Tunney, the Toronto promoter who played the role of WWF president on TV, that the referee's decision had been reversed, because it was clearly shown that the Rougeaus had used Jimmy Hart's megaphone. The titles reverted back to the Hart Foundation. Television interviews were produced for the Quebec market, explaining this decision. (In those years the results of the house shows weren't as readily available; bookers had more freedom when only local fans really knew what had transpired on a given card.)

This kind of ending, in which the titles were given back to the champions following a reversal of the referee's decision, was the specialty of Dusty Rhodes, former wrestler and NWA booker. "This way of doing things became known as a Dusty Finish, due to Dusty's overuse of it, mainly in house shows," Lono explains. The aim of a Dusty Finish here was to create, locally, a team that would be recognized by the average fan as being the real champions. This would on paper create a team that would sell tickets for a specific market." he adds. Raymond Rougeau explains what went down from an insider's point of view. "At the political level, the Americans didn't want French-Canadian babyface tag team champions. But Pat Patterson thought that, for Montreal, it would be good for us to win the titles. So they had to find a way that would allow us to win the titles in the province without having to lose them back in the U.S. It was Pat who came up with this idea."

So it probably wasn't a surprise when Vince McMahon had his own idea for the brothers, namely to turn them heels — a first in the Rougeau dynasty. As bad guys the Rougeaus were called upon to work with a very popular team, The Rockers, Marty Jannetty and Shawn Michaels.

Despite being veterans when they moved to the WWF, the Rougeaus had to earn the respect of a new locker room. Even before the infamous British Bulldogs incident, when Raymond and Jacques first began touring with the company, Ted Arcidi came into the locker room one night after his match. Arcidi was famous for being a strong man, but, seeing Arcidi exhausted, Raymond cracked a simple joke: "Hey, Ted. What are you huffing and puffing for?" Taking offence, Arcidi showered Raymond with insults. After a couple of minutes Raymond stood up and fired back. "You overblown steroid piece of shit. Who the fuck do you think you are?" Raymond was ready to fight — but Arcidi wanted to put his wrestling boots back on first! But even before this weird exercise was over, seeing that Raymond was still there in front of him, Arcidi said: "Man, I don't wanna fight you. I'm sorry!"

On another occasion there was an incident with Bob Orton, Randy Orton's famous father. Raymond was to go over Orton, so he went to see him to know what he wanted to do during the match. Orton, in front of his friends, ridiculed Raymond — making it clear that he wasn't happy having to lose to the newcomer. Once they were inside the ring, Orton potatoed Raymond three times. "After the third time, I told myself, 'I'm not gonna take this anymore!' and swung a left hook right on his chin." Orton decided to go home right away — the match lasted just two minutes, nowhere near its scheduled 15 minutes. The next time they faced off, Orton worked as light as a feather. "I didn't feel any shots at all, and he flew like a ballet dancer all over the place!"

After a successful run in 1989, Raymond decided to tell Vince McMahon he wanted to retire. He didn't want to mortgage his health; the many nagging injuries he'd picked up over his career had begun to pile up. In spite of McMahon's persistence, Rougeau stuck to his guns. Vince didn't want to lose such an exemplary, valuable employee, so he offered him a job as a commentator and interviewer. McMahon respected Raymond for his loyalty even more when the WWF went to war against WCW, and his brother Jacques joined the competitors. Wanting to invade the Francophone market of the Montreal territory, WCW had even offered a contract to Raymond — but Rougeau's decision to stay with the WWF essentially earned him a job for life.

Born on February 18, 1955, Raymond Rougeau worked as a professional wrestler and used it as a springboard to guarantee himself financial security at a very young age. The fact that he retired from the ring at 34 bears this out. After 18 years as a wrestler, 13 years as a commentator and 20 years after his last match in the WWF, he can say, "Mission accomplished!" He earned the respect of the wrestling world.

MICHEL DUBOIS, SOVIET JUSTICE

Born in Saint-Lin on February 9, 1947, Michel Lamarche had two completely different wrestling personas. If you talk to American wrestling fans, his name was Alexis Smirnoff. "We French-Canadians are so talented that we can play all kinds of roles!" says Ivan Koloff, another French-Canadian who played a Russian. Montreal fans, however, knew him as Michel "Justice" Dubois. "It was Bob Langevin who came up with the name Dubois. The Dubois brothers were very well-known thugs in Montreal in the 1960s," Lamarche remembers. "Then, in one of my matches, I screamed out the word 'Justice!' and the nickname followed me ever since." It was primarily in the Montreal territory that Lamarche would play character, coming to the ring in a judge's robe and hat, giving the impression that he was judge, jury and executioner!

In both 1973 and 1981 he was the Montreal territory champion. In the 1970s he was also a tag champ with Fidel Castillo, as he was in the 1980s with Pierre "Mad Dog" Lefebvre. He was U.S. champion in San Francisco, as well as a tag team champion, and he was one of the few Quebecers to have won a title in Japan, the IWA heavyweight championship. But Lamarche didn't have it easy at first. In fact when Langevin came up with the name

EDDY CREATCHMAN, MICHEL DUBOIS AND JEAN-JACQUES FORTIN ON "SUR LE MATELAS" (ALYSSA SILVER COLLECTION)

Dubois, it was during Lamarche's second run for Johnny Rougeau's promotion. Indeed, after having been trained by Édouard Carpentier, Lamarche had his first match on TV in the spring of 1969. "It was a two-minute squash against Abdullah," he remembers. Later he was told to play the character of the Green Hornet. "Cowboy Jones and I would be the masked wrestlers playing superheroes," he says. The adventure lasted just a month, because Johnny Rougeau didn't think he was ready. "He told me that his promotion wasn't a wrestling school." These words drove him to get better. He moved to the Maritimes, at promoter Rudy Kay's invitation, and they kept him the whole summer. "Leo Burke and Bobby Kay helped me get better," he says.

At the end of 1969 he found himself in Kansas City for promoter Bob Geigel, but some immigration problems would interrupt his stay and he would only remain two months in Missouri. So he came back to Montreal one Monday and decided to go say hello to the boys at the Paul-Sauvé Arena. "Paul and Jos Leduc had seen me in the Maritimes and they spoke for me to the office, saying that I had improved and that I was now a good wrestler," Lamarche says. "The Rougeaus were so impressed with me that I replaced Dick Taylor against Johnny in Quebec City," Lamarche adds.

Between 1971 and 1974 Lamarche worked in the U.S. under the name Mike "The Judge" Dubois, in an attempt to translate his Quebec character. He wrestled primarily in the Carolinas and Georgia, and he even worked one match with the WWWF in Pittsburgh in 1972. "I also spent my summers in the Maritimes," he adds. One day in August 1972, when he was in the Maritimes, one of the Kay brothers told him that he needed to get to Montreal right away: they needed a sub for The Sheik, who wasn't going to show up for a Jarry Park Stadium show. That match, teaming with Abdullah the Butcher against the Rougeau brothers, was to be his first big Montreal main event. In 1974, as wrestling in the province was slowly dying, Lamarche returned to the U.S. for good, for Mid-Atlantic, one of the most reputable territories of the time. He formed a tag team with Freddie Sweetan. Later he would work in Texas for the Funks, before returning to the Carolinas, where he was to team with another Quebecer, Sgt. Jacques Goulet. Together they main evented a tournament in April 1977 for the NWA Mid-Atlantic tag team titles, losing to Tim Woods and Dino Bravo. Goulet and Lamarche wrestled together for two years.

It was in 1974 that another wrestler who found success in Montreal was to change the course of Lamarche's career.

"I was on the same tour with Ivan Koloff, and he told me that I was hard-working, a good wrestler . . . but because of my French accent I would never be over," he remembers. He kept mulling over the idea in his head, and in January 1977 Pat Patterson called to say that he spoke with Roy Shire, the promoter in the San Francisco territory, and they wanted him. "I was flying between Detroit and Montreal while reading a magazine. One of the advertisements was for Smirnoff vodka; that's how I got the name."

He arrived in San Francisco with the character of Alexis Smirnoff in tow and he had tremendous success. "I won the U.S. title in San Francisco in a loser-leaves-town match against Pat Patterson. Everyone was screaming at the top of their lungs . . . Pat had been in San Francisco for 14 years. You could hear a pin drop," Lamarche remembers. He spent most of 1977 in San Francisco, wrestling with Ray Stevens, Harley Race and The Sheik, as well as up-and-comers like Sgt. Slaughter, Roddy Piper and Jimmy Snuka. Afterward Lamarche started wrestling in Japan for the IWA, the third most important Japanese promotion at the time. He was successful there, too, thanks especially to a feud with Rusher Kimura during which they exchanged the promotion's top belt. He also wrestled for All Japan and New Japan, and had excellent matches with both Inoki and Baba. Lamarche was, without a doubt, one of the most successful Quebecers in Japan. "I started going to Japan in 1971," he recalls. "During the next 10 years I went there three times a year to participate in about 30 tournaments. I worked with Fujinami, Tsuruta, Brody — in short, with almost everyone. I earned $6,000 a week, 15 weeks a year in Japan," he says today. Lamarche and Maurice Vachon are the only Quebecers who have won major singles titles there.

Lamarche also made the most of an opportunity to tag with the wrestler who had suggested he change his character for the United States, Ivan Koloff. From late 1979 until the end of 1981, they criss-crossed the Georgia territory, winning the titles on their way. Their last match together took place in 1982 in Charlotte against Giant Baba and Genichiro Tenryu. "We wrestled a few matches in Florida. I know the AWA wanted us, as well, but Koloff was angry over some personal matters that, in fact, I had nothing to do with, and so we never teamed again . . . We actually didn't talk to each other ever since." From there he returned to Quebec, primarily as a tag team wrestler, partnered with Pierre "Mad Dog" Lefebvre. "I really loved working with him," Lamarche remembers. "I took him under my wing."

While he was based on the west coast he wrestled for the WWF when they presented shows in the region. He wrestled against many well-known WWF wrestlers, including Bret Hart, and occasionally he'd replace Nikolai Volkoff alongside The Iron Sheik. "Bret worked really stiff at that time," he remembers, laughing. After having worked with the WWF for a few years, Vince McMahon called him to join a tour of Kuwait in 1987. He also wrestled in Hawaii and Australia during those years. In 1986 the AWA called upon his services. "Ray Stevens was the booker and he was a good friend of mine," Lamarche says. Verne Gagne gave him the name "The Machine" Cecil Dubois, making a reference to his Francophone origins and to the name he used in Montreal. "I didn't like working for Verne, but I couldn't refuse the money he offered," he explains. With the AWA he would work with a young Curt Hennig and also Leon White, who would become Big Van Vader.

After having retired as a wrestler he would operate a wrestling school out of San Francisco. "I had the school from 1988 to 1993. The most well-known talent I trained there was Chris Benoit. I met him in Japan and I had him with me for six months, mainly to polish him," Lamarche reveals. In 2000 he returned to Montreal to take part in a match for Jacques Rougeau Jr.'s promotion. "I went there to help Jimmy [Jacques]," he explains. He remains close to the Rougeau family.

Lamarche also found television and movie work during the years he spent in California. Aside from car dealership commercials he landed parts in movies like *Bad Guys*, *Body Slam* and *Alcatraz 2000*. He also acted in the *The Fall Guy* series with Lee Majors. "Gene Lebell got me the role I played in *Bad Guys*," Lamarche explains.

Even though he found success stateside he learned a great deal from the years he spent at home. "When you stay in Montreal too long, you just burn out. You have to come for six months at a time. If you're not the boss you can't be a solid babyface. As a heel you can reach the top, but you make more money in the States," Lamarche says. "With Koloff I earned $1,800 to $ 2,500 a week, much more than what I could earn in Montreal. I wanted to work full time as a wrestler and I made it. But I have to say that I still had a lot of fun in Montreal."

"THE RUSSIAN BEAR" IVAN KOLOFF

"When I went to Japan with Red McNulty I saw him wrestle and I told myself that, if he shaved his head, he'd make a damn good Russian. I told him if he came to Montreal we would give him a push, and he'd make money. He said yes right away — he was starving in Vancouver," Jacques Rougeau Sr. remembers proudly. "Coming back to Montreal I told my brother Jean that we would call him Ivan Koloff and that he was going to be a hit. He filled

MICHEL DUBOIS AS ALEXIS SMIRNOFF WITH IVAN KOLOFF
(MICHEL LAMARCHE COLLECTION)

the buildings all over the province." he adds. The Russian Bear confirms it: "He saw potential in me. They were true to their word and they give me the name . . . Koloff came from Dan Koloff, who used to wrestle in Montreal a long time ago. They also thought that I was a Lenin lookalike!"

This is how one of wrestling's most legendary Russian gimmicks was created in 1967. Koloff filled the Forum more than once against Johnny Rougeau and became the MAC's International champion twice. Finally the young Francophone, who was born Oreal Perras on August 25, 1942, on a farm in Ontario, was to become world champion in 1971. "Jean had subsequently called Vince McMahon Sr. and proposed Koloff's services to him. He made a lot of money in New York," Rougeau Sr. said. He became WWWF champion on January 18, 1971, ending the living legend Bruno Sammartino's seven-year reign. In the 1980s he returned to Montreal for Varoussac and entered into a brief rivalry with Raymond Rougeau. His national career would continue until the end of the '80s, mainly with the NWA, where he was world tag team champion many times with, among others, the wrestler who would become his "nephew," Nikita Koloff. Ivan Koloff would continue wrestling sporadically until the early 2000s. In his autobiography he underlines the importance of the time he spent in Montreal: "I owe my career to getting that break. For that I want to say 'thank you' to Jacques Rougeau."

FRENCHY MARTIN, THE MERCENARY JOKER

Nobody will ever be able to say that Frenchy Martin can't keep a straight face. "It's really upsetting that people don't know wrestling any better than this . . . How much money would it take to change my ranking?" he asked.

Jokingly, of course, that's how he attempted to bribe his way to a higher position in our top 25 list (see ranking on page 401). He's clearly someone who enjoys life and cherishes each moment. "For some guys, they always want to know whether they are going to win or to lose. If you get a few hundreds of thousands along the way, it's not really that big of a deal," he explains.

Frenchy Martin spent the last years of his career with the WWF, from '87 to '90, as the manager of Dino Bravo. At that time he used to walk around with a sign that read *USA is NOT OK* and wore an artist's smock. He was also

THE ASSASSINS COVERED IN BLOOD: PIERRE LEFEBVRE AND FRENCHY MARTIN (LINDA BOUCHER)

the host of a Francophone version of "Piper's Pit" called "Frenchy's Studio." Remembers Frenchy: "The artist was Gorilla Monsoon's idea. I reminded him of Salvador Dali. And becoming a manager didn't offend me. I was there to make money. I wasn't a young boy just starting in the business. If you wanted to get a good payday . . . they'd tell you how they wanted you to work. You can't ask to be paid . . . and do it your own way," he says, philosophically, seeing the role as simply a new phase of his career.

Born Jean Gagne in Quebec City on July 19, 1947, he was a barman when his good friend Michel Martel began wrestling. His curiosity was piqued and it would change his life forever. "What attracted me was a match I went to see at La Tour de Quebec, a cage match between Maurice Vachon and Jos Leduc. I told myself: 'I have to do this one day.'"

In 1971, after some training in Quebec, Michel got himself a spot with

FRENCHY MARTIN WAS A MAJOR STAR IN PUERTO RICO, HERE SEEN FACING BRUNO SAMMARTINO
(FRENCHY MARTIN COLLECTION)

the famous Hart family's Stampede Wrestling. "One person who helped me a lot in Calgary was Chin Lee, a guy originally from Montreal. Thank god I wasn't trained by Stu Hart," he deadpans, referencing the fact that the patriarch of the Hart family had a reputation for being hard on his students. During the first years of his career he would work mainly in Canada under the name Don Gagne. "In the summer I worked in New Brunswick for Emile Dupree and in the winter for Stampede . . . Bret Hart used to referee my matches!" It was at that time that The Mercenaries, donning their hallmark berets, were to come together. They proceeded to travel around the world, from Japan to Puerto Rico, making stops in Montreal for Johnny Rougeau's All Star Wrestling. They actually won the WWC tag team titles in 1975 and held the IWA titles in Japan. "We had a good time. We were the same kind of people. Michel wasn't close with his money . . . nor am I," Frenchy Martin recalls during an interview with *SLAM! Wrestling*.

From 1975 to 1978 Martin and Martel teamed in Puerto Rico for Carlos Colón's WWC. Frenchy was then wrestling under the name Pierre Martel.

"We just clicked . . . There was no animosity, there was no, 'Who's the brain?' No competition at all . . . I complimented his ideas or, if I came up with one, he'd put it aside and then later on, he'd come back and grab it and use it . . . He was very intelligent. And, naturally, when I was booking I was very good, too, because I kind of followed his idea. In a way, we had the same mind. We didn't have the same life, but we had the same mind," Martin says. "Puerto Rico was the best. We were really over. But we got also too much heat at times. We had to leave the arena hiding in an ambulance many times."

He met his wife, and his children were born while he was in Puerto Rico, where his tag team earned a victory over Bret and Smith Hart. "Smith and I teamed up for a six-minute TV match with Frenchy Martin and Michel Martel, the hottest heel team in the territory had ever known. We were going to get squashed, which was fine by us. I liked Frenchy and Michel, and I was happy to do my small part in helping them get over," Bret Hart says in his biography.

Unfortunately an accident was to put an end to not only their business partnership, but also their friendship. On June 30, 1978, Michel Martel suffered a fatal heart attack. "When Michel died, I almost drank myself to death. It was terrible. I was so close and then, boom. Life is like that," Martin said to SLAM!Wrestling. In spite of the loss of someone who had become a real brother, Puerto Rico remained his home base. "I even wrestled against Ric Flair for an hour in Puerto Rico for the NWA championship. I beat him in a non-title match in the Carolinas. They showed this match on TV to build up our encounter." Even though he worked in Puerto Rico most of the time, he still travelled. "I worked many tours in Japan. Michel and I even won the tag team championship when we wrestled for Baba." Michel's death led Frenchy to forge a strong friendship with Michel's brother, Rick. The two of them tried to work together as much as they could. "In the late 1970s I was in New Zealand and Hawaii working for Rick Martel, who was the booker."

Opportunities in Montreal were hard to come by early in Martin's career. He wouldn't begin spending extended periods in the territory until the 1980s, when he started working with International Wrestling. "Gino Brito was the booker when I worked for International Wrestling. The name Frenchy Martin came when we were doing TV in Sherbrooke for Grand Prix.

He had tremendous success for Brito wearing his famous beret and would be a part of a formidable team with Pierre "Mad Dog" Lefebvre. But, in December 1985, tragedy struck again. Martin saw his partner Pierre Lefebvre die in a car accident. With the world of wrestling transforming at the same time, Frenchy decided to move on. Thanks to Terry Garvin, he got a chance to work with the WWF. He wrestled briefly, then quickly transferred into other roles, including becoming the Francophone heel TV commentator, partnered with Édouard Carpentier and Guy Hauray.

Talking about his career as a WWF manager, Martin points out there were many wrestlers besides Dino Bravo under his tutelage. "I was about to manage Jos Leduc in New York as The Headbanger. It wasn't the gimmick . . . Jos just didn't work out in the WWF," Martin remembers. Finally, before a show in Des Moines, Iowa, he almost joined his former partners. "In 1990 I had my first heart attack and put an end to my career with the WWF." Some years later he was to go on the first tour of the Montreal territory with Jacques Rougeau and would manage Abdullah the Butcher, but the adventure was short-lived. He would make some appearances with the ICW in the 2000s, trying to help his son get started in the business.

When Frenchy Martin talks about his career and an era where people believed in the illusion, one can't help but note his nostalgia. But, as usual, he turns serious issues into a laughing matter. "At times I, myself, believed that wrestling was real . . . at least when I was in the ring with certain guys!"

Frenchy Martin keeps bringing his ranking back into the discussion, and even through his jokes there's a hint of disappointment. "It makes me happy to be ranked. But 21? I will have to say it's my age," he says. No matter how he's ranked he can, nonetheless, take comfort in the fact that he has been inducted into the Quebec Wrestling Hall of Fame. Rick Martel sums up Frenchy Martin's character like this: "Frenchy is like my own brother. Just having him around makes me feel happy and close to my brother Michel. But he's such a character, that Frenchy."

And as far as Frenchy Martin is concerned, "In spite of everything, I would start all over again without changing anything."

DON LEO JONATHAN, MORE THAN THE MATCH OF THE CENTURY

He first wrestled in Montreal in 1952, won the territory title twice in the 1950s and drew thousands of fans, but it wasn't until 1972 that Don Leo Jonathan made it to the top. A feud against Jean Ferré, still talked about today, put him there.

On January 12, 1972, during their very first show at the Montreal Forum, Édouard Carpentier defended his title against "The Mormon Giant" Don Leo Jonathan in a well-crafted story conceived by Grand Prix promoters. Near the end of that match Jean Ferré intervened in favour of his friend and fellow countryman. The champion was disqualified. Even though Jonathan won the match he had just lost any chance of winning the title. This confrontation, in front of the biggest crowd in the short history of the promotion, initiated a feud everyone would remember — the Giant's first in North America.

DON LEO JONATHAN, ONE OF THE MANY GIANTS TO WRESTLE IN MONTREAL

It wasn't until four months later, on May 31, 1972, that the Giant wrestled Jonathan for the first time, losing via disqualification. This match of the century drew 16,164 people, the biggest crowd in the history of Grand Prix. The return affair, on August 2, 1972, broke this record with 20,347 spectators — the biggest crowd Grand Prix *ever* drew at the Forum. Jonathan won that match as well, but Ferré gave him three piledrivers afterward. The rubber match took place on September 7, 1972, in front of a respectable crowd numbering 12,000. That would be the only win Ferré had in the feud. "One of the best matches that I've ever seen was the one opposing the Giant to Jonathan," Luke Williams remembers. The three matches, combined with the success he had already achieved, definitely established Jonathan as one of the most important non-Quebecers in the territory's history. Ultimately he would be one of the most successful Americans in Montreal — ever.

Born Don Heaton in Hurricane, Utah, Don Leo Jonathan had the physique for the job. Measuring 6' and weighing some 240 pounds he was "the most impressive wrestler I've ever seen. He's as strong as a bull," Jackie Wiecz says. After starting out in California, Jonathan, considered a very agile wrestler in spite of his imposing physique, moved to the east coast. In the '50s Montreal was a territory everyone wanted to be booked into, and on June 8, 1955, Jonathan beat Pat O'Connor for the Montreal title. He would exchange the championship with Yvon Robert, losing it on August 17, only to claim it back the following week before losing it again to Killer Kowalski for good on December 14, 1955. His match against O'Connor aside, the other three matches drew at least 14,000 fans each.

In fact the 1955 match in which Robert took his title from him drew 18,972 to Delorimier Stadium, the biggest crowd in the world that year. Jonathan was the biggest heel in the territory and the best draw, which explains why five of the biggest crowds of the year, as well as seven out of the best 10, had Jonathan main-eventing. He came back in the spring of 1956 for feuds with Édouard Carpentier and Killer Kowalski, but by the late 1950s things became quieter, with Jonathan mainly wrestling in tag teams with Kowalski.

Jonathan would not return as a Montreal regular until the 1970s, when, at the age of 40, he faced Rene Goulet on December 15, 1971, for Grand Prix. Following the Montreal feud with Andre the Giant, Jonathan moved to the WWWF for feuds with Pedro Morales and Bruno Sammartino in 1973–74. He challenged both men for the championship. Ironically Jonathan's last match was a six-man tag affair, teaming with a rising star, Roddy Piper, and the man with whom he had the most important matches of his Montreal career, Andre the Giant. His exploits secured his induction to the *Wrestling Observer*'s Hall of Fame, as well as the Quebec Wrestling Hall of Fame. Montreal and Vancouver were the Canadian cities in which Jonathan had the most notable success, but he also had good runs in Toronto, Winnipeg and Calgary. "I have wrestled so much in Canada that people think I'm Canadian," Jonathan, who has been residing in a suburb of Vancouver for 40 years, says.

GILLES "THE FISH" POISSON, THE STRONG MAN FROM LAC-SAINT-JEAN

Gilles Poisson once lifted a car on live television. "The car weighed 2,200 pounds," Poisson says. And, as François Hébert recalls, "Gilles Poisson picking up a car on Télé 7 TV remains part of the lasting and vivid memories of the wrestling programs that aired on every Sunday mornings before the arrival of the WWF."

Born on October 30, 1944, Poisson first donned the boots for Stampede Wrestling in Calgary. "It was Mad Dog Vachon who sent me," Poisson remembers. Afterward he worked in Portland, as well as for All Japan Pro Wrestling. It was a few years before he started wrestling with Grand Prix. "When I started wrestling in Montreal, I already had two years of experience . . . it was Maurice Vachon . . . who brought me back." He was supposed to wrestle Andre the Giant for the 1973 Grand Prix show at Jarry Park Stadium, but the match never took place. André's local wrestling licence had expired, and the MAC wouldn't let him

ONE OF INTERNATIONAL WRESTLING'S MANY TAG TEAMS: THE HANGMAN AND GILLES "THE FISH" POISSON

(LINDA BOUCHER)

compete. "I have, nonetheless, wrestled against Andre the Giant about a hundred times. I was even one of the few wrestlers to bodyslam him," Poisson says. He also wrestled under the name Louis Cyr in the WWWF in 1976 and Pierre Poisson in the AWA. His last regular matches in Montreal happened in the 1980s for International Wrestling.

While Poisson made his mark away from Quebec, many foreign wrestlers were coming to the province to try to make theirs — Montreal wasn't just a nice place to live back then, it was also a great place to wrestle.

THE HOLLYWOOD BLONDS

Fans today might associate the name with Steve Austin and Brian Pillman in WCW, but the first team to have success as the Hollywood Blonds was formed by Jerry Brown and a young Canadian, Dale "Buddy Roberts" Hey. If the Leduc brothers were the biggest acquisition for Grand Prix in its war against All Star Wrestling, The Blonds were certainly a close second. "When the two Hollywood Blonds left the territory Grand Prix collapsed. It hurt because they were a big draw when they were on top," Gilles Poisson explains. The team was created by Bill Watts in 1970, and they were almost immediately successful. "I became partners with Leroy McGuirk for Championship Wrestling in 1970 and I brought in Dale Hey, who I'd seen in Minneapolis. He was a jobber, but I knew he had potential. Jerry Brown's partner was injured, and we didn't want him anymore. So, I teamed up Dale and Jerry, and the Hollywood Blonds were born," Bill Watts recalls.

In 1972, when they moved from All Star to Grand Prix in Montreal, they added a third member to the act when Sir Oliver Humperdink became their manager. "They wanted to come back with something different, and I was the something different. Grand Prix Wrestling was running head to head with the Rougeau brothers . . . I was lucky enough to hook up with those guys in main events right from the get-go. It was really exciting and a great time in my life. I really enjoyed those guys," Humperdink explained to SLAM! Wrestling. "They had exceptional timing," Billy Two Rivers recalls. One of the highlights of The Blonds' Montreal run was working the semi main event at the famous Jarry Park Stadium show of 1973, where they faced Édouard

Carpentier and Bruno Sammartino.

Dale Hey had worked for Johnny Rougeau in the '60s under his real name. As Buddy Roberts he would eventually become the third member of the Fabulous Freebirds when he partnered with Michael Hayes and Terry Gordy. The famous trio would work in Montreal during the dying days of the International Wrestling promotion. Currently retired, Hey has many health problems. In 1988 Humperdink would

THE HOLLYWOOD BLONDS AND SIR OLIVER HUMPERDINK WERE A HOT TEAM IN THE '70S (BERTRAND HÉBERT COLLECTION)

come back to Montreal with the WWF as Bam Bam Bigelow's manager. He died in March 2011, following a long illness. Jerry Brown enjoys a peaceful retirement outside of the wrestling world. He told *SLAM! Wrestling* the years he spent in Montreal were special: "The crowds were intense. I loved it, because they're a little bit hot-natured . . . It was just fun to be around."

JACKIE WIECZ

Jacques Magnin, hoping to capitalize on the success of his mother's brother, Édouard Carpentier, came to Quebec in 1969. "It was Jack Britton who had the idea of bringing me here to team up with Édouard," he reveals. He was renamed André Carpentier to make the most of the familial tie, even though he would team more often with Andre the Giant and Rico Garcia. "I had a guarantee for a week and a round-trip plane ticket in hand. I had nothing to lose," he explains.

But, like his uncle, he never left. He has been living in the province for

THE REAL-LIFE NEPHEW OF ÉDOUARD CARPENTIER.
JACKIE WIECZ (JACKIE WIECZ COLLECTION)

40 years and has settled down near Mont-Laurier, a few hours north of Montreal. Although his uncle most certainly played a role in the start of his Canadian career, Magnin didn't come empty-handed. He already had 10 years of experience in Europe after beginning his wrestling career upon finishing military service in 1960. And before he stepped foot in a Montreal ring he had many amateur wrestling, bodybuilding and weightlifting titles to his name. Born on December 8, 1940, he was coached professionally by Bollet Delaporte, a huge name in catch, as wrestling was, and still is, called in France.

Magnin enjoyed success with Johnny Rougeau's All Star Wrestling, going around the province while his uncle toured to give the promotion a Carpentier to present to the public. He signed with Grand Prix at its inception and readopted the name Jackie Wiecz he used in France when he teamed with Édouard. "With Grand Prix, my career reached its peak . . . It opened so many doors for me." In fact Wiecz would later join New Japan under the name Jacky Carpenter and then would cross Canada, winning titles in the Maritimes in the process. He had some success with The Sheik's promotion but would never make a real breakthrough in the United States, where working without a green card meant he could have been deported to France. Married with a young child, he couldn't come to terms with the risk. "When I got the chance of going for the WWWF, The Mongols told me that they would take care of me. Maurice Vachon also told me to go. This is the only thing I regret in my entire career. I would have loved to know what would have happened if I had gone to the States."

By 1976 he began cutting back on his schedule: "One night after a disastrous show, attendance-wise, the promoter put the gate on a table in the locker room and we divided it amongst ourselves. I knew then that I had to find a new job to take care of my family." In 1980, one year before he retired from the ring for good, he faced Hulk Hogan twice for the fledgling Varoussac. "He was intelligent and he was already quite the businessman," Wiecz says about Hogan.

SAILOR WHITE

Ed White made his debut in 1972 in Larry Kasaboski's territory but quickly found his way to Montreal and Grand Prix Wrestling. He would wrestle in Montreal for more than a decade. On October 10, 1976, while wrestling was in the midst of a business low, White won the International title from Billy Two Rivers. Next, in the early days of International Wrestling, he had a long feud with Dino Bravo, where, ultimately, according to a stipulation following a loss, he would lose his hair at the hands of Menick, a famous Montreal barber. White went on to win the tag team titles with Gilles Poisson. Ultimately, however, he's best remembered for his association with Rick Valentine, with whom he also won the tag belts. In an epic feud White and Valentine drew 15,300 fans at the Colisée de Québec against Dino Bravo and Rick Martel on July 11, 1984. At the time they were, perhaps, the most hated heels in the territory. In the '80s, as a singles wrestler, his biggest success came in winning the newly created TV championship.

White worked in the WWWF as Moondog King, of the famed Moondogs tag team. After running twice as a candidate in federal

THE PRIDE OF NEWFOUNDLAND. ED "SAILOR" WHITE
(BERTRAND HÉBERT COLLECTION)

elections in his native Newfoundland, White died on August 25, 2005, from injuries he suffered in an accident while driving his cab.

YVON ROBERT JR.,
NEVER EASY TO BE THE SON OF GOD

After earning an MBA from UCLA, Yvon Robert Jr. decided to follow in the footsteps of his famous father. Like many second-generation sportsmen, his genetic heritage didn't ensure guaranteed success. Robert Jr. would never earn the recognition or enjoy the success of his famous father. In his wallet he would carry a scrap of paper with this inscription, quoting Victor Hugo: "What was done, and done well, is not to be done again." Ultimately the son would make peace with the monument that was his father in wrestling history. "I said, 'After the Expo, Dad, I think I'm going to try it.' He said, 'It's up to you,'" Robert Jr. recalled in an interview with SLAM! Wrestling. "I didn't want to get to 60 years old and regret not having tried," added Robert Jr., the godson of former boxing great Joe Louis.

Born on October 19, 1936, he would eventually wrestle for a decade before leaving the business for good in 1977. Early in his career he worked in St. Louis under the names Bob Brunnel and Beau Brunnelle, trying to learn the craft without the gigantic shadow of his father looming over him. Brunnelle, in fact, was his mother Leona's maiden name.

When he finally returned home, the Rougeau family's wrestling monopoly made it difficult for him to get the chance to showcase himself. His father's desire to find a place for him in Montreal was one of the reasons behind the launch of Grand Prix. In the new promotion he was mainly known for a championship tag partnership with Édouard Carpentier. "He was very much like his father and everyone loved him," Paul Vachon said upon the death of a wrestler with whom he worked closely. This ease with which he made and kept friends in the difficult world of wrestling was what allowed him to make appearances for International Wrestling, mainly as a referee, but also as an "agent" for King Tonga. His credibility consolidated the switch of Tonga from the role of Dino Bravo's worst enemy to that of his partner. Robert Jr. had many health problems in the last years of his life,

THE THREE MUSKETEERS: ÉDOUARD CARPENTIER, JEAN FERRÉ AND YVON ROBERT JR.

(BERTRAND HÉBERT COLLECTION)

including losing a foot to complications resulting from diabetes. On April 30, 2008, he died of a heart attack, like his father before him.

ZARINOFF LEBOEUF HASN'T BEEN SEEN NEAR A WRESTLING RING IN MONTREAL FOR MORE THAN 25 YEARS (BERTRAND HÉBERT COLLECTION)

ZARINOFF LEBOEUF, ANOTHER RUSSIAN FROM QUEBEC

Réjean Gagnon adopted the name Zarinoff with Grand Prix in the 1970s. It was then that the Quebecer was "discovered" in his own territory as a foreigner, thanks to his awesome Russian cobra sleeper. His Russian character can be traced back to runs in Memphis and Charlotte, North Carolina, where he wrestled as the Russian Stomper. Leboeuf also enjoyed success in tag teams, first with Rene Goulet in The Legionnaires and then with Yukon Eric (Scott Irwin, not Eric Holmback) under the name Yukon Pierre. The team was called the Yukon Lumberjacks and, under the guidance of "Captain" Lou Albano, they won the WWWF tag team titles from Dino Bravo and Dominic Denucci on June 26, 1978. In the early 1980s he wrestled for Varoussac and had a feud with Dino Bravo that culminated in a Russian chain match. But after he took liberties in the ring with Armand Rougeau, Raymond ran him out of town. Born in Montreal on February 13, 1939, he disappeared from the business and was never to be seen again. According to his friend Gilles Poisson, he currently lives in the United States, where he has found a second career in the fields of insurance and real estate.

RICHARD "LE MAGNIFIQUE" CHARLAND, MAD DOG'S PROTÉGÉ

Born on September 26, 1956, this hometown boy from Ville-Émard was certainly the Montreal wrestler whose career was most affected by the demise of International Wrestling. In 1987 he found himself in the uncomfortable position of not being able to work at home and with no place in the WWF. He was discovered by Maurice Vachon and began his career in 1972 with Grand Prix. In addition to Vachon, he'd had Édouard Carpentier, Luigi Mascera and Omer Marchessault as trainers by the time he made his debut at the age of 16. Montreal fans have always known him under the name Richard Charland, but in the late 1970s he was also Garth

RICHARD CHARLAND AND KING TONGA WERE INTERNATIONAL WRESTLING TAG TEAM CHAMPIONS IN THE '80S (LINDA BOUCHER)

Vader for The Sheik in Detroit and Mauler Malone for the WWWF. In the 1980s he rose above preliminary matches. After he had worked for promoter Denis Lauzon's opposition group, Varoussac brought him back in. He turned heel, attacking Leo Burke, who had just beaten him for the new TV championship, destroying the trophy on Burke's head. "There's nothing

TWO REAL-LIFE BROTHERS: BOB "UFO" AND ROCKY DELLASERRA (LINDA BOUCHER)

better than being bad. That's my drug," Charland said to *SLAM! Wrestling* in 1999.

He was later part of Tarzan Tyler's stable and his association with the number one manager in the territory would take him to yet another level. In 1985 he also wrestled for Maple Leaf Wrestling, as the WWF's Toronto office used many Quebecers. He strengthened his position in Quebec by becoming King Tonga's partner. Teamed with the number one heel in the territory, he became a tag team champion on March 11, 1985. Because of this partnership Charland was right in the mix when Tonga made his inevitable babyface turn.

When other Quebecers left for the WWF he became the most experienced local wrestler and won the tag team championship with Sheik Ali (Stephen Petitpas). After International Wrestling shut down he became a bit of a wrestling nomad, doing occasional shows for the WWF in Canada. Finally he hooked up with Bill Eadie when the former WWF star was looking for a partner to form another Demolition team on the independent circuit. He abandoned the idea of wrestling full time in 1991, but he remained active until the early 2000s. "Richard Charland was one of the best talents in the province. He could have become as big a name as Rick Martel," former wrestler Fernand Frechette says. "They didn't pick up my number. I didn't get that break," Charland concedes.

BOB DELLA SERRA, THE UNKNOWN UFO

Bob Della Serra was known around the world as Johnny Heffernan, UFO, Karl Steiner and Bobby Heffernan, but it was as Bob Della Serra, his real name, that he is remembered in Montreal. He won championships and was successful in Europe and Puerto Rico, but in Montreal he was never able to transition from mid-carder to star. He tagged with Don Kent in Puerto Rico in 1982 under the name the New Fabulous Kangaroos, playing the role of Johnny Heffernan Jr., cousin of Roy Heffernan, an original member of the famous duo. In Montreal he enjoyed some success with his masked character, UFO, for Grand Prix in the 1970s. His career came to a slow halt in the 1990s, when he tried his hand at acting. His younger brother, Rocky Della Serra, also wrestled and ended up promoting in Vancouver.

DOMINIC DENUCCI, A HARDCORE TRAINER

Born in Naples, Italy, Dominic Nucciarone moved to Montreal at the age of 18. "I came from Italy to Nova Scotia in February 1953 and then I took the train to Montreal," Denucci remembers. After having been coached by Tony Lanza he started his career in the early 1960s. "The guys told me that if I wanted to make money I had to wrestle in the United States," he recalls. From the very start he became a star in San Francisco for promoter Roy Shire. His feud with Ray Stevens would actually produce two matches that are considered among the best draws in Cow Palace history. Subsequently he went on to resounding success in Australia, where he won both tag team and single titles. Dominic Denucci was, according to Jim Barnett, his

2012: DOMINIC DENUCCI AND MICK FOLEY AT THE PRO WRESTLING HALL OF FAME (BERTRAND HÉBERT)

most successful drawing card in World Championship Wrestling in Australia during the mid-1960s when it was considered one of the top promotions in the world. Denucci won the world title of the same division three times after capturing the WWWF International tag team title with Bruno Sammartino, sharing the straps the last time in 1978 with Dino Bravo. He started to wrestle in Montreal regularly with All Star Wrestling in the late '60s and then moved to Grand Prix in the '70s. In 1977 he became the International champion, defeating Johnny Valiant. He was also often teamed up with other Italians, like Gino Brito, Tony Parisi, Luigi Mascera and Tony Marino.

In the 1980s he decided to open a wrestling school in Freedom, a suburb of Pittsburgh, where he still lives today. Among his students, two have gone on to well-known careers. The first is Troy Martin, who, under the name Shane Douglas, was NWA and ECW world champion. The second, and most famous, is Mick Foley. On a December 29, 1988, show (broadcast on January 4, 1999) Foley won the title that his mentor could never secure: the WWF world title. "I credit my turnaround to hard work and persever-ance, but, above all else, the dedication of that old 'son of a bitch' Dominic Denucci," Mick Foley writes in *Have a Nice Day!*

NEIL GUAY, A HANGMAN AMONG WRESTLERS

Neil Guay had an international career that many people don't know about. He was Hulk Hogan's partner in the WWF in 1980 and 1981, and "Classy" Freddie Blassie was their manager. When he wrestled in single it was against the biggest stars of the time — men like Bruno Sammartino, Pedro Morales and Bob Backlund. He actually wrestled at the famous Shea Stadium show on August 9, 1980, where Sammartino faced his former protégé, Larry Zybysko, in what was voted match of the year, while Hogan faced off — as a heel — against Andre the Giant. Guay worked with another Quebecer that night, Rene Goulet. In September 1980 he made his Madison Square Garden debut. It was also the debut for another Quebecer, Rick Martel. "Working for McMahon Sr. was like working for your own father. He liked me a lot as a wrestler. I didn't get along with the son, and after the death of Senior it was the end of my career in the WWF," Guay explains.

Born in Matane, Quebec, on July 21, 1942, Guay is another product of the famed Loisirs St-Jean-Baptiste. "I met Denis Gauthier at his gym. Jacques Rougeau Sr., his father-in-law at the time, advised me to try the Loisirs St-Jean-Baptiste, rather than training with the Grand Prix wrestling school." Working as a police officer at the time and dissatisfied in that job, Guay took Rougeau's advice to heart and made his debut at the Loisirs under the guidance of Pat Girard in 1971. As is often the case, his first match was as a last-minute replacement. "I had to substitute for Dick

"THE HANGMAN" NEIL GUAY WITH FRED BLASSIE AND HULK HOGAN (NEIL GUAY COLLECTION)

Taylor. Paul Leduc dyed my hair blond for the match," he explains. "I contacted Rudy Kay in New Brunswick and he hired me for six weeks. We were well paid, much better than in Montreal. I was a jobber in Montreal. I didn't do anything outstanding. That's why I chose to leave home." Afterward he moved to Calgary, where he wrestled under a mask as Towering Inferno. From there he would go to Japan for New Japan Pro Wrestling. "They liked me . . . I worked with Inoki, Sakaguchi and Kobayashi. They paid you very well and treated you like a king," he explains.

While in Japan, he made an important ally. "In Japan I met Paul Vachon. The fact that we spoke French allowed us to become friends. He told me that he would bring me to Los Angeles. It was at that time that Leo Garibaldi, the booker, gave me the name Hangman. I became champion and stayed there for a year," he recalls. After this he teamed with Jos Leduc, using the name Jean Louis, in Tennessee. It was also at this time that he worked for the WWF. Guay worked for International Wrestling in the '80s on an irregular basis, winning the International tag team championship twice, first with Pierre Lefebvre in 1980 and again with Swede Hanson in 1981. After suffering a serious concussion in a match with Andre the Giant, and then another in a car accident, he was forced to put an end to his career after 20 years.

Guay's fondest wrestling memory came against Sgt. Slaughter, with whom he once partnered in the AWA as the Super Destroyer Mark III. "Maurice Vachon told me that the promoter's son, Greg Gagne, was so into the match that he saw him jumping like a little kid," he says of his best wrestling moment.

While being a Francophone was, at times, an obstacle for men like Guay trying to make it in the States, being an English-speaking wrestler in a French province was no piece of cake, either.

LEN "KOJAK" SHELLEY

"I was in Japan in 1976 when I decided to shave my head . . . It went without saying that people started to call me Kojak. Subsequently, in Tennessee, I took up Telly Savalas's gimmick in the TV program, the lollipop." That's how Len Shelley explains the birth of his character, a cutting-edge choice at the time. He became quite popular among young fans and enjoyed real success almost everywhere he wrestled — though comparatively little in his native province of Quebec. "The promoters told me I was Anglophone, that my name was Shelley, so I wouldn't draw a dime," he says, with a hint of bitterness. "With Grand Prix, it wasn't really better. In Montreal Gino Brito was the first promoter to give me a chance as International tag team champion with Richard Charland." (This occurred in the early 1980s.) "I even wrestled at Paul-Sauvé Arena against Hulk Hogan before he became a big international star," he adds, explaining how long it took him to finally get a chance in Quebec.

He started training in 1963, 17 years prior to this run. "The teacher told me to find a better place . . . He felt I was good enough to succeed. So I enrolled in Tony Lanza's school. Wrestlers had to have a licence at the time, and it took me only six months to get one." He left five years later, in 1968, after having tried in vain to become a wrestling star in his native territory. "Subsequently I was part of The Scorpions tag team, wearing a mask . . . And my style was so different that no one recognized me," he adds.

Born on March 13, 1941, Shelley, like many other Montreal wrestlers,

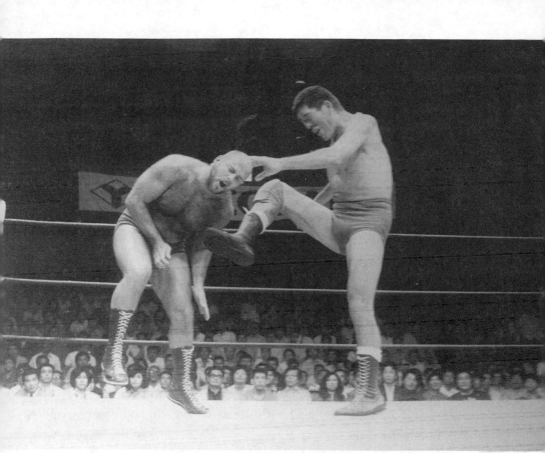

LEN SHELLEY WRESTLING GIANT BABA IN JAPAN (LEN SHELLEY COLLECTION)

went to Calgary before heading for the States. He worked many of the American territories, including Louisiana, San Francisco, Portland and Oklahoma. "I have also wrestled for Giant Baba in Japan. I really loved working there, but I had a hard time with the food. After two or three tours there I found it even more difficult. Above all I never went to the clubs; it was really difficult to fit in, and I didn't think that you could mix up sport, on the one hand, and drink and drugs, on the other," he explains. Then, in the early 1980s, a tragic event altered the course of his career. "In New Brunswick I was main-eventing against Randy Savage. On my way to the show I had a car crash. I didn't wrestle for 20 months. I came back for three months, but I had to take another year off because my back was so badly injured. But, even after taking a year off, I was always in excruciating pain. And I didn't want to undergo surgery because there was only a 50 percent chance of success." In 1987, at the end of things for International

Wrestling, he attempted a comeback; the death of the promotion put an end to this. Some years later he trained his son Eric Shelley and was even able to have some matches with him. Eric would go on to wrestle on *Monday Night Raw* as part of the WWF's original light heavyweight tournament. In the 1990s Len went on to train a few other guys who had some indy success, including Nightmare, Nightstalker and Steve Ace.

EDDY CREATCHMAN, THE MOST HATED MAN IN QUEBEC WRESTLING HISTORY

"I make money profusely and I change my Cadillac every year. When I see the Rougeaus I see red, and the more I think about them, the more I come to the conclusion that I like animals more than them." There's a shining example of why the one and only Eddy Creatchman was hated by fans. But the notorious manager wasn't just hated by the crowds who came to watch the shows in the different arenas of the territory between 1963 and 1987; he was also able to play the heel with the MAC, which, rightly or wrongly, wasn't fully wise to the secrets of wrestling. This is one of the reasons why, in August 1973, the commission decided to suspend Creatchman's licence. "The MAC suspended him, and wrestlers decided to go on strike!" Paul Leduc remembers, smiling. "Five thousand people went to the commission screaming, 'We want Creatchman!' As for me, I only want men with thorough knowledge of my sport to take care of wrestling, instead of men who have never practised my sport and who want to tell me how to go about my business," Creatchman explained in a radio interview. Ironically all the controversy around his suspension revealed exactly how much Montrealers loved to hate him. "It was the only time that Creatchman was a babyface," Leduc recalls.

Actually his family knew his babyface side, as well. "We have very fond memories of a very close-knit family, and, unfortunately, Eddy became very sick and was taken away from us too early. Eddy was a loving and warm father/husband/grandfather. Outside of the ring he was a wild character, but he lived a wonderful family life, with a lot of love," his daughter Cheryl and granddaughter Alissa remember. On the other hand, for fans who knew

EDDY CREATCHMAN AND STEVE STRONG IN THE 1980S (LINDA BOUCHER)

Eddy Creatchman as the greatest manager to ever work in Montreal, it was almost impossible not to harbour some hatred toward him — he was that successful in leaving a mark on the collective consciousness of the province.

So how did he manage it? Even when you analyze wrestling today you can't help but hate Creatchman. "His aggressive interviews were small masterpieces of intimidation responding to society's need to let off steam," *La Presse*'s journalist Guy Émond explained when wrestling's first manager to earn the nickname The Brain left the world for good on March 9, 1994. Édouard Carpentier confirms Guy Émond's analysis: "He put on such a show. He was able to pack the Forum with people, playing this role and doing it so intensely he caused small riots!" He impressed wrestlers of succeeding generations. "I have never seen a guy with so much courage. This guy was brave and invested himself 200 percent in what he did. In the 1970s he found himself amidst riots and was scared of no one . . . He would come back to the locker room and think it was funny," Rick Martel says.

Creatchman could have become a successful actor if the opportunity had arisen. He had an innate talent for show business. In fact he participated in one of the first movies on wrestling. *I Like to Hurt People* was produced in Detroit, The Sheik's territory. The Sheik put his trust in him and made him his manager after having seen him work in Montreal. In one scene Eddy Creatchman and Abdullah Farouk (Ernie Roth, a.k.a. "The Grand Wizard of Wrestling") were arguing. "The two were yelling at each other, the director called for a cut . . . and the two started laughing loudly. It's one scene I hope I can find and add back into the film," producer Bryan Greenberg and director of photography explained during an interview with *SLAM! Wrestling*.

Creatchman was born on February 27, 1928. He began wrestling in the 1940s, then recycled himself as a referee. It wasn't until Johnny Rougeau made his return to wrestling that he became a manager. "Those were all special memories. Even though Creatchman was the villain, and Johnny Rougeau was the babyface, they were still extremely close friends," his daughter explains. In the 1970s Creatchman was everywhere — and he was evil incarnate. He had a whole army behind him, spearheaded by Abdullah the Butcher and The Sheik. Wielding his own electric cattle prod, a cane and a cigar, he infuriated the entire territory. Less well-known is that he also performed in the States. He worked in the Detroit territory with The Sheik and Abdullah the Butcher and, in fact, became the official manager of The Sheik when Ernie Roth left for the WWWF. With The Sheik, he also worked in Toronto, Pittsburgh and St. Louis. In Pittsburgh, in December 1973, he managed The Sheik against Bruno Sammartino, probably the only time that Creatchman worked, even if indirectly, for the WWWF. St. Louis was a different story altogether. In August 1974 promoter Sam Muchnick agreed to bring in The Sheik, even though he wasn't a fan of his style. Muchnick's worst fears were realized when The Sheik and Creatchman did what they did best and essentially caused a riot. A couple of years later, in 1978, Eddy managed Dick the Bruiser in Indianapolis. Naturally Bruiser was the biggest babyface in the territory, and, of course, faithful to his habits, working with the good guy was just one of Creatchman's ruses. It was in Indianapolis, working for the WWA, that Creatchman partnered with the other "Brain" — Bobby Heenan — to try to eliminate Bruiser.

Upon his return to Montreal in the 1980s, Eddy Creatchman would be a central figure on the heel side of International Wrestling, doing his all to find monsters who would eliminate Dino Bravo and the Rougeaus from pro wrestling. He would be in the corner for a who's who of bad guys: Pat Patterson, Pierre Lefebvre, Billy Robinson, Sailor White, Kamala, Swede Hanson, The Bourreau, Gilles Poisson, Scott and Bill Irwin, Michel Dubois, The Sheik, Dick Taylor, Frenchy Martin, Rick Valentine and his main attraction, Abdullah the Butcher. From late 1984 and all of 1985 he was absent from TV. "Eddy's wife, Mrs. Goldie Creatchman, became very ill with cancer; she passed away in 1985. It was a difficult time for the family, and Eddy and Floyd didn't have the same will to work after this hardship," his daughter reveals.

Unfortunately, after his return in 1986, the federation fell on hard times. And with the departure of Bravo and Martel, Creatchman invested his own money in order to help the company continue fighting. But it was in vain. "He lost $40,000," Gino Brito reveals. "Our competitor, the WWF, took our territory. It's difficult . . . for two wrestling organizations to survive at the same time," he told journalist Tom Lapointe. Creatchman would spend the last years of his life fighting against the legislation of a new sports commission — he believed it was damaging wrestling even more than the commission it had replaced. "I'm very angry. I'm fighting to save local wrestling because it's my life. I'm ready to go with my boys to Chicoutimi and Sept-Îles. There's enough room if everyone is reasonable, because people love this . . . because they get a lot of fun out of it," he said in an interview with La Presse in the early 1990s.

It was during this period that he partnered with Richard Charland and Réjean Désaulniers to form the FCL, a wrestling promotion in Sorel (45 minutes southeast of Montreal) that still exists today, based in Shawinigan (two hours northeast of Montreal).

Shortly before his death the majority of the restrictions imposed by the new commission were dropped. Eddy would be very proud to see that local wrestling has taken back its rightful place in the Montreal territory.

Could Creatchman, if he'd been younger, have continued with the WWF, being bilingual? Édouard Carpentier thinks so. "Creatchman would've been perfect with the WWF. He was a showman above all."

IVAN KOLOFF SIGNS HIS CONTRACT TO FACE JOHNNY ROUGEAU,
WITH TONY ANGELO AND BOB LANGEVIN WITNESSING
(PAUL LEDUC COLLECTION)

TONY ANGELO, THE PIONEER OF MANAGERS IN MONTREAL

Tony Angelo, whose real name was Hank Pardi, preceded Eddy Creatchman as Abdullah the Butcher's mouthpiece with All Star Wrestling. He's something of a forgotten figure in Montreal's wrestling history, but he was the first Quebecer to become well known in a manager's role. His career wasn't limited to Montreal, however, as he would follow Ivan Koloff to the WWWF after their success here. "His role was that of a loud, overbearing guy . . . kind of how you think somebody in the Mafia would be. I thought he was great," Koloff explains in his autobiography. Angelo also managed another Quebecer, Brute Bernard, when he was teaming with Skull Murphy, as well as The Mongols, Bepo (Nikolai Volkoff) and Geeto (Newton Tattrie, a wrestler from Nova Scotia). Angelo wrestled in the early 1960s and even became a tag team champion in Florida as the Russian Crusher with his partner Boris "The Great" Malenko. The father of the well-known wrestler and WWE agent Dean Malenko, Boris was an institution in Florida, and their team had a notable feud with the Kentuckians, Luke Brown and Grizzly Smith (who's the father of famous wrestler Jake "The Snake" Roberts).

THE GREAT ANTONIO, A NATURAL ATTRACTION

Born Antonio Barichievich on October 10, 1925, in Zagreb, Yugoslavia, the Great Antonio was known worldwide for feats of strength, especially for pulling four buses at once. But, like many strongmen, when he arrived in Montreal in 1946 he also had a wrestling career. In fact, because promoters didn't want to use him at first, he decided to promote his own shows under the name Antonio Promotions. He wrestled for Stampede Wrestling and New Japan, among other promotions, and he actually had trouble with two of the three biggest stars in the history of Japanese wrestling. In the early 1960s Antonio refused to lose to Rikidozan, the legendary father of Japanese wrestling. More than a decade later, in 1977, he refused to sell for Antonio Inoki in a match that can be viewed on YouTube today.

THE GREAT ANTONIO WITH HIS FRIEND AND MANAGER, DEEPAK MASSAND (PAUL LEDUC COLLECTION)

In return Inoki treated him to quite a few stiff kicks. "He had a concussion because of those kicks," Deepak Massand, Antonio's manager for the match, remembers. "He made a considerable amount of money from wrestling, as he made use of his exploits as a strongman to advertise his matches," Massand continues. "In the middle of the street he blocked the traffic for hours to pull buses in order to advertise his match with Inoki." He did have his name in the *Guinness World Records* books in the '50s and '60s, and was a guest on such programs as *The Ed Sullivan Show* and *The Johnny Carson Show*. But, in spite of all the money he earned in his career, in the end he roamed the streets of the Plateau Mont-Royal and Rosemont, two Montreal neighbourhoods, with his belongings and memories in bags, homeless, before dying from a heart attack on September 7, 2003. "He finished his life poor in the streets of Montreal because his ex-wife took all of his money," Massand, who knew him for more than 25 years, concludes.

(RICK MARTEL COLLECTION)

RICK MARTEL, A MODEL IN AND OUT THE RING

On May 13, 1984, in Minneapolis, Rick Martel became the AWA world champion, scoring a pinfall over Jumbo Tsuruta. In some circles the choice of Martel as a champion was met with raised eyebrows. But to a great champion like Nick Bockwinkel, who the Quebecer met in Hawaii in the 1970s, Martel was an excellent choice. "I've always said to Verne Gagne [AWA promoter] that we waited too long before making him champion. He was such a good wrestler and he was also younger and more handsome

WORLD CHAMPION BOB BACKLUND [CENTER] AND TAG TEAM CHAMPIONS RICK MARTEL AND TONY GAREA WERE AT THE TOP OF THE WWF IN THE '80S

than me! As someone who would replace me, he was a logical choice," says Bockwinkel. Although he couldn't have known it at the time, Martel was to become the Quebecer who has had the longest reign as world champion. As well, he was arguably the last great AWA champion at a time when the promotion still had some weight in the wrestling world, along with the WWF and the NWA.

For 18 months Martel defended his title around the world, from Minneapolis to Winnipeg, through New Jersey, Chicago and even Japan. The first time he put his belt on the line was on May 14, 1984, against Bockwinkel in Montreal. In October 1985 he wrestled against the NWA world champion Ric Flair in a 45-minute match in which both men were counted out. Ric Flair mentions a rematch in his book: "In Quebec City one night, Rick Martel and I headlined a twelve-match show . . . We gave the people a phenomenal sixty-minute match. Unfortunately, for every Rick Martel, there's a Rufus R. Jones." After having defended his title against many renowned wrestlers like Harley Race, Bob Backlund and Terry Gordy, it was at the Paul-Sauvé Arena in Montreal that he successfully defended for the last time, against Jimmy Garvin. Eight days later, on December 29 1985, he would lose to Stan Hansen.

Martel succeeded in becoming what his brother Michel had always wanted him to become. "After the death of my brother in 1978 I felt that I had a big mission to accomplish: becoming the great champion that Michel had always wanted me to become," he confided to Le Lundi in 1984.

He was born Richard Vigneault on March 18, 1956, and it was actually thanks to his elder brother that Martel decided to become a wrestler. "The first time I saw a professional wrestling match, my brother was wrestling and I must have been 12. From that moment on, this was what I wanted to do." The only professional training he got was with his childhood friend, Quebec City wrestler Bob Boucher. After he encouraged him and pushed him to go beyond his limits, Michel was to open doors for him. In 1973, working for promoter Rudy Kay in the Maritimes, his brother made the call that changed his life. "A wrestler was injured just before the tour, and Michel suggested to the promoter that I replace him," Martel relates. He began his career on the East Coast as Pat Kelly (the name of the wrestler who was injured; after all, the programs had already been printed).

That same year, in Montreal, Johnny Rougeau was backing another young upstart — his own nephew, Raymond. This left little or no room for Martel. "I had to leave Montreal! I don't resent Johnny Rougeau. I even thank him because, if I had stayed here, I would probably not have had the international career I had." For 1973 and 1974 Rick would primarily work in the Maritimes and Calgary territories. He also made a brief appearance in Japan. Following Kevin Sullivan's Calgary stay in 1974, Martel was invited to make his debut in Florida in 1975 for Eddie Graham.

Later in 1975 he moved to Georgia, but following a financial disagreement with promoter Jim Barnett he finished the year in the territory that would become World Class Championship Wrestling. In 1976 he returned to Georgia Championship Wrestling, appeared a few times in Montreal for Johnny Rougeau's All Star Wrestling and returned to Japan with his brother Michel and Frenchy Martin. In 1977 he went to New Zealand and Australia. "It was a turning point in my career. Mark Lewin, who I met in Atlanta in 1976, brought me," Martel says.

After a short stay in Puerto Rico following the death of his brother

Michel, who was only 34, he went back to New Zealand and Hawaii. He would buy into the Hawaii territory and discover another side of the wrestling business. "I was 23 when I bought shares in the promotion and I became the youngest booker in wrestling at the time. I was able to do this because I had learned a lot from Mark Lewin." At the end of 1979 he would leave the Pacific Ocean territories to join Don Owen in Portland.

"It was there that I got to know Roddy Piper. We were roommates, and he became like my own brother," Martel says. Piper sings from the same hymn book in his autobiography. "Rick ended up becoming one of my best friends. He is not only an amazing wrestler, but he is also a truly amazing man." This relationship would eventually lead to Martel playing a crucial role in the national expansion of Vince McMahon Jr., playing a part in the feud that led to the first *WrestleMania* with Roddy Piper against Hulk Hogan. In fact, some years later, Martel roomed with Hogan when the two wrestled for the AWA. Martel says that he was so close to Hogan that he was right there for the negotiations that led to his return to the WWF. "In 1983 they [Hogan and McMahon] met secretly in Phoenix, and I was there. Sometime later Hulk signed a 10-year contract with Vince." In his book Piper directly credited Martel for the feud with Hogan. "Hogan is a great guy and a great businessman, but I don't think either one of us had much love for the other at that particular moment. But we did have one thing in common. We had a mutual friend named Rick Martel . . . He had told each of us that the other guy was a decent guy, and we both valued Rick's opinion." The rest is now part of wrestling history.

In June 1978 Martel returned to the south for another stint with Georgia Championship Wrestling. At the time GCW had a national audience on channel 17 WTBS, and Rick began to interest other promoters. It was in Portland that he eventually received a call from Vince McMahon Sr. In September 1980, after honouring his obligations to Don Owen, Martel began wrestling full time for the WWF. This brought him closer to home than ever, as the WWF was broadcast on channel 22 ABC in Burlington, Vermont. Quebec fans clamoured for the brand new Varoussac Promotions to bring him in.

In November 1980, in a practically forgotten part of Montreal's title history, he became International champion by beating Pierre "Mad Dog" Lefebvre. He forfeited the belt three months later to Michel "Justice" Dubois.

He continued to wrestle regularly in the province, but he was doing too well with the WWF to come back here for good. Teaming with Tony Garea, he won the federation's tag team titles twice. "We quickly became friends, as I had spent a lot of time in New Zealand, his country of origin," Martel remembers. In spite of his success in New York, he went to Minneapolis in June 1982. "When the AWA called, things were going well with the WWF. However it's better to leave when you're on top, as the saying goes," Martel explains. "I loved the years I spent with the AWA, although it was difficult to work for Verne Gagne, who was far from being an easy boss."

RICK MARTEL WITH HIS GOOD FRIEND RODDY PIPER
(RICK MARTEL COLLECTION)

He decided to return full time to Montreal. In addition to wrestling he became booker for International Wrestling, in which he had bought shares in 1983.

This part of his career was marked by an infamous feud with Steve Strong (Steve Disalvo in Calgary), a Martel creation. "I had to make do with the talent available. We were looking for a heel to work with me. After having seen his photos, we brought him in." But things don't always go the way they were planned. "We had a lot of success . . . But, after all this, when it came time to losing to me in a cage match in Chicoutimi, he refused. I was the booker and one of the owners, and he refused to lose — in spite of the fact that I created his character and had helped him to train and reach this position," Martel says with some bitterness. "Later he told me that he made a mistake. I told him that it was such a pity that he had to kill a town in order for him to understand that. 'After all I've done for you, couldn't you just

RICK MARTEL AND RIC FLAIR, AWA AND NWA CHAMPIONS RESPECTIVELY, IN JAPAN

(RICK MARTEL COLLECTION)

have trusted me?'" When Strong got a WWF tryout at the Montreal Forum, it was no surprise that Martel didn't put in a good word.

By the beginning of 1986 the world economy and the U.S. exchange rate, as well as the constant pressure exerted by the WWF, made it clear that International Wrestling wouldn't survive for long. A decision was fast approaching. "I secretly went to see Vince . . . and I proposed forming a team with Tom Zenk under the name Can-Am Connection. He told me: 'Rick, you have the magic wand, I trust you.'" The Cam-Am Connection took off like a rocket. American magazines even compared them to the Rock 'n' Roll Express, then the most popular team in the United States, mainly among women. The pressure, the travelling and the success quickly changed the attitude of Zenk, a young man who had wrestled for almost nothing in Oregon just a year earlier. Nothing seemed good enough for him; even

Martel lost patience. "I told him the problem wasn't Vince or the others, it was him!" Philosophically, today, Martel wonders whether he wasn't to blame for the tension with Zenk. "Ever since I had been fired by Jim Barnett, I decided not to discuss money matters with other wrestlers . . . I did the same thing with Tom, and he put it in his head, or some other people put it in his head, that I made more than him. But as far as Vince was concerned, if you were in a tag team, you earned the same amount of money."

Ultimately, in the middle of a feud with The Islanders (Haku and Tama), Zenk packed up and headed for home, leaving Martel a simple note of thanks. WWF officials attempted to change his mind, in vain. At the same time Tito Santana was about to retire and headed on a path toward a career in commentary for Spanish TV, beside Petro Morales. Instead he was chosen to replace Zenk and would ultimately step in to "save" Martel, left to defend himself against The Islanders, who, in turn, had "injured" his Can-Am Connection partner. The new team relaunched Santana's career. "We enjoyed chemistry together and were very good, so the fans backed us from the start," Santana says in his autobiography. The new team became known as Strike Force, but for a while it seemed they would have another moniker: Vince McMahon wanted them to be called Border Patrol. With so many Mexicans dying of heat exhaustion while trying to cross the border at the time, Santana talked him into changing the name, so he wouldn't be heel south of the U.S.

Strike Force won the tag team titles against the Hart Foundation on October 27, 1987. After much success the team finally gave up the belts against Demolition at *WrestleMania IV*. Martel would take the remainder of 1988 off to stand by his wife Johanne's side and help her overcome an illness. "If Rick didn't have to leave for personal reasons, Vince wouldn't have split the team," Tito Santana says, nostalgically. In 1989 Rick Martel returned to wrestling with an idea: resuming his career as a heel. "I have always wanted to be a heel, but Vince laughed at the idea. I told him that I was giving him my notice. Two weeks later Vince called me to tell me that the WWF didn't need Rick Martel, and Rick Martel didn't need the WWF, either, so why not reach an understanding." After having abandoned Santana in a match at *WrestleMania V*, he finally turned. "Many of the ideas for characters were formulated when Vince, Pat and I were sitting by the pool. Rick is a polished worker, but how can we give him more substance? He looks like a male model. That was one of those moments when, at the instant the comment was made, we each all knew that it would work," J.J. Dillon relates in his book.

Rick Martel was hesitant at first, but inspiration would finally fire his imagination. "The perfume called Arrogance and the vignettes were all my ideas, and I had 'carte blanche' to do anything I wanted." The character was a success, and there was a natural feud with Santana to explore. Slick would join him as a manager and help put emphasis on The Model's character.

After suffering an injury in June 1990, Martel came back in October of that year and embarked on a rivalry that culminated in *WrestleMania VII*'s "blindfold match" against one of the biggest stars of the time, Jake "The Snake" Roberts. Shortly after this Martel left the WWF, again, this time to take care of his own interests. "It was because of Stan Stasiak," he explains. "When I saw such a great champion finishing his career in Oregon as a referee, it was then that I decided not to go through what he went through. I was resolved to prepare my life after wrestling."

He returned to wrestling at the end of 1991. "In 1992 it wasn't 100 percent Rick Martel anymore. The best part of my career was between 1978 and 1991." But he was very much in demand because of his experience. During SummerSlam 1992 Martel and the brand new heel Shawn Michaels wrestled for the affection of Sensational Sherri Martel. "Shawn asked me whether he could travel with me because he wanted to understand the psychology of the heel in order for him to improve his character."

Michaels confirms what Martel says in his biography. "My encounter with Rick Martel at SummerSlam turned out to be a small but important step up the card." During the rest of 1992, as well as in 1993 and 1994, Martel would commute between the WWF and the independent circuit. It was actually during one of these tours on the independent scene that he met Don Callis, a meeting that would play a key role in his last run in 1997. "The professional in me was demanding that I finish my career the right way," Martel recalls. "I was 42 and I needed a young wrestler to team with. I had the idea of coming back and creating the Super Models team with Don Callis because he had the mic skills, while my strength had always been the work I did in the ring. The story was planned as follows: Don was to end up betraying me, and I would subsequently become the favourite of the crowd once again. At the end of the story, I would be able to leave with the sentiment of a job well done."

Vince McMahon loved the idea, and they agreed upon a one-year contract. "I hadn't wrestled for two years, so we got booked with Emile Dupree's Maritimes tour. Each night we worked with Adam Impact and Christian Cage, better known under the name Edge and Christian," Martel remembers. "Nights in, nights out, we put in at least 30 minutes. Some night we went close to an hour. That was Rick Martel's work ethic. He wanted to get in ring shape for his final run," Edge says in his autobiography.

When the WWF's contract finally came it was for just three months, instead of a year. Their justification was that the young Callis wasn't a safe bet. For the WWF, memories of Tom Zenk might have lingered. Being a good businessman, Martel called Eric Bischoff, the man in charge of WCW. "I negotiated with him the biggest contract of my career." Bischoff wanted Martel in singles action and offered just a basic contract to Callis. Callis finally signed the same type of contract with the WWF. In January 1998 Rick Martel returned to wrestling for one last run. One month later he would become the WCW TV champion, defeating Booker T. Unfortunately injuries interfered with Martel's plans. "I appreciated my last year. I had a lot of fun, but after three injuries in six months, it was high time for me to leave," he says.

WCW tried to change his mind, but this time he was dead set on retiring. He would finish out the year as a French commentator for WCW with Marc Blondin and Michel Letourneur. Today Martel attends the Legends Convention and occasional shows where he's being honoured. In an interview with the British tabloid The Sun, he says that WWE has twice offered him an agent's position. "I thought about it for a few minutes, and said, 'No.' I have a young daughter and couldn't go back on the road."

After a 25-year career Rick Martel is deservedly ranked among the best wrestlers in the history of the Montreal territory (see ranking on page 401). "Third . . . it's such an honour. I immediately thought of my brother Michel, who sacrificed so much to fund my dreams. I said to myself that he would be proud of me mainly as I respect the wrestlers on this list a lot. They have all left their mark on wrestling on the Montreal territory." Inducted into the Quebec Wrestling Hall of Fame in 2004, Martel's career and the way he behaved outside of the ring make him an example to be emulated by wrestlers today, and he couldn't have left a better legacy for his sport. Let's give the last word to Guy Hauray, one of the craftsmen behind the return of wrestling on TV in the 1980s in Quebec: "Rick Martel: a gentleman, a nice person with whom one could have a serious business discussion, a man who respected his commitments."

DINO BRAVO, THE BABYFACE OF ALL BABYFACES

"If you just consider the number of spectators he drew in the '80s, Dino Bravo must be ranked among the best draws in the history of Montreal. The guys in the preliminaries used to make $300 or $400 per night when he was on the card," Gino Brito explains. In fact Bravo ranks fifth of all time behind Robert, Kowalski, Hogan and Carpentier. On October 14, 1985, he teamed with King Tonga against Brutus Beefcake and Greg Valentine, and their match drew 18,997. Two years earlier his match against Masked Superstar, on July 25, 1983, drew 18,394. These are just a few examples of his box office prowess in Montreal.

At the height of his success, and considering the strong relationship between the WWF and International Wrestling, Bravo longed for a WWF championship match. "My dream would be to obtain a WWF world championship match against Hulk Hogan at the Olympic Stadium. Whether I win or I lose, I could at least say that I got my chance," Bravo explained to Jean-Paul Sarault of Le Journal de Montréal in 1985. In Sunny War Cloud's opinion it would have worked: "His objective was to beat Hulk Hogan at the Olympic Stadium. I'm sure he would've packed the Big O." A record-breaking crowd would have consolidated Bravo's place in Montreal history, but Bravo's dream match wouldn't take place until four years later, at the Forum, in front of a respectable crowd of 17,340. "The most goose bumps I have ever had in my career were when I refereed the match between Hulk and Dino at the Forum. The energy exuded by the crowd was just incredible," Nelson Veilleux remembers. Unfortunately the house show match was not part of the WWF's general programming. It was based on the fact that Bravo "injured" Hogan at an earlier Forum show and had forced him to leave the ring on a stretcher. In 1985, with Bravo seen as a demi-god in the territory and Hogan at his peak, the possibilities would've been mind-boggling.

Dino Bravo became interested in wrestling at a young age and had the right contacts. "I knew him when he was three," Gino Brito says. "I used to live at 7755 Bordeaux, and Dino lived at 7745 Bordeaux. One day Dino came to see me because he trained a lot and asked me to help him become a wrestler." When Dino Bravo spoke about this period, his passion was obvious: "I started practising amateur wrestling at the age of 12 or 13 and I trained a lot because deep inside I knew that one day I'd practise this sport," he told Revue Lutte in 1983.

He was born Adolfo Bresciano on August 6, 1948. Promoters wanted something easier for the fans to remember. One of the wrestlers from Jack Britton's Detroit territory was called Dino Bravo — it was his real name. The original Bravo had teamed with Dominic Denucci, who worked with him as Dominic Bravo. Denucci ironically would also team with Bresciano a couple of years later.

It was Gino Brito who asked his father to contact the original Bravo. "Jack Britton asked me, and I said, 'Yeah, go ahead.' I knew I was out of it," the original Dino Bravo said during an interview with Greg Oliver of SLAM! Wrestling. Brito was pleased: "I told myself Gino Brito, Dino Bravo; it's gonna work. Jacques Rougeau Sr. told me then that it was good idea. All this took place in 1971." The fact is that Brito wanted to become Bravo's tag partner. "When I decided to debut him I put myself in tag team with him in order to help him make a name for himself," Brito explains. The Italian Connection was born.

In the early '70s there weren't many opportunities for wrestlers in Montreal. All Star Wrestling presented, at most, five or six matches per card, which left little room for a young talent. Bravo, however, benefited from the creation of Grand Prix. "I told Johnny Rougeau that I would rather send Dino to Grand Prix," Brito remembers. "I asked my father to tell Lucien Grégoire that I had a guy for him at the new office. He was hired the next morning. I then told Dino that I was going to join him in six months to a year. During that time he became a top guy with Grand Prix."

The friends became tag champions with Grand Prix and enjoyed great success there, but the Grand Prix venture would come to an end in 1974, and Dino Bravo would have to continue his career abroad. "In 1973 the match that really opened doors for me was my first major defeat against Kowalski. After the match he came to the locker room to tell me: 'Kid, you're gonna go far, 'cause you're aggressive,'" Bravo told Revue Lutte. In 1974 he went

(LINDA BOUCHER)

DINO BRAVO WAS THE LAST MAJOR LOCAL CHAMPION IN MONTREAL

to Europe but had little success, at first. At the end of the same year he worked for the WWA, a territory based in Los Angeles, for promoter Mike LeBell. He would finally make it outside Montreal, enjoying a good run partnered with Victor Rivera and winning the tag belts. "The breakthrough was really difficult to reach. However, the sun started shining once I won the tag team championship," Bravo explained to *Livre de la Lutte*. Later he would team with Édouard Carpentier for the same promotion.

The year 1975 marked his return to Canada, and he worked for Toronto's Maple Leaf Wrestling. He would also work for Championship Wrestling in Florida, where he wrestled against Frank Goodish — before he became world famous under the name Bruiser Brody. In 1976 he was able to get himself noticed in one of the most important territories, Jim Barnett's Mid-Atlantic, when he won the tag titles with Tim Woods against Ole and Gene Anderson. He made the acquaintance of Masked Superstar there, and this would lead him to Montreal in the early 1980s.

In 1977 he earned NWA championship matches against Harley Race and performed well. In 1978 he moved to New York to work for Vince McMahon Sr. and won the tag team titles with Dominic Denucci against Toru Tanaka and Mr. Fuji. During this period he successfully wrestled other Quebecers abroad, including Stan Stasiak and his former boss with Grand Prix, Paul Vachon. He also teamed with Andre the Giant a few times, a formula that would be replicated in the days of Varoussac. American wrestling magazines spoke of him as a possible successor to the great Italian champion Bruno Sammartino. In 1979 he returned to the Atlanta territory and this, ironically, brought him closer to home because of its ties with Toronto. He went on to beat Greg Valentine for the Canadian NWA championship in a tournament, and the belt was presented to him by "Whipper" Billy Watson. At the end of the year he won the title a second time and feuded with Ken Patera. He finally made the jump to Verne Gagne's AWA and would become a contender for the world championship title after he scored a surprise victory against Nick Bockwinkel.

In 1980 he formed a new tag team with another of his Grand Prix bosses, Maurice Vachon. He also began a big feud with the mammoth "Crusher" Jerry Blackwell, and for a while Dino was recognized as the AWA Canadian champion. He worked full time for Gagne until 1981, when he came back to Montreal to win the International title from Michel Dubois. "Bravo was very muscular and strong, but he was also agile and quick," Dubois remembers. "The U.S. experience was very enriching; however, I know that I can have similar experiences in the province of Quebec," Bravo told Livre de la Lutte on his return to Montreal. In 1982 a unique opportunity presented itself, and Bravo went on an Asian tour for Antonio Inoki's New Japan, where he wrestled against Hulk Hogan for the first time and also teamed with him. He also had a bloody fight there with Abdullah the Butcher that would boost their rivalry in Montreal. "And that was such a match. When there're people who support you, when the bleachers are packed, wrestlers always make an extra effort," Bravo told the Livre de la Lutte. That match is definitive, according to many fans of this generation, and the tape is still very much in demand by collectors.

In 1982 Bravo and Rick Martel also teamed for the AWA. The irony, of course, was that they wrestled together in the AWA when they feuded in Montreal! "Dino was like a brother to me," Martel says. On April 8, 1985, their match against the Road Warriors drew 15,016 people at the Forum. "Bravo and Martel were, in fact, the Mega Powers of the Montreal territory," says François Poirier, referring to the infamous Hulk Hogan and Randy Savage tag team.

In order to guarantee Bravo's long-term commitment to Montreal, Gino Brito sold him shares in the Varoussac at the end of 1982, a tactic commonly used by promoters looking to keep their top stars happy. From 1983 to 1986, in Sunny War Cloud's eyes, Bravo reached a legendary status: "Dino Bravo . . . was a giant in the wrestling world, as much as Yvon Robert in his days." He was a four-time International champion and his presence on a card often determined whether there would be a full house. In addition to programs against King Tonga and Masked Superstar, his wrestling highlights included feuds with "Big" John Studd, Billy Robinson, Sailor White, Gilles Poisson, Rick Valentine, Zarinoff LeBoeuf and Rick Martel. He was, in short, the icon of Montreal.

In 1985 the WWF played off this popularity and recognized his International championship as its Canadian championship — he participated in shows across Canada for the WWF through Maple Leaf Wrestling. In the end, over a period of 10 years, he was recognized by the three major associations in the United States as their Canadian champion. At the time when Martel, Flair and Hogan held the three world championship titles, Dino Bravo was one of the few men in the world who could claim victories over each. Varoussac had a new belt made for him and it was considered among the most beautiful in all wrestling. By the end of 1986 he finally sold his shares in International Wrestling and left Montreal to join the WWF as a full-time performer. "In 1985 he was very ambitious and thought he would be able to work on an equal footing with Vince in Montreal," Guy Hauray explains. When this became unworkable, the hero of the Montreal territory took fans by surprise and turned heel before leaving for the WWF.

Bravo would replace Brutus Beefcake in the Dream Team, partnering with Greg Valentine and with Johnny V as their manager. In order to make sure there was no ambiguity for Montreal fans, he savagely attacked the Rougeaus at the Forum. In spite of everything, one could feel that this turn of events wasn't really his first choice. "I don't always understand people. However, I've never insulted Quebecers. But when you're on the heel side, these things are to be expected. But this will change when I become world champion," he told the *Journal de la Lutte* newspaper in response to being booed. He and Valentine enjoyed a good feud with Jacques and Raymond Rougeau, and they would even main-event the big show presented at the Palais des Sports in Bercy, France, very much like Johnny Rougeau and Yvon Robert had before them.

Some fans remember Bravo for a feat of strength: bench-pressing "710 pounds" (as the weight was represented) during the very first WWF Royal Rumble in 1988. He set this record with the help of Jesse Ventura, future governor of Minnesota. Obviously it was all part of a storyline. But if lifting 710 was fiction, Bravo's real brute strength wasn't. "According to several wrestlers, during that time period, which was the height of the WWF's emphasis on the monsters, Bravo, even though he was already 39, was one of the two strongest (along with Warlord) when it came to bench-pressing and, realistically, could max out in the 550-575 range," Dave Meltzer reported in 1993. It was no surprise that Bravo earned the nickname the Canadian Strongman.

By 1988 he had returned to singles competition and he would go on to participate in each of the *WrestleManias* presented during the time he wrestled for the WWF, even though he never regained the status he had in Montreal. Over the years he battled against Don Muraco, Ronnie Garvin, Jim Duggan, Hercules and Kerry Von Erich, but one of the highlights of his run was being involved in the tournament to crown a new WWF champion at *WrestleMania IV*. To help him transition from tag team action he was assigned Frenchy Martin as a manager. "I wrestled a little bit and then they made me Dino Bravo's manager . . . he needed something extra," Frenchy Martin says. In 1990 Martin's health problems forced him to retire, and Jimmy Hart became Bravo's manager. Soon Bravo was involved in one of the most important programs of his WWF career: introducing a former sumo wrestler from Vancouver, John Tenta, as Earthquake. In order to help establish his new partner, Bravo and Earthquake battled Hulk Hogan, either in singles matches or facing Hogan and Tugboat as a team.

In 1991, after *WrestleMania VII*, Bravo began commuting between the WWF and the WWC in Puerto Rico, wrestling primarily against TNT (who would become Savio Vega), as well as the territory's promoter, the legendary Carlos Colón. The WWF prepared a local scenario that would allow Dino to bow out in a Forum farewell match in the role of the hero —but destiny decided otherwise. His last match at the Forum took place on January 20, 1992, with a victory over The Barbarian. For reasons still unknown today, the farewell night never took place.

Three months later he would put an end to his career once and for all after a short tour in Europe, where he wrestled against Jim Duggan, Bret Hart and Tito Santana. "He confided in me during our last European tour," Rick Martel says. "'I got offers to do business that I don't want to do,' he told me. I even called Pat Patterson to try to keep him in the WWF. I told him we could team together. Dino would be the strong man and I would take the bumps." Unfortunately it never happened.

On March 10, 1993, less than a year after his last match, Dino Bravo was assassinated inside his home in Laval. He was 44. "I will be happy as long as I can wrestle; after that, I don't know," Bravo told *Revue Lutte* in 1983.

"At about 240 pounds, Bravo combined the tag team flying manoeuvres that young babyfaces were expected to use in the '70s, but was also known for his impressive strength and was pushed as being able to bench-press in excess of 500 pounds, which was an incredible figure during that time period," Dave Meltzer argues. "Bravo worked well and worked hard," adds Leo Burke, who knew Bravo in Montreal. Former manager Oliver Humperdink says, simply, "He had it. He had the X factor."

After professional wrestling in Montreal hit its lowest point in years, Bravo, Martel and a new generation of Rougeaus restored its glory — they were the core of what is today simply known as International Wrestling.

FROM VAROUSSAC TO *WRESTLEMANIA III*
THE RISE AND FALL OF
INTERNATIONAL WRESTLING

On March 29, 1987, the WWF presented *WrestleMania* III at the Pontiac Silverdome in Michigan. At the same time International Wrestling was agonizing over the idea of closing its doors. Almost all of the men most responsible for making the seven previous years a glorious period for wrestling in Montreal were on the WWF roster. Clearly Montreal is one of the territories that suffered the most from the expansion of the WWF. The Rougeau brothers, Dino Bravo, Rick Martel, Tom Zenk, Little Beaver, Frenchy Martin, Pat Patterson, Édouard Carpentier, Guy Hauray and Jean Ferré had all been part of Montreal wrestling in one way or another. *WrestleMania* III's main event, Andre the Giant versus Hulk Hogan, had played to 7,283 fans at the Paul-Sauvé Arena on August 25, 1980 — the first full house in the history of the new Montreal wrestling company, when it was still known as Varoussac Promotions. The most important name missing from the list of men who went to the WWF is Gino Brito, the promoter of International Wrestling, and one of its stars until the very end. Andre the Giant asked Brito to attend his *WrestleMania* rematch with Hogan. "He was a friend. He offered to pay for me to go to *WrestleMania* III, but I didn't want to see Vince. It would not have been good for me," remembers Brito.

In 1980, when Gino Brito launched his career as a promoter, the future seemed bright. His father, Jack Britton, took the promoter's licence from Bob Langevin in 1977, a black chapter in the history of local wrestling, as it was following the successes and difficulties associated with the rivalry between All Star Wrestling and Grand Prix Wrestling. From 1977 until the early 1980s, Britton was the principal promoter in town, organizing shows at the Paul-Sauvé Arena and occasionally at the Verdun Auditorium. These

MITSUO YOSHIDA

RIKI CHOSHU GOT SOME EXPERIENCE IN MONTREAL AS MITSUO YOSHIDA (PAUL LEDUC COLLECTION)

had been Montreal's primary venues since the 1970s — only the Forum was more popular or prestigious, but it was inaccessible without a television presence. Even with a good mix of well-known wrestlers and youngsters like Randy "Dandy" Savage, Eddie Farhat Jr. (son of The Sheik), Bepo Mongol (Nikolai Volkoff), Abdullah the Butcher, The Sheik, Khosrow Vaziri (The Iron Sheik), Grizzly Adams and Matsuo Yoshida (Riki Choshu), the crowds and gate were small. Even Raymond Rougeau and the Vachon brothers couldn't turn things around. "The fullest house that my father had in those years was for the match opposing Pat Patterson to Lou Albano on February 11, 1980 — the match drew 2,000 people. Burlington TV was broadcasting in Montreal, and that's why they drew such a big crowd. They more than doubled their usual gate," remembers Gino Brito. At the time Patterson and Albano were with the WWF. The success of the card was sadly ironic. "My father died on the eve of the show, on February 10. So he didn't even get to see the fullest house he drew," explains his son.

The death of Brito's father spurred change. "I went to New York to find someone ready to invest in a promotion with me," remembers Brito. "I learned from my father's mistakes. My father tried to do this on his own. Vince McMahon Sr. advised me to approach Frank Valois." Jean Ferré, whose career was managed by Valois at the time, also took part in the adventure. "The name Varoussac is derived from our names," explains Brito. "Va (Valois) rouss (Roussimoff) ac (Acocella)." This acronym was to reinvigorate wrestling in the province under the banner Superstars of Wrestling. To set the record straight with the wrestling magazines of that era, Varoussac was not part of the IWA and would never affiliate itself with the WWF, NWA or AWA.

Their first year was spectacular, thanks to the match between Hogan and Ferré and the acquisition of a TV contract. Hulk Hogan was still a heel at the time, and in order to attract a crowd that would break records Varoussac used a simple but efficient formula: Hogan destroyed everything in his way. After the international champion, Édouard Carpentier, had been defeated twice in non-title matches (the second time he lost in only 30 seconds) another French wrestler, his nephew Jackie Wiecz, lost a match quickly as well. The newspapers announced that Hogan wanted the other Frenchman, Jean Ferré, or a championship match against Carpentier. Even Gino Brito lost to Hogan — his sole objective was to fill Paul-Sauvé by pitting the Giant against Hogan. To top everything off, the American wrestling broadcasts beamed into Quebec advertised the first major match between Hogan and Ferré on August 9, 1980, at Shea Stadium in New York. The *Showdown at Shea* was presented to a crowd of 36,295 and also featured a number of matches involving other Quebec wrestlers, including "The Hangman" Neil Guay, Rene Goulet and Pat Patterson. This match between Hogan and Ferré was eventually willfully forgotten by both history and the promotion behind the match. In fact what made the events of *WrestleMania III* even more appealing to fans in '87 was the fact that the WWF didn't hesitate to say that Hogan and Ferré had never fought before, and that Hogan was reticent about wrestling André because he considered it like facing his own brother. Reality, however, was that this match took place many times in the late 1970s and in the early 1980s. On August 25, 1980, when Varoussac presented the historic revenge match, the future was full of hope.

It was Guy Hauray, an acquaintance of Édouard Carpentier, who managed to get a television deal with Télé 7 and its associated stations. Varoussac launched throughout the province. Before getting this contract the promotion used to rely only on the New York stars and the Quebec wrestlers available. Montreal fans knew the wrestlers, thanks to the WWF wrestling program that could be followed on ABC station 22. Gino Brito, who had to pay a percentage to the New York office although he paid for the talent, invited the fans to follow this program in the advertisements he placed in newspapers. On Sunday, December 7, 1980, these advertisements invited people to follow

Télé 7 the following Sunday (December 14), instead, as wrestling made a return to Quebec's airwaves. Thanks to this program, Varoussac was always at the vanguard when it came to making use of talents from other territories, and over the years many wrestlers came to get experience in Montreal.

In 1981 Varoussac continued to use WWF stars, but the promotion also invited wrestlers to come from other territories. The Destroyer, the masked wrestler whose real name is Dick Beyer, came back to Montreal (he had appeared for Grand Prix). Beyer, also known as Dr. X when he was with the AWA, was a superstar in Japan. "I am the only human being on the planet who can go to and come back from Japan with a mask on his head," explained Beyer to the magazine Lutte Professionelle au Québec in 1982. At the beginning of the year he was feuding with Maurice Vachon, but the latter got involved in a bigger feud, the battle of the Mad Dogs with Pierre Lefebvre. Michel "Justice" Dubois returned home and became the International champion. Dubois, being heel, was in charge of putting over the biggest star of the company, namely Dino Bravo. In fact Bravo came back home after making a name for himself in the United States and became the International champion. From that moment the belt became an inseparable part of him. "Dino defeated all creatures that walked on two legs," remembers Rick Martel, laughing.

"Quickdraw" Rick McGraw, a talented wrestler who is now largely forgotten, was equally part of the roster and was even an International tag team champion with Gino Brito. He also wrestled alongside Andre the Giant later with the WWF. Unfortunately his short stature limited his success. Today he's remembered mainly because he was the first wrestler to die at a very young age due to a heart attack caused by the abuse of steroids and other drugs. The year ended with the annual Christmas show on December 28, 1981, at the Paul-Sauvé Arena. The principal arena of the promotion was full. Eight thousand watched Ferré, who only wrestled big shows, perform in the main event against "Big" John Studd. As for Dino Bravo, he wrestled Abdullah the Butcher. "The kids convinced me at the last minute to go. But, much to our surprise, once we got to the arena we were told that the show was sold out," remembers Gerald Hébert, a former NCW announcer.

In 1982 WWF wrestlers continued to appear in Montreal, including Greg Valentine, "Big" John Studd and Bob Backlund. The latter came to defend the WWF title against Raymond Rougeau and The Destroyer at the beginning of the year and against Billy Robinson near the end of it. Robinson was presented as the British Empire champion, a title recognized by the AWA at the time — and he came to the ring with his manager, Lord Alfred Hayes. The latter would become a commentator and work behind the scenes in the WWF a couple of years later. Robinson stayed in Montreal for some time and had great battles with Dino Bravo. "Look at Billy Robinson! He's the most exquisite wrestling machine that I have ever had to wrestle," explained Bravo to the magazine *Lutte Professionnelle au Quebec*. Robinson is a wrestler who was trained in the famous Snake Pit of Billy Riley in Wigam, Britain, a wrestling school that looked more like a concentration camp than a school. Years later Robinson became the trainer of the Japanese wrestlers who launched the shoot style in the UWF. This led him to train MMA participants like Kazushi Sakubara and Josh Barnett.

On April 5, 1982, the fans were treated to a match between Hulk Hogan and Bravo. The week after a return match opposed Hogan and Ferré. During the same show there was also a match between Dino Bravo and Stan Hansen. Raymond Rougeau and Pat Patterson won the tag team championship for the second time, but this time Patterson turned heel in spite of the fact that they were still champions. This compelled the champions to find each a partner on Frank Valois's order, and the winning team would be the new champions. Patterson chose Pierre Lefebvre, and they became one of the best teams in the history of the territory, while Raymond chose Billy "Cool Cat" Jackson for lack of a better choice. Raymond and his partner lost, creating a storyline where Raymond was looking for the right partner to get his revenge on Pat Patterson. Their feud would spread over two years. "Those were some of the best years of my career!" says Rougeau when talking about his feud with the wrestler who claimed to be the Dream of Quebec. At the beginning of the year a young Mike Rotunda made his Montreal debut. He graduated from the University of Syracuse in New York and chose The Destroyer as his mentor. "I called Frank Valois . . . I told Mike to meet me at exit 36 of the New York Thruway and to bring enough clothes for a week," Dick Beyer says. Still known today as Irwin R. Schyster, the name he adopted a couple of years later in the WWF, Rotunda would wrestle in the preliminaries in Montreal and acquire considerable experience under the Destroyer's tutelage.

On July 26, 1982, about 14,000 spectators filled the Forum to witness

ALOFA, BEFORE HE WAS RIKISHI, AS INTERNATIONAL
WRESTLING'S TELEVISION CHAMPION (LINDA BOUCHER)

the return of wrestling to the hockey temple. That night Jean Ferré wrestled in the main event against Stan Hansen, and Dino Bravo wrestled Abdullah the Butcher — with Yvon Robert Jr. as the referee. This match stirred a lot of controversy, and the title would be suspended. Robinson would win the title after winning a tournament final against Rick Martel later in the year. "The decision to organize a show at the Forum was easy. On six occasions we had a full house at Paul-Sauvé. I was sure that I would attract a big crowd. Unfortunately the managers of the Forum didn't hire enough employees at the ticket windows. About 2,000 people had to be turned away," Frank Valois told *Le Journal de Montréal*. Things were going well as Varoussac toured the territory, presenting its shows around the province. "When you are well organized and your matches are well balanced the fans trust you. I would add that our wrestlers can even fight with the wrestlers of the golden period of wrestling in Montreal," Valois said in the same interview.

At the end of 1982 Jean Ferré sold his shares to Gino Brito. Brito offered his shares to convince Dino Bravo to be available full time for Varoussac. According to Brito, Pat Patterson was also interested in buying in, but one can see that the friendship between Brito and Bravo played in Bravo's favour. If one analyzes the situation closely, it was certainly the best choice to make, given the fact that, some years later, Patterson would become the right-hand man of Vince McMahon.

In 1983 everything seemed to work for the group. They even launched a wrestling school in February called the Brito and Bravo Wrestling School, with Édouard Carpentier as the trainer. "There are very few Francophone stars. Dino and I are doing our best to amend this situation. If we can manage to develop only one wrestler like Rick Martel, the experience will be worth it," explained Gino Brito to Le Journal de Montréal back in '83. Unfortunately the school produced only two wrestlers who would enjoy real success — and even that was after the company had closed down — Nelson Veilleux, who was Pierre-Carl Ouellet's partner in Europe, and Luc Poirier.

Aside from his work for the WWF as a jobber, Nelson Veilleux had some success when teamed with Pierre-Carl Ouellet in Europe. They wrestled under the name Double Trouble. In the early 1990s they worked regularly in Europe and South Africa. While Veilleux came back to Quebec to nurse an injury, Ouellet went as scheduled to Puerto Rico, where he first met Jacques Rougeau. After that Veilleux continued to wrestle on independent circuits until he retired in 2008.

In the ring fans had the opportunity to see the much-hyped feud between Ray Stevens and Jimmy Snuka. Stevens's savage attack on Snuka filmed for WWF was broadcast on Télé 7, and Frank Valois congratulated himself on air for having succeeded in bringing the confrontation to Montreal. Tony Parisi, Gino Brito's partner, also wrestled regularly in the territory. The Italian Connection was a crucial ingredient of the Varoussac machine and played an important role in fighting the stable led by "The Brain" Eddy Creatchman. In April 1983 Superstar, better known as Masked Superstar or Demolition Ax (Bill Eadie), made his first appearance. According to Gino Brito, Superstar was one of his biggest attractions. "Before the Garvins and the Rougeaus, our feud which attracted the biggest crowds was Superstar versus Bravo," remembers Brito. He never won the title against Bravo, but the intensity of the two men and the brutality of their wrestling always guaranteed a breathtaking spectacle. On July 25, at the Forum, 18,394 fans showed up for a double main event: Jean Ferré versus Blackjack Mulligan and Superstar versus Bravo.

Also in '83 Montreal fans were treated to an unprecedented grouping of the three Rougeau brothers in one wrestling match. Raymond, Jacques and Armand performed together for the very first time. Ken Patera, The Samoans, Nick Bockwinkel and Ivan Koloff also wrestled during the year. "Our ambition is to bring back the golden era of wrestling . . . when Eddie Quinn attracted the best wrestlers in the world. The crowds constantly filled the Forum and

JIMMY SNUKA, LORD ALFRED HAYES AND
INTERNATIONAL CHAMPION BILLY ROBINSON
(LINDA BOUCHER)

the Delorimier Stadium and wrestling rolled in money," explained Dino Bravo to *La Presse* in 1983. Varoussac brought back Hulk Hogan, but this time as a babyface because he'd just been featured as Thunderlips in *Rocky III*. He would team with Dino Bravo and Jean Ferré in the only wrestling show ever held at the Velodrome (now known as the Biodome).

The end of 1983 saw the first changes that had a negative impact on a promotion that had managed to extend its territory everywhere in Quebec and make incursions into New York and Vermont, as well as in Ontario and the Maritimes. The Paul-Sauvé Arena suddenly changed its policy concerning the maximum number of standing spectators, lowering the number to 1,000 from 2,000. Moreover the number of seats allowed at ringside decreased by 600 compared to the Forum, although the sizes of the rinks were the same. Varoussac was forced to refuse 2,000 potential spectators at its December 26 Christmas show, one of its biggest events of the year — and the last time Jean Ferré would wrestle for the promotion. Before leaving he tried to convince Brito, his friend, to join the WWF. "Vince wanted to get the territory. André came to see whether I would go to New York full time with him. 'Vince will find a spot for you,' he told me," says Brito, who was to remain faithful to his own promotion.

At the beginning of 1984 new partners joined the trio of Brito, Bravo and Valois. In fact Rick Martel and the promoter from Hull, Tony Mule, became shareholders. This change of ownership was followed by a name change. Varoussac morphed into International Wrestling that spring. "When Ferré officially left they wanted to get rid of the 'rouss' from the promotion's name," explains Françoise, Frank Valois's daughter, who worked for the office.

In addition to new owners, a new booker came to give Brito a hand with creative decision making. Near the end of 1983 Leo "The Lion" Burke, a member of the Cormier family in the Maritimes, came to Montreal. No stranger to the territory, he had briefly worked for Johnny Rougeau in 1969. He occupied the position of booker until the middle of 1985. "This is how we worked with Leo . . . We used to meet on Mondays, and I asked him to write the whole week . . . We would sit together for a couple of hours, and he would explain to me what he would like to do. I told him to change certain things or make do with them," reveals Brito. As for Burke, it's clear that Gino Brito was the boss during that period, but Dino Bravo was also involved in making decisions. In 2005, during WrestleReunion 2, the Great Samu made a statement that backed this up. "In Montreal, the decisions were made both by Gino and Dino."

LEO BURKE WRESTLED AND ALSO BOOKED THE MONTREAL TERRITORY (LINDA BOUCHER)

Says Burke: "I loved working in Montreal, and it's such a pity that young wrestlers are now deprived from such a place." Unlike many wrestler-bookers, fans would not have to get sick of seeing him in main events. Montreal had its star: Dino Bravo. Still Burke would be the first to give a chance to Richard Charland, who would turn heel against him after a Burke television victory. Charland would stand out in the role of the bad guy and became one of the most important talents on the International Wrestling roster.

Fans today know Burke as the trainer who helped refine many WWF wrestlers in the 1990s. "In Calgary I trained guys like Test, Edge, Christian, Mark Henry and Ken Shamrock," he explains. The year 1984 was a strong one, thanks to the rivalry between Bravo and Martel and in spite of the fact

DINO BRAVO VS RICK MARTEL, THEIR FIRST MATCH IN QUEBEC CITY

(LINDA BOUCHER)

that Martel joined the AWA. "I'd just settled down in Quebec City in 1984 when the AWA — Nick Bockwinkel, more precisely — suddenly called me to seriously discuss the belt with me," remembers Martel. This would allow for a symbiotic relationship between the AWA and International Wrestling to develop, permitting the Montreal territory to refresh its supply of foreign stars. "Verne Gagne and I, we exchanged talent," explains Brito. "This allowed me to vary my talent."

Bravo versus Martel stands out as definitive of the era. It was a rivalry between the two biggest stars of the territory, both at the provincial and international levels. The first of these three fights took place at the Colisée de Québec on September 21, 1983. This match was presented as a special attraction, as it was meant to be the only match opposing the two wrestlers. Moreover Édouard Carpentier was the referee; Verne Gagne, the AWA promoter, was in Martel's corner, and Gino Brito was in Bravo's. Portions of this match were aired on an International Wrestling TV program on Télé 7, but the end of the match was never shown. Fans were simply told that the finish was controversial. Carpentier apologized profusely, but TV viewers didn't know what really happened, aside from the fact that Bravo was still the champion. The end of the match was finally broadcast. Bravo won, and as he propelled himself to take the fall on his rival he landed on Martel while having both feet on the second rope. Carpentier didn't see any of this and counted the 1-2-3.

YOKOZUNA CAME TO MONTREAL EARLY IN HIS CAREER AS KOKINA (LINDA BOUCHER)

The animosity that this controversial ending created made both men defy each other, week after week. Bravo said that he didn't want to fight Martel anymore and that he didn't cheat — at least not consciously. He also commented on the chauvinism of the wrestling fans in Quebec City and of Stan Marshall, the promoter. As for Martel, he denounced the injustice of the outcome. The fans also remembered that he was robbed of the AWA title in a similar way by Nick Bockwinkel. He even brought a picture of the controversial ending to an interview. Such a photo finish proved that his "friend" cheated.

After many months of controversy, two return matches were announced. One of them was to be held at the Colisée de Québec and the other at the Forum. The match they had in September 1983 was broadcast twice on TV, and the two men spoke their minds to Carpentier. However each of them had his own logical way of interpreting their first contest. Even 25 years later this angle is still compelling, especially compared to today's storylines. At the time the NHL rivalry between the Montreal Canadiens and the Quebec Nordiques was at its peak, so it was logical for the promoter to attempt to take advantage of that natural animosity between Montreal and Quebec City.

The return match in Quebec City, on March 5, 1984, saw Martel trying to prove he had been robbed of his victory in the first encounter. This time Yvon Robert Jr. was the referee. The match also had a controversial ending, as Martel won by count out. The rubber match took place a week later at the Montreal Forum. Pat O'Connor, former NWA world champion, was to be the ref. Neither wrestler was to vanquish the other, as they were both counted out. "The tension we created due to our feud was so intense that when we made peace and wrestled as a tag team, the fans were so pleased since they believed we were stronger together," Martel says today.

This rivalry put aside, Frenchy Martin, who came in near the end of 1983, ruled the roost, and with Pierre "Mad Dog" Lefebvre as his partner they became tag team champions. In May 1984 Killer Kowalski returned to Montreal after a 10-year absence, first as a referee and then as Gino Brito's partner, wanting to exact revenge on Lefebvre and Martin.

Rocky Johnson, the father of The Rock, came to Montreal during this period, as well as AWA stars like Crusher Blackwell, Nick Bockwinkel, Ken Patera and Kevin Kelly. The latter would become Nailz in the WWF. Jumbo Tsuruta, the big star of All Japan and an AWA world champion, also came to Montreal. Ric Flair came in to defend the NWA championship against Gino Brito, Raymond Rougeau and Rick Martel. Brito and his group would have liked to have had him come more often, but because International Wrestling was not a member of the NWA, accessing dates with Flair was, to say the least, difficult. "My plan was to oppose Flair and Bravo in a main event at the Forum, but it was too complicated to bring Flair and build the program on TV," recalls Brito. "Valois, the promoter, invited the best international wrestlers to come wrestle in Quebec. This is why I wanted to come back to wrestle in Quebec," says Martel in a radio interview. What really happened, however, was that a former partner was actually behind the invitation of foreign wrestlers to Montreal. "Ferré helped us get some wrestlers from abroad. He had wrestled everywhere and knew all the promoters and wrestlers. Ferré and Verne Gagne helped us a lot in inviting foreign talents," explains Brito.

Leo Burke brought in Kerry Brown, a wrestler from Calgary. Brown used the name Rick Valentine, a gimmick he used in the Maritimes, calling himself the "brother" of Greg Valentine. He would team with Sailor White, and they had Tarzan Tyler as their manager. A staunch rivalry developed

A VERY GOOD HEEL FACTION: RICK VALENTINE, SAILOR WHITE AND TARZAN TYLER (LINDA BOUCHER)

between him and Dino Bravo. This feud would lead to a reconciliation between Bravo and Martel. After a vicious attack by "Valentine," who used a hanger as a weapon, Martel seemed to be in real mortal danger and about to lose consciousness. Seeing his rival in need, Dino Bravo came to his aid, even though they had not spoken since their last match. "I had seen Roddy Piper do something similar in Portland in 1980 and I thought that it could be a good idea," remembers Martel. "But the hanger left large spots on my neck and it really hurt, even days later," he adds.

After the first incursion of the WWF into the territory in June at the Verdun Auditorium — marking the return of Jacques Rougeau to Quebec — International Wrestling pulled out the stops by bringing Jacques back and putting the tag team belts on him and his brother Raymond. "Jacques performed in the first two WWF shows because he quarrelled with Dino Bravo," explains Sunny War Cloud. "I had seen him in Saguenay before the other WWF show in Verdun, and he told me to thank Pat Patterson for all he did, but that he decided to return with International."

On July 23 Jacques Sr. came out of retirement to team, for the very first time, with his three sons. The four of them wrestled together all across the territory that summer.

The summer of 1984 was also made special by the arrival of a wrestler who impressed every real fan of wrestling in the territory, King Tonga. In September the promotion added a second TV program, on Trois-Rivières channels 9 and 13, when it absorbed the time slot used by Denis Lauzon, a competing promoter. The situation, however, didn't last for long. In December Guy Hauray left International and turned over the Télé 7 airtime to the WWF. December had never been kind to the company: it always seemed to harbour some ill omen in the coming year.

The last big year for the promotion really was 1985. It was marked by the regular presence of the AWA world champion, Rick Martel, a feud between Bravo and Tonga that continued to draw the crowds and the arrival of Hawk and Animal, the Road Warriors — the new special attraction for the fans all over North America and Japan. Also dubbed The Legion of Doom, they headlined shows against all the top babyfaces of Montreal. "The Dog-Faced Gremlin" Rick Steiner made his debut with the promotion at the beginning of the year. Steiner wrestled principally as a team with Scott Duran. Although Duran looked a little like Rick's brother, Scott, they were definitely not the same person. Scott began his career in 1986 when Rick Steiner had already left Montreal. Rick and Scott Steiner went on to be one of the best tag teams in the world in the 1990s, with WCW, WWF and New Japan Pro Wrestling.

A logistical challenge had emerged for International Wrestling: "The Paul-Sauvé Arena has become too small for our international cards. We must now present six to eight programs at the Forum," Valois told *Le Journal de Montréal* in February 1985. The truth, however, was also that the Paul-Sauvé Arena was being renovated, and this is why many cards were held at the Verdun Auditorium that year.

Having lost his International title in the match that opposed him to Bravo, King Tonga became the latter's partner following a vicious end to his association with manager Tarzan Tyler. He then signed a "contract" with Yvon Robert Jr., who was to act as his "agent." Robert convinced Tonga to forge a team with Dino Bravo and fight the Road Warriors during the show held on June 24. This day, however, was better known for the match opposing the

THE ROAD WARRIORS AND "PRECIOUS" PAUL ELLERING, WHAT A RUSH IN MONTREAL! (LINDA BOUCHER)

Rougeaus and the Garvins and became known as the St-Jean-Baptiste Massacre. King Tonga was then replaced by Butch Reed in Tyler's stable. Coming from Missouri, Reed would team with Charland, but only stayed two months before going back to the Mid-South. Later he would join the WWF as The Natural and also the WCW, where he teamed with Ron Simmons (Farooq).

The Montreal territory was different from the other territories in North America. The business relationship between the Montreal office and the local media was so strong that International Wrestling was the only group able to force the WWF to present joint events during its national expansion.

On December 22 Rick Martel came back to Montreal for the Christmas show at a time when he was about to lose the AWA championship. As for the association with the WWF, Brito spoke his mind. "Some important developments may take place before the end of the year," he said to Jean-Paul Sarault. The end of the association with the WWF actually went unnoticed. Then, on December 24, 1985, Pierre Lefebvre, Tarzan Tyler and

Adrien Desbois died in a tragic car accident on their way back from a show in Chicoutimi. A year full of glories had been darkened.

The WWF was no longer interested in working with International Wrestling after holding one last big show in January 1986, showcasing Hulk Hogan. Because of this, Rick Martel's numerous connections made him the ideal booker for Gino Brito, Frank Valois, Tony Mule and Dino Bravo. But things soon became complicated. "I received a phone call from Gino Brito at midnight: 'The Rougeau brothers are joining the WWF!' The Rougeaus, Dino and I would've worked together. That is the way I saw things, and everyone would've had his share," explains Martel. Pat Patterson brings the WWF side of the story: "At that time Vince wanted Quebecers because our television was broadcast in Quebec in French. He told me to get the Rougeaus, Bravo, Martel . . . Afterwards, rumours started that I was bringing my friends and they would get a break because they were Quebecers. The boys didn't understand why we were doing this. We wanted to come in the territory and drew big crowds with the Quebec guys."

"Signing with the WWF means we will be coming back to the Forum once in a while. But, one thing is certain, once we sign the agreement we will certainly miss Montreal," declared Jacques Rougeau to La Presse. Resetting after the Rougeaus' last match at the Paul-Sauvé Arena on February 3 was difficult. "Frank Valois is not really happy about the departure of the Rougeaus. However we managed to survive at Paul-Sauvé in the past. We will do it again. We just have to work hard and unearth new prospects. Anyways, I don't see how we can deal with this otherwise," said Tony Mule to La Presse. Today Gino Brito notes that Raymond respectfully came to him in person to say their deal with International Wrestling would be coming to an end. "I wanted to be the one who announced the news to him. I also wanted to give him enough time to find other wrestlers to replace us," confirms Raymond. In order to replace the Rougeaus, a team was put together that consisted of Tom Zenk and Dan Kroffat (Phil Lafon). They were very successful and were to establish an interesting rivalry with the Long Riders (Scott and Bill Irwin). At the end of 1985 a new wrestler came in to attack Dino Bravo. This wrestler was no other than Sheik Ali, better known in the Maritimes under the name of "Big" Stephen Petitpas. He actually had wrestled under that name for Varoussac in 1980. Foreign wrestlers were always good heels; the success

YVON ROBERT

THE LION OF FRENCH CANADA WAS THE FIRST AND BIGGEST LOCAL SUPERSTAR

THE ROUGEAUS: RAYMOND, ARMAND, JACQUES SR., AND JACQUES JR., A WRESTLING DYNASTY

ANDRÉ ROY AND PAUL LEDUC WITH HOCKEY PLAYERS MIKE BOSSY AND BOB SAUVÉ AND THE STANLEY CUP

HULK HOGAN APPEARED IN MONTREAL IN THE EARLY '80S WITH A WHOLE DIFFERENT LOOK!

GIANT CAKE FOR A GIANT WRESTLER: FERRÉ WITH HIS FRIENDS VALOIS AND ROBERT JR.

DON EAGLE WAS ONE OF THE MOST POPULAR WRESTLERS IN THE U.S. WHEN TV ARRIVED

TARZAN TYLER WAS AS WELL KNOWN IN MONTREAL AS HE WAS IN THE FLORIDA TERRITORY

"MAD DOG" VACHON

FROM 1964 TO 1966, "MAD DOG" VACHON WAS THE AWA CHAMPION ON SIX DIFFERENT OCCASIONS

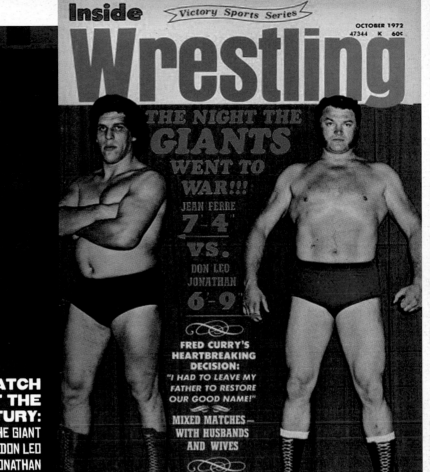

Inside

Victory Sports Series

OCTOBER 1972
47344   K   60¢

Wrestling

THE NIGHT THE GIANTS WENT TO WAR!!!

JEAN FERRE
7'-4"
VS.
DON LEO JONATHAN
6'-9"

FRED CURRY'S HEARTBREAKING DECISION:
"I HAD TO LEAVE MY FATHER TO RESTORE OUR GOOD NAME!"

MIXED MATCHES— WITH HUSBANDS AND WIVES

THE MATCH OF THE CENTURY:
ANDRE THE GIANT VERSUS DON LEO JONATHAN

JOHN CENA COULD CERTAINLY BE A POWER FORWARD FOR THE MONTREAL CANADIENS!

DINO BRAVO AS A BLEACHED BLOND HEEL IN THE WWF

MANY GENERATIONS OF MONTREAL WRESTLING: THE DESTROYER, PAUL VACHON, DON LEO JONATHAN, BRET HART AND MAURICE VACHON

MONTREAL EXPOS' ANDRE DAWSON AND MAURICE VACHON, TWO HALL OF FAMERS

ENEMIES IN THE WRESTLING BUSINESS, EDDY CREATCHMAN AND JOHNNY ROUGEAU WERE ACTUALLY GOOD FRIENDS

LUFISTO, THE CHAMPION FOR A NEW ERA, HOLDING THE NCW FEMMES FATALES TITLE

BESIDES WORKING FOR THE WWF, LUNA WAS ALSO A STAR IN JAPAN

VIVIAN VACHON MADE HER BROTHERS PROUD WITH HER CAREER

MARYSE, THE FIRST WWE DIVA COMING FROM THE PROVINCE OF QUEBEC

NWA WORLD CHAMPION RIC FLAIR VERSUS RAYMOND ROUGEAU AT THE FORUM IN 1984

EDDY CREATCHMAN WITH THE LOVELY MISS ELIZABETH BACKSTAGE IN MONTREAL

JOS LEDUC

AS HEEL OR BABYFACE, IN MONTREAL OR MEMPHIS, HE WAS OFTEN COVERED WITH BLOOD

MONTREAL HOSTED THE REMATCH BETWEEN HULK HOGAN AND ANDRE THE GIANT IN 1980

THE DESTROYER, BOB BACKLUND AND REFEREE ADRIEN DESBOIS BATTLE FOR THE WWF TITLE

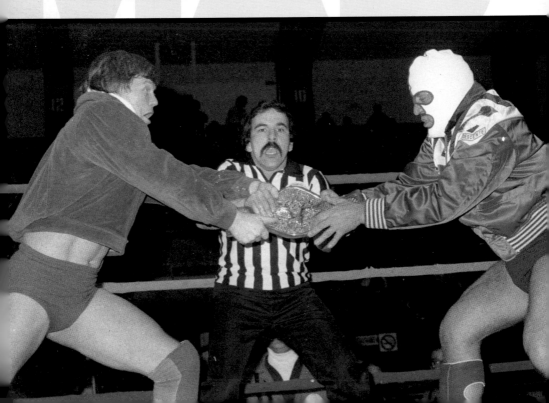

IN 1997, JACQUES ROUGEAU HEADLINED THE MOLSON CENTRE AGAINST "HOLLYWOOD" HULK HOGAN

FRIENDS BEFORE ENEMIES: PAT PATTERSON AND RAYMOND ROUGEAU

THE QUEBECERS, WORLD TAG TEAM CHAMPIONS, CENTER ICE AT THE JOE LOUIS ARENA IN DETROIT

KING TONGA WAS THE FIRST ONE TO DEFEAT DINO BRAVO FOR THE TITLE

RENÉ GOULET AND KARL GOTCH, WWWF WORLD TAG TEAM CHAMPIONS

PIERRE "MAD DOG" LEFEBVRE HAD A SHORT RUN IN 1980 AS THE INTERNATIONAL CHAMPION

ÉDOUARD CARPENTIER

ARRIVED IN MONTREAL IN 1956. HE WAS SUPPOSED TO STAY JUST A FEW WEEKS — HE NEVER LEFT.

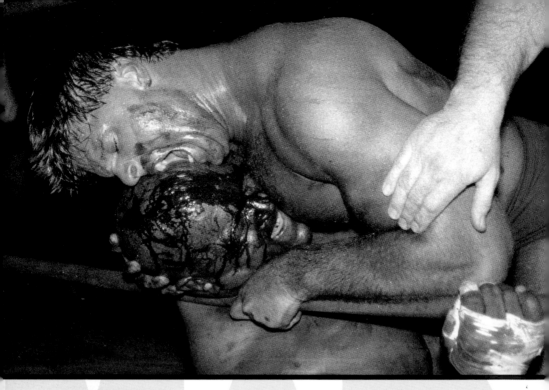

JACQUES ROUGEAU WENT TO WAR WITH ABDULLAH THE BUTCHER JUST LIKE HIS FAMILY BEFORE HIM

A BOXING MATCH LIKE NO OTHER IN MONTREAL BETWEEN RAYMOND ROUGEAU AND THE LATE OWEN HART

EL GENERICO AND KEVIN STEEN, ROH TAG TEAM CHAMPIONS

QUEBEC PREMIER RENÉ LÉVESQUE WITH HIS VERY GOOD FRIEND JOHNNY ROUGEAU AND PAUL LEDUC

RICK MARTEL & DINO BRAVO

RICK MARTEL, AWA WORLD CHAMPION, AND DINO BRAVO, INTERNATIONAL CHAMPION

THE ISLANDERS TONGA KID AND KING TONGA DEBUTED IN MONTREAL BEFORE GOING TO THE WWF

(LINDA BOUCHER)

of The Iron Sheik and Nikolai Volkoff in the WWF at the time was undeniable. A student of Emile Dupree, Petitpas had his debut with the Grand Prix promotion in the Maritimes, where he won the championship both in singles and in tag teams with partner Leo Burke. In 1985 he won the International tag team championship with Richard Charland, titles that were left vacant by the Rougeaus. The WWF took everyone by surprise in February, when it presented its first solo show at the Forum on a Monday night, the very day when International Wrestling usually held its matches at Paul-Sauvé Arena. International Wrestling was forced to cancel its card for a week.

International Wrestling had Kamala come in, but he wasn't that successful and quickly left. But in a year's time his match against Hulk Hogan at the Forum for the WWF would draw a crowd of no less than 19,000. The power of TV had become all the more evident. The program broadcast by International

A YOUNG LUDGER PROULX, THE LINK BETWEEN THE LAST GOLDEN AGE AND THE INDY ERA

(LINDA BOUCHER)

Wrestling was losing pace when compared to the program broadcast by the WWF. The latter was able to instantly create a wrestler who people wanted to pay to see. International Wrestling did its best to improve its presentation and respond to the demands of distributors by using a new logo created by a computer. "Stan Marshall and I went to a studio in order to create the logo," explains Martel. But the revenues that International Wrestling derived from TV were decreasing. The federation also invited Michael Hayes and Buddy Roberts, the Fabulous Freebirds, to come to Montreal during this period. Roberts was returning to the territory. The two men didn't stay long, and even someone like Sgt. Slaughter, a strong draw from his time with WWF, failed to change things for Brito and Valois's company. In April another major incident made things go from bad to worse. International Wrestling champion Dino Bravo had to have his appendix removed and miss many months of action. He and Rick Martel had been invited to participate in the first Crockett Cup, a tag team tournament presented by the NWA. They were scheduled to wrestle against Steve Williams and Terry Taylor in the first round, but because of Bravo's illness Martel had to forfeit for the team.

"I was so scared. The doctors blamed the pain tearing through my lower abdomen on stress. I wanted to keep this from them in order to be able to wrestle on April 28, but I only got out of the hospital on Saturday," confided Bravo to *La Presse*. Rick Martel chose Austin Idol as his new partner in Quebec, but no American wrestler really wanted to stay long enough to get the attention of the fans, given the low exchange rate on the Canadian dollar. Even the return match for the AWA title on June 9, opposing Rick

Martel and Stan Hansen, failed to fill the Paul-Sauvé Arena. On June 30 Dino Bravo lost the International title for the last time, when Gino Brito threw in the towel to end the match and concede the victory to the Great Samu, Bravo's rival, in order to spare Bravo permanent injury when he came back too soon from his operation.

While some wrestlers had come to Montreal to fill their pockets, others came to learn. This was the case for Toshiaki Kawada, a Japanese wrestler who, at the time, was only known by his first name. Kawada would later become one of the most important wrestlers for All Japan Pro Wrestling in the 1990s, along with Kenta Kobashi and Mitsuharu Misawa. He used to fly like a cruiserweight when he worked in Montreal. His style was totally different from the strong style that would bring him fame in Japan.

Then it was Frank Valois's turn to quit the promotion. "Some told my dad he was out of touch," says his daughter. His shares were bought by Brito, Bravo, Martel and Mule.

The Road Warriors came back a number of times, but aside from drawing a huge crowd in Quebec City, they were no longer the attraction they were two years earlier and even they couldn't help make things better for International Wrestling. Finally newspapers announced that Bravo, Martel and Tom Zenk were leaving International Wrestling to join the WWF. "A show took place at the Paul-Sauvé Arena on September 28. Martel was present but he was not wrestling. I went to ask him whether he was really going to join the WWF . . . When he said yes, I knew that the end of International Wrestling was fast approaching," remembers François Hébert. Dino Bravo wrestled his last match for International Wrestling on September 8, and Rick Martel bid farewell on September 22. Gino Brito bought their shares in the company. "When Dino came to see me and tell me that he was going with Vince, he was crying like a baby. But I told him to go. I also told him that I would send my own son, if Vince would take him," Brito says, philosophically.

Jos Leduc returned to International Wrestling at this point, after having been fired in December 1985, for refusing to lose to Raymond Rougeau. On October 13 International Wrestling presented Mad Dog Vachon's last match after a big retirement tour all over the Montreal territory. After this the glory days of International Wrestling seemed over. The Great Samu was done, and the International championship belt was passed on to "Dr. D" David Schultz. What made the promotion choose Schultz remains a mystery — his reputation was poor and he'd been dismissed from the WWF after having hit a journalist just a year earlier. "When you are desperate you try anything," says Brito. The title was declared vacant after a match opposing Schultz and Hercules Ayala, who came from Puerto Rico. Only 800 spectators were in attendance, even though it was the annual Christmas show. Brito, however, walked with his head held high. "I admit that International Wrestling is going through hard times. But it will certainly survive this," he said at the time. Twenty years later hindsight had changed his perspective. "The last year I lost $385,000. I almost lost my shirt . . . It was really difficult. I was constantly losing money," he says, sadly.

The promotion rebounded slightly in early 1987, when Bruiser Brody came to Montreal to continue his worldwide feud with Abdullah the Butcher. "Brody and I ran numerous independent shows around St. Louis and when things were hot on television from Texas. Brody suggested we bring Abby in. While I don't recall Brody specifically talking about Montreal, I do know that Abby would return the favour of picking up a payday," recalls former St. Louis announcer and wrestling historian Larry Matysik. This was the first time Abdullah was promoted as a babyface in Montreal — as with Schultz, Brito was trying anything to give the company a shot in the arm. After recovering from a broken leg, Steve Strong, who had an intense rivalry with Rick Martel the year before, came back as a babyface. The promotion wanted to turn him into its own version of Hulk Hogan. At first he teamed with Abdullah the Butcher, which allowed Abby to turn heel on him and, in theory, make Strong into a bigger babyface. But he was simply not a Quebecer — and fans remembered all too well that Martel was better than him.

Sheik Ali, Leo Burke, Sweet Daddy Siki and The Sheik: none of them could fill the gap left by the local stars. It's worth noting that one of the most famous foreign wrestlers in the history of Mexico trained in Montreal and made his debut as a professional wrestler with International Wrestling. In fact Ian Hodgkinson, from Thunder Bay, Ontario, better known as Vampiro, was trained by Louis Laurence and Abdullah the Butcher. "I met him on the way to Sudbury, Ontario. Unlike everybody else, he started to learn the business from outside before starting his actual in-ring training. Ian lived in my basement for a couple of months," says the wrestler, who went by the name "The Farmer" Louis Laurence in the documentary *Vampiro: Angel, Devil, Hero*. As Bill Fury he wrestled in Montreal using a Billy Idol gimmick. North American fans would best remember him for his involvement with WCW in the late 1990s. "Everything that happened to me in wrestling was thanks to Louis," says Vampiro in the documentary.

On Sunday, May 3, 1987, International Wrestling presented its last card at Paul-Sauvé Arena. Sunday shows had replaced Monday night cards there, perhaps because the promotion wanted to benefit from lower rental costs or get dates on some wrestlers. On Monday, June 1, Gino Brito came out of retirement to wrestle Abdullah at the Verdun Auditorium. But there was no gas left in the tank. The promotion no longer had access to French television, and the new Quebec Sport Commission established bylaws that only the WWF could afford to follow. "The Americans and the government have stifled us," explained Eddy Creatchman on the radio.

Finally the inevitable occurred. On Tuesday, June 23, 1987, International Wrestling held its last Quebec show, at the Laval Coliseum, with a cage match opposing Gino Brito and Abdullah the Butcher. At the end of the show a return date, July 7, was announced but it never took place. Ironically, on the same day the WWF recorded matches for its TV programs that featured such Montreal territory wrestlers as Martel, Bravo, the Rougeaus and Tonga. "What allowed us to survive until the month of June," says Brito, "were two shows that were held in Ontario . . . These were the only two shows we organized in 1987 that were not financial fiascos. We still had access to TV in Ontario. We did a program with Tray Travis, the former boxing manager for Eddie Melo, who was in my son's corner against Chuck Simms. My son was the television champion at the time, as I knew I could rely on him, that he would never leave me." At the end of June 1987 International Wrestling ran its last shows in Ontario, namely in Scarborough and Owen Sound. Too busy covering a championship boxing match featuring Matthew Hilton and the closure of the Montreal Alouettes, journalists didn't note the end of an era. On the other hand those same journalists were riveted by the June 29 card promoted by the WWF that presented no fewer than four Quebec wrestlers in its main event. "This was the final nail in the coffin," says Brito.

In spite of his not attending *WrestleMania III*, Gino Brito eventually worked for the WWF, replacing Édouard Carpentier as the promoter for the new Quebec Sport Commission. "I was looking for work. So I called Pat Patterson, who arranged for a meeting between Vince and me. Given my connection with Ronald Corey and Serge Savard, I was the best candidate for the position of promoter," says Brito. This association lasted until Brito was eventually replaced by Donald K. Donald, a promoter for the music concerts booked into the Forum.

It had been a remarkable few years. "In my opinion International Wrestling was second only to the WWF. The long list of wrestlers who went to New York later goes to show to what extent there were quality wrestlers," former English commentator Milt Avruskin said.

Every golden age in Montreal wrestling history featured the debut of a new Rougeau. The last golden age was no exception.

JACQUES ROUGEAU JR.

Jacques Rougeau wasn't even 11 when his great-uncle, father and older brother wrestled for his uncle Johnny's promotion. He was predestined to follow up in their footsteps. "Since my childhood I was attracted to wrestling . . . I followed my father everywhere around the territory. I had it in my blood," Jacques told Le Journal de Montréal. His professional debut was more complicated than he wished. "My father didn't want me to become a wrestler . . . he contended that I . . . had the physique of a ballet dancer. He said that I wasn't ready and that he didn't want me to wrestle in Montreal," Jacques continued. Without knowing it, the very first obstacle in his path was to become a hallmark of the wrestler who would become the last icon of Montreal wrestling.

Born on June 13, 1960, Rougeau was still an adolescent when he finally competed. "I was 17 when I had my first match at the Verdun Auditorium in 1977 against Michel Gagnon." Given the fact that his father didn't want him to become a wrestler, Jacques took the necessary steps. "I secretly borrowed $350 from my mother and called promoter Stu Hart in Calgary to offer him my services. Afterward I had tours of the U.S. and Mexico until my return to Montreal in 1981," Rougeau explains.

While his brother Raymond made a triumphant debut at the age of 16, supported by both his father and uncle, Jacques made his low-key initial appearance in Verdun, while the Montreal territory was at its lowest level in 40 years. "Raymond had the chance to begin his career in a prosperous era . . . If I had the same opportunity I would've used the name Rougeau right from the start," he explains. "I did use, though, the name Jimmy Rougeau in Calgary, but in the States I used Jerry Roberts, so I wouldn't tarnish the family name." After Calgary, Jacques went to Nashville in 1978 to

JACQUES ROUGEAU JR. AS JERRY ROBERTS, THE ONLY ROUGEAU TO WRESTLE UNDER ANOTHER NAME
(BERTRAND HÉBERT COLLECTION)

work for Nick Gulas, considered by many as, perhaps, the worst-paying promoter in wrestling. Jacques would learn that the hard way. "I was 18. I earned $25 a night and I travelled with the Poffo family, Randy Savage in the lead. But I ate canned tuna fish," he told Réjean Tremblay of La Presse. "He called me, I was in Florida, and he told me: 'I'm fed up with eating baked beans,'" Jacques Sr. remembers. In Tennessee Jacques feuded with Terry Taylor and Jos Leduc and won many titles.

He also wrestled for what is now CMLL in Mexico, the company managed by the Lutteroth family. "In Mexico I learned a wrestling style that wasn't well known in North America at the time. When I came back I wasn't better than anyone else, but I had the chance to work with different people and with different styles. I was wrestling under the name of Rorro Rouyo, which means Babyface Rougeau," reveals Jacques. Afterward he wrestled in Florida for Eddie Graham and then, finally, in Atlanta. "It was Raymond who helped me get in. I got my first break and I could finally pay my rent!" Rougeau told Le Lundi magazine. "I had the chance to work an eight-minute match with NWA champion Harley Race. The fans didn't know I was a

THE ROUGEAU BROTHERS,
A NEW GENERATION OF CHAMPIONS (LINDA BOUCHER)

Rougeau, but the boys backstage knew and were calling me Jobber Rougeau."

His return to Montreal in the early 1980s would bring many successes. First wrestling as a full-time team in 1982 for International Wrestling, the Rougeau brothers were an immediate hit. They won the International Wrestling tag team titles on four different occasions between 1982 and 1985, enjoying epic battles for the titles with such teams as Pierre Lefebvre and Pat Patterson, Frenchy Martin and Pierre Lefebvre, Rick Valentine and Sailor White and King Tonga and Richard Charland. By 1984 Jacques had big ambitions. He told *Revue Lutte*: "I'm happy to have returned to the province of Quebec. My dream would be to organize a world tag team championship in Montreal. It would be our way of thanking the fans here who have always supported us."

In '85 Jacques and Raymond would have the most celebrated tag feud in the history of International Wrestling against Ronnie and Jimmy Garvin. "The match with the Garvins had such a strong angle that the feud became legendary," Jacques told RF Video. But in 1986 the Rougeau brothers were to leave the province for good to join the WWF. "We're privileged to wrestle in a period during which wrestling blossomed," Jacques explained to *Le Journal de Montréal*. "Imagine, our Monday night match was broadcast on TV across the U.S.A. In next to no time, we will become two of the most well-known Quebecers throughout the world."

They were to have a fantastic career with the WWF, sometimes simply billed as the Rougeau brothers, and at other times as the Fabulous Rougeau Brothers. If Raymond wasn't overly bothered by the fact that they were never the tag team champions, the same couldn't be said for Jacques: "I lost a little bit of respect for Vince, when Tully Blanchard and Arn Anderson passed right in front of us, getting the belts, although we had been there for four years, giving 150 percent of ourselves." For so many wrestlers, titles are little more than a better position on the card and, in some cases, a better paycheque. Jacques, who had worked so hard to achieve his position, saw winning the tag team championship as a validation of his career choice.

The Rougeaus finally turned heel, like many Quebecers with the WWF, and had an important feud with The Rockers, Shawn Michaels and Marty Jannetty. "Our matches were scheduled last everywhere in North America, even after Hulk Hogan's match. No one could follow us!" Raymond remembers. This feud made Jacques Sr. particularly proud. "They wrestled such great matches. People were standing on their chairs," he explains. As the Rougeau brothers were becoming storyline heels, Jacques was involved in a real situation that's still talked about in wrestling locker rooms everywhere today. It had nothing to do, however, with a wrestling match.

THE ALTERCATION WITH DYNAMITE KID — THE WHOLE STORY

Jacques was involved in a locker room incident with Dynamite Kid (Tom Billington) in 1988. "Dynamite was a bully who wasn't playing nice and who, above all, didn't like Jacques personally," Raymond says. "I asked Mr. Perfect to keep an eye on my stuff. But he pulled a rib on me and made me think that the British Bulldogs were responsible. At the same time he made the Bulldogs believe that we thought they were responsible . . . and that we would stooge them to the office," Jacques says.

"Dynamite Kid came in with his whole gang: 'Bad News' Brown, Davey Boy Smith, Don Muraco, The Ultimate Warrior, Jim Powers and Jim Neidhart," Raymond continues. "Jacques was playing cards with Perfect, and he hit my brother on the back of the head, calling him a dirty stooge. My brother and I didn't understand what was going on. Dynamite looked at him and said "You want to stooge?' and then he took a swing . . . and hit him square in the middle of the face. My brother hadn't yet understood what was going on, but he was punch-drunk. Dynamite had laid him out on the floor and was about to kick him in the face, but my brother blocked him. Here I intervened and I stopped the whole thing. I had a leg injury . . . Dynamite pushed me, and I said: 'You want to beat up my fucked-up leg, too?' He tells me that they are going to wait. A locker room is exactly the same as a prison; if you don't make people respect you, you will just be crushed. I was injured, so I couldn't do anything. I wouldn't have been able to beat my own dog," he says.

"The following day we took a plane bound for Chicago, and the flight attendant made an announcement on the mic right before we left the plane: 'I would like to congratulate the Fabulous Rougeau Brothers on their new boxing career!' Obviously people found this really funny. I told my brother that we had to avenge ourselves: be it you or me. If it's me, I will have to wait until I can walk again and that would take at least a month or two . . . But my brother said: 'I got to do it.' I told him that I would help him. My brother wasn't the best fighter, but he was not afraid of anything; he'd fight a pitbull. We put a mattress on the wall of our hotel room, and for two days I showed him how to hit with authority and weight. The outcome of the fight would be determined by the first shot. If you hit him good and proper right from the start, it's going to be okay, because one has to admit that Dynamite was a good and dangerous amateur wrestler. My father told us to use a roll of quarters for a bigger impact," remembers Raymond.

"The days after the incident, Dynamite walked around like a peacock, thinking that he had broken us. I let him think that he had won, knowing full well that we were preparing a comeback. The guys came to see us and said that this was crazy stuff, nothing more, as they didn't want to antagonize Dynamite. Dino Bravo was one of them. Without picking sides, he warned us about the seriousness of the situation . . . My brother and I agreed that it would take place in Fort Wayne, Indiana. We were going to do interviews that day and would spend the whole day in the arena. We told ourselves that he was certain to be on his own at some point during that day. Usually he walked around with his gang . . . During this time I kept on training my brother, showing him how to hit and many other tricks that my father taught me . . . In the afternoon Vince passed by and said that he would like to talk to us later. My brother told me that we had to do it right away, because Vince was in the know. He got wind of the whole thing. Pat Patterson knew about it and let him in on it because Pat knew me; he heard of some other business I took care of. I've never sought a fight, but I knew how to make people respect me. Pat told Vince that it wasn't over and that he knew us too well. We didn't want to lose our jobs. So we had to do it before Vince talked to us," explains Raymond.

"We were in the corridor, close to the cafeteria where Dynamite and his gang were. Suddenly Patterson came and started talking to us. I was speaking to Pat but I kept on looking out of the corner of my eye at the cafeteria. Muraco passed by, Neidhart passed by, Davey Boy passed by, 'Bad News' Brown passed by, and fewer and fewer members of his gang remained there. My brother told me that he was coming, but Pat didn't know what was going on, so he carried on speaking. I positioned myself facing Pat in such a way as not to make Dynamite suspicious. My brother was there with a book in his hands; he read all the time, but he had the roll of quarters buried in his hand. In order to inspire confidence in Dynamite, Jacques nodded in his direction. Dynamite went by like the bully that he was. Pat continued to speak, but I could no longer hear what he was telling me. Then Jacques told me he was going to do it. And I heard the blow. I changed sides and I see blood all over the place, but Dynamite was still standing; he wasn't on the floor. He was literally frozen and couldn't control his limbs anymore. But my brother froze, too, as he wasn't expecting that Billington would remain standing. Pat was going to make a move, but I pushed him against the wall and told him not to get involved in this. He started screaming out for help," Raymond recalls.

"I was walking with Jacques and Raymond towards the cafeteria. Dynamite arrived and Jacques punched him in the mouth. There was blood everywhere. He almost broke his jaw. Geez, I didn't even know this was coming. They thought I was in on it; it was a living hell for a while," adds Patterson.

"I swung as hard as I could . . . right in his freaking teeth. I couldn't believe it; his knees buckled but he was still standing. I had hit him with the force of a sledgehammer. He grabbed me! I thought it was finished. My brother screamed, 'Jab, sacrament . . . jab, tabarnac!' And I hit him again," Jacques confirms.

Raymond continues: "It was as if I was playing a video game. I screamed jab, boom, jab, boom, and each time my brother hit Dynamite. Dynamite tried to come to his senses, then the gang started coming in. 'Bad News'

Brown came and told me that it was two against one. I told Bad News that my hands were clean and that Jacques did it all by himself. But Dynamite had lost four teeth. I told my brother that it was high time we went to speak to Vince . . . When we arrived at Vince's office he was with Hogan, and we asked Vince if we could speak to him. Vince told us that he was busy. I said to Vince that we had to talk to him right away and pointed at Jacques' hands, which were dripping with blood. Vince said, 'Ah shit!' insinuating that he didn't speak to us in time. And Hogan just said, 'Hey brother, come on in,'" he continues.

"Vince asked us what went wrong and after having told him what happened, I said to him that if he was going to fire us . . . I could live with it and that I could still look at myself in the mirror, but if we hadn't done anything, we wouldn't have been able to look at ourselves in the mirror . . . Vince said that he didn't want to fire us, but that it had to stop now. After having asked around, he came back and told us that the Bulldogs went to the hospital. He told us to leave the arena immediately, but not to stay in town as a precaution. We had to wrestle in Cleveland the following day. I then told Vince that there was only one problem, as our belongings were in the locker room right in the middle of their gang. We did this on purpose to make sure that no one suspected anything. I told Vince that it would be a good idea if he came with us. The guys looked at us with daggers in their eyes. Vince accompanied us to the parking lot. He told us that he wanted to see us the next day in Cleveland.

"Upon our arrival in Cleveland, we were checking whether everything was safe, but Blackjack Lanza was waiting for us in the parking and told us not to go to the locker room and to go directly to Vince's office. Vince didn't want to fire us . . . He liked us and didn't blame us for what happened. He was actually happy . . . He knew that Dynamite had it coming for a while. He started the meeting out by congratulating us. He said that if we wanted to have a visual impact, it was well done. Dynamite looked bashed and his face was all swollen with teeth missing . . . Dynamite told Vince that he wanted to break our legs and he wanted to have us killed.

"Vince allowed him to blow off steam and then asked him where this was going to lead. He told him that, 'Judging from the reaction of the Rougeaus, you know, it's not going to stop here. You attack him in Miami, you get a comeback in Fort Wayne; here he gets out of the ring and is hit with a baseball bat, then a month later going out to a restaurant with your wife in Calgary, you are hit with a baseball bat in return. . . But, I tell you, this has to stop here.' Then Vince told him he was going to fire all four of us if anything else happened," he recalls. "Dynamite and Davey Boy gave him their word, saying that it was over and then Vince said, 'I'm not telling you not to be on the lookout, but I tend to believe them. As far as you're concerned, I think everything is okay, too, right?'

I told him that everything was okay . . . We were attacked, we had a comeback, and that's all. But Vince told us that there was one condition . . . We had to pay for Dynamite's teeth. I said no, that was out of the question. Vince told us to calm down. He was going to pay for them, but in front of the boys, we were to pay for them. Maybe we unknowingly paid for them through our paycheques . . . I sincerely don't know," he says.

"The following week Vince told us that he had a bad piece of news to give us. The Bulldogs had given their notice they would be finishing up at the Survivor Series in five or six weeks. So they were no longer afraid of being fired. During the first weeks we weren't in the same cities, but the last 10 days we were, and on the last night, at Survivor Series, we were to wrestle in the same match. I said to Jacques that we must not be naive or crazy . . . We were very intelligent in choosing our moment and so might they be . . . What we did over the last week was not take our showers at the same time. One of us went to the toilet while the other remained close by. I know it's not pleasant, but that's the way it was. However I said to Vince that one thing was clear: Dynamite was too proud and too much of a bully . . . He would want to save face. We can meet in the corridor, and he could make a movement in my direction and finally just comb his hair . . . So if he's within my reach and he makes an abrupt or abnormal gesture, I will hit him. I won't spend a whole week keeping an eye on him each time he passes by.

"So Vince called a meeting one week before our last week together. He invited us to the meeting at the San Francisco airport, near the security gates, so that no one could have weapons. Vince isn't stupid — he knows that some-times people get killed for less. We hadn't seen each other since the incident . . . a month and a half. Each day we had been told that we were getting a comeback and that we needed to check our backs, that we were not safe.

"Vince spoke and then Dynamite said that he had given his word, but that there was something that he wanted to clarify . . . He pointed at Jacques, saying that he gave him no credit for what he had done, that he gave me all the credit for it, and that Jacques only did what I told him to do. Jimmy [Jacques] is sometimes too proud . . . and wanted to start the whole thing all over again, saying that Dynamite had started it all. I looked at Jacques and told him to shut up in French. We didn't need to start the whole thing all over again. I told Jacques that it was a way for him to save face. It was Jacques who hit him . . . And everyone on the planet knew it was Jacques who hit him. I had nothing to do with it, just some encouragement. I told Dynamite that I thought he was a man of his word, Davey Boy, too; and, as for us, it was over. We shook hands and left.

"In Dynamite's book he told a whole bunch of lies, saying that he kicked our asses. Now he's in a wheelchair. That goes to show you that what goes around comes back around," Raymond concludes.

What people don't talk about is the way this adventure was to allow Jacques to protect the Quebec midget, Tiger Jackson, a couple of years later. Jacques defended him at least twice, at a time when the boys used to relentlessly rib Tiger. The things he learned from Raymond and his father gained him respect and helped his friends to be respected, as well.

Jacques, who had essentially been a tag specialist since returning to Montreal, was to see his destiny change in 1989, when Raymond decided to call it quits. After a short period away from wrestling, Jacques returned to the WWF and had his best moments in single competition.

In 1991, after vignettes to introduce his new character were broadcast on WWF programming for several weeks, Jacques Rougeau became The Mountie — wrestling's version of the Royal Canadian Mounted Police officer, wearing the red and black uniform and the world-famous RCMP hat. His first match as The Mountie took place at Royal Rumble 1991, where he beat Koko B. Ware. After a feud with Big Bossman he would become the second Quebecer to win the Intercontinental title. Unfortunately the title came under less than ideal circumstances. In fact, for some time before the Royal Rumble of 1992, the rumour was that Bret Hart was going to join WCW. Hart, who was Intercontinental champion at the time, if the rumours were true, was going to leave the WWF and appear on WCW's program with the belt, much like Ric Flair would do upon his arrival in the WWF.

Not wanting to be vulnerable, Vince McMahon decided to have Hart lose the title at a house show in case the rumours happened to be true. Jacques wore the belt for three days before losing it to Roddy Piper at the Royal Rumble. It was the first title the legendary Piper had ever won with the WWF. History would prove the Hart rumours just that — rumours. He was to become the next WWF world champion just a few months later.

The year 1992 brought Jacques other concerns: RCMP complaints meant he was no longer able to use his gimmick in Canada. He wrestled as The Mountie in the U.S. and as Jacques Rougeau in Canada. "Representatives of the federal constabulary service discussed some of the personality traits of the character the Montreal wrestler impersonated with the management of the WWF at the beginning of the week in Ottawa," Constable Yves Juteau, the spokesman of the RCMP, told the Canadian Press. At the same time Le Journal de Montréal published an article headlined "Jacques Rougeau makes the RCMP sweat."

In 1993, after another sabbatical, Jacques returned once more to the WWF, this time in a tag team with a new partner. "Pierre-Carl Ouellet . . . I met him in Puerto Rico, and he really impressed me," Rougeau said, explaining his choice of partner to succeed Raymond to le Journal of Montréal. Jacques finally made his tag team dreams come true, and the two men quickly became world tag champions. They dominated the tag team division and would become heroes to wrestling fans all over the province. The Quebecers, as they were called, were, however, to incur the wrath of none other than the Montreal Canadiens — mainly because of their heel tactics and because their manager Johnny Polo (who would become Raven in ECW) was wearing a Canadiens sweater when they won the title. "What was shown doesn't reflect our image," the spokesman of the Canadiens, Bernard Brisset, explained to Le Journal de Montréal. "We're hardcore fans of the Canadiens. It was a stunt to spite Americans. I want to absolve my bosses in the WWF of all responsibility in this affair, as this was done on my own initiative," said Jacques Rougeau in a subsequent apology in the same newspaper.

Despite the success Jacques wasn't satisfied with the working conditions he faced in the WWF. He announced his retirement after winning these tag team titles for a third time and drawing a record-breaking crowd at the Forum against Ouellet in October 1994. Humble and at peace during a press conference, he thanked Gino Brito, Tony Mule, Frank Valois, Tony Ross, Jack Britton and Pat Girard, people who helped him further his career. He also explained his decision. "If I decided to call it quits, it's because of my family. That's the main reason." The match was memorable and would unite the Rougeau family. After Jacques's victory, his father would whisper in his ear: "Son, I'm proud of you." For Jacques Rougeau Jr. it was such a moving moment that it brought him to tears. "This was what my heart had striven to hear for a long time. Those were the most beautiful 30 seconds of my life," he confided to Le Journal de Montréal.

But his retirement wouldn't last for long. After a big disappointment in the promotional field following a failed attempt to convince Vince McMahon to hold a wrestling show at the Olympic Stadium, he failed a second time when he tried to relaunch wrestling in what was no longer the Montreal territory of old. The only interesting note about this attempt to revive a local promotion was the arrival of a new team, The Doormen (Michel Payette and Ron Trottier, two hugely muscled guys), and the beginning of the career of Carl Leduc, Paul Leduc's son. In Jacques's defence, it has to be noted that wrestling simply wasn't as popular as it had once been, and it was even more difficult to compete with what the WWF and WCW offered. So Jacques decided to make another radical change and return to the ring.

In 1996 he laced up his boots again, this time for WCW. "The team was supposed to be called The Quebecers, because they couldn't change the fact that we were Quebecers," Ouellet recalls, but WCW didn't want to take risks, legally speaking. "The name The Canucks was also considered; but finally we became the Amazing French-Canadians." Unfortunately Ouellet and Jacques would never be used to their full potential. In his last year with WCW Jacques promoted a match between Hulk Hogan and himself at the Molson Centre, scoring a victory to the surprise of the 17,023 spectators. During this time his brother Raymond and his sister Joanne both worked for the WWF. It would have been interesting to eavesdrop on the conversations at family dinners!

At the end of 1997 Ouellet and Rougeau finally returned to the WWF. Jacques and his entire family were presented to the crowd at the Molson Centre just before the famous Survivor Series. Unfortunately the team had lost its lustre — the WCW booking team had tarnished its glory forever.

In 1999 Jacques Rougeau opened another promotion, International Wrestling 2000, as well as a wrestling school. His international experience was beneficial to his students. "Jacques showed us things that many guys in the province don't know, like the selling aspect. When you're selling you look at the crowd and hold your head high," Kevin Steen, one of Rougeau's most successful students, says. "There're lots of things that Jacques taught me and that I still use today."

WCW called Jacques again in 2000, asking him to participate in some events with Lance Storm's Team Canada. When Jacques refused to be beaten by The Cat at a TV taping he left the promotion. "I told Vince Russo that I didn't want to be used as a jobber," Jacques says.

Jacques has been promoting wrestling for 10 years now, all over the province of Quebec. He manages to draw thousands of spectators and is the only promoter in the province who can afford to hold shows at legendary buildings like the Verdun Auditorium. In 2001 he was ranked ninth-best promoter in the world. "Jacques Rougeau's promotion is the most important one in Canada," adds Dave Meltzer, backing up his statement by pointing to the crowds that Jacques manages to draw to see him and his students at work. Indeed Rougeau's school had developed many wrestlers at the local scene, as well as at international levels over the past decade.

He currently produces the Jacques Rougeau family shows — refusing to call these cards wrestling shows and using promotional techniques that would shock wrestling purists.

"Jacques has a personality that draws heat," says his brother Raymond, laughing. Again and again he's had to cut his own path or prove others wrong. His father didn't want him to wrestle; he had to leave home to learn and even wrestle under other names; he broke another wrestler's teeth and wasn't given credit for it; he became Intercontinental champion under particular circumstances; his character sounded the alarm among the RCMP; he became tag team champion when the WWF didn't have the greatest tag team division; his local tours in the mid-1990s weren't successful; his victory over Hogan put a lot of heat on him with WCW; he would be caught in a feud with his own family during the war between the WWF and WCW; WCW considered him a mere jobber during his second stay there; and, finally, in spite of the fact that his family spectacles draw more than any other promotion in the province, they don't appeal to all wrestling fans. If that doesn't single him out as a black sheep, what will?

"Jacques is someone who defies all conventions. He doesn't give a hoot about what others do. He comes up with a new product and it works. He invests himself 100 percent and no one is ready to do that," says Nelson Veilleux, who worked for Jacques and who was partnered with Pierre-Carl Ouellet before him. In spite of all of this he's a media and fan favourite, and many consider him Quebec's last true wrestler. Like a singer or an actor, he's invited to appear on popular local TV shows, and he's the authority as far as wrestling is concerned for the news media.

In October 2010, a 50-year-old Jacques announced a farewell tour that took him to many cities in the province; it began at the Verdun Auditorium, where he had his first match, and ended on May 28, 2011, in Drummondville. "I was with the WWF for 10 years with three characters who were popular: with my brother Raymond in the Fabulous Rougeau Brothers, The Mountie and with Pierre-Carl Ouellet as The Quebecers," Jacques said in 2008. "My spectacles have been presented to full houses for over a year in more than 11 cities," he adds.

Black sheep or not, how can you argue against success?

PIERRE LEFEBVRE, THE *OTHER* MAD DOG

We can't help but wonder what the history of wrestling in Montreal would look like if Pierre Lefebvre hadn't left this world so tragically early, in December 1985, in the automobile accident that also took the lives of Tarzan Tyler and Adrien Desbois. This question really is legitimate — the majority of the Montreal stars of the time moved on and joined the WWF following his death. In 1987 one has to believe that the WWF would have made use of the Assassins of the Ring as part of its rich tag team division. This is actually what Frenchy Martin himself thinks. "He was excellent. Together we would've made a breakthrough in the WWF. No question!" Rick Martel thinks the same way. "With Frenchy they were a good tag team. It's obvious they would've made it to the WWF. Pierre had a lot of talent." And Jacques Rougeau says, "If I were to compare him to someone everyone knows it would be Arn Anderson."

Born on February 24, 1955, in L'Assomption, Quebec, Pierre Lefebvre was a childhood friend of Raymond Rougeau, and he was coached by his friend. Lefebvre's hero during his youth, Jacques Rougeau Sr., also participated in his training. On the other hand, in 1972, when the Montreal territory belonged to Johnny Rougeau, only one young wrestler was given a chance to make a name, and it was Raymond. "Seeing that there was no room left for him in addition to his having met his soulmate and gotten married, Pierre stopped wrestling

JACQUES ROUGEAU WITH TWO YOUNGSTERS, NEIL GUAY AND PIERRE LEFEBVRE (PAUL LEDUC COLLECTION)

in 1974 to work as a welder," his best friend Raymond Rougeau remembers. He hadn't wrestled for two years, except for a match here and there, but, like all real wrestlers, wrestling called to him again. In 1977 Raymond, who made a name for himself in the Atlanta territory, put in a good word for Lefebvre.

This time his career would take off. He stayed in Atlanta for two years, working for promoter Jim Barnett. He wrestled in the same territory as many wrestlers who were to become synonymous with the sport over the course of the next decade, men like Ric Flair and Ricky Steamboat. Very few trustworthy records of the results of this time period remain, but we know that Lefebvre worked under his real name. During the summer he returned to Montreal, along with Raymond, to work in the territory for promoters who produced summer tours. They often worked together, thus paving the way, without knowing it, for their feud in the early 1980s. In 1977 the two buddies would also go on a three-week tour of Germany. Clearly it was in the late 1970s that Lefebvre acquired considerable experience and made a name for himself. It was also during this period that a wrestling promoter in America, also originally from Quebec, gave him the nickname that would change forever his place in wrestling history.

In an interview with the *Revue Lutte* in 1983, Lefebvre explains the origin his Mad Dog moniker. "No one should think that I wanted to copy Mad Dog Vachon. It came from a promoter in Detroit, George Cannon. He offered me a match in his territory and came up with the name. When I came back to Montreal, promoters here copied Cannon, and so I have been called Mad Dog ever since." Raymond Rougeau remembers the resemblances between the two men. "His physiognomy is similar to that of Maurice, with the hairy body, the beard, his corpulence, and at the time his style became very aggressive." It's easy to think that promoters of the day saw dollar signs and a natural feud between the young Mad Dog and the original Mad Dog — especially because Vachon was one of the best draws in Montreal. And they did have matches against each other. Their feuding yielded the expected results, but because Vachon wasn't in Montreal full time Lefebvre would keep the name and would breathe life into it for a new generation of wrestling fans.

"It's my first memory of wrestling, an interview with Pierre Lefebvre in the studios of Télé 7 in Sherbrooke . . . He promised vengeance against Raymond Rougeau at the next show at the Paul-Sauvé Arena for a leg injury he incurred in a match against Rougeau a couple of months back. It's been 30 years now, and I'm still as crazy about wrestling as I was at the time," relates François Hébert. Lefebvre's rough voice made him a hit on the mic, also evoking Maurice Vachon. Added to this there was a barely suppressed, deep-seated anger, only waiting for the next match to explode. It's common to see him lose his patience during an interview, to get so on the verge of exploding that he would tell his partner or manager to take over. He gave the impression that he was a guy who needed to focus all of his concentration just not to lose control or do things that he may later regret.

It was actually an impression that was to follow him throughout his life. And an incident that took place in January 1981 would make newspapers headlines and give him a major piece of his character's puzzle. During a show at the Paul-Sauvé Arena, Lefebvre, according to his own account, was hit in the face by a cigarette butt. After identifying the perpetrator, he decided to take matters into his own hands. The altercation left an 18-year-old man with a black eye. When it was all said and done, Lefebvre had to pay a $300 fine and spend five days in jail. Before he was sentenced, just after the incident, the MAC suspended him for a couple of shows.

Upon his return wrestling fans would avenge their peer, greeting Lefebvre at each of his appearances with the words "in jail." Lefebvre sensed an opportunity to build heat and made the best of the unfortunate incident. His manager at the time often started off the interviews by asking people not to scream "in jail" at his man. Of course the opposite occurred. Mission accomplished.

In the 1980s he would be the cornerstone of the Varoussac tag team division. Promoter Gino Brito still speaks very highly of him: "He was a hard-working wrestler. I put him on all of my shows, and he never put me to shame. He wasn't a Guy Lafleur, to draw a comparison with hockey, but he was a Claude Lemieux. Everyone wanted him on their team."

In 1980 and 1981 Pierre Lefebvre teamed with Michel "Justice" Dubois. Between 1982 and 1985 he would win the International Wrestling tag team championship five times with three different partners. Those five championships can be added to his two previous reigns with "The Hangman" Neil Guay in 1980. In 1981 Lefebvre needed to have surgery on one of his knees. It was announced that he would be out for some time due to an injury caused by Raymond Rougeau, in order to add fuel to the feud which was to continue until Rougeau joined the WWF. In 1982 no one was surprised to see Pat Patterson choose him as a partner after having brutally put an end to his partnership with Rougeau. Raymond, with the help of many partners, would attempt to avenge himself, in vain, for more than a year. In the first half of 1983 Lefebvre would also find himself as tag team champion with Billy Robinson. This partnership was short-lived because it was used as a way to turn Robinson babyface when he was done with his singles program with Dino Bravo. The two men, nonetheless, had enough time to become champions and feud with Gino Brito and Tony Parisi.

Lefebvre and Pat Patterson would take the titles from the Rougeaus at the Paul-Sauvé Arena in the summer of '83. Then, finally, Frenchy Martin came into the picture, teaming with Lefebvre until his tragic death in December 1985. The two men terrorized the territory with their aggressiveness and their success lead them quickly to the tag belts, first with Tarzan Tyler as their manager and then again in Eddy Creatchman's stable. On TV Édouard Carpentier nicknamed them the Assassins of the Ring. Even though it was never officially their team name, it fit them like a glove.

Although history remembers Lefebvre as one of the specialists of Montreal's tag team action, it seems to have forgotten that Lefebvre was also twice International champion for the Varoussac promotion, winning the title twice in 1980, each time against none other than Édouard Carpentier. He would then successfully defend the championship against Pat Patterson, but he would lose the title in November of the same year against Rick Martel. On March 25, 1984, Lefebvre wrestled against Akira Maeda at Madison Square Garden during a TV taping for the WWF's All-American Wrestling. Maeda won the match and became WWF International champion, a title with which Maeda would start a new promotion, the UWF, a mixture of wrestling and mixed martial arts. Even though it didn't last for long, the UWF was a forerunner of Pride and the UFC. Lefebvre even did an interview in Montreal sometime later wearing a UWF T-shirt.

Lefebvre also took part in some shows organized jointly by International Wrestling and the WWF in 1985, wrestling against Rick McGraw and Tito Santana. Considering his positioning and his Mad Dog nickname, one can rightly think that he would've gotten a chance to make his mark, mainly given the fact that both Raymond Rougeau and Pat Patterson were working for WWF. "Without a doubt," says Patterson. "It's sad because he was such a good worker. He loved the business and was working really hard. I liked Pierre a lot. We had a good chemistry as a team. I was very saddened when I heard about his accident," he adds.

In spite of his untimely death, he had left his mark on his era so successfully that 22 years later he was inducted into the Quebec Wrestling Hall of Fame.

History repeated itself once again in the early '80s. Foreign-born stars, like in the old days, came in to tour the Montreal territory and benefited from the general popularity of the sport.

DINO BRAVO VERSUS KING TONGA, A GREAT FEUD IN THE 1980S (LINDA BOUCHER)

KING TONGA

First managed by Floyd Creatchman and then by Tarzan Tyler, King Tonga sparked a lot of interest. Born 'Uli'uli Fifita on February 10, 1959, on the island of Tonga, King Tonga was trained in Japan by Giant Baba and Jumbo Tsuruta. On October 9, 1984, he became the first man in the history of International Wrestling to beat Dino Bravo 1-2-3 via pinfall on TV, winning the International title in the process. "I met Frenchy Martin and Pierre Lefebvre in Puerto Rico and they're the ones who talked for me in Montreal," reveals Tonga. When asked who was the toughest and most dangerous man they had known, or who they would like to have alongside them in a real fight, many wrestlers of the generation would name Tonga. "He was a teddy bear, that guy . . . but everyone was looking for him all the time," Rick Martel relates. "Once in Victoriaville, he went looking for a fan in the sixth row who insulted him!"

"King Tonga is a man of his word. I was the one who served as an intermediary for him to join the WWF. I saw him in action in Quebec City once. Some people were looking to pick a fight with him, and he emptied out the biggest bar in town," says Guy Hauray. His feud against Bravo got so heated that 19,500 people were on hand at the Forum on December 23, 1984, for the Christmas super show, to see if Bravo could win his championship back. After losing the title back to Bravo in 1985, Tonga won the tag team titles with Richard Charland and this would ultimately lead to his babyface turn. "I was still green at the time and Bill Eadie (Superstar) taught me a lot about tag team wrestling while in Montreal," remembers Tonga. He then started to team with his former arch-rival. Bravo and Tonga wrestled the best teams in Montreal and even teamed together when International Wrestling and the WWF did their joint shows. They faced the likes of The Iron Sheik and Nikolai Volkoff, Greg Valentine and Brutus Beefcake and the Hart Foundation. Soon after, when he made the switch to WWF he teamed with another wrestler who used to wrestle in Montreal in the '80s, Tonga Kid (Tama), and they became The Islanders. Before he retired, he also wrestled as Meng in the WCW.

PHIL LAFON WOULD BECOME THE SECOND WRESTLER NAMED DAN KROFFAT (LINDA BOUCHER)

PHIL LAFON/DAN KROFFAT

Born in Ontario, but brought up in Montreal, Philippe Lafond would be trained in Calgary after having been discovered by the British Bulldogs. It was in the Montreal territory that he would make a name for himself. After a first run under the name "Flying" Phil Lafon, he would come back in 1986, this time under the name Dan Kroffat. He teamed with Armand Rougeau, and the two became tag team champions. He would also be part of a successful tag team with Alofa the Polynesian Prince. Alofa was the young Rikishi, working his first territory. Kroffat would become an international star with All Japan Pro Wrestling teaming with Doug Furnas. The two men won the ECW tag titles in the late 1990s before joining the WWF. Unfortunately Lafon was in a serious car accident while on his way from Montreal to Ottawa, along with Flash Funk and Sid Vicious, that would prevent him and Furnas from having enough time to adapt their style for the WWF. "Kroffat was among the most underrated in-ring performers of this generation," said Dave Meltzer.

THE GREAT SAMU

Born Samula Anoa'i, the Great Samu is part of the great Anoa'i wrestling family. He's actually the son of Wild Samoan Afa. "While I was in Japan someone put me in touch with Gino Brito and Dino Bravo," Samu remembers. "Montreal is the first territory in which I succeeded on my own without the help of my father or uncle [Sika]. I was proud of that." Although he first

VICTORY! EDDY CREATCHAMN, MAN MOUNTAIN MOORE, GREAT SAMU AND FLOYD CREATCHMAN

(LINDA BOUCHER)

came in 1985, it wasn't until a year later that he had real success in the territory, winning the International title on June 30, 1986, against Dino Bravo. He was then managed by Floyd Creatchman.

There was actually a controversy concerning Samu and the International belt. It must be noted that Gino Brito had a hard time with his champions. "One year I spent $10,000 on belts," says Brito, "because the guys used to lose them all the time." One version of the story that's told in Montreal is that Samu took the belt and never came back. On the other hand, this isn't confirmed by Brito, who remained vague when asked. However, as far as Samu is concerned, the truth is clear: "I was travelling back and forth from Florida to come wrestle in Montreal and, from what I remember, I went back home when I was still champion, and they never brought me back." This was when International Wrestling was having serious financial issues at the end of 1986, trying to compete with the WWF. "It was probably because of financial reasons," Samu says. "Gino offered me shares in the office, but I wasn't ready to settle down. If I had to do things all over again, I would probably accept the offer." What about the belt? "My apartment was broken into and the belt was stolen," Samu explains. Other young members of the Anoa'i family would wrestle in Montreal in those years. Besides the aforementioned Tonga Kid and Alofa, former WWE champion Yokuzuna, under the name Kokina, worked a few shots in Montreal, too.

As in every era, local performers were also able to make a name for themselves in the Montreal territory at this time.

SUNNY WAR CLOUD

Born May 10, 1956, in Jonquière, Quebec, Robert Rancourt is the real deal. He has a passion for wrestling that's defied Mother Nature for years. "I have always wanted to be a wrestler. I went to see my first show in the Georges-Vézina arena in Chicoutimi when I was five. It was in 1960," he says. It would be wrong to assume that he started his career in the 1980s for Varoussac, even though that's when he got his first taste of real success. "My first local match was in 1971 against Mario Raté on channel 10 for *Sur le Matelas*. I was 15 and I got $15," Rancourt remembers. In the 1980s he finally decided

SUNNY WAR CLOUD REPLACED IVAN PUTSKI AGAINST RANDY SAVAGE AT THE FORUM (LINDA BOUCHER)

to put everything into his passion under the tutelage of his idol, Édouard Carpentier. "Carpentier told me that anyone could work at a factory, but not everyone has the talent for wrestling." After having made his first steps in the business in Chicoutimi, he was to improve by training at the Loisirs St-Jean-Baptiste and worked some TV tapings for International under his real name. "I remained with the Loisirs until the creation of Sunny War Cloud. At the time Dino Bravo didn't want us to wrestle for free for Pat Girard because he was paying us with the big office," explains the wrestler, who is now called Sunny, even by his wife. He owes his character, to a large extent, to advice given to him by Édouard Carpentier. "He told me, 'If you want to get out of here, take up the character of an Indian. It always works in a territory.' Then I went to see Dino Bravo, who accepted the idea, and he gave me the name Sunny War Cloud, based on a former Native American worker, Suni War Cloud, from Buffalo. Afterward I invested in a credible costume."

While International Wrestling was in decline and had little local talent, he was offered a good opportunity in a tag team. "Leo Burke teamed me up with Joe Lightfoot in an Indian tag team, and we finally got a good position." But unfortunately it was too late. There was no more money, and everyone was pulling in a different direction. After going to the Maritimes he started touring to make a living as a wrestler. "In 1987 I went to Germany and when I came back I saw on TSN that I was to start wrestling with Stampede. I had only sent in my photos and an application! Finally Ross Hart called me, and I loved Calgary," he says, laughing. It was there that he became friends with Shinya Hashimoto, who worked with Stampede under the name Hashiv Khan at the time. That would get him the chance of wrestling in Japan for New Japan. "I also worked in Memphis and Kansas City, but, at that time, the arenas were empty, and I was starving." While on a Germany tour, he also worked with WWE future superstar Chris Jericho.

In 1985, while International Wrestling worked with the WWF, he also participated in shows presented by Maple Leaf Wrestling in Ontario. Unfortunately, when he might have had the opportunity to join the WWF for real, his life was out of control. "When Tatanka got his chance in the WWF in 1992, it was impossible to reach me — I didn't even have a phone," War Cloud explains. As the rumour goes, although it has never been confirmed, War Cloud was the person the WWF really wanted. There were other possible opportunities, but the stars never aligned again. "In 1994, in Shawinigan, I went to a show with Nelson Veilleux because Pierre-Carl Ouellet was wrestling against Razor Ramon. I went there with an envelope containing all the required documents for them to consider my application, and I gave it to Rene Goulet. Upon leaving the arena I saw the envelope in the garbage bin. That was one of the biggest disappointments of my career," he says, sadly. In 2000 he relaunched wrestling in Quebec City as a promoter with a company called CCW, and it was successful for a few years. Now in his 50s, he still wrestled almost every week until quite recently. But on December 3, 2010, after a career of almost 40 years, Sunny War Cloud called it quits for good. The announcement of his retirement made headlines in Quebec City.

LUC POIRIER

Born June 9, 1962, Luc Poirier wrestled in Montreal from 1983 to 1985 under the name la Merveille Masquée (the Masked Marvel) but used his real name in the WWF when the federation was trying to create its own local star, even though that relationship didn't last long. "It was not too good. I don't have very good memories of it. Obviously I was not prepared at all. I should have been sent somewhere I could have learned without the pressure of the WWF. It was too much too soon," remembers Poirier. After the WWF, his trainer, Édouard Carpentier helped him to get work in France where he worked as Sergeant O'Connors. Then English promoter Peter Williams brought him to Germany. "Peter Williams and Otto Wanz came up with the name Rambo. At the time, the movie was very popular," he recalls.

LUC POIRIER, CWA CHAMPION AS RAMBO (LUC POIRIER COLLECTION)

In 1992, Poirier became the CWA champion in Germany for most of the year, losing the title to Road Warrior Hawk. He won it back in 1993 and held it for three more years before losing to Ludvig Borga. He also wrestled for New Japan, often teaming up with Vader and Brad Rheingans against Riki Choshu, Masahiro Chono, Keiji Muto and even Antonio Inoki. After winning the CWA title a third and final time, he got a second chance with the WWF in 1997 as one of the members of the South African Truth Commission, wrestling under the name Sniper. "Owen Hart and I were very good friends and he told me they were looking for a big guy who could work. He told me he had told a few words to Bret and Vince about me and it was up to me to give it a try," the 6'6" giant reveals. He was finally let go in 1998. After refusing a contract with WCW, he retired. Poirier now lives in Florida and takes part in some reunion shows in Europe from time to time, even appearing as Rambo in April 2011.

FLOYD CREATCHMAN

"Floyd was a very colourful person. He had a unique style, spunk and a larger than life character," his sister Cheryl and niece Alissa explain. His wrestling

FAMILY BUSINESS: FLOYD AND EDDY CREATCHMAN

(LINDA BOUCHER)

career was short, but he had time to travel. In the '70s he wrestled in Toledo, Detroit, Cincinnati and Memphis, under the name Leslie Floyd Creatchman III. The only important match he had in Montreal was a tag team contest, where he and his father faced Raymond Rougeau and Lionel Robert in August 1976. In 1984 Eddy's son joined the family business and became a manager, too.

"Floyd had the same type of mouth as his father. Very natural with promos; it all flowed very easily for both of them," his sister says. He would actually be King Tonga's corner man upon his arrival in the territory. He then challenged wrestlers to beat King Tonga for the suitcase that was handcuffed to his wrist and purported to contain $10,000. Born on June 25, 1957, Floyd would play a key role in the last years of International Wrestling, managing Sheik Ali, Bruiser Brody, Richard Charland and the Great Samu. He was also a commentator on the English television show and hosted "Floyd's Penthouse" (also called "Creatchman's Corner"), the Montreal version of "Piper's Pit," with the charming valet Sugar by his side. "Floyd put his heart and soul into wrestling — it was in his blood. He loved every minute of it," his sister says. But after International Wrestling shut its door in 1987, his career came to an end. On October 25, 2003, "Pretty Boy" Floyd Creatchman died at the age of 46. "Floyd had other businesses and was also sick with Crohn's disease, so he wasn't really interested in the WWF. We think both Eddy and Floyd would be amazed to see countless fans . . . dedicating websites to their careers and keeping their memories alive. To see fans, to this day, post old wrestling videos of them on YouTube, or to discuss their roles in Quebec wrestling . . . It's nice to see that their memory lives on and that they won't be forgotten," his two relatives conclude.

ANDRÉ ROY

André Roy got into the business, like many young fans, by offering to help and doing anything the promoter needed during the presentation of a wrestling show. Roy would take on a variety of jobs, working as part of the ring crew, selling tickets or even ringing the bell, until he finally became a referee. "My husband has always loved wrestling; his father Ovila was a wrestler. We actually first met at a wrestling match," his wife, Ghislaine, says. "I was the favourite driver of the wrestlers. The boys would say, 'Send me Roy; he's going to drive my car.' I got a break in wrestling this way," he says in the documentary Les Saltimbanques du Ring. In the 1980s he would be one of the main referees of International Wrestling, even though he had to be accredited by the MAC before being allowed in the ring. He went on to referee the Hulk Hogan versus Jean Ferré bout in 1980 and an NWA world championship match between Ric Flair and Raymond Rougeau at the Forum.

His son, Claude Roy, was a wrestler who performed from 1981 to 1984 and who participated in a WWF show at the Verdun Auditorium. "I had the chance to work one match refereed by my father, my first match. I would've loved to have him more often in the ring with me as a guide," Claude says. In fact in addition to his considerable career as a referee, André Roy was first a wrestler in the early 1960s and was even a manager under the pseudonym Lloyd Spiro, wearing a top hat and brandishing a walking stick. After the demise of International Wrestling he became a referee for the WWF at the Forum. The commission at the time forced the group to use local officials. He would retire in 1990, after refereeing his last match, featuring Haku and Davey Boy Smith. "Wrestling was my drug. I was a wrestling maniac," he says in Les Saltimbanques du Ring. André Roy died on May 14, 2007.

ADRIEN DESBOIS

"Adrien Desbois had no business getting involved in that match!" a young François Hébert wrote to Revue Lutte after Desbois reversed the decision in the return match between Bravo and Tonga at the Forum in 1984. "Desbois disqualified Bravo after his victory," he explains now, laughing. After he trained at the Loisirs St-Jean-Baptiste in all the roles of the business, it was finally as a referee that Desbois made his way into the roster of the big

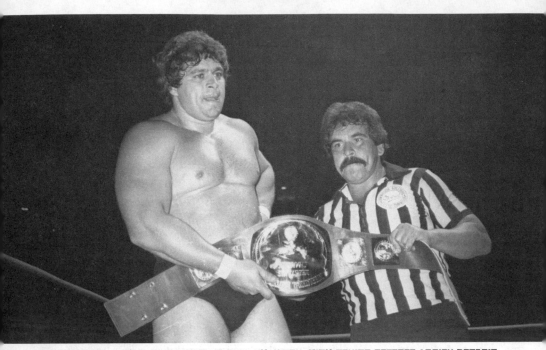

DINO BRAVO, A FOUR-TIME INTERNATIONAL CHAMPION, WITH SENIOR REFEREE ADRIEN DESBOIS

(LINDA BOUCHER)

office in the 1980s. He was often involved in the main angles of the promotion, particularly if the referee had to speak on television. "Adrien put on quite a show," adds his colleague Michel Renaud. He was, without a shadow of a doubt, the most famous and recognized referee in the history of International Wrestling and probably one of the three best referees the territory has ever had. In the 1990s his son Dany Desbois would become a wrestler and perform for years with the Proulx family's ICW and Paul Leduc's FLQ. "When you needed a referee for a program, for a well-determined gimmick, Adrien was the best," concludes Gino Brito. Desbois died tragically in December 1985, alongside Pierre Lefebvre and Tarzan Tyler.

THE ST-JEAN-BAPTISTE MASSACRE, ROUGEAUS VERSUS GARVINS DRAWS THE MEDIA'S ATTENTION

Jimmy and Ronnie Garvin, with the help of their valet Precious, savagely attacked Raymond and Jacques Rougeau, as well as their father Jacques Sr.,

ONE OF MONTREAL'S BEST FEUDS EVER. THE ROUGEAUS VERSUS THE GARVINS

(LINDA BOUCHER)

at the Montreal Forum on June 24, 1985. The media dubbed the episode the St-Jean-Baptiste Massacre because it took place on the St. John the Baptist Day, a holiday in Quebec.

Just before the summer of '85 Dino Bravo, one of the owners of International Wrestling, asked Rick Martel, then AWA champion, to spend the summer in the territory. But there was no real opponent for Martel to work with. "Dino told me to send someone and that he was going to get him ready," Martel explains. Immediately he thought of Jimmy Williams, who was better known as "Gorgeous" Jimmy Garvin. "I had excellent matches with him," Martel adds. Jimmy's wife Patty (Precious) was originally from North Bay, Ontario, and with Montreal being just a couple of hours away it made perfect sense.

Coincidentally Ronnie Garvin decided to spend the summer in Montreal, something he hadn't done for about 20 years. "I called Dino in the spring of 1985 to get booked for a match per week, as I wanted to spend the summer in Montreal with my parents. I had not seen Jimmy for two or three years when we found each other again in Montreal. We didn't consult or anything," explains Ronnie. "Honestly at first I didn't think the feud with the

Rougeaus was a good idea and I didn't want to wrestle full time. But the angle was so hot that I really had no choice." Seeing a good opportunity, the management of International Wrestling changed gears, deciding to team Jimmy and Ronnie as the Garvin brothers and to establish a rivalry between them and the most popular team of brothers in the territory, the Rougeaus. "It was Gino Brito who approached me about this," Raymond Rougeau says. But, once again, the situation left Rick Martel with no opponent. Dino Bravo made it clear it was a necessary business decision. "So I decided to take the summer off," Martel says.

After putting the Garvins together as tag team, they finally wrestled the Rougeaus on the St-Jean-Baptiste super show card. As soon as they entered the Forum's ring, Jacques Rougeau Jr. was blinded by Precious, who sprayed his face with hair spray. Raymond attempted to defend himself as best as he could, but he was at a disadvantage, two against one. In order to even things out, Jacques Sr. jumped in. But the Garvins were ready and waiting for him, and he eventually left the Forum on a stretcher. In the end both Jacques and Raymond were covered in blood. Mass hysteria erupted.

This is how Jimmy Garvin remembers the event: "I've wrestled for 23 years. I went around the world four times, but that was one of the most violent situations I've ever seen. The fans wanted to literally kill us, and if it weren't for the security guards, they would have!" Ronnie Garvin felt the same way: "It was as if we had beaten the Pope to death."

The rivalry spread to the four corners of the territory. "We even broke attendance records in many cities that summer," remembers Jacques Rougeau Sr., who was his sons' corner man. The first return match at the Forum was the main event in July, and it was the last show there presented solely by local promoters. It was also immortalized by being the first commercial VHS release by International Wrestling. Finally the climax of the feud took place at the Forum, on August 26, 1985, as part of the first co-promotion between Gino Brito's International Wrestling and Vince McMahon's WWF. The Rougeau versus Garvin match took place in the semifinal of the main event match between Dino Bravo and King Tonga against the former WWF tag team champions, The Iron Sheik and Nikolai Volkoff. That night, in front of 21,500 fans, the Rougeaus avenged themselves. "The fans screamed so loud that night that the noise created a ringing in my ears. It was the . . . loudest in my career," Raymond says.

After the match Vince McMahon wasn't at all complimentary. "Whether this match was on the card or not, it wouldn't have affected the number of people in the crowd," is what Gino Brito remembers as his response. But Raymond Rougeau thinks differently: "You could gather from the reaction of the people that this was the match they wanted to see." Jimmy Garvin agrees: "You could even have scheduled only that match between us and the Rougeaus on the card, and you would still have a full house."

But when the crowd didn't react as well to the main event, Brito looked at McMahon and said, "The fuck you know!" It's not surprising that, after this, things started to sour between the two promoters. As far as the people involved were concerned, however, McMahon's comments were of no importance. They still speak of this feud as one of the most beautiful moments in their careers. "For the rematch there were more people in attendance than at the Rolling Stones show," Jimmy Garvin says, proudly. "Wherever we wrestled the place was jam-packed," Ronnie remembers.

REFEREE PIERRE MORRISON IN BETWEEN EARTHQUAKE AND HULK HOGAN AT THE FORUM
(PIERRE MORRISSON COLLECTION)

1986 TO TODAY
THE WWF/WWE ERA

Although International Wrestling still operated in 1986, that was the year that the WWF really took control of Montreal for good. The WWF didn't come alone — with the company came the new star who would become a smash hit in Montreal, as he would everywhere else.

HULK HOGAN

On May 14, 2002, after having just won his sixth WWE world title, Hulk Hogan was given an ovation at the Molson Centre that would last for more than 12 minutes — the kind of reception fans in Montreal usually reserve for their biggest sports heroes, men like Maurice Richard and Guy Lafleur. "The crowd reaction in Montreal was out of this world. I had certain towns where the Hulkamaniacs were wilder and louder . . . Montreal is an exception . . . Montreal was the place . . . If I had to live my second life I would move to Montreal," Hogan says in an interview for the DVD *Hulk Still Rules.* "For me it was very emotional. I'm from Montreal; it made me feel good that wrestling fans in Montreal gave Hogan the biggest ovation of his life. I was all choked up — we had never seen anything like that," Pat Patterson says in the same documentary. So how did an American from Florida manage to conquer the hearts of Quebecers as if he were one of their own?

"First, in my opinion, good looks play a key role in the popularity of any future wrestler. And if you look good you've already got an important asset," Yvon Robert once said to *Lutte et Boxe* magazine in December 1951. The most legendary of Montreal wrestlers, without knowing it, just described the primary asset of the wrestler who was to be born Terry Bollea two years later.

After making his debut in 1977, Hulk Hogan received the gift that would make him a character known by everyone in North America: Sylvester Stallone offered him a role in *Rocky III*. Neil Guay remembers this episode: "When Stallone came to see him in New York, Hulk didn't believe him and thought it was a joke. He was just about to not go to meet him." Vince McMahon Sr. would put a lot of pressure on Hulk Hogan at the time, not thinking much of the movie deal. McMahon Sr. asked him to choose: *Rocky* or the WWF. "Hangman, it's time to find another place to wrestle," is what Guay remembers Hogan saying on the day he made his choice. After the movie Hogan left for the AWA, where he would become a crowd favourite and where Hulkamania was really born.

From the first *WrestleMania* with Cyndi Lauper and Mr. T to the battle of the Titans between Hogan and Andre the Giant at *WrestleMania III*, Hogan earned the unanimous support not only of the fans, but also of his colleagues. "Being a star didn't change him. As far as I'm concerned, he's the same. I respect him a lot," said Rick Martel to *Le Journal de Montréal*. *WrestleMania III* was such an important event that before a show at the Montreal Forum, the WWF held a press conference organized at the Ritz Carlton to promote the card. "I will prove that I'm still the strongest," André explained. In reality the Giant was preparing to pass the torch to his heir. The match would be broadcast on closed circuit at the Forum as well as at the Colisée de Québec and at the Georges-Vézina arena in Chicoutimi. Hogan's victory was announced on the front page of *Le Journal de Montréal* in an article entitled "The fans want a return match at the Olympic Stadium." For Hogan, it was the apotheosis of his career.

During the '80s the presence of Hogan on a card at the Forum would guarantee a big crowd. He broke all attendance records at the Forum for a match against Don Muraco on August 18, 1986, when 21,700 were in the house. "Scalpers were asking for $50 for a standing-only ticket. It was incredible! We had to go back home because it was out of our price range . . . Ringside seats sold for half of that back then!" remembers former NCW announcer Gerald Hébert. After a victory over Big Boss Man in front of 16,000 spectators, Hogan would be the only star on the front page of *Le Journal de Montréal* under the flamboyant headline "Hulk Hogan shakes the Forum!" He had clearly replaced even the most well-known local wrestler as the true star of Montreal wrestling. "Incredible! Hogan has become the real star of the Forum, better than such Canadiens players as Stéphane Richer or Mats Naslund. He's so spectacular that even the local stars' matches seem to lack something compared to him," Serge Amyot said in Le Journal de Montréal. It would have been unthinkable just a couple of years earlier.

In 1993 Hogan left the WWF when his contract expired. He had his last match at the Forum against Ric Flair in January 1992. In the summer of 1994 he signed with WCW, and two years later, wearing new colours and with a new attitude, Hulk Hogan would change the face of wrestling again by helping WCW dethrone the WWF and Vince McMahon as the industry's leaders. Montreal fans would have to wait five long years before seeing Hogan in the ring again, when he finally wrestled Jacques Rougeau in April 1997. After McMahon bought WCW in 2001, Hogan finally returned to the WWF. During this period he made some appearances in Montreal for Raw and SmackDown tapings. And he also main-evented the second WWF pay-per-view presented in Montreal, No Way Out, in February 2003. In 2009 he joined TNA, but his last Montreal appearance was in 2005 with WWE. Many still think that the presence of Hogan on a wrestling show in the territory would guarantee a huge crowd. As a matter of fact Hogan is the third-best draw in the history of Montreal wrestling, only behind Robert and Kowalski, and before super-popular workers like Carpentier, Bravo and Johnny Rougeau. In the late '80s journalist Serge Amyot of Le Journal de Montréal explained what Hulkamania represented very well: "In Montreal, wrestling had been Yvon Robert's business, then the business of Jean Rougeau and now, it's Hulk Hogan's business!"

Even though Montreal was close enough to New York to become one of the cities Vincent J. McMahon could have run regularly, he never did so. The belief is that he had some kind of a working agreement with the promoters of the time, Eddie Quinn and Johnny Rougeau. Everything really started to change in the early 1980s, when more and more WWF wrestlers came to Montreal. "We did the promoting ourselves and we simply paid a commission for the use of talent the way promoters do today with TNA wrestlers," Gino Brito explains. One of these talents was Hulk Hogan, in his pre-Hulkamania period, as well as the WWF world champion, Bob Backlund, and some local talents like Rick Martel and Pat Patterson. Then, in 1984, the WWF demanded exclusivity from its wrestlers. For the first time two shows were presented under the sole banner of the WWF at the Verdun Auditorium, with Hulk Hogan on top. Surprisingly the impact was relatively minor, but the fact that WWF TV was only presented in English was clearly a factor. And with International Wrestling having exclusive rights to present wrestling at the Forum, the WWF found itself in something of a dead-end situation.

By 1985, however, the territory was clearly falling in love with the WWF and its stars. To truly seduce the fans, the WWF would have to do something it had never done before, and has never done since: presenting joint wrestling shows with another promotion. Simply put, they needed International Wrestling in order get into the Forum. And there was clearly a demand for this: WWF programming was finally being presented in French — by the very men who had been the voice of wrestling in Montreal for five years, Guy Hauray and Édouard Carpentier. *Le Journal de Montréal* devoted an important article to this: "If the World Wrestling Federation has had unprecedented success since it invaded Montreal, it's thanks to its numerous stars, the matchless Hulk Hogan in the lead, but also to two experts who are the spokespersons of the WWF: Guy Hauray and Édouard Carpentier."

Because the Colisée de Québec didn't have the same exclusive deal with International Wrestling, a solo WWF show was first presented there that would draw 10,000 spectators, with the U.S. Express defeating The Iron Sheik and Nikolai Volkoff in the main event. That was five times the number of spectators than the last International Wrestling show held in the same building. This fan infatuation continued into August, when a record-breaking crowd packed the Forum. "There were 21,500 spectators at the Forum last night for the wrestling matches, more than at the Olympic Stadium for the Expos game. If there was more space, they could have packed in another 5,000 fans," Réjean Tremblay told *La Presse*. This three-way dance between the public, the WWF and International Wrestling would continue until January 1986.

In October '85, however, four wrestlers no-showed a card presented at the Forum: Mike Rotundo, Barry Windham, Superstar and Ivan Putski. (It did mark the first Montreal appearance of Terry Funk and Randy Savage.) The public wasn't happy about four stars going MIA, but it wasn't just the fans who were critical of the WWF. "Montreal wrestlers mustn't be forgotten," Dino Bravo complained to *Le Journal de Montréal*. Édouard Carpentier

JOS LEDUC PUT HIS HANDS ON THE INTERCONTINENTAL BELT BUT WAS NOT ALLOWED TO KEEP IT

(LINDA BOUCHER)

seemed to wash his hands of the affair, even though he was officially the WWF's promoter in Montreal: "Mr. Ronald Corey and Irving Grundman told me that they gave their word to International Wrestling and that I had to negotiate with this group. I can't present cards solely with WWF wrestlers."

In November and December 1985, cards were presented jointly that would involve enough local talent for the federation to buy peace. Andre the Giant made his return after a two-year absence in a match against King Kong Bundy. In December Bravo was in the main event against Randy Savage for the Intercontinental championship; the crowd was the smallest since the joint shows began, even though it was still a respectable 14,000.

Hulk Hogan's first WWF Forum appearance took place in January of 1986; he faced "Cowboy" Bob Orton in front of more than 15,000. This would be the last show presented with International Wrestling. The dream match, opposing Dino Bravo to Hogan, was put aside, despite being announced months earlier. Bravo was the only International Wrestling star on the card, and he faced "Big" John Studd, an opponent he'd wrestled against many times and defeated at the Paul-Sauvé Arena five years earlier.

Little by little the WWF and Hulk Hogan *became* wrestling, and eventually an enormous colour picture of the Hulkster even adorned the front page of *La Presse*. "Irving Grundman ended up yielding to Vince McMahon. The latter was in Grundman's office yesterday night to reach a new agreement that would give the World Wrestling Federation, the New York Titan Sports office, the exclusive right to present wrestling shows at the Forum," Réjean Tremblay wrote. "To give up its rights at the Forum, Frank Valois's group made the WWF give up another city, Quebec City, and television rights there. On the other hand, it isn't impossible for the two groups to unite and organize a joint show at the Olympic Stadium during the next summer season," added André Rousseau in *Le Journal de Montréal*. The dream project would never see the light of day, because, as Rick Martel explains, "Vince's machine moved forward very fast. He no longer needed us." As for the Quebec City deal, it was over by the end of the year. Sometime after this the WWF was to administer the coup de grâce to International Wrestling — by signing the Rougeau brothers.

In February 1986, in their first solo show, the WWF did its best to win Quebecers by presenting Maurice Vachon in a last match at the Forum, a battle royal. In March the Rougeau brothers returned to wrestle the Hart Foundation. The first *WrestleMania* was broadcast on closed circuit at the Verdun Auditorium, but *WrestleMania 2* through *VIII* would be broadcast at the Montreal Forum.

Finally Martel and Bravo jumped ship — Bravo having put his problems with McMahon's company aside in exchange for a very profitable contract. With the Rougeaus, Martel and Bravo on its payroll, the WWF would often present matches in Montreal with storylines specific to its territory. This was the case in November 1986, when Can-Am Connection Rick Martel and Tom Zenk were put in the main event against the British Bulldogs for the tag championship. "We did our interviews between matches at the Forum specifically for Montreal," recalls Marc Blondin, who had replaced Édouard Carpentier. With an average of about 15,000 spectators per show, the WWF concluded 1986 as the uncontested ruler of the territory.

In 1987, when International Wrestling shut its doors, an era of near WWF exclusivity began and it would last until the deregulation of wrestling by the Quebec Sports Commission in the early 1990s. In January 1987, 20,302 fans came to see Raymond Rougeau (substituting for his brother Jacques) wrestle against Dino Bravo in their only one-on-one match of their career, as well as a main event that featured Randy Savage and Ricky Steamboat in a brilliant contest. On February 27, 19,202 fans filled the Forum again for another Savage/Steamboat showdown. In April it was the first match between Jacques Rougeau and Dino Bravo in singles, as well as the WWF debut of Frenchy Martin. On August 31 the WWF returned, this time with Mr. T as a special referee for a main event "hair match" between Pat Patterson and Brutus Beefcake. In September the first appearance of Strike Force, Rick Martel and Tito Santana, took place. In the preliminaries a young wrestler from Texas called the Dingo Warrior made his debut. He would eventually become The Ultimate Warrior and one of the biggest stars of the federation. The attendance average was just under 15,000 people, thanks mainly to Savage and Hogan.

The year 1988 started with 16,308 on hand to see Savage against the Honky Tonk Man in January and then, in both February and March, more than 18,000 were happy to be visited by Hulk Hogan. The March card was even more special, as the WWF paid tribute to Maurice Vachon, who had just had lost his leg five months earlier in an accident. In June 300 spectators would attend the first softball game of WWF wrestlers and the La Presse-CKOI team made up of, among other celebrities, Montreal Canadiens players. "I organized this softball game with Dino, Jacques, Raymond, Rick Martel, as well as Jake Roberts and Jim Duggan," Marc Blondin remembers. The WWF wrestlers, Quebecers or not, were now part of the Quebec sports world, the same way the Canadiens or the Expos players were. During the remainder of the year Dino Bravo tried to get the WWF title from Randy Savage, and the Rougeau brothers adopted an all-new attitude and turned heel. In fact, out of the four major Montreal wrestlers with the WWF, only Martel was still a babyface. Still the WWF was able to increase its average attendance to almost 15,000 per show, thanks to a great start and the feud between Bravo and Savage. When Savage died on May 20, 2011, every major Montreal media outlet reported the story, demonstrating that he clearly left an indelible mark on the fans of the era.

In January 1989 Hogan was back, teaming with Jim Duggan and Ronnie Garvin against Dino Bravo and the Rougeau brothers. This was the last main event program specific to Montreal until Jacques Rougeau's retirement match of 1994. To everybody's surprise, Dino Bravo put a bear hug on Hogan and made him pass out — injuring his back so that he would actually leave the Forum on a stretcher. The mythical match between Bravo and Hogan was finally going to take place. On March 10 the Hulkster would defeat Bravo — a rare occurrence in Montreal — when Bravo tapped out to Hogan's own bear hug in front of a crowd of 17,340. The match was two years too late and had lost some of its lustre. Bravo was a heel, and it clearly didn't generate the same passion the same match would have in 1986.

On June 2 of the same year Dusty Rhodes wrestled his first match for the WWF, substituting for Jake Roberts against Ted DiBiase. On June 30 Montreal had the right to a unique event. Two years after his retirement Roddy Piper came back to wrestling and had a match against Randy Savage, even before returning to television. Only 4,500 spectators would be present, showing that only local talents in major matches could have an impact on the tickets sales. Indeed the WWF witnessed a considerable drop in attendance in 1989, averaging only 10,000 spectators. On October 20, without even knowing it, the fans would see what would turn out to be the last match of Andre the Giant in Montreal, when he faced The Ultimate Warrior.

On January 1990 Dino Bravo was in the main event for the last time at the Forum, going down to The Ultimate Warrior. In October the Road Warriors made their return. Now called the Legion of Doom, they teamed with The Ultimate Warrior against the three members of Demolition. Le Journal de Montréal reported a meagre attendance of around 8,000 spectators, which is a very small crowd compared to what Hawk and Animal were drawing with International Wrestling in the 1980s. Nothing was working for the WWF:

the crowds were becoming smaller and smaller, and the shows further and further apart. Montreal fans, used to being treated to a dozen shows a year, saw the WWF only six times in 1990. The WWF was then drawing an average of just over 7,000 spectators, less than half the crowd of just two years earlier. "New York wanted to fire Gino Brito and replace him with a Toronto promoter. We demanded that we keep a spokesman in Montreal. At least we've saved one job," explained Mario Latraverse of the new Quebec Sports Commission to La Presse. In fact it was the excessive regulation of the commission that had killed indy wrestling in the province. The WWF was the only party capable of affording the exorbitant costs of holding an event. Montreal, which had been infatuated with wrestling for a decade, was no longer the territory the WWF had invaded in 1985.

On February 15, 1991, Gino Brito presented his last show as a promoter. His last show featured, ironically, the first Montreal appearance of The Undertaker. The next WWF show, in April, would be produced by Donald K. Donald, but only 6,000 fans showed for a card that did not include a single Quebecer — a first for the WWF in Montreal. Francophone television stations stopped airing wrestling at the same time.

In 1992 fans continued to desert WWF shows at the Forum in spite of the fact that the company lowered ticket prices. Jean-Paul Sarault of Le Journal de Montréal, who had always defended wrestling, made a shocking accusation: "The WWF doesn't respect its clients at all and laughs at its fans." The province and the WWF were on the verge of parting ways and things continued to deteriorate. Hulk Hogan was to make a final appearance for the WWF in Montreal on January 20, facing Ric Flair, but it took all of Hogan's popularity to draw a meagre 10,000 spectators to what should have been a dream match. It was actually the last crowd numbering more than 6,500 that year — and it was the first time that Flair defended the title he had just won at the Royal Rumble the day before. On that same show Dino Bravo wrestled for the last time in Montreal, scoring a victory over The Barbarian. In December 1992 the year-end show was, for the first time, presented without Hulk Hogan on the WWF roster. The main event match between Ric Flair and Bret Hart drew 6,200.

Wrestling wasn't just on the decline in Montreal; the same kinds of things were occurring pretty much everywhere in North America. The early

1990s were disastrous for the WWF, and the company clearly had no idea what to do to rekindle the popularity it had enjoyed just a few years earlier. The WWF family-friendly formula had become stale and outdated — the federation had painted itself into the corner.

In 1993, after a show at the Forum in March during which you could have heard a pin drop, the WWF decided to present its next show in July in the more intimate setting of the Forum Theatre. This venue had a different seating configuration that accommodated about 5,000. In March Lex Luger (Larry Pfohl) wrestled in Montreal for the first time. He was part of the CFL's Montreal Alouettes football team, before turning pro wrestler with the NWA and the WCW. On November 26, in its third and last Montreal show of the year, a light emerged at the end of the tunnel. The WWF world tag team champions, The Quebecers (Jacques Rougeau and Pierre-Carl Ouellet), defended their belts in their own city against the Steiner brothers. A total of 13,800 people bought tickets to support their champions — forcing the last-minute decision to open the Forum completely. The main event opposed Yokozuna to The Undertaker, but the publicity revolved around the two local boys. The facts show, again, that if local talents were positioned as equal or superior to other wrestlers, the WWF could draw good numbers in Montreal even in a down period.

The year 1994 started off quietly, but became hot when Jacques Rougeau's retirement match was set up for October. Luna Vachon made her first appearance in Montreal as a WWF wrestler during the Rougeau retirement set-up show in June. Once more just three shows had been presented at the Forum that year, but the last two drew more than 12,000 people — a good sign. "Montreal has been the WWF's best house show city for the past year," reported Dave Meltzer in 1995.

After such a strong end to 1994, Quebecers expected big things for 1995, but it turned out to be rather mediocre. The WWF tried hard, hiring a local promoter — none other than Joanne Rougeau, the sister of Jacques and Raymond. In February Pierre-Carl Ouellet, after a five-month absence, was called upon at the last minute to wrestle Shawn Michaels. In May the first show under the guidance of Joanne Rougeau saw some success, as Razor Ramon beat Jeff Jarrett in a ladder match to win the Intercontinental title. Jarrett won the belt back two days later in Trois-Rivières, and the title switches were

JOANNE ROUGEAU AND LINDA MCMAHON AT A
PRESS CONFERENCE IN MONTREAL (BERTRAND HÉBERT)

mentioned during *Monday Night Raw*, a rare occurrence. Pierre-Carl Ouellet made his official return, beating Jerry Lawler, with the latter making his first appearance at the Forum as a wrestler. Ouellet was introducing his pirate character, Jean-Pierre Lafitte, to the Montreal fans for the first time. In September 1995 two matches featuring Lafitte were held, one in Montreal and the other in Quebec City, against the world champion, Diesel. These matches would ultimately lead to Ouellet's departure from the WWF. Unfortunately the Forum card didn't even draw 6,000, primarily because Diesel was one of the worst draws as WWF champion. The evening wasn't completely unremarkable, though: it featured the first Montreal appearance of Triple H, the man who would become an important star in the ensuing years and even a member of the McMahon family.

January 12, 1996, was a sad day in the history of Montreal wrestling. The last ever wrestling show was presented at the Montreal Forum but no Quebecer made it onto the card. Nonetheless many Montreal wrestling legends were present, including Paul Leduc and Jacques Rougeau Sr. On August 2, 1996, the WWF made amends during its first show at the Molson Centre as one Quebecer, Carl Leduc, was the first to wrestle in a match where he pinned future world champion, Justin "Hawk" Bradshaw (JBL). A boxing match specific to Montreal was also presented between Raymond Rougeau and Owen Hart. A big press conference was held to promote the event, with boxer and actor Deano Clavet acting as the trainer for Rougeau, while the former Canadian heavyweight boxing champion George Chuvalo was in Owen Hart's corner. It's also important to note that this was the first time Montreal fans would see Stone Cold Steve Austin and Mick Foley, the latter working as Mankind. On November 22 Carl Leduc was defeated in a match against The Sultan (his last match with the WWF), and this meant the return to square one for Quebecers in McMahon country. Except for the last show at the Forum and the first in the brand new Molson Centre, which both drew a little bit more than 10,000, it was yet another disappointing year at the box office for the WWF in Montreal.

The year 1997 started off with a show in Quebec City followed by a show in the afternoon the day after at the Molson Centre. Quebecer Martin Roy was on the card as his Judas character and would lose to Savio Vega. More importantly Rocky Maivia made his local debut, and in just a few years' time he would be better known as The Rock. Today he's one of Hollywood's biggest stars under his real name, Dwayne Johnson. On June 13 Ken Shamrock, the former UFC champion, made his first appearance in Montreal, refereeing a match between Legion of Doom against the team of Crush and Judas. Twelve years later the UFC would draw one and a half times what WWE does at the Bell Centre. The last show of '97 took place on November 9, and it would become the most well-known wrestling show ever presented in Montreal: Survivor Series 1997. The famous screw job match between Bret Hart and Shawn Michaels, which we'll put aside for a later chapter, headlined the first PPV event broadcast from Montreal, a moment that the fans in Montreal had been dreaming of for 10 years. Montrealers responded well to the event, and a crowd of 20,593 made it the largest in the territory in 11 years. One former International Wrestling talent worked that evening, the announcer, Albert DiFruscia who made the French and English introductions. The card was also significant for the return of Steve Austin after a serious neck injury. Kane's first major match since his recent arrival in the WWF, against Mankind, also took place. Ultimately it was the last time that Montreal fans would see Bret Hart in a WWF ring for almost 15 years.

After the event the Attitude Era and the Monday Night Wars saw wrestling enjoy an unprecedented surge in popularity. The WWF visited Montreal just five times over the next two years (although a sixth event was scheduled for May 29, 1999, but was cancelled after the death of Owen Hart six days earlier). Montreal, in spite of its faithfulness since 1985, was put aside as new markets opened up. In March 1998 the Quebecers came back home and they wrestled for the WWF one last time in their city on August 2. On November 8 a four-way match between Austin, The Undertaker, The Rock and Kane was presented to an almost sell-out crowd. The July 2, 1999, show was the last presented by Joanne Rougeau, who would be replaced by a permanent team based out of the WWF's Toronto office. The WWF finished the century with a show on November 21, with a main event between The Rock and Triple H that drew 12,418 fans.

The WWF enjoyed its best Montreal attendance in years, with the five events drawing a little bit more than an average of 11,000. Steve Austin and The Rock had almost replaced Hulk Hogan in the hearts of fans.

The beginning of the new millennium saw the WWF come to Montreal for just three shows in two years. In 2000 the WWF drew 11,534 people to see The Rock in the main event. In 2001, after a house show on a Sunday night that surprisingly drew 12,351 fans, the WWF returned to Montreal on October 16 to present a broadcast of SmackDown, the first TV taping shot in Montreal. Rob Van Dam, wrestling in Montreal for the first time, and Kurt Angle were the main event of the show that drew 14,068 fans, the biggest crowd since the Survivor Series. This would actually be the first of six successive similarly successful television events.

On March 18, 2002, in front of 13,000, a live broadcast of Monday Night Raw was presented at the Molson Centre the day after WrestleMania X8. It was, of course, Raw's first visit to Montreal. That night the WWF announced it would divide into two companies, namely Raw, managed by Ric Flair, and SmackDown, managed by Vince McMahon. Vince was also to get his first taste of the "You screwed Bret" chants that Montreal fans would never forget to greet him with. In the main event Hulk Hogan and The Rock teamed up for the first time in order to dispose of Scott Hall and Kevin Nash by disqualification. Randy Orton, newly arrived from OVW, the WWF development territory, had a dark match at the beginning of the show. But the wrestler who made the most impressive debut was Brock Lesnar. One year later he would be in the main event of WrestleMania XIX.

On May 14, 2002, after stopping the night before in Quebec City, the WWF returned to the Molson Centre to tape SmackDown. The WWF seemed to be in love with Montreal fans, again, with a second TV broadcast from Montreal in less than two months. It was Sylvain Grenier's first match that night, losing to Christian in a dark match. On October 14, 2002, the WWF, now called WWE, presented Monday Night Raw at the Bell Centre — which had also just changed its name. Eric Bischoff was the new general manager of the brand and made his first appearance in Montreal.

Montreal was again a hot wrestling territory. And WWE rewarded its fans accordingly with a second PPV event. On February 23, 2003, No Way Out came to town, showcasing The Rock and Hulk Hogan on top. Steve Austin returned after an eight-month absence to face his former WCW boss, Eric Bischoff. Chris Benoit wrestled for the first time in his native province, and Rey Mysterio also wrestled in Montreal for the very first time. The first official presence of Sylvain Grenier in WWE also took place, as he refereed the match between The Rock and Hogan. The crowd responded well, with 15,114 in attendance, in spite of a snowstorm.

On July 7, 2003, WWE returned for Monday Night Raw, and Pierre-Carl Ouellet had a dark match to the delight of the fans gathered at the Bell Centre. "Aside from the big stars, I was the one who got the biggest reaction," Ouellet remembers, proudly. La Resistance, Sylvain Grenier and Rene Dupree, world tag team champions at that time, made their first appearance together in Montreal. It was also the episode of Raw where Steve Austin forced Kane to show his face, as he had lost his mask a week earlier. WWE finished its Montreal year with an afternoon show in November, thus putting an end to the string of consecutive television shows that had started in October 2001.

WWE returned with a Monday Night Raw on May 31, 2004. Jean-Frédéric Clément (Handsome JF) and Éric Mastrocola, two graduates from Jacques Rougeau's school, lost during the Sunday Night Heat taping against The Hurricane and Rosey in a rare match that included some Montreal indy wrestlers. If the main event between Eugene and Kane wasn't anything spectacular, La Resistance of Sylvain Grenier and Robert Conway, dressed in the colours of the Quebec flag, won the WWF tag team titles against Edge and Chris Benoit. The fans were ecstatic witnessing Grenier and Conway showing they would continue to react with fervour and passion every time a Quebec wrestler was involved in something important. It would actually be the only time in the history of WWE that a Quebec wrestler won a title at home.

After a house show in October 2004 played to just 4,000 spectators, WWE would come back on January 18, 2005, with a taping of SmackDown. The program was just coming out of a year during which it was voted the worst wrestling program on TV and, without knowing it, would be embarking on another year that was going to be mediocre, at best. The Montreal show was no exception, and the crowd didn't answer the call — less than 4,000 people attended.

On August 15, 2005, Raw returned to Montreal with the re-emergence of Shawn Michaels who got a lot of reaction for making the fans think that Bret Hart was in the building. Lita and Edge received a lot of heat from the 12,000 in attendance. But once again Hulk Hogan was the star, main-eventing against Kurt Angle. Once the TV broadcast was over, Hogan teamed with John Cena and Batista against Angle, JBL and Shawn Michaels in a dark match. Unfortunately, this was more than likely the last time that the fans in Montreal would see Hulk Hogan in a wrestling ring.

Even a SuperShow (Raw and SmackDown on the same day) held in September 2006 that drew 13,500 couldn't inspire Montreal fans. Montreal was nonetheless the first Canadian city to receive a visit from WWE, 11 months after the Chris Benoit tragedy; however, the promotion didn't see fit to make Montreal's own Maryse Ouellet the women's champion in Montreal, instead giving her the title in Toronto (of all places) in December 2008. On September 13, 2009, Breaking Point, a third PPV event in Montreal, drew just 12,000 and was voted one of the worst wrestling shows presented worldwide that year.

In 2010 only one show occurred, an afternoon Halloween event at the Bell Centre, and it drew no more than 5,900. 2011 saw no WWE event, a first since 1984. McMahon's promotion came back stronger than ever in 2012 with a noisy house show in March and then with the return of Monday Night Raw. Besides the return of Bret Hart, Raw was publicized locally as the Pat Patterson appreciation night. In the end, however, the show would be remembered for one of the scariest scenes most of the 10,000 plus in attendane would ever witness. Around 10 p.m., Jerry "The King" Lawler suffered a massive heart attack while doing live commentary. If it wasn't for Dr. Samson and the EMTs, the scene would have been even more tragic. Lawler stayed in Montreal a full week before going back to Memphis. "I was lucky it happened there," said The King in a press conference. The show kept going but it wasn't until the final segment that the crowd got back to life. In one of the best interviews ever given in Montreal by WWE stars, CM Punk, Bret Hart and John Cena tried to give the crowd a happy ending after a crazy night. To top it all off, Cena spoke French during the segment and received

CM PUNK, BRET HART AND JOHN CENA TRIED TO GIVE THE CROWD A HAPPY ENDING

(MINAS PANAGIOTAKIS)

a babyface pop like he hadn't received in years. Once again, something historic had happened in Montreal.

The sad truth is that only two Quebec wrestlers who hadn't wrestled for International Wrestling in the 1980s have enjoyed WWE success. The two actually had similar career paths, with each man winning many tag team championships.

PIERRE-CARL OUELLET

"I wanted to be the next Hulk Hogan . . . I nurtured this dream up until 2010. Wanting it that much allowed me to make it in the business, first as world tag team champion and to also wrestle for the world championship — the same one Hulk Hogan had held. But there comes a time when you know that you have given wrestling everything you had. Unfortunately you reach that moment when you realize that you won't be reaching your goal. It's then time to move on," Carl Ouellet said in February 2011 on CKAC. He became the last wrestler of our top 25 (see ranking on page 401) to announce his retirement. "I wanted to slowly disappear from the scene without making any official announcement. Today I share this with the wrestling fans and sports fans of Montreal, to thank them for having supported me and my dream."

Ouellet's last years in the wrestling business played out something like the main character in the film *The Wrestler*, but without Randy "The Ram" Robinson's demons. Robinson wrestled with the dream of returning to the big time. Ouellet did, too, with as much conviction and dedication he had on his first day in the business.

Born in Greenfield Park on December 30, 1967, Ouellet had by the time he was 14 decided he wanted to be a professional wrestler. The heroes of his youth are the men ranked with him in our list of the top 25 Montreal territory wrestlers, guys like Dino Bravo, Rick Martel and the Rougeaus. In the mid-1980s a friend of his father took him to the famous Loisirs St-Jean-Baptiste.

Because Pat Girard was already 70 at the time, it was mostly Nick Rapone who trained him, though Ludger Proulx and Guy Ranger also helped. He spent two years at the Loisirs before going to Édouard Carpentier's school. It was there that he would make the acquaintance of Nelson Veilleux, a man he would cross paths with later on. After a wasted trip to Calgary he was told to take the bus to Edmonton, in case they needed a substitute wrestler. "When Bruce Hart wanted me to pay for more wrestling classes, I came back home," he says.

Ouellet subsequently received a phone call from Emile Dupree, the well-known Maritimes promoter Quebecers had seen wrestle locally in the days of Grand Prix. Dupree asked him whether "Crawford" was coming east this summer. Ouellet said no, he was in Calgary. Emile Dupree was referring to

Bob Crawford, while Ouellet, who clearly didn't understand Dupree's accent, thought it was Kroffat, referring to Dan Kroffat (Phil Lafon), who was to spend the summer in Calgary. Meanwhile, Nelson Veilleux, a.k.a. Bob Crawford, heard nothing more from Dupree, which was odd, considering he regularly worked summer tours in the Maritimes. Veilleux ended up calling Dupree, and when the latter explained the situation to him Veilleux didn't find it funny. "I didn't

DOUBLE TROUBLE: NELSON VEILLEUX AND PIERRE-CARL OUELLET, TAG TEAM CHAMPIONS IN SOUTH AFRICA

even know that Crawford was Nelson, and I really heard Kroffat," Ouellet remembers. "Knowing Emile, when he speaks on the phone, it's so true that Crawford sounds like Kroffat," Veilleux agrees. Veilleux would finally go to New Brunswick during the summer and wrestle against Ouellet and Eddie Watts, who were called the Super Bees. "Emile was known for copying WWF gimmicks," explains Ouellet. He also wrestled against Masa Chono that summer, and Chono went on to become a legend in Japan.

Ouellet thought that Veilleux had talent and wanted to team with him. "I kept on telling him that he was good, that he was talented," Ouellet remembers. Thanks to one of Ouellet's contacts, the two friends got booked in England as Double Trouble. They wrestled against such guys as David Taylor, Steven Regal and David "Fit" Finlay. They appeared there three times, staying for about three months on each tour. They also went to South Africa, where they were very successful, and to Germany, where they wrestled for Rene Lasartesse, as well as to France for a short three-to-four-week tour.

In time Germany's Otto Wanz contacted the Quebecers about joining the CWA, but only Ouellet was hired in the end. "When you wrestled for the CWA you get closer to the WWF," Ouellet says. He was to find himself in the same locker room as Regal, Taylor, Finlay, Alex Wright, Eddie Gilbert, the Road

Warriors, Jimmy Snuka and Luc Poirier. Then Ouellet went to Puerto Rico for Carlos Colón. In the meantime Veilleux also got an offer to go to Puerto Rico through Frenchy Martin, but for Savio Vega's IWA. Veilleux, however, developed appendicitis and had to undergo surgery, which prevented him from going. "We would've tried to form Double Trouble again over there. I think that if we had made the run together in Puerto Rico, we would've done it. Whether in the WWF or WCW, we would've made it together as a team," says Ouellet. It was at this point that Ouellet and Veilleux parted ways as far as their careers were concerned. By the end of 1992, Ouellet was on the verge on making it big. "I had positive feedback from WWF, WCW and USWA," he recalls. But Puerto Rico changed Ouellet's career path. He went there in January 1993, and in March of the same year Jacques Rougeau was scheduled to appear on a big show. After having met Ouellet and seen his track record, as well as a couple of videos and a match in person, he was really impressed. "Jacques told me: 'I'm going to help you get into New York,'" Ouellet remembers. However he was incredulous until Rougeau called Vince McMahon directly from Puerto Rico, and, after having praised Ouellet, Vince responded that he would give him a tryout in South Carolina. In spite of a match where Jim Powers didn't really give him much of a chance to show-case his talent, the WWF agents liked what they saw. Six other wrestlers were getting tryouts at the same time and all six were hired. In addition to Ouellet, there were the Smoking Gunns, Adam Bomb (Bryan Clark), Curtis Hughes and Bastion Booger (Mike Shaw).

After a short stint with Wing in Japan, Jacques called him to let him know that they were going to start teaming in the WWF. Judging from what Jacques told Ouellet, Vince asked him whether he got along with him well enough to be his partner, to which Jacques answered in the affirmative. According to some other people, Rougeau's return ticket to the WWF was to get himself a partner. Carl Ouellet thus became Quebecer Pierre. Ouellet actually had his own theory on the name he was given: "They thought Carl didn't really sound like a Quebec name. Because Pat Patterson's real name is Pierre, I imagine that's where they got the name they gave me." On the other hand, Rougeau urged Ouellet to keep his identity, so when news-papers in the province talked about him they called him Pierre-Carl Ouellet.

Soon after their debut they won the tag team titles in a match against

Rick and Scott Steiner on September 13, 1993. "The Steiners didn't want to put us over, so that's why we won by DQ in a Quebec rules match," Ouellet relates. At the '94 Royal Rumble, their match against Bret and Owen Hart would be voted the best match of the show. "Such tag team moves have never been witnessed before in the WWF," says Ouellet, speaking about the Quebec bomb and other manoeuvres in their arsenal. Then, between January 1994 and April 1994, The Quebecers lost and won the titles twice before finally losing them for a final time to The Headshrinkers in Burlington, Vermont. It was then that they parted ways. According to Rougeau, he wasn't very happy with the fact that the WWF wasn't keeping its promises to him and he decided to leave. His match against Ouellet at the Montreal Forum filled the building and received enormous media coverage. "It really put me on the map in Montreal," Ouellet remembers.

After this he took on the character of Jean-Pierre Lafitte. Ouellet had submitted a scenario to the WWF based on his real-life disability — he had lost an eye in a childhood accident. The plans were modified and gave birth to the character seen on television. In fact Jean Lafitte was a real-life pirate, and Pierre was added to the first name for continuity, making it appear he was a descendant. Ouellet wasn't really happy. "You'll be the first pirate in the history of the WWF," McMahon told him, trying to convince him. "He knew what to say to make you leave his office on cloud nine," Ouellet says, laughing.

After In Your House 2 the WWF decided to test Ouellet in a dark match main event against Bret Hart. Bruce Pritchard was impressed by the match, and Ouellet began a feud with Hart, the most important match being the main event of a house show at the legendary Madison Square Garden. "Bret thought highly of me. He even suggested that they put the Intercontinental belt on me. I actually sent him a letter from Germany some years later to thank him," Ouellet says. After a series of victories and an unfortunate incident with Diesel and Shawn Michaels, which will be discussed in more detail later, Ouellet left the WWF. He went back to teaming with Jacques Rougeau, this time in WCW, but the partnership would last only last a year.

After a short stay in Germany for Ouellet, he and Rougeau returned to the WWF in 1998, but only for a couple of months. Rougeau was let go, but Ouellet got his contract renewed for another year. Then he got invited to the Brawl for All competition, the WWF's attempt to schedule a shoot

fight tournament. According to Ouellet it was 100 percent real, but WWF officials tried to tamper with the outcome of the matches. Ouellet's first opponent, Steve "Dr. Death" Williams, was clearly supposed to win. In fact Road Warrior Hawk went to see Ouellet to tell him to take a dive after Williams's first shot in order to avoid getting injured. Ouellet's answer was unequivocal: "Well, Mike, go back to Steve and tell him that I'm not laying down for anyone and that he's in for the biggest fight of his life." The match wasn't very good — the referees stopped the match eight seconds before the end in favour of Williams. "It was fucking bullshit!" Ouellet remembers.

In 1999 he wrestled in Memphis in the WWF development territory where he worked, among others, with Kurt Angle. Subsequently he was to wrestle for All Japan Pro Wrestling, where he teamed with Vader and also worked against Japanese legend Kenta Kobashi. In 2000, after having been freed by the WWF, he made a rare appearance in what was left of the Montreal territory, wrestling for NCW to a full house at Challengemania 8 against Glen Kulka who had also recently been released by WWE. "I wanted to give the young wrestlers what I got when I started in wrestling, the hope to make their dreams come true," he said on MusiquePlus (French MTV). In the meantime he called Rhino, who he'd met in Germany, to help him join ECW. He got a tryout — against Rhino. The trial was a success. He wrestled some squash matches and finally received a title match at the ECW Arena against Justin Credible. He sent the "Queen of Extreme" Francine through a table to a big reaction from the rabid and knowledgeable ECW fans.

In September 1999, through Sid Vicious, another peer with whom he'd developed a close friendship, he got a tryout with WCW, but nothing came out of it. The WWF gave him permission — even though it was the tail end of the Monday Night War and he was still under contract. Later, through Vince Russo, he was brought into the Canadian angle with Lance Storm, Bret Hart and Jacques Rougeau. But after Rougeau refused to lose to Ernest "The Cat" Miller and left the federation, the whole storyline failed, and Ouellet was never brought back.

From 2003 to 2008 Ouellet wrestled for TNA under a mask as Mr. X, became IWS champion in Montreal, wrestled in Puerto Rico and pretty much everywhere in the province of Quebec, spent one year in England and obtained interviews and dark matches with WWE.

He remained focused on his dream, but went through many ordeals during this period. In one instance Jacques Rougeau didn't want his student Éric Mastrocola to lose against Ouellet in Montreal in a dark match, so neither Mastrocola nor Ouellet got to perform. Another time, in Montreal, Vince McMahon pretended not to know him. In England Ouellet waited until one a.m. after an event to thank Vince, but McMahon pushed him against the wall without even listening to him. John Laurinaitis (WWE executive vice president, also known as Johnny "Ace" Laurinaitis, who PCO knew well after his stint with All Japan) left him waiting on the phone without ever getting back to him. After making peace with Shawn Michaels over what happened between them a few years earlier, Ouellet proposed a scenario and got a dark match against Charlie Haas, who, during the match, pretended to have forgotten the spots that would've made Ouellet look good.

In spite of all that Ouellet told himself that he made many mistakes and that he could have done certain things differently. "Even after 20 years in the business, we learn on a daily basis," confides Ouellet, humbly.

"I gave up so many things in the hope of achieving my dream of becoming WWE world champion," Ouellet says. Then, with his young daughter, London, occupying an important place in his life, he realized it was time to make the decision. "When you choose to have a career in professional wrestling, it becomes your life. Then you realize that there are other things in life aside from wrestling. However I'm positive that what I've learned throughout my career as a professional wrestler will be put to good use for the rest of my life," he says. "It's hard but I've turned the page. I wrestled in 50 countries, in five continents and in 49 American states. I was the main event at shows held at the Montreal Forum. I worked for WWE, WCW, ECW and TNA. I really did have a good career." The PCO character was done, but Carl Ouellet can continue his life proudly. He's just starting a motivational and educational conference, took part in a spectacle of Cirque Éloize and he has a new objective: to be cast in a movie. "I would really love to act in a big fight scene in a major motion picture, another big dream!"

SYLVAIN GRENIER

Not all wrestlers start the same way. While working as a model Sylvain Grenier ran into one of the most influential personalities in WWE, Pat Patterson, on a golf course. Patterson convinced him to enter the Tough Enough contest in 2001. He succeeded in the auditions, but his Canadian citizenship prevented him from participating in the show. Through Patterson he was, however, invited to train in Florida at Rocky Johnson's school. He went to learn from The Rock's father. "I had the opportunity of working with The Rock early on, as it was the best experience that you could have as a rookie," Grenier remembers. After many months there he was invited to a training camp in Cincinnati. On September 18, 2002, WWE signed him to a development contract but a visa issue delayed his arrival at OVW. He would spend some time in the province, mainly working for the NCW. He also participated in some training sessions with Jacques Rougeau. In February 2003 Grenier was finally called upon to make his big debut. His first work came refereeing the match between The Rock and Hulk Hogan in Montreal at No Way Out. "I had to train as a referee for two to three weeks on the road with Mike Chioda," he remembers. "Hulk was my hero when I was young. I loved guys with that big physique like him, Hercules and the British Bulldog," Grenier adds.

(PAT LAPRADE COLLECTION)

SYLVAIN GRENIER AND ROB CONWAY, AS LA RESISTANCE, WON THE WWE TAG TEAM CHAMPIONSHIP AT HOME

Since the departure of Pierre-Carl Ouellet and Jacques Rougeau, few Quebecers wrestled in WWE, and none of them had been really successful. Ironically he was teamed with another French-Canadian, Rene Dupree, in a tag team called La Resistance. He would win the tag team championship once with Dupree. Then La Resistance would become Grenier and Robert Conway, and it was with the latter that he was the most successful, winning the tag team titles on three different occasions. Being a four-time world tag team champion is an exploit that very few Quebecers or wrestlers can brag about. "Sylvain had a wonderful look, he was a great talent and with his foreign accent, he was the perfect heel to me," says John Bradshaw Layfield.

In 2007, after he was booked again with Dupree, this time with the new ECW and after short stay with OVW, Grenier's adventure with WWE came to an end. Since then he's mainly wrestled in Quebec, where he was NCW champion and TOW champion in addition to winning both promotions' tag team titles with his faithful partner, Rob Conway. He was also CRW champion, wrestled for ROH and toured France after getting back in touch with his first partner, Rene Dupree. From 2009 to 2012, he ran a wrestling school in Montreal.

Born on March 26, 1977, Sylvain Grenier continues to wrestle big names coming to the territory like Abyss, Shelton Benjamin and Al Snow and the best local talent like Kevin Steen, Franky the Mobster and Dru Onyx. He hasn't completely put aside the idea of returning to WWE one day. "If they let me be who I am, they will see the difference," he concludes.

With the arrival of the WWF and International Wrestling closing shop, it was understood that the 1990s weren't going to be business as usual. Jacques Rougeau would be involved in the last two matches of importance that involved a wrestler from Montreal, in Montreal.

ROUGEAU VERSUS OUELLET AND ROUGEAU VERSUS HOGAN: JUST LIKE IN THE DAYS OF YVON ROBERT!

On April 11, 1997, Jacques Rougeau achieved what very few wrestlers can boast: he scored a pinfall victory over Hulk Hogan. "It's the most important win of my career," Rougeau claimed years later. This victory has long been an enigma, especially for wrestling insiders, as many people, including other wrestlers on the same show, wondered how it even became possible. Without taking anything away from Jacques Rougeau's career, in '97 Hulk Hogan was still synonymous with wrestling worldwide. Hogan, who had for so long been dressed in red and yellow, had turned heel and started wearing black and sporting a beard of the same colour. Moreover he was world champion of the biggest wrestling promotion at the time, WCW. To understand how it all occurred you have to first go back to 1994.

In '94 Jacques set wheels in motion, planning his retirement because he was unsatisfied with the way he was being treated by the WWF. "Jacques . . . wanted to leave immediately after *WrestleMania* X for WCW," Ouellet explains. On June 25 at the Forum in front of 12,248, during a match for the tag titles held by The Headshrinkers, The Quebecers, wearing gears made out of the Quebec flag, seemed on the verge of winning the coveted belts for a fourth time. But to everybody's surprise the match ended with a shocking moment: Pierre-Carl Ouellet betrayed Jacques Rougeau and, with manager Johnny Polo, gave him such a beating that he would leave on a stretcher, despite his brother Raymond's run-in. The table was set for Jacques Rougeau's "final" match against his former partner on Friday, October 21, 1994, at the Forum.

A very serious press conference was organized at the Westin Hotel in Mount Royal on August 9, 1994. Vince McMahon himself came in to promote the event. Killer Kowalski also travelled from Boston to attend this press conference, joining Bob Langevin and Yvon Robert Jr. in representing the glorious past of the sport in Montreal. Vince McMahon, recognizing the importance of Rougeau to wrestling in the territory, made the following comment: "I hope now that Jacques's farewell night will be something really special." No staff of the WWF, including Jack Tunney and Pat Patterson, really

PIERRE-CARL OUELLET GAVE JACQUES ROUGEAU
THE MATCH OF HIS LIFE ON OCTOBER 21, 1994
(BERTRAND HÉBERT)

believed what they heard, but Vince McMahon had just predicted the future!

"I wouldn't want to miss Jacques's farewell match for all the money in the world," a headline in *Le Journal de Montréal* said, quoting Édouard Carpentier a couple of weeks before the event. On October 21, 16,843 people paying $214,000 were to imitate the Flying Frenchman and fill the Forum, the best crowd for a wrestling card in Montreal in several years. The promotion for the match reached a fever pitch in the non-wrestling media, something never before seen, even in the glory days of International Wrestling. The two men walked a very thin line between fiction and reality, and made comments that stirred the curiosity of fans and laymen, all the while making the most sceptical of sceptics think that maybe, this time, it was all going to be real.

In an interview with *Le Journal de Montréal*, Jacques Rougeau fired the first salvo. "He was disrespectful to me. I can't forgive him for the comments he made . . . saying I was over the hill and that he was always the one who did all the work in our tag team matches," Ouellet answered with inflammatory words in the same newspaper. "This is so much like Rougeau. He seems to believe that he's the only one who knows how to wrestle." By the night of the match it was Ouellet who had a sense of mission accomplished. "Some of my friends called to ask me whether I really betrayed Rougeau! I can't wait for this to end, as the last two weeks were hard for me. Being the villain in Montreal isn't easy. My mother doesn't find the situation very funny," he said to La Presse. It should be noted that the match essentially represented the only game in town. Since August 12, 1994, Major League Baseball had been on strike, so the Expos weren't in the papers. At the same time, beginning October 1, 1994, the National Hockey League had locked out its players, so the Canadiens, who had won the Stanley Cup 16 months earlier, weren't active, either. The two men pretty much had the sports pages to themselves. "Mario Tremblay and Pierre Trudel on CKAC devoted their entire program Les Amateurs de Sports to the match on the eve of the big night. Vince McMahon himself called in to put more heat on the fire. "I pushed Jacques following Vince's declarations and left the studio in a fury. I think that Trudel and Tremblay still hold a grudge toward us for having made a scene and for having made them believe in our story during their show," Ouellet says, smiling, today.

The match was broadcast live on CKAC and, for the last time in history, all the sports journalists of the major daily newspapers and television were at ringside. "It was the first wrestling match to be broadcast on CKAC, one of the oldest radio stations in North America," Rougeau remembers. Réjean Tremblay explained the situation very well in La Presse the day after. "First, there was no hockey or baseball. People were dying for a roller coaster ride at the Forum. More importantly, because the two stars are Quebecers, guys from the territory, and Quebecers liked to cheer their own stars a thousand times more than such cartoons characters like The Undertaker and IRS." Bertrand Raymond of Le Journal de Montréal talked about the festive atmosphere that reigned that night: "One hour after the last match, two to three thousand spectators blocked Maisonneuve Street, as if it was a Stanley Cup night!" The two men were the last Quebecers to main-event a show together at the Forum, a throwback to the good old days of Yvon Robert, Maurice Vachon, Jos Leduc, Dino Bravo and Johnny Rougeau. "After the retirement match Vince and Pat, actually all the WWF office, was in love with me! Because no one thought we were going to have such a good crowd," Ouellet reveals. In fact ticket sales were very slow at the beginning, but they would dramatically rise at the end with all the coverage.

It would take Jacques two years to come back to wrestling after such a send-off, this time with WCW and alongside Ouellet again. "I've never signed such a good contract before. We're to wrestle eight to 10 times a month, compared to 25 times with the WWF, and our salaries are double," Jacques told Le Journal de Montréal, explaining his decision.

Immediately after their WCW debut it was reported that the company itself would debut in Montreal at the beginning of the following year. On February 4, 1997, Hulk Hogan and The Giant (WWE's Big Show today) came to Montreal for a press conference, announcing a big wrestling card at the Molson Centre on April 11, with the long-awaited match between Jacques Rougeau and Hulk Hogan. In reality, however, it was Rougeau who was actually promoting the show.

In spite of their new partnership, things between Jacques and Pierre-Carl Ouellet were tense and on the verge of exploding. "Our biggest quarrel was after the press conference for the show at the Molson Centre," Ouellet says. "The Giant, my opponent, pushed me and I picked up a chair to defend myself. The following day, the only newspaper that talked about it on its front page was The Gazette — and there was a photo of myself with The Giant . . . not Jacques and Hogan. He blamed me . . . I've never understood why The Gazette chose this picture, instead of the one featuring Jacques and Hogan."

The pressure that Jacques had put on his own shoulders was unbelievable, not to mention the financial investment. Regarding this Ouellet refutes one of the many tall tales about Montreal wrestling. "$25,000 wasn't the price Jacques paid to defeat Hogan; it was what Hogan cost at the time, period. And it cost us another $20,000 for the rest of the WCW talent who were on the show. Fortunately the gate that night rose to $240,000. I think that it was a good deal, given Hulk Hogan was with the nWo at the time on WCW's Monday Nitro." The show drew 17,023, making the event a big success on a financial level with the ticket prices being the highest in the history of the Montreal territory. It must be noted that since WCW didn't give Jacques and Ouellet a television push, the two men had to do a colossal promotional job, going all over the province.

HULK HOGAN AND JACQUES ROUGEAU SET MONTREAL ON FIRE ONE LAST TIME (JF LEDUC COLLECTION)

But WCW did record event-specific interviews for the Quebec broadcast of its show. In one Hogan slapped Rougeau, accusing him of calling himself the Hulk Hogan of Montreal. On April 11, when Hulk arrived at the airport, Jacques was waiting for him there — with all the media in tow — to return the favour. "The slap in the face of Hogan at the airport was my idea," relates Ouellet, proudly. This little scripted moment would give them priceless media coverage on the day of the event.

If the finish of the Ouellet/Giant match was terrible — The Giant took off PCO's eye patch in order to get himself disqualified because he didn't want to lose by pinfall — the finish of the Rougeau-Hogan match made the show legendary. "Hogan decided to lose to Jacques . . . It wasn't for money, and it was only decided upon that night. Hogan told him: 'It's your town, brother. Tonight, I'll put you over!'" Ouellet remembers. Though this had often been believed to be an urban legend, Hogan confirmed the story on Twitter in 2012. "True, he deserved it," simply said The Hulkster. "Hulk had a lot of respect for the Rougeaus, mainly for Jacques, who put Dynamite Kid in his place in 1988 in the WWF," Ouellet concludes. Even though for

Jacques this was one of the most important matches of his career, people often forget that the crowd, who hadn't seen his opponent in Montreal in more than five years, welcomed Hogan like a long-lost family member while greeting Jacques with boos. The reaction was so unusual that Hogan, at the peak of his game as the heel leader of the nWo, couldn't help but ask fans he met in the bar of his hotel after the match this: "I thought that Jacques was really popular in Montreal?" What nobody figured into the equation was that Hogan was even more popular. Marc Blondin, who was the ring announcer that night, recalls that the boss of WCW wasn't happy. "I remember that Eric Bischoff blew a fuse upon learning of his star's defeat with a small package," he says.

"This victory has given me a lot of prestige locally. At first, I told Hogan that he must have wanted to piss off Bischoff . . . But he said, 'Jacques, you have been on the road with me for 10 years. Your brother Raymond and you opened up for me so many times this is my way to say thank you,'" Rougeau says in an interview with RF Video. As far as Pierre-Carl Ouellet is concerned, it remains an event that hasn't received the credit it really deserves, because of the way Jacques talks about it today locally. "I find it sad that Jacques has taken away some of the credit he deserves, being so humble and not mentioning nearly enough the fact that he had worked hard, to the point of getting sick, to make the event the success it was. Also . . . this victory was well deserved for years of hard work and the value of the name Rougeau in the eyes of Hulk Hogan." As it turned out, the fall-out of that match was partly responsible for both men being let go by WCW a few months later.

In spite of the criticisms levelled at him for having tunnel vision, Jacques Rougeau is a relentless promoter. Almost 15 years after the fact, the following question was asked in a survey for the French version of *Family Feud*: Name a well-known wrestler? The top two answers? Jacques Rougeau first, followed by Hulk Hogan — which says a lot about the popularity these two guys had and still have. Rougeau deserves a lot of credit for having known how to revive the good old days of wrestling in the Montreal territory.

While Jacques Rougeau tried to retire, Ouellet, put over by the match against Jacques Rougeau, became the heir apparent of professional wrestling in Montreal. Unfortunately he was to face almost insurmountable difficulties, the most important of which was no other than the WWF champion.

PIERRE-CARL OUELLET
VERSUS KEVIN NASH:
14 YEARS OF WAR!

When the Internet phenomenon took over professional wrestling, many of the things that were secret, and which should have stayed in the locker rooms, became known to the whole world. Among these secrets was the friendship that developed between Shawn Michaels, Diesel, Hunter Hearst Helmsley, Razor Ramon, 1-2-3 Kid and Aldo Montoya in the WWF. They even had a nickname outside the ring, The Kliq. The rumour mill always said The Kliq had too much influence for its own good between 1995 and 1996. This story concerning Pierre-Carl Ouellet proves it.

Let's go back in time. After the Rougeau retirement in October 1994, Ouellet submitted a scenario to the WWF that would change his character. Ouellet wanted to use the fact that he had one good eye to his advantage and make a gimmick out of it. The WWF saw things a bit differently and decided to give him the character of a pirate and the name Jean-Pierre Lafitte. The WWF asked him to stay home and grow his beard. Vince McMahon also told him that he wouldn't wrestle in Montreal again for two years, not until he reached the top of the hill and returned to Montreal as a hero.

But in February 1995 Vince himself called Ouellet. He asked him to do him a favour and wrestle on a show at the Montreal Forum against Shawn Michaels. IRS was injured and he had to find a good substitute. Even though the two years hadn't yet elapsed, Ouellet accepted. In the meantime he contacted Jacques Rougeau and asked for advice. Rougeau wasn't on good terms with the WWF at the time, because the WWF had refused his idea of a show at the Olympic Stadium and wanted Ouellet to leave the WWF. "Maybe he wasn't the best person to ask for advice," admitted Ouellet 14 years later. In fact Rougeau told him that if he lost against Michaels in Montreal, his career would be over in the territory and that he would never be able to do anything with him as a promoter.

On the night of the show George Steele, who was an agent, told Ouellet that he was losing to Michaels. Ouellet explained his point of view and let him know that he didn't want to lose. "You don't want to put me over? I have just won the Royal Rumble — 29 guys put me over and you, you don't want to do it in Montreal, you piece of shit?" Michaels said to

Ouellet after having heard of it. Ouellet answered: "Let me think about it, I'm not sure." Finally Ouellet went to see Steele and Michaels and apologized, saying that he didn't know what he was thinking and that of course he would do the job, he would do the right thing for business. But Ouellet still didn't want to lose clean, so they agreed on a finish in which Michaels would pin Ouellet with his feet on the ropes. "But as of that moment hatred had settled in between Michaels and

PIERRE-CARL OUELLET AS WWF'S FIRST PIRATE, JEAN-PIERRE LAFITTE (CARL OUELLET COLLECTION)

me . . . Even though I had changed my mind. He didn't like the fact that I hesitated," remembers Ouellet.

For some reason Vince McMahon wasn't made aware of this or at least he didn't make a big deal out of it, if he knew about it. Ouellet finally came back as Jean-Pierre Lafitte and received a mega push during which he wouldn't lose for a long time. Then he started travelling with Hunter Hearst Helmsley. It must be noted that when the latter came to the WWF, Ouellet was the first to make room for him in the locker room and welcomed him, as Sid Vicious had done for him a couple of years back. The two men got along very well. "We were good friends," notes Ouellet about Triple H. But the latter started to side with Michaels, and sometime later The Kliq was born.

In a TV taping Kevin Nash (Diesel) went to see Ouellet and let him know that next month in Montreal they would wrestle against one another for the WWF world championship. He added that he would use his big boot and Jackknife powerbomb to go over right in the middle of the ring. "This was the first time that I was given a finish a month prior to a match!" Ouellet recalls, adding that Nash wanted to make a statement because of what happened with Michaels six months before.

"This was a big deal for me. I was only 27 or 28. I was confused and I was wondering whether I had made the right decision in staying — what if I had listened to Jacques's advice and left instead?"

The closer the September show date in Montreal got, the more Ouellet dreamed about the world title, in spite of Nash's statement. "I win in Montreal. I win in Quebec City. I drop it back in Toronto," Ouellet remembers when he was contemplating his perfect scenario to make his dream come true. He convinced himself that it was going to happen this way. On the day of the show agent Tony Garea met him and asked him to do a good match: nine to 10 minutes, big boot, Jackknife and to put Kevin over, to which Ouellet answered: "I don't think so!" Without thinking about what he was doing, he told him clearly that he didn't want to lose to Nash. "Listen, Tony, if I lose to Nash, you're not going to have a main event. I'm going to take my things and leave. I live 20 minutes away from here; I couldn't care less!"

In the locker room, in front of the other wrestlers, Nash went to see him and asked him whether it was true that he didn't want to lose to him. In a moment of ultimate arrogance, Ouellet simply answered yes, that he didn't want to lose, that it was either going to be a double disqualification or a double count out. "I didn't think about the fact that he could beat me up right there," Ouellet says, laughing. Then it was Shawn Michaels's turn to talk to him: "You motherfucker! You're not a fucking businessman. I'm going to get you fired; I'm going to fucking kick the shit out of you!" Michaels screamed, before taking hold of his Intercontinental belt and preparing to swing it at Ouellet. "Swing at me, motherfucker, but don't miss me . . . 'cause if you miss me, I'm going to fucking kill you!" Ouellet replied.

Finally cooler heads prevailed and the match took place. It was a curtain match — as the wrestlers call it — where the wrestlers watch it from behind the curtains in the hopes of seeing the guys settle scores in the ring. But the match unfolded correctly and the outcome was a double count out. The following morning Gerald Brisco and Bruce Pritchard called Ouellet, who told them he was resigning. But they convinced him to go to Quebec City and apologize to Nash. Ouellet had to pay a $1,500 fine to the WWF, the pay he was supposed to get for the Montreal show.

Only half sincere, but still not wanting to burn all of his bridges, he apologized to Nash and the others. He wrestled against Nash again in Quebec City, practically the same match as the previous night. He climbed on the third rope for his legdrop, a manoeuvre he did regularly, but accidentally hit his heel straight into Nash's face. "I really didn't intend to do so, but with the heat that there was, it wasn't really the right time to give him a potato!" Ouellet says.

Nash's friends didn't see it as an accident, and Michaels and Razor Ramon, from the hockey player's bench in the Colisée de Québec, screamed out for Nash to beat the shit out of Ouellet. "Everyone wanted a shoot fight," Ouellet recalls. An avalanche of elbow blows were swung at him in the corner, making him punch-drunk. This was followed by a big boot and a powerbomb. Nash pinned Ouellet, who didn't get up. He had had enough heat as it was.

As he was going through the curtain to head backstage, Ouellet jumped Nash, but they were quickly separated without further trouble. "I think the agents knew they made a mistake," explains Nash in an interview with Tim Baines in the *Ottawa Sun* in May 2009. "They should have insisted that he do what he was told to do or they should have pulled the match." Going to Toronto on the following day, Ouellet had the firm intention of settling the score with both Michaels and Nash. When he reached the arena Sid Vicious, the Smoking Gunns and Bob Holly went to see Ouellet and told him that they were on his side, if anything happened. But Kevin Nash himself defused the bomb, taking the floor and saying in front of everyone that they were all adults and that this had to stop here. "You could really cut through the tension with a knife," remembers Ouellet. Finally the agents changed the Toronto card. Diesel wrestled against Waylon Mercy, while Ouellet wrestled against Fatu (Alofa, Rikiski).

At this point the WWF left for a tour in Europe. "To piss them off even more, I was going over against Aldo Montoya, one of The Kliq, each night in the opener," Ouellet remembers. "The Kliq wasn't too happy about it, saying that putting over a guy who wasn't business was absolute bullshit." Subsequently, during a house show in Cleveland, to everybody's surprise, Vince McMahon showed up. A meeting was planned to talk about the future of the WWF, which was the reason for Vince's presence. In this meeting there were Yokozuna, The Undertaker, Diesel, Shawn Michaels, Triple H, Razor Ramon and some others, a maximum of 10 wrestlers.

Michaels, Nash and Ramon pushed for Ouellet to go, but McMahon didn't want this to happen. From that moment on, however, Ouellet became a jobber. After one month he called Jacques Rougeau to tell him that he was really thinking of joining him with WCW, which he ended up doing, making his debut in September 1996.

However what Ouellet didn't know at the time he changed camps was that Nash and Scott Hall (Razor Ramon) were also going to WCW. "With the experience I now have, I should have been patient and stayed with the WWF," Ouellet says, humbly. After one year Ouellet and Rougeau's contracts were not renewed. Nash and Hall generated a lot of reaction with Hogan and the nWo, so timing was really bad for them. Four years later Ouellet and Rougeau returned to WCW, as they were involved in the storyline of Lance Storm and the Canadian Rules. "Nash didn't know that I was booked. One day after he saw me I lost the hardcore title." When asked whether the heat he had with The Kliq in the WWF had a role to play in all of this, Ouellet says: "In my opinion, there was some Nash influence in there."

Life works in mysterious ways, however, and 14 years after the beginning of this feud between Ouellet and Nash, the IWS, an independent promotion in Montreal for which Ouellet wrestled from time to time, wanted to organize something big for its 10th anniversary show. After having discussed it with Ouellet, the idea of bringing in Kevin Nash, who then wrestled for TNA, was on the table. It was a dreamed-of opportunity for Ouellet to settle his scores once and for all. The announcement went off like a bomb; the wrestling media in Canada and the U.S. immediately ran stories about the old feud. Le Journal de Montréal even devoted an entire page to it on the morning of the show, May 30, 2009.

The match was presented to the fans as a shoot. Nash even declared that "he wasn't coming back to Montreal to lose." But, as with any good Hollywood scenario, Ouellet avenged himself and came out as the winner. There aren't that many feuds in professional wrestling that last more than a few months, and only the most heated last anywhere close to a year. But a 14-year-old feud? That's rare, very rare. Ouellet's victory over Nash ended a long cycle — and, in all reality, the last decade and a half might have been very different without the spectre of that rivalry on his shoulders.

Real-life feuds like this don't happen too often in wrestling. However, the first WWF PPV presented in Montreal also ended with the crowning moment of wrestling's perhaps most unprecedented rivalry.

THE MONTREAL SCREW JOB:
THE DAY WRESTLING CHANGED FOREVER

At Survivor Series 1997, in the middle of the ring in Montreal's Molson Centre, Shawn Michaels won the WWF world championship. Earl Hebner called for the bell, signalling a submission following a sharpshooter. It was Bret Hart's finishing move, but it was being applied by Michaels. In itself? Nothing special. But the events which followed — including Bret Hart spitting in Vince McMahon's face in front of the cameras and the crowd — made it one of the most memorable occurrences in the history of wrestling. "One of the most famous and almost surely the most talked about match ever in North American wrestling history," is what Dave Meltzer calls it.

On November 9, 1997, a total of 20,593 people witnessed a change in the direction governing the WWF and a turning point in the history of the business. If the most knowledgeable fan understood some of what had just happened, everyone else was asking serious questions. Since then the Montreal Screw Job, as it's become known, has been a matter for debate and speculation.

"All I know is . . . we worked a really hard match. A sort of hasty truce was made earlier that day. Shawn implied . . . he didn't want trouble and wanted to be left out of it. He was very cooperative," remembers Bret Hart in *Survival of the Hitman*, a documentary presented on the Fight Network in 2010. "It was more a conflict between Bret and Vince," confirmed Shawn Michaels in 2003. Then suddenly everything collapsed. "I could hear someone say: 'Ring the bell!' That's when I knew it was Vince McMahon . . . I finally realized that they screwed me," Bret Hart recalls bitterly in the documentary *Wrestling with Shadows*. He wasn't alone. The Molson Centre crowd was in shock: it was that obvious the bell was rung without Bret giving up. "Earl Hebner was a very good friend of mine. I don't blame him for what he did. I felt bad that they put him in this predicament. They caught him like a gangster just before he went through the curtain; his job was at stake, even if he promised to protect me on the eve of the match," Bret says, philosophically. "Had I been in his place, would I have done the same thing? Probably," affirms Jimmy Korderas, a former official for WWE, supporting his colleague's decision. "You don't have the time to think, and it's either this or you lose your job . . . A big contract waited for Bret, not the referee," says Korderas.

"I elbowed my French colleague, commentator Jean Brassard, and told him that he had just been screwed," says Raymond Rougeau, who was at ringside. "When Bret started to destroy the equipment and began drawing the letters WCW in the air, there was no doubt that we had just seen something extraordinary. A piece of history," remembers François Poirier. "I felt terrible. I felt like I let everyone in the country down. It became clear to me that everyone knew I got screwed. I could have been the Pied Piper and turned over a car in Montreal that night and set fires . . . I didn't want anyone to get hurt doing something stupid like that. My brother Owen helped me the most, telling me: 'If you don't look bad, it's them that look bad.' It was possibly the most real thing that ever happened in wrestling, ever," Bret has said.

In the locker room the situation was not much better. "I was backstage with The Undertaker. It was like a movie. Suddenly everyone went from shock to anger. I have never seen it like that backstage to this day. I thought it was going to be a real close call . . . where there would be a riot. There were a lot of angry people," Carl DeMarco, former president of WWE in Canada, says. "It should have been a DQ, the Hart Foundation was to come in, then Hunter and then the referees were to pull them apart," relates Korderas. "I was backstage and was waiting for my cue, which never came. I was wondering what was going on and when I finally saw what had happened, I told myself: 'Oh, shit!'" Back in the locker room Hart was both furious and disappointed. "What hurt the most, I thought that I had built up a library of some of the greatest matches of all time. Vince and I always talked about an anthology. When I punched him in the dressing room I knew that it was not going to happen. My whole body of work, it was all going to get locked away in a basement somewhere. Without Bret Hart being visual, without seeing him, I don't mean anything. I just fade away, fade like Bruno Sammartino. I hated that they took that away from me," explained Hart in the *Survival of the Hitman*. "Almost a fitting end to The Hitman character . . . because he never sold out and never lost his integrity . . . What they did is they murdered The Hitman character," says Hart.

"God as my fucking witness, my hands are clean on this one. I swear to God," that's what we hear Shawn Michaels say in *Wrestling with Shadows*. Six years later the truth came out on a WWE Spike TV show: "Yes, I knew.

I was asked to do something by the man who has given me the opportunity to have everything that I have in my life. A man who has stuck by me that I stuck with. He asked me to do it, and I did it. I'm not sorry for it." But on the DVD *Greatest Rivalries: Shawn Michaels vs. Bret Hart*, Michaels has a different take: "I had a ton of guilt, but I honestly felt I was a soldier doing what I was told to do. It was by no means a moment in my life and career that I relished. I will tell people there was not one desirable thing about doing that."

SHAWN MICHAELS WAS ABOUT TO DO UNKINDLY THINGS TO THE CANADIAN FLAG (JF LEDUC COLLECTION)

Afterward Vince McMahon had no other choice but to apologize to Bret, to keep guys like The Undertaker happy. His excuse was that he couldn't take the chance that Bret might walk into WCW still WWF champion. Heated words ensued, and Bret asked him to leave. Vince did not oblige. What happened next occurred in the dressing room of the legendary Montreal Canadiens. "Somehow Vince ran into my hand. I drilled him as hard as I could . . . It was the right thing to do. There was no other choice but to get up and punch Vince one time and then let it go. That's a Stu Hart judgment call," recounted Bret in *Wrestling with Shadows*. "I was in the locker room with Bret when Vince came in. Vince told Bret that he did what he had to do for the business and if Bret wanted to take a shot at him, he could. Bret acted like he was going to leave, but turned around and threw a punch at Vince. Then he looked at Shane McMahon and told him he was next and then looked at Gerald Brisco and told him he was next, so I decided to interfere. Bret told me he had nothing against me so I told him that if that was the case, to stop now and leave the room," revealed Sgt. Slaughter.

A DAY LIKE NO OTHER IN MONTREAL FOR BRET HART
(JF LEDUC COLLECTION)

Many wrestling scenarios conceived since have tried to showcase themselves as representing moments that would change wrestling for good, but the truth of the matter is, nothing will ever match that night. "The biggest name in wrestling and the biggest promoter in wrestling on national television saying: 'It's fake!' I can no longer kayfabe. To me that's why it's such a watershed moment . . . The kayfabe era died that day," says former wrestler Lance Storm. "For the first time, with the screw job in Montreal, the curtain was pulled back . . . You could see what was going on behind the scenes. You got to see how the strings were pulled, how nasty and how manipulating the business could really be," adds journalist and historian Heath McCoy.

From that moment on, the WWF seemed freed and finally able to change its destiny. Until Montreal the company was in the red, losing the battle against WCW. In the six months before Survivor Series 1997 the WWF managed to crack a 3.0 rating for Raw just three times. After November 10, 1997, and up until the last WCW broadcast on March 26, 2001, *Monday Night Raw* scored less than a 3.0 just once.

In the six months that followed the screw job, the WWF put an end to more than 80 weeks of consecutive dominance of WCW's Nitro. "I don't want to say that the screw job saved the WWF, but it was one of the things that allowed for the re-emergence of the company, mainly because Vince McMahon became an excellent heel," adds Korderas. The WWF found itself with an owner it could cast as the evil boss, the type of tyrant everybody had to deal with in the course of their lives. "That whole incident was the start . . . making Vince McMahon the biggest heel in the business history. He didn't want to be, by the way, but everyone around him told him he just should run with it," Carl DeMarco explains. "Without Montreal Vince McMahon probably wouldn't have become a character," confirms Dave Meltzer.

But the truth behind how that night unfolded remains unclear.

"It's so hard to find a hero anywhere. I was proud of that Hitman character. He fought for the right causes; he spoke up and told the truth. I loved being a hero to people around the world. If you think of India, where these kids waited a whole afternoon just to meet me, it was real — this is something you can never buy," Bret Hart said in *Wrestling with Shadows*. And this seems to be the heart of the problem. For Bret it was real, but for Vince McMahon and the WWF it was a show — a show that was losing money and was in danger of disappearing for the first time since 1984. Bret Hart signed a 20-year agreement one year earlier for less money than the WCW had offered him. This agreement, however, allowed him to graduate to a role backstage in the organization after the end of his career and also guaranteed him some creative control during the last month of his work as a wrestler. "Everything I have ever done and plan on ever doing, I owe it all to my WWF fans and I will be with the WWF forever!" Bret said at the announcement of his decision on *Raw* in 1996. But the company's critical financial situation compelled Vince McMahon to free Bret from his contract and to let him negotiate with WCW — a deal that would ultimately make Bret a multi-millionaire. The contentious point in this whole situation was that Bret Hart was the WWF world champion when this was happening. In fact the problem was made worse because of who the WWF wanted to put over and where the match was to take place. The WWF had settled on Shawn Michaels.

"Bret didn't want to lose to Shawn Michaels . . . The two even had battles in the locker room," explains Raymond Rougeau. The two men didn't trust each other anymore, to the point that it was hard for them to work together, even for the well-being of the company. Also, from the get-go Hart refused to lose in Canada. But if there was one place in Canada where Hart could have lost, it was Montreal. Because of the language barrier, he was never as popular here as elsewhere in Canada. He was never a box-office draw like the Rougeaus or the Vachons were.

On the day of the match the news of Bret's imminent departure was everywhere, even in the headlines of the most important Canadian newspapers. His departure was no longer a secret. The disagreement between Bret and Shawn was no longer a secret, either. But in a shocking twist it helped the WWF. Because of this, Survivor Series 1997 beat WrestleMania in buys — 250,000 against 237,000 — becoming the only PPV ever to do so. "Rather than hurt business, it led to incredible — by the standards of a weak WWF at that time — late interest in the match," says Meltzer.

"A lot of people were very uneasy that day. You could feel tension in the air," remembers Gerald Brisco, who was among the few privy to the secret outcome of the match. "I only learned about it when it happened in the ring, as it was top secret," says Rougeau. The other people in the know were Vince Russo, Sgt. Slaughter, Earl and Dave Hebner and Triple H. Both Ross and Pat Patterson maintained they didn't know. In order to convince both men to get in the ring, Vince McMahon simply said yes to the scenario Bret Hart proposed for the match, which would've led to a disqualification and a battle between DX and the Hart Foundation. But instead of pitting Vince's words against those of Bret, the documentary Wrestling with Shadows secretly recorded their conversation. "Going into the meeting with Vince, it occurred to me, why don't we put the mic on you? Under Canadian law it's legal to tape someone, as long as one party is aware of it . . . Our lawyer said it was okay to use the conversation in our documentary," explains Paul Jay, director of Wrestling with Shadows.

This is how the truth came to be known. Up until the fatal moment Bret Hart wasn't comfortable about how his career was ending with the WWF — he considered Vince McMahon to be like a father. "His emotional attachment was clear to Vince and the WWF," explains Gord Kirke, his former agent. It was precisely the human dimension of the situation that hurt Bret Hart that night. Over the ensuing years the WWF launched an attack on his character for his refusal to lose the belt, with no other explanation, reducing a very complex situation to its simplest iteration. "I think he was a lot madder about being double-crossed than losing the title and being double-crossed against Shawn Michaels. He'd have lost the title without a problem and agreed to do so, so that wasn't really the big issue. I think he wanted to do it on his terms, and his contract gave him that right. So he was probably madder about signing a contract in good faith and negotiating rights and turning down a bigger offer in the process and then getting double-crossed," Dave Meltzer says. "Gerald Brisco told me Bret wanted to see me. That he had threatened to beat the shit out of me . . . I will go over there and let him get his free shot in. I felt like I owe that to Bret," Vince McMahon admits, talking about the punch Hart gave him backstage after the match.

The match outcome is now the most copied in the history of wrestling. Over the years any tour of the WWF in Canada inevitably implied an attempt to recreate the finish, mainly in cities like Calgary, Edmonton and, of course, Montreal. During the No Way Out PPV presented in Montreal in February 2003, the end of the main event between Hulk Hogan and The Rock involved a similar finish, with Sylvain Grenier as the sellout referee. At the end of 2009 another Montreal PPV revolved around a similar finish in the match between The Undertaker and CM Punk, with Teddy Long in the role of Vince McMahon this time. Even WCW got into the act, using the finish immediately after Hart's arrival in December 1997 which left a bitter taste about the match that made the largest amount of money in the history of the company, Sting facing Hulk Hogan at Starrcade 1997. In 2010 TNA copied the controversial outcome, with Hogan this time playing the role of the boss, swindling Kurt Angle. It's arguable that wrestling's obsession with this finish is directly related to the fact that the original was real.

When Bret Hart finally joined WCW their ineptitude became transparent: WCW didn't even try to use him to open up the Canadian market. "They should have gone into Canada, but they were doing such strong business in 1998 in the U.S. that they didn't think about opening new markets," explains Dave Meltzer. "They never saw Canada as much of a market. During their years on top they basically just ran Toronto and Vancouver," adds Greg Oliver of SLAM! Wrestling. After some rough years in WCW Bret suffered a stroke in 2002 while riding his bike. He almost died. "Vince called me up when I had my stroke and we talked. Emotionally, for me, it was important for him to know I wasn't bitter about what happened with Owen. I felt somehow, through the family squabble, he didn't really understand my position. It wasn't this hatred I had for him and everything he stands for. It wasn't about that at all. The truth is, I was so grateful for the opportunity to have the career I had and the chances he gave to me. When he called me and said we could still do that anthology . . . That was a really big turning point . . . That's what I wanted," Bret Hart reveals in *Survival of the Hitman*. In 2005, WWE proudly put up a picture of Vince and Bret shaking hands, as Bret had just started working on his DVD anthology. In 2006 he was inducted into the WWE Hall of Fame, but refused to attend *WrestleMania* the following night.

This story was told all around the world, and obsessed wrestling fans haunted Vince, Shawn and Hebner with the famous "You Screwed Bret" chant each time they had the chance. On the other hand McMahon clearly invited fans to do it in the scenarios he presented. After Breaking Point it got to the point of making one wonder which had to stop first: Vince or the fans? "I don't think people are still obsessed with it . . . It's fun to chant things at Shawn Michaels or Earl Hebner, but I don't think that constitutes an obsession. It's just fun," Greg Oliver argues. "In Montreal it wasn't forgotten, and we kept on waiting for a resolution at each visit. If to do this we had to go against the current and make fans see Shawn or Vince in a bad light, then we had to do it, so that it would never be forgotten. After all Quebec's motto is Je me souviens (I remember)," François Poirier explains. This message, after having fallen on deaf ears for years, seems to have been finally heard by both parties.

On January 4, 2010, Bret Hart made his return to WWE as a guest host. "It was time to forgive, see if I could turn a negative into a positive. If we could turn this whole thing and have a little fun with it," he says in *Survival of the Hitman*. Bret was the one who opened up talk for the return everyone wished for, but that no one believed would happen. "In the end my decision was that I wanted to go out, let people see the old Hitman from 10 years ago come back. It felt strange, but I can tell you that when I did my little thing . . . It seemed that I was gone for about 10 minutes and not 12 years. I don't think I ever did it with emotion like that in WCW," he explains today in the same documentary. On his Facebook page Bret Hart said that his meeting with Shawn Michaels in the ring that night was the first real meeting since Montreal. "It's worth mentioning that although I did see Shawn earlier in the afternoon in the cafeteria, our in-ring faceoff was unrehearsed and heartfelt on both sides, and I can finally say that Shawn and I have finally made peace in what has been a long, draining and sometimes pointless war of personalities." Shawn himself admitted after *WrestleMania XXVI*, as he was announcing his retirement, how important Hart's forgiveness was to him. "I've got to thank Bret Hart. I cannot tell you how much I drove that poor guy crazy. I want to thank him . . . to have forgiven me . . . And I will forever honour his friendship," says the wrestler, who has been a born-again Christian for many years now. *WrestleMania XXVI* would mirror for one last time the careers of the two men. Hart returned as a wrestler for the last time to fight Vince McMahon, and Michaels had his retirement match against The Undertaker.

The last time the two men will discuss the matter in public is more than likely on the three-DVD set about this feud. But Hart's return to the Bell Centre on September 10, 2012, for *Monday Night Raw* is probably the final chapter of the story. "Since we sort of got back on good terms again, I always thought: 'I wonder what will happen when they're in Montreal' . . . whenever that happens, it will be a *Monday Night Raw* eventually . . . they'll have to think that maybe it would be a good idea to bring me into that," Hart told the *The Gazette*. "I didn't expect it in some ways and wondered if it would ever happen, and here it is." Bret received a hero's welcome in a city that never forgets. Ironically, he's more popular in Montreal now than he was in 1997. "I don't think they thought it would get the reaction that it did. I think they thought it wouldn't be a big deal. As you can see, I had a better feel for how that audience was going to react. But I'm grateful to WWE for doing it. It was really satisfying," Hart told the U.K.'s *The Sun* after the event, to put an end to the long saga of the Montreal Screw Job.

THE ERA OF
THE INDEPENDENTS

Since the demise of International Wrestling many independent promotions have popped up in Montreal. The fact is, these promotions had always existed in the territory, but since the end of the 1980s they've taken control of the local business, given the absence of a major league local promotion.

THE PROMOTIONS

After International Wrestling closed, the only well-established promotion left was the Loisirs St-Jean-Baptiste. Around 1989–90, following a disagreement, Pat Girard fired Ludger Proulx. In December 1990 Proulx, who had already promoted a few shows and who had helped Girard with booking at the Loisirs, founded ICW in the Hochelaga-Maisonneuve neighbourhood in Montreal, alongside Carl Langlois, Randy Côté, André Moreau and Réal Massicotte. During that time Girard fired everyone at the Loisirs. Why? Because it was his way of retiring and making sure to help Ludger get started with his promotion. "I didn't realize it when it happened, but Pat knew me, I was like him, and he wanted to force me to start my own promotion, and by firing everyone he kind of forced them to come to ICW," says Ludger. After a short while some workers brought Proulx, against his will, to see Girard, and when he saw him Girard gave a big hug to his student, making Proulx understand what really went down.

Within a year all of Ludger's partners had left the promotion. Ultimately his brother Serge would become his longest associate in the venture. Throughout the years, on top of all the guys from the Loisirs, wrestlers such as Jos Leduc, Frenchy Martin, Gino Brito, PCO, Richard Charland and Sunny War Cloud performed there. Many veterans of independent wrestling in the province wrestled or even made their debuts with ICW. It was the only federation of any value in Montreal in the early 1990s and its 20-year history made it the oldest wrestling promotion on the island of Montreal. The Loisirs and ICW were definitely the bridge between International Wrestling and the era of the independents in Montreal.

SERGE PROULX IS CONSIDERED ONE OF THE BEST HEELS OF THE INDY ERA (PAT LAPRADE)

But just before International closed down in 1986, François Poirier, Eric Jalette and Philippe Bélanger, three guys from Joliette, a town 44 miles north of Montreal, founded a wrestling promotion in their high school. First known as the AWA (Amateur Wrestling Association) it became Lutte Lanaudiere in 1992 and finally took up the name NCW (Northern Championship Wrestling) in 1996 and relocated itself in Montreal, while still presenting shows all over the province. Twenty-five years later, after having presented wrestlers such as Pierre-Carl Ouellet, Lance Storm, Sylvain Grenier and Tommy Dreamer, NCW is still as active as ever and has the title of the longest-running promotion in Quebec wrestling.

In 1999, after having promoted some shows in the mid-1990s, Jacques Rougeau opened his wrestling promotion, International Wrestling 2000. This independent group would become the one that would draw the most spectators throughout Canada. Local talents like Keven Martel, Iceman and Kevin Steen would be a part of its roster, in addition to international stars like the Road Warriors, Abdullah the Butcher and Bret Hart.

Still in 1999, a promotion that was more underground than Rougeau's emerged, namely the IWS. With Manny Eleftheriou in the lead, it would take over 10 years later as the most important wrestling promotion in the province.

CM PUNK CAME TO MONTREAL TO WRESTLE PCO BEFORE JOINING THE WWE (YAN O'CAIN)

It had a crucial role to play in the careers of such wrestlers as Ring of Honor's El Generico and Kevin Steen. Unfortunately, after more than 10 years of existence, the IWS decided to close up shop following its show on October 9, 2010.

In 2000 two wrestling promotions made their Quebec debut. In Montreal former wrestler Paul Leduc opened, almost without his family's knowledge, a promotion that he called the Federation de Lutte Quebecoise (FLQ). Many local wrestlers would go on to wrestle at one time or another for the FLQ — its mission was to train the youth of Quebec.

At the other end of Hwy 20 Sunny War Cloud opened up his promotion in Quebec City, CCW. The latter would become a benchmark for wrestlers in the area with, among others, the talented Keven Martel, who was to take care of training new wrestlers. Upon its closing down in December 2003 one of CCW's wrestlers, Eric Picard, with the help of two other associates, bought the promotion assets and renamed it EWR. Even though EWR was only in business for two years it revolutionized wrestling in the province, bringing in independent wrestlers both from the U.S. and Canada. "Bringing in all these wrestlers, the EWR allowed the territory to open up. It all started with the success of bringing in Christopher Daniels," Patrick Lono says. Among the wrestlers who came to Quebec City were Petey Williams, Raven, Steve Corino, Homicide and A.J. Styles. Since 2011, Steve Boutet's NSPW has been the main promotion in Quebec City.

At the same time Marc Pilon, wrestler and coach with NCW, started promoting big events twice a year with the cream of the crop of Quebec wrestlers and some big names from the independent American scene. Former

TNA world champion Samoa Joe was brought in before his TNA run, and former WWE world champion CM Punk headlined one of the shows against Pierre-Carl Ouellet. With the EWR these shows helped put the Montreal territory back on the map again. After the end of these two promotions the IWS would continue to forge ahead, bringing in Sabu two days before his debut with WWE, as well as Sid Vicious, Christian Cage and Team 3D.

In January 2005 an important event occurred on the independent scene when the NWA officially set foot in the territory for the first time. In fact Rodney Kellman became partners with the owner of the CWA in Montreal to present shows there under the banner of the NWA Quebec. Although this association was only to last three months, the NWA Quebec tried to start again in 2007, presenting some shows in Laval. The CWA-NWA Quebec was the only promotion in Montreal in 2004 and 2005 to give a hard time to the much more established IWS with Steve Charette, Patrick Lono, Philippe Leclair, Geneviève Goulet (LuFisto) and Hugo Roy at the helm.

In 2006 the Association de Lutte Féminine (ALF), the very first female-only wrestling promotion in the territory, was created by Kim Leduc, daughter of Paul Leduc. "The ALF was of crucial importance to female wrestling in the province as it gave the girls an opportunity to be the stars of the shows. The guys were the special attraction, contrary to what was usually the case . . . The female wrestlers had the opportunity of developing as they intermingled with girls having different experiences," Geneviève Goulet says. Unfortunately the promotion closed down in 2009, but in September of the same year female wrestling had its place again, thanks to the NCW Femmes Fatales, sister promotion of NCW, founded by Geneviève Goulet, Stéphane Bruyère and Anthony Tonin. The best female wrestlers in the world come to Montreal for Femmes Fatales. Among these were Awesome Kong, Cheerleader Melissa, Jazz, Sara Del Rey, Mercedes Martinez, Madison Eagles and Ayako Hamada. Since 2010 it has been considered the third-biggest promotion of its kind in North America, after SHIMMER and WSU and the best-known promotion outside the province.

In 2007 a new promotion, TOW, made its debut with the announcers of TNA Impact on RDS Marc Blondin, J.F. Kelly and Pierre-Carl Ouellet in the lead. Ouellet would leave his spot to Sylvain Grenier near the end of 2007. The TOW brought to its different shows such stars as Abyss, Honky Tonk

Man, Matt Morgan, Al Snow, "Hacksaw" Jim Duggan, Beer Money Inc., Demolition, Shane "Hurricane" Helms, Shelton Benjamin and "Rowdy" Roddy Piper. It also paid tribute to many former local wrestlers, including Rick Martel, Pat Patterson, Édouard Carpentier, Gino Brito, Paul Leduc and Abdullah the Butcher. Its 1,800 fans in March 2010 made up the biggest crowd for a regular promotion since the beginning of the indy era, excluding what Rougeau's promotion managed to draw.

During the last 20 years many other wrestling promotions were successful in the province. FCL in Shawinigan, CPW and C*4 in the Hull-Ottawa region, RWR in Verdun, ISW, Battlewar and CRW in Montreal, MWF in Valleyfield, JCW in Jonquière, GEW in Granby, SCW/ALE in Sherbrooke and, finally, R2W in Quebec, completed an already impressive list of promotions, keeping the territory alive.

THE WRESTLERS

Fans have seen many wrestlers come and gone over the years. During the 1990s and the early 2000s it was difficult for a Quebecer to break through in America. There were fewer big independent promotions, and the WWF, WCW and the ECW dominated. So it would be subjective and unjust to name just a few of the Quebec wrestlers from the era.

On the other hand, Quebec wrestling witnessed a turn of events in 2004, as two matchless talents struck the territory like lightning.

EL GENERICO

El Generico, or The Generic Luchador as people call him, made his debut in 2002. He was a bit player at the time, so much so that very few people would ever have believed that he was to become one of the best wrestlers in the world.

After a match against Pierre-Carl Ouellet and Kevin Steen in 2003 and after his feud with Steen in 2004, he started drawing the attention of our neighbours south of the border. El Generico had his first chance in the U.S. with CZW in a match that also involved Sexxxy Eddy, Exess and Kevin Steen. It was the beginning of a nice saga for him as for Steen. From that day on El Generico

EL GENERICO AS IWS CHAMPION IN MONTREAL, BEFORE TOURING THE WORLD (PAT LAPRADE)

has become a very well-known name around the world. He was PWG champion and tag team champion of the promotion located in California.

From 2007 to 2011 he has been a regular with Ring of Honor, the third most important promotion in North America. His matches are frequently presented on iPPV. They have also been presented on HDNet in the U.S., as well as on Sinclair Broadcasting Group. In 2007 he was voted the best wrestler in the province, taking over from his good friend Kevin Steen. In 2008 he featured in ROH championship matches and he won the ROH tag team titles with Steen. "I've never wrestled against Generico before 2007 and I found that he was great. He brings in so much energy and exudes a lot of charisma," notes former WWE world champion Daniel Bryan. In 2009 he was ranked as second-best wrestler of the decade in the province, in addition to having been voted wrestler of the year.

The year 2010 was fruitful for El Generico and he made his debut for the prestigious Mexican AAA promotion, in addition to becoming PWG tag team champion with former WWE tag team champion Paul London. Even if he didn't participate in the TV tapings, he was invited by WWE for *Raw* and *SmackDown* shows held in Toronto and Ottawa. After his former partner Steen turned on him at the end of 2009, he had the upper hand in their final match at the ROH *Final Battle 2010*, ending a year-long feud that was voted the best in the world for 2010 by the *Wrestling Observer* newsletter. In 2011 he got a tryout with TNA and added the ROH television championship to his trophy case. He also finished 46th in the *Pro Wrestling Illustrated* 500 rankings, one of only five Quebec wrestlers to crack the top 50. 2012 was another good year for the Laval-born wrestler, as he won titles in countries like Sweden, Japan and Germany. He has been wrestling in Europe on a regular basis for a couple of years, having visited France, England and Russia. He also visits Japan a few times a year for Dragon Gate or DDT promotions. He has actually worked in close to 30 different countries so far in his career. In the U.S., he now works on a more frequent basis for Dragon Gate USA and Evolve.

El Generico isn't about to retire any time soon and could easily become one of the best wrestlers that the province has ever had. "Generico is currently the best wrestler in the province of Quebec," says veteran Sunny War Cloud. "He's a great guy, a very good wrestler. He has great potential for either TNA or WWE. I would recommend him anytime," says former WWE wrestler Sean Waltman, better known as X-Pac.

His future evolved in parallel to Kevin Steen, with whom he went around the world for four years. "He has an incredible talent! Bravo-Rougeau and Ouellet-Grenier already took the big step to WWE . . . The next duo to make it could be Steen-Generico," Pierre-Carl Ouellet says.

KEVIN STEEN

This is what Dwayne "The Rock" Johnson had to say about Kevin Steen on Twitter in July 2012: "My boy Curt Hawkins introduced me to Steen's matches. Been a fan ever since. #Innovator." But before getting the thumbs up by one of the best wrestlers of all time, Steen's journey began some 13 years ago.

He was coached by Jacques Rougeau Jr. when he started wrestling for

IW 2000, and many already saw him as a future star. "Very good . . . He had potential," Raymond Rougeau recalls.

In 2004 the EWR in Quebec City offered him a golden opportunity to wrestle against one of the best wrestlers in the world at the time, Christopher Daniels. This match propelled Steen to the

KEVIN STEEN, THE BEST OF HIS GENERATION AND ROH WORLD CHAMPION (PAT LAPRADE)

indy peak and he would never look down again. Afterward there was a series of successes for the wrestler who fans would nickname him Mr. Wrestling. He won the PWG title in California, the IWS and EWR titles in Quebec, the CZW Iron Man title and the PWG tag team titles, in addition to participating in many tournaments in the U.S., wrestling in Europe and having gone on a long tour of Japan for Dragon Gate.

After a brief stay in ROH in 2005 Steen returned in 2007 to team with El Generico. For three years Steen and El Generico were one hell of a team. Their feud with the Briscoe brothers in 2007 was one of the most violent and gripping in the history of Ring of Honor. In 2007 they were actually ranked the third-best team in the world by *Wrestling Observer*. The following year they were voted the second-best team in the world by *Wrestling Observer*, second only to their long-standing enemies, the Briscoes. In '09 they ranked 7th for a third consecutive top 10. For the first decade of the 2000s they were considered the fifth-best in the world. "As a team they were fantastic. They had a great chemistry. They were definitely one of the most entertaining teams on the scene," Daniel Bryan says. "As a team they definitely have the potential to be part of TNA," says Samoa Joe.

After a year-long hiatus from ROH, Steen came back stronger than ever at the end of 2011. He quickly became the most popular wrestler on the roster and on May 12, 2012, in Toronto, he won the ROH world title against Davey Richards.

"He has a very good attitude and is always learning," former ECW and ROH champion Jerry Lynn says, explaining Steen's success. In the province of Quebec he wrestles regularly with NSPW, TOW, C*4 and some other promotions.

Between 2004 and 2008 he was voted the best wrestler in the province three times. From 2003 to 2007 and again in 2010 and 2011 he was involved in the match of the year locally. "In the days of the junior heavyweights in Montreal he would've been a top guy," Gino Brito says. In 2009 he was voted the wrestler of the decade in the province, ranking ahead of other wrestlers like Pierre-Carl Ouellet, Sylvain Grenier and LuFisto. In 2012 he was ranked 20th in the well-known PWI 500, the second Quebecer ever to crack the top 20. "In spite of his weight and build he's agile," Dan Murphy, one of the editors of the PWI 500, comments. In 2010 and 2011 he won the Bruiser Brody Memorial Award, awarded to the best brawler. "I'm very proud and happy for him," admits Jacques Rougeau Jr.

Steen is, without a shadow of a doubt, one of the best Quebec wrestlers of the indy era. "I think that he has the talent that would allow him to join WWE; he has the attitude, he has the guts, he has what it takes," Pierre-Carl Ouellet says. "If only he had a body, he would main-event WWE right now. He's better than guys who are doing main-events in the WWE and one of the best promo guys in the business," said Dave Meltzer.

THE FUTURE

Other wrestlers from the province work hard and hope to get noticed. The 6'10" Darkko is well known by WWE officials; Dru Onyx and Franky the Mobster have had tryouts for WWE. Each man could get the break they're waiting for. Others had the chance to grow up in this business.

JEAN-JACQUES, CÉDRIC AND ÉMILE ROUGEAU

Wrestling fans in the 1960s and the 1970s had an opportunity to see the Rougeau brothers, Johnny and Jacques, in action. In the 1980s and 1990s they watched the team of Jacques Jr. and Raymond. But wrestling fans could see a third generation of Rougeau brothers.

Jean-Jacques, or J.J., as he's nicknamed, is Jacques Rougeau Jr.'s first son. He was named thus in honour of his great-uncle Jean and his grandfather. He performed at a very young age, becoming a fourth-generation wrestler for the Rougeau family. Near the end of his adolescence J.J. started wrestling in tag team with his father, a little bit like Jacques Sr. did with his own son. "J.J. is the Édouard Carpentier of the Rougeaus," his father simply explains.

Cédric developed his passion for wrestling later in his life. At only 19, he stands out at 6'5" and his 260 pounds. "Cédric is the Jos Leduc or the Dino Bravo of the Rougeaus," says his father, proudly. With his height and physique, he's the prototypical WWE performer. "When he's ready I will call the WWE, and he will get a shot. I'm positive. I can even be his manager!" says Jacques. For a few years now WWE has mainly hired either wrestlers with an imposing physique or second- and third-generation wrestlers. Cédric has the advantage of having both.

And if ever Cédric and J.J. need reinforcement, the young Émile wouldn't

A PROUD DAD WITH HIS SONS ON HIS FINAL RETIREMENT: CÉDRIC, J.J. AND ÉMILE ROUGEAU

(KAREN BROADWAY)

be that far behind. "He's the Johnny Rougeau of my boys. He's charismatic and always wants to be in front of the cameras, just like me when I was his age," Jacques explains. Émile has already started wrestling at the age of 11. "J.J. is an acrobat, Cédric is a strong man, and Émile's an actor," concludes their proud father.

ALEX SILVA

Born in Montreal on January 23, 1990, Alexandre Freitas started his career at the young age of 14. Son of local indy talent the late Tommy Rose, he was invited by OVW in 2010 and decided to move to Louisville, Kentucky, without any guarantee. The gamble paid off as he became a regular, winning the television championship three times. It paid even more when Silva became the first wrestler featured on TNA Impact Wrestling Gut Check segment on April 26, 2012. The following week, he was originally scheduled

ALEX SILVA GOT THE CHANCE OF A LIFETIME WHEN RIC FLAIR GRANTED HIM A TNA CONTRACT

(JF KELLY COLLECTION)

to be denied a TNA contract, but he convinced Ric Flair to change his vote by delivering a very emotional promo and was awarded with a TNA spot. "It's awesome. The best day of my life!" Silva told RDS.ca after the show. "He's still a rookie, but he has potential, he looks good and works hard. He's still young, but he has guts. When you want to play with the big boys, you have to leave the security of your own territory and that's what he's done," explains Jim Cornette who worked closely with OVW for years. Since then, he returned to OVW, now the developmental territory for TNA, waiting to be called up to the main roster.

THE HISTORY OF WOMEN'S WRESTLING IN MONTREAL

When it comes to women's wrestling, names like Mildred Burke, Mae Young, Fabulous Moolah, Wendi Richter, Sherri Martel and Chyna, not to mention Japanese wrestlers like Chigusa Nagayo, Jaguar Yokota, Lioness Asuka and Manami Toyota and more recently Canadian wrestler Trish Stratus stand out. But Montreal has also had also its share of female wrestlers.

VIVIAN VACHON

Although she was born on the other side of the border, in Newport, Vermont, Vivian Vachon, whose real name was Diane, didn't grew up in the U.S. Apart from having been born on January 23, 1951, at a hospital five minutes away from the Canadian border, Vivian grew up and spent her childhood in the Eastern Townships, where the Vachon family lived. "She's the only one in the family who wasn't born at home," says her brother Paul. She started her career when she was still a teenager, in the late 1960s. Her brothers Paul and Maurice didn't want her to wrestle, but Vivian was determined to succeed. So Maurice sent her to train with Lilian Ellison, better known as the Fabulous Moolah, and her career started from there. It was actually Maurice who found the ring name for his sister. "Marilyn Monroe was very popular during her days. Her initials were M.M. Maurice wanted to find something similar for our sister. So he came up with Vivian Vachon, so that the initials were identical, like those of Marilyn," says Paul. In the 1970s she wrestled in the United States, Japan and Australia and, of course, in Canada. On February 26, 1971, she won the California women's title, and on November 4 of the same year she won the AWA championship. At the time she was considered

THE QUEEN OF WRESTLING, VIVIAN VACHON

(LINDA BOUCHER)

one of the best female wrestlers in the world; the public dubbed her the Queen of Wrestling."

An article published in *The Wrestler* magazine in December 1972 debated who could wrestle the world women's title away from Fabulous Moolah, saying: "Vivian Vachon, of course, is the most likely. A dynamic wrestler, Vivian has the size, speed, and savvy needed for the rigorous schedule the women's champion must follow. She can be brutal when necessary yet is a master of scientific wrestling. Her best facet, however, is that she seems to have no flaws at all. In fact, if anybody upsets Moolah for the championship, it's likely to be Vivian Vachon."

According to the newspapers and magazines published at the time, Vivian was more popular in the U.S. than in her own province. "Vivian was very strong and wrestled like a man," her niece Luna remembers. During those years she wrestled in small towns, but not in Montreal, where women's wrestling was only accepted in the early 1980s by the Athletic Commission. "Claude Provost, who was acting as the deputy mayor under the reign of Jean Drapeau, brought about that change," Gino Brito remembers. "We could see that women's wrestling worked in the U.S. and in smaller towns in the province. Provost was a big fan of wrestling and always came to the shows. So, we asked him to talk to the Athletic Commission because he had some contacts there. Shortly after that the commission legalized women's matches in Montreal."

In spite of her popularity Vivian was famous as one of the best heels in the business. She performed in the movie *Wrestling Queen* in 1975, after having retired one year earlier. "I wanted to have a family," Vivian explained in an interview in 1986. It was actually the year that she returned to the ring for her brother Mad Dog's retirement tour. She wrestled mainly against the Lock and Candi Divine. The 1980s also saw her return to Japan. Unfortunately on August 24, 1991, she died, along with her daughter, in a car accident. "The accident occurred in Mont-Saint-Grégoire. Vivian was about to turn on road 104 on her way to Masonville when she got hit by a drunk driver. He was going twice the speed limit," remembers journalist Ghislain Plourde who was at the scene. Vivian had retired again from wrestling in 1987 and was 40 at the time of the tragic accident.

LUNA VACHON

A lot of things no one knew about Luna Vachon surfaced at the time of her death. For example, despite fans believing that Luna was Paul Vachon's daughter, she wasn't his biological child. Her real name was Gertrude Wilkerson and she was called Trudy by everyone; she was the daughter of Paul's second wife, Rebecca Van Pierce. "She was three and a half when I entered her life. I'm the only father she has ever known," Paul says. "My father means so much to me," Luna said after receiving an award at the Cauliflower Alley Club in 2009, thus confirming that a father isn't necessarily the one who begets the child, but, rather, the one who accepts and takes upon the role. "I was crying when I received the award, just because my father and uncle were present." In spite of having been born in Atlanta on January 12, 1962, she was, without a shadow of a doubt, a full-fledged Vachon.

Vivian greatly influenced her niece. Like his sister, Paul didn't want his daughter to become a wrestler. When he was in the WWF she went to the ring with him, so he taught her some things, but didn't want her to make wrestling her profession. Luna was, however, as obstinate as Vivian. "Vivian and her husband Buddy Wolf started coaching me. Then my father sent me to Moolah in Columbia, North Carolina," Luna remembered. She was still young and only weighed 110 pounds at the time. "I was told that I was too skinny to be a heel. But I wanted my aunt to be proud of me, so I persevered. It's funny because today all the divas are very skinny," related Luna, whose aunt Vivian was her idol. His first match was for Moolah at the age of 21. She won a match against Peggy Lee Leather and lost on the same card against Donna Christanello. Subsequently she left Moolah and settled down in Florida. It was there that everything really started for her.

As she was playing the role of a journalist who was giving a prize to Kendall Windham in the ring, Windham slapped her and she fell violently to the mat. "Backstage I went to Windham, looked him in the eye and with the voice of my uncle Maurice, I asked him if this was the best he could do," she remembered, laughing. "It was then that Jake Roberts started yelling, 'You're a Vachon. You're Mad Dog's daughter!' No one knew that I was a Vachon at the time," she said. Mike Graham, the promoter of the territory, asked her whether she was interested in working in Florida and whether she was ready to shave off half her hair. Graham wanted her to be part of Kevin Sullivan's clan, and in this group there was a wrestler called Bob Roop, who had already shaved half his head. Vachon accepted the offer. "At the beginning they wanted to call me Moaning Mona, but Nancy Sullivan, Kevin's wife at the time, said that I didn't look like the moaning type. So she proposed Luna, short for lunatic. It was actually Nancy who shaved my hair. She was one of the rare female friends that I've ever had," remembered Luna, who also wrestled under the name Angelle Vachon.

Luna would travel a lot. "I toured Japan over 17 times," she recalled. She was managed by her father during her first trips to the land of the rising sun and teamed with The Lock. "Bull Nakano copied our gimmick," Luna said pointing out the influence that her style and look had in Japan. She also wrestled in Australia, Singapore, Europe and Dubai. She also participated in the only PPV event in the history of the AWA, SuperClash III.

Her WWF adventure started in 1992. She had a hard time getting along with some of the WWF divas. "My first choreographed match was against Sable," said Luna. "I wanted to help her at the beginning, but she told me that she didn't need to learn how to fall, as she was going to become a champion anyways." In an interview with WWE.com, Luna explained: "Sable wasn't a wrestler until I made her one. A real wrestler can wrestle a mop and make it look like the mop is kicking their ass, and that's what happened that night. She beat me, and when we got to the back there was champagne and confetti, and everyone wanted to celebrate with Sable. I kept walking until Owen Hart came up to me and told me I had just put on the match of my life. It meant a lot to have someone like him say that to me."

It's actually surprising that Luna was never WWF champion. "I was scheduled to win the title three times. Once I was caught smoking a cigarette in front of the fans, and the other two occasions Sable forgot the belt in her hotel room. She did it on purpose, I'm positive about that," Luna said with conviction. But Sable wasn't the only one with whom Luna got into trouble. "Madusa and I had more matches in the locker room than in the ring," she explained. They wrestled against each other in the WWF, as well as in the WCW.

Luna wrestled at *WrestleMania X*, teaming with Bam Bam Bigelow

ONE TOUGH COMPETITOR, LUNA VACHON
(SCOTT TEAL COLLECTION)

against Doink and Dink. "Many people credit Sunshine and Precious with pioneering the cat fights. I say Sherri and Luna perfected it in 1993," former valet Missy Hyatt holds. Unfortunately Sherri left the company in August 1993, which put an end to a feud that worked very well. Luna was also part of ECW. "The first time I wrestled against a man was against Stevie Richards in ECW. He was very nice and allowed me to do so many things in the ring," she remembered. "Luna was the first Queen of Extreme. She was my first manager," remembers Tommy Dreamer.

Aside from Bigelow and Dreamer, Luna also served as the valet of Bull Nakano, Goldust, Shawn Michaels and Tom Nash, as well as Gangrel. And she actually married the last two men. She was also part of a stable called The Oddities in the WWF. In the 2000s she wrestled mainly for independent federations all over the U.S. She finally retired in December 2007. "I have so many problems with my neck and back that surgery would be useless," concluded Luna, explaining why WWE didn't get in touch with her for the women's battle royal presented at *WrestleMania XXV*.

Those long-term injuries would have tragic consequences. On August 27, 2010, Luna was found dead in her house by her mother, probably because of an overdose of painkillers. The wrestler who was famous for her sturdiness, her in-ring abilities, as well as her particular look, was also an incredibly nice girl, who helped all those she loved and would go to battle for them. "She was willing to beat up a drunken New Jack for disrespecting me," says Missy Hyatt. She also inspired many wrestlers like Nattie Neidhart (Natalya), Lita and Daffney. The latter even said that she had watched Luna's performances for hours to learn the art of women's wrestling. "She was ahead of her time as far as her look, character and wrestling are concerned. Today she would've been much more popular," says Jim Korderas.

"Thank you for all the years," said an emotional Vachon to WWE.com when talking about her career. "Thank you to those that knew me back then and those that still remember me today. Thanks to everyone that ever screamed at me, cheered for me, spit at me or threw beer on me. I want to thank them for everything," she said.

"I would like to think that Luna is in heaven, since the devil was afraid that she would take his spot," Missy Hyatt says. "She would be happy to be described this way," concluded her father.

LUFISTO

Geneviève Goulet's interest in wrestling was sparked when she saw performers like Nakano, Toyota and Hokuto on tape. But Goulet had an idol in Montreal. "It was Luna Vachon, because of her look, how solid she was in the ring and her way of involving the crowd. She was a heel, but I loved her!" After having been coached in her native Sorel by Pierre Marchessault and Patrick Lewis, she met former wrestler Lise Raymond. "Mulling over that today, I can say that meeting her was more than crucial . . . Lise Raymond told me to stand tall, fight for my ideas and never to allow the wrestlers who didn't want women in their world demean me. She even told me that it was better to be a bitch and secure one's spot than to get along with them, that wrestling's a cut-throat profession and that I should always keep my head held high in order to be considered a serious wrestler," she relates.

This is exactly what Goulet did. Under the name Precious Lucy at first, and now under the name LuFisto, she's wrestled across the Montreal territory, Ontario, British Columbia, the U.S., Mexico, Europe and Japan. After having adopted a very popular extreme style in the late 1990s and early 2000s, the wrestler, who was nicknamed the First Lady of Hardcore, was rewarded for her choice. She was invited to participate in some extreme wrestling shows in Mexico for the LLF, where she's actually still the extreme champion. Moreover, in 2003 she went to Japan for a two-month tour. "I didn't intend to do extreme wrestling. I was given the

THE SUPER HARDCORE ANIME FROM MONTREAL, JAPAN, LUFISTO (GILDA PASQUIL)

opportunity to do it in a match and I saw it as a way of trying new things and challenging my own limits. I also wanted to prove, one more time, that girls were able of being as good at this as the guys were. Finally it allowed me to make a name for myself, be different and contribute a new style to female wrestling," relates the wrestler, who has been coached over the years by Len Shelley and the Proulx brothers.

She's achieved many things over the course of her career, including winning the CZW Iron Man title and the King of Death Match Tournament, as well as the Queen of the Death Match Tournament and the ALF title. She's also very popular with the Quebec media. "She's worked hard to get where she is," notes Kevin Steen. During her travels she won men's titles and that's something she's perhaps most proud of. Her ability to wrestle against men even KO'd the Ontario Athletic Commission's wrestling department, which, at one point, refused to allow her to wrestle against men. The department eventually gave up — and is no longer in charge of professional wrestling in Ontario.

A regular with SHIMMER, the biggest women's wrestling promotion in North America, LuFisto has also worked for most of the biggest independent federations in the U.S., including CZW, PWG, WSU and ROH. In Quebec she's considered almost a demi-goddess by other women wrestlers. Many among them chose to become wrestlers because of her, and they are often impressed when they work with their hero. Furthermore Goulet has taken many young women under her wing over the years and helped them improve and develop. One of them is Granby's Kalamity, who's the actual Femmes Fatales champion and was ranked 35th in the PWI Female 50 in 2012.

Since 2001, except for when she was injured in 2007, LuFisto has been voted best independent woman wrestler in Quebec. Since 2002 she's been one of the 50 best wrestlers in the province (men or women), in addition to being one of the most popular wrestlers year after year. In October 2010 she became the first Femmes Fatales champion. In 2012 she was voted 17th in the PWI Female 50. She also celebrated her 15th year in pro wrestling June 23, 2012, by having a try-out with TNA. Although no ranking of the sort in the past was done at this level, historically she comes right after Vivian and Luna as the best female wrestler in Montreal history. "She's been the best female wrestler in the province over the last decade," concludes Sunny War Cloud.

If the Femmes Fatales title is the most important women's title in the Montreal territory, WWE, TNA and SHIMMER women's titles are certainly the most important ones in the world. The WWE title, called the Divas title, has actually been held by a Quebecer.

MARYSE OUELLET

After a six-year period during which there were no Quebec women's wrestlers in WWE, Maryse Ouellet registered in the Diva Search contest in summer 2006. Born on January 21, 1983, she already was a wrestling fan.

"I started watching wrestling in 2001–2002 because of Jeff Hardy," Ouellet reveals. Although she was eliminated from the contest, WWE signed her to a development contract shortly after. "I couldn't have won the contest. Because of some regulations people from Quebec aren't allowed to win this kind of contest in the U.S. That's why I had to lie and say I was from New Brunswick. In fact, I was born in Deux-Montagnes, Quebec," explains Ouellet. Between August 2006 and January 2008 she spent her time commuting between OVW and FCW, the development promotions for WWE. Then, in February 2008, she became a regular in the SmackDown women's division. She actually won recognition on December 28, 2008, when she took the Divas title from Michelle McCool. In spite of an injury she incurred a couple of days later she kept her title until her return in February 2009. In April 2009 she was transferred to Raw, WWE's number one ranked show, and became one of management's favourite divas.

"I've heard that I have a lot of sex appeal and that's really something I try to use when I get on stage," explains Ouellet, who has been dating former WWE champion Mike "The Miz" Mizanin for a few years. On July 26, 2009, she lost her title against Mickie James. After she returned from her injury, WWE used her Francophone background as part of her character, with Maryse regularly performing some of her dialogue in French. "For me being French-Canadian doesn't seem to be that exotic, because that's who I am. But for the fans, especially in the United States, it's something really interesting," Ouellet told SLAM! Wrestling. On February 22, 2010, Ouellet won the Divas title for a second time, keeping it for a little more than two months. ProWrestling Illustrated magazine actually ranked her as the ninth-best female wrestler in 2009 and 10th in 2010. For the rest of her tenure with WWE, she was mainly used as a valet, working primarily with Ted DiBiase Jr. "I liked it, it was different. All the girls were having two-minute matches while I had 10 minutes of TV airtime," says Ouellet. But on October 2011, she received a phone call from John Laurinaitis, senior vice president of talent operations. "The conversation lasted 30 seconds. He told me they decided to let me go. I thanked him for the six great years I spent with the WWE and that was it!" recalls Maryse. "I would've left anyway. I wasn't interested in doing short matches and barely being used. I always said what I thought. I had no problem going to Vince and let him know how I felt about something. And I've made a lot of sarcastic

MARYSE OUELLET HELD THE WWE DIVAS TITLE TWICE (MIKE MASTRANDREA)

comments on the two-minute matches. That's why I was let go. My relation with Mike [The Miz] had nothing to do with it. We were always very professional," concludes Ouellet.

Vivian Vachon started her career as a wrestler more than 40 years ago. In a short period of time she was crowned world champion. Four decades later, after Luna Vachon's and LuFisto's successes, Montreal had another world champion in Maryse Ouellet. Will women's wrestlers from the province be able to continue to develop and achieve an international level of stardom? "I'm confident," Goulet concludes. "We have talent in the province."

MONTREAL
THE BIRTHPLACE OF
MIDGET WRESTLING

Most accounts of the history of midget wrestling in North America say that Jack Britton started the whole thing in the late 1940s. But the truth of the matter is that it began even earlier.

Gérard Phillips, who wrestled under the name Gerry Phillips at the Atwater Market in the late 1940s, was actually responsible, to a large extent, for midgets becoming wrestlers. Sometime in 1947–48 Paul Downing, a police sergeant in Montreal, was one of the wrestling promoters at the Atwater Market. Phillips sold tickets, wrestled there and took 25 percent of the promotion's gate. The shows took place on Tuesday evenings, but on Sundays, the wrestlers went to the ring and practised. There was an interesting lone spectator each Sunday. "When we practised Marcel Gauthier, a midget, came to the ring and started picking a fight with the other wrestlers. He said: 'Bring, other midgets and I'll beat them!' This didn't fall onto deaf ears," Phillips remembers. One day a friend of Phillips, Rolland Reid, former amateur wrestler who trained at Loisirs St-Jean-Baptise, introduced him to someone. "That's when I met Jean Roy. He wasn't a midget, but, rather, a short adult." Roy was training at the Loisirs, and Phillips took the opportunity to invite him to the Atwater Market. "I convinced Paul Downing to give them a tryout on Sunday during the practice. After having practised together, it worked," Phillips relates. So, during the next show, Gauthier climbed onto the ring to challenge anyone of his weight class. Roy, who was sitting in the crowd, accepted. "We advertised the match in la Voix Populaire and le Montréal-Matin, two newspapers," Phillips remembers. "We usually drew 500 to 600 spectators, but on this occasion we drew around 1,600!" Taking place in 1948, it was the first midget wrestling match on record, according

THE MASTERMIND BEHIND MIDGET WRESTLING,
JACK BRITTON [LEFT], WITH LITTLE BEAVER
AND BOB LANGEVIN IN HAWAII (PAUL LEDUC COLLECTION)

to Phillips. "In my opinion this was the first midget match in North America. Then Raymond Sabourin, another midget who heard about the match, showed up and expressed his interest to be part of the promotion. The matches scheduled either two midgets against a regular-sized wrestler or three midgets against two regular-sized wrestlers," Phillips explains.

Shortly after this, around 1949, Jack Britton's role in this story begins. "Britton wrestled against me at the Atwater Market," Phillips notes. Having seen that midgets drew considerable crowds and as he had already wrestled in the U.S., he decided to start his own midget wrestling touring group. "He realized that this thing could go far," Phillips says. And even though Britton wasn't only the promoter associated with the early days of midget wrestling, he paid the midgets well, while making a lot of money himself.

What makes the story all the more interesting is that Gauthier, Roy and Sabourin became famous, but under other names. Marcel Gauthier became one of the best midget wrestlers in the world, Sky Low Low. Jean Roy became Tiny Roe, and Raymond Sabourin became Pee Wee James. "Sky, Tiny Roe and Pee Wee James were part of the first crew of midgets," Gino Brito adds. Brito remembers precisely how his father worked. "He sent in four guys on the road with four midgets each. There were always 16 midgets on the road. At some point there were 24 midgets!"

SKY LOW LOW

Deciding whether Sky Low Low or Little Beaver was the best midget wrestler in history is as difficult as trying to determine whether Alexander Ovechkin is better than Sidney Crosby. If Sky was considered the better technician, Beaver was considered the more spectacular. "Without question [Sky is] the most famous midget pro wrestler of all time," Dave Meltzer says about him. Gino Brito saw things differently. "Beaver was the star, but Sky was hard to beat. He was the general in the ring." As far as Little Brutus is concerned the choice is easy to make. "Without hesitation the best midget was Sky Low Low." If we are to rely on the ranking provided in this book, Beaver is a couple of positions ahead of Sky Low Low. (See ranking on page 401.) "There's no big difference between the two," Brito says, trying to give both their due. Recently *The Wrestler* magazine focused on the best midgets of all time, and its choice was Sky Low

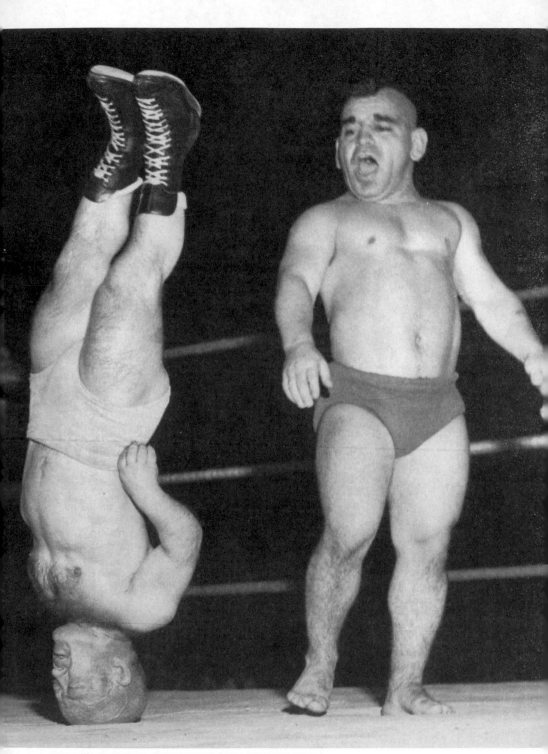

THE TWO GREATEST: SKY LOW LOW AND LITTLE BEAVER (TONY LANZA)

Low followed, of course, by Little Beaver and Hornswoggle, who has been performing for some years now in WWE. No matter whether Sky or Beaver was really the better wrestler, their careers crossed paths more often than not.

Marcel Gauthier's life changed dramatically when Jack Britton decided to go around the world with a group of midgets. In 1949, under the supervision of Britton, he officially became Sky Low Low. That same year the legend says he won a tournament in Paris, becoming the very first world champion in his category, a title that was later partially recognized by the NWA. In the 1950s Sky and Little Beaver exchanged this title many times.

Little Beaver was actually the man he'd wrestle most often. As a matter of fact it was doubtlessly the best and longest rivalry in the history of the Montreal territory; although it took place more often than not outside the province's boundaries. They even wrestled against each other in front of Queen Elizabeth II and King Farouk of Egypt. "Sky didn't like it when other wrestlers were successful, because he didn't want another wrestler to take away his spot. But with Beaver it was different. He realized that the crowds were bigger and that he was ultimately going to make more money himself," Brito says. Little Beaver's character, with his Indian look, was so popular it made it easy for Sky, who looked old even at a young age, to be the heel. Sky is actually often referred to as the father of midget wrestling, a statement substantiated by Little Brutus, who says that Sky paved the way for the others.

He wrestled on many cards at Madison Square Garden after 1957, when the New York Athletic Commission lifted its ban on midget wrestling. Like the other wrestlers in his division, Sky went around the world. "My father took them to Japan, Europe and everywhere in between," remembers Brito.

Very often promoters presented midget tag team matches, most probably because four men always seemed to be travelling together. In the 1950s Sky's regular partner was Tiny Roe. In the 1960s it was Fuzzy Cupid, while in the 1970s it was Little Brutus. In singles competition one of Sky's acts was to offer $100 to any midget who could beat him for two out of three falls. In 1975 he won the midget of the year award given by Pro Wrestling Illustrated, in addition to finishing second the following year, right after Lord Littlebrook. Sky was known for being quick in the ring, for having an excellent dropkick and for the ability to stand on his head without falling. He was also very strong and fearless — which played tricks on some people.

While he was in Chicago in 1973 signing autographs after the show, there was a guy harassing a girl he knew. At one point the young man touched the young woman's breasts, yelling, "You don't wear a bra!" Seeing an opportunity to help a lady in distress, Sky stopped signing and went toward the young man, who obviously didn't take him seriously. That's when Sky punched him below the belt, asking, "You don't wear a jock?"

Near the end of his career he wrestled for the McMahons (father and son), from 1981 to 1987. In 1982 in the WWF he worked his last feud — a series of tag team matches in against his sworn enemy, Little Beaver. He called it quits in the Maritimes, and his last recorded match dates to July 1988 in a tag team match with Bob Crawford. In 2002 he was inducted into the Professional Wrestling Hall of Fame and in 2004 the same honour was bestowed on him by the Quebec Wrestling Hall of Fame. In 2000 singer Mark Cutler, an American from Rhode Island, called his album *Skylolo* in honour of Sky, going so far as to put a picture of him on the album cover. This shows the extent to which his reputation transcended wrestling. Marcel Gauthier died on November 6, 1998, of a heart attack at the age of 70, after a 36-year career. So Sky Low Low or Little Beaver? Brito gives an answer that no one can refute: "Sky Low Low *and* Little Beaver!"

LITTLE BEAVER

On March 29, 1987, at *WrestleMania* III, Little Beaver was involved in a six-man tag team match, battling with Haiti Kid and Hillbilly Jim against Little Tokyo, Lord Littlebrook and the behemoth King Kong Bundy. "The stadium was so big that I tried to imagine . . . I was at the Montreal Forum in order to keep my emotions under control," Beaver said. All those who watched remember that, at the end, Bundy squashed Beaver and was disqualified because he was not supposed to face one of the two midgets. "I don't want to brag about the match, but I think that I've stolen the show from the others," Beaver said to *Le Journal de Montréal* afterward. What the fans probably don't know is that Beaver was left with a serious back injury that basically put an end to his career at the age of 52. "My lower back hurts so much, I got to see my doc every day," Beaver told Jean-Paul Sarault in April 1987. In an interview conducted with him in 1998 Bundy said: "I remember that Little Beaver kicked me with his

LITTLE BEAVER WAS ONE OF THE MOST EXCITING WRESTLERS TO WATCH

(MUSÉE BAILLARGEON COLLECTION)

moccasins and it hurt me badly. So I was a bit hard on Beaver on that night. You know what I mean? But he deserved it. But, you know, I hope I'm not to blame for his hasty death. I don't want to have that on my conscience."

In an autobiography published in 1979 Little Beaver, born on April 18, 1934, tells a dark tale, saying that he was disappointed with his career and with the promoter who came to get him from Saint-Jérôme in 1950. He says Jack Britton promised to make him a millionaire and that he failed to do so. Ultimately he seems disappointed in the years he spent as a wrestler and never fully accepted the fact that he was a midget. Yet if there's one midget's name that fans of any generation of wrestling remember it's his.

"Little Beaver was definitely the biggest star," says Little Brutus. He was the icon of this division for years. "One of my teammates, when I played junior, saw a photo of Little Beaver in the newspaper and told me that I looked like him — that I was as tall as him! That's how I got my nickname. Gordie Howe still calls me the Beav when he sees me," says hockey hall of famer Marcel Dionne, whose nickname was Little Beaver. His Native American look, with

A VERY YOUNG LITTLE BEAVER WAS TRAINED BY JACK BRITTON (TONY LANZA)

the Mohawk haircut, the feathers and Indian shirt was distinctive. "The Native American community saw Little Beaver in a good light because he respected our ancestor's traditions through his character," affirms Billy Two Rivers. Of course it was a gimmick. The wrestler who played the Indian for all those years was actually a young man called Lionel Giroux. "A cowboy character in an American comic strip . . . had a sidekick who answered to that name, and I was given that name," said Beaver in an interview. He was referring to the Red Ryder, whose sidekick Little Beaver was a young Navajo.

If you take the time to read his whole autobiography, you quickly realize that Beaver contradicts himself. He says he never made a lot of money, but then he says he changed cars two or three times a year. "At one point he used to drive a Thunderbird and a Cadillac," affirms Brito. "A regular midget performer earned $200 to $300 at Madison Square Garden, but Beaver and Sky earned something between $1,500 and $2,000 per match in New York," says Brito.

If Sky Low Low was considered the better technician, Beaver never allowed anyone to steal the show from him in the ring. He regularly managed to perform high-flying manoeuvres, as well as dropkicks, during his matches. He was credited with developing the comedic style that made midgets so successful for years in North America. But his career took him a lot further. Midgets were a draw wherever they went. Whether it was in California, New York, Europe, Japan, Australia, New Zealand or Canada, they had the same tremendous success.

Montreal fans still remember Paul Leduc's wedding in the ring at the Forum, but 10 years earlier Little Beaver, only 16 at the time, got married after a wrestling match in Santa Monica, California, in front of 6,000 spectators. His only son came from the marriage. In the 1950s the NWA recognized a world midget champion, a title that Beaver held twice, the first time in the 1950s and the second time in the early 1970s. His title defences were, unfortunately, never recorded — one single defence of the title was found for Beaver on July 5, 1974, in Calgary against Frenchy Lamont. He was chosen the midget of the year by *ProWrestling Illustrated* in 1973. In 1982 he participated in many tag team matches for a number of WWF wrestling shows between the months of August and December. Each time one of his opponents was Sky Low Low. He also wrestled for International Wrestling in the '80s, with Gino Brito wanting to continue the work his father had begun. "He worked almost only at the Paul-Sauvé Arena and at the Forum, often with Tiger Jackson," Brito remembers. "I also spoke to Beaver about his book a couple of years before his death, and everything turned out all right," he says, making a reference to his comments about Britton, who, by the way, died just after its publication. "He knew that it talked about him, but he didn't want to read it," Brito reveals.

Surprising as this may seem, in spite of all the success he had it was the last match of his career that is most remembered today. After two months of convalescence he returned to the WWF, serving only as Hillbilly Jim's manager. On December 4, 1995, after a long struggle with a lung illness, Little Beaver died of emphysema. He was 61. In 2003 he was inducted into the Professional Wrestling Hall of Fame and in 2004 he was inducted into the Quebec Wrestling Hall of Fame.

TINY ROE

After taking part in the first ever midget match Tiny Roe went around the world with Jack Britton's team. The Montreal athlete stood 4'10", which made him taller than most of his colleagues. So he wrestled more often with the bigger little people, against men like Mighty Schultz. Before he was called Tiny Roe, Roy briefly wrestled under the name Mickey Langlois. "He managed to work well with anyone. He could guide those who had some difficulties and could follow those who were better," remembers Brito. Born in 1927 he started his career in his early 20s, a career that wouldn't come to an end until the 1960s. After having settled in Windsor, Ontario, close to Detroit, where Jack's wrestling office also was, he died in 1986 at the age of 59.

PEE WEE JAMES

After making his debut at the Atwater Market, Raymond Sabourin wrestled under his real name for some time in Quebec and Ontario. But shortly after this his name was changed to Pee Wee James — a ring name he kept throughout his career and under which he was the most successful. Born in Montreal in 1933, James is rightly known as one of the founding fathers of midget wrestling. He was a heel throughout his career, but was paradoxically considered to be a real comedian, who went so far as to play music in order to entertain the crowd. "Pee Wee James was the journeyman of the midgets," remembers Brito. "In a 15-minute match he only worked for four or five minutes, because he wasn't able to follow the best wrestlers at the technical level," Brito says. In spite of his weaknesses it's easier to name the places where he didn't wrestle. Sabourin put an end to his career in 1968, after having spent 20 years in the world of professional wrestling. On September 16, 2008, at the age of 75, he died in Ottawa, where he had lived since the 1970s.

RAYMOND SABOURIN A.K.A. PEE WEE JAMES WAS ONE OF THE FIRST MIDGET WRESTLERS

(SCOTT TEAL COLLECTION)

LITTLE BRUTUS

Jean-Jacques Girard — Little Brutus — had a successful career. Born in 1937 in Lacolle, near the U.S. border, he began wrestling in 1954 and had his first tag team match in Detroit with Tito Infante against Fuzzy Cupid and Mighty Schultz. At the time he wasn't called Little Brutus, but Tiny Tim Girard. "It was Bert Rubi's wife who named me Tiny Tim," recalled Girard in an interview in SLAM! Wrestling. After having wrestled under this name for about 10 years, Girard changed it and

LITTLE BRUTUS, HERE WITH SKY LOW LOW, WAS ANOTHER PIONEER IN MIDGET WRESTLING

(ROGER BAKER)

his attitude, turning heel. "There was a normal-sized wrestler from Quebec named Jim Bernard, who also worked at that time. He was also known as Brute Bernard, so I decided to become the little brute, Little Brutus," he explained. He, too, worked all over the world and went into partial retirement in in 1974. He would enter the ring occasionally in the late 1970s and 1980s, working for both the WWF and the NWA, as well in the Montreal territory and the Maritimes. After a glorious career, the wrestler called Tiny by the fans died on April 1, 2010.

MIGHTY SCHULTZ

Rolland Dubé is another Quebec wrestler who followed in the footsteps of the pioneering midgets. "I think he came from Abitibi," Brito says. "He lived there, anyway." He wasn't given the name Mighty Schultz for show. "He was a very strong midget," Brito explains. "He could lift Beaver, stretching his arms to their limit. He really had a good build for a midget." Schultz is often considered as one of the most hated heel midgets, second only perhaps to Sky Low Low," Brito says, "When he wrestled the crowd didn't find it funny. He had a lot of heat . . . The crowd really hated him."

TIGER JACKSON

In the late 1970s the wrestler who was to become the last famous Montreal midget, Claude Giroux, began his career. Because Little Brutus grew up in St-Jean and in the '70s lived in Iberville, he trained Giroux, who came from the same region. "I worked at the military college when Brutus trained me," Giroux remembers. "I started training in October 1978 and had my first match in December of the same year, teaming with Little Beaver against Sky Low Low and Brutus." These three wrestlers were all his mentors. "Brutus showed me the basics, while Beaver and Sky put the finishing touches on my work," he adds. Under the name Tiger Jackson, he wrestled for the NWA, the WWC in Puerto Rico and also in Germany. "I was on the show in which Bruiser Brody was killed," remembers Jackson. "At the time we had to give a $500 deposit to the promoter as a guarantee for our presence. My life was worth much more than $500."

In the early 1980s he also had a couple of matches with the WWF. "I wrestled in Calgary, Kuwait, Italy, Hawaii and the Bermudas," says Jackson. He returned there at the end of 1992, teaming with The Bushwackers. Throughout 1993, when he wasn't wrestling with Butch and Luke, he was involved in a feud with Little Louie or was being used to play the roles of Little Macho Man and Little Hulkster. In November 1993 he started wrestling under the name Dink the Clown, the gimmick with which he is mostly known outside the Montreal territory. As Dink he was called upon to accompany and team with

SKY LOW LOW INFLUENCED A LOT OF MIDGET WRESTLERS, AMONG THEM TIGER JACKSON

(LINDA BOUCHER)

Doink the Clown. "Ray Apollo played Doink at this point . . . And I got along with him very well." In 1994 he spent the first months of the year in a feud with Bam Bam Bigelow and Luna Vachon. Although he had no issue with Luna, the same couldn't be said about Bigelow. Midgets are known to have a rough time in wrestling locker rooms. "This was often a matter of jealousy. Midgets were popular with the crowds, and this didn't work for everyone. I had a hard time with Bam Bam at the beginning and went to see Pat Patterson and told him that if it didn't work, I was just going to leave. But we finally got along."

He was in a match at *WrestleMania X* in New York, finishing his feud with Doink against Bigelow and Luna. Jackson would spend the remainder of 1994 in another feud, this time against Jerry "The King" Lawler. At Survivor Series he teamed with Doink, Wink and Pink against the team of Lawler, Queazy, Sleazy and Cheesy. Finally, on May 16, 1995, Tiger would wrestle as Dink for the last time. "This was not only the last time I wrestled for the WWF, but also the last time in the U.S.A.," explains Jackson. "I had my own business at the

TIGER JACKSON. WHO ALSO PLAYED DINK IN THE WWE. WITH LITTLE BEAVER (LINDA BOUCHER)

time, so I started to wrestle less and less." In 1997 he was on the undercard of the Rougeau/Hogan show in Montreal. He also briefly worked for WCW. "Tiger's contract with Vince didn't come to an end, but he wasn't happy because he didn't get his promised cut of PPV money. So he accepted a deal to wrestle for WCW. We were both in a match, a four-versus-four, at the MGM Studios in Florida, where we were dressed like Luchadores with masks. This way no one could recognize him," explains Pierre Villeneuve, another midget wrestler who often travelled with Giroux. Today Giroux still occasionally participates in shows for Jacques Rougeau — and he even brought back the Dink character for him in December 2010, playing the clown for the first time since he left the WWF.

Wrestling allowed Giroux to work elsewhere in show business: "I took part in American TV, films and commercials. I worked with the Cirque du Soleil, in addition to performing stunts and standing in for kids." When he looks back on his career Claude Giroux seems satisfied. "I loved working for Vince McMahon Jr., Gino Brito and Afa. I had a good career."

History shows that midget wrestlers were stars everywhere around the world. And they all owe it to Jack Britton, who had the foresight to launch a worldwide midget wrestling tour. But without Gérard Phillips's perspicacity, who knows what would've happened. "Britton was quicker than me," Phillips philosophically concludes some 60 years later.

QUEBEC WRESTLING FAMILIES

Two of the most popular sports in the province of Quebec are hockey and wrestling. Many families have left their mark in both disciplines. Although hockey is the sport that has occupied the biggest place in the hearts of Quebecers, wrestling has more families who have been successful from generation to generation. If the names Dufresne, Presenza and Ranger are known mainly by hardcore fans in Montreal, some others are known throughout the world.

THE BAILLARGEONS

There were six brothers, Jean, Charles, Adrien, Lionel, Paul and Antonio (Tony). They originally came from Saint-Magloire near Quebec City where today a small museum stands in their honour. They all had wrestling careers starting in the 1940s and ending with Antonio in the '70s. They would showcase strength and acrobatic performances before their wrestling matches. Early on, they often did all their promotions by themselves. Their sister Geraldine was also a strong

CHARLES AND ANTONIO BAILLARGEON WITH MONTREAL CANADIENS' GUY LAFLEUR (PAUL LEDUC COLLECTION)

JEAN, PAUL, ADRIEN, LIONEL, CHARLES AND ANTONIO BAILLARGEON (MUSÉE BAILLARGEON COLLECTION)

woman and she took part in the show, proving that their incredible strength did indeed come from their grandmother. But unlike her brothers, she never wrestled. "Wrestling is tempting, but I don't really entertain the idea. It's unworthy of a woman," she said in an interview back then. Many people consider them the strongest brothers in the history of the world; when they were at their peak, they even made newsreels before movies! One of the first Quebec wrestling families to distinguish themselves, the Baillargeons were tag team champions in both Montreal and the San Francisco territory. Paul, Tony and Adrien actually received votes for a place among the best Quebec wrestlers of all time.

Jean Baillargeon Jr. speaks with passion about his famous family: "They loved wrestling. My dad, who could tear up a phonebook with his bare hands, was also wrestling sometimes as The Angel." Paul was well known for a crazy feat of strength: lifting a horse on a telephone pole. "Maybe not crazy, but today when I think about it, maybe not the smartest stunt!" he would say years later. Paul is remembered for having had the best career in North America, among other territories in Calgary and Minneapolis. He was so popular in Quebec City that Yvon Robert would play a subtle heel as the two of them were drawing big houses.

FATHER AND SON: GINO BRITO AND GINO JR. FIGHTING TO KEEP INTERNATIONAL WRESTLING ALIVE

(LINDA BOUCHER)

THE ACOCELLAS

Luigi Acocella, who is of Italian origin and who started his career in 1932, was the first member of his family to become a wrestler. Then two years later his brother Gabriel started his own career. "My father wrestled for money in carnivals," relates his son Gino. "Then my uncle convinced him to get involved in wrestling." After having had some matches in Boston, promoter Paul Bowser told them to come back in a year because he had too many Italians. "So they went back to see Bowser and asked him whether he would take two Irish wrestlers, as there were lots of Irish people in Boston," Gino says. These new characters were to change their lives. Luigi became Lou Kelly, while Gabriel became Jack Britton. The two, however, had short-lived in-ring careers. Britton would subsequently have tremendous success as a promoter. "When thinking of Quebecers who were influential in wrestling on a major league level, one of the first names that should come to mind is Jack Britton. He started midget wrestling, women's wrestling with Moolah, he owned five percent of the office in Johnny Rougeau's promotion and had contacts all over the world," Paul Leduc says. "When I was young they called me Little Britton, and all I was thinking is that I needed to change this to a more Italian name,

JACK BRITTON, FATHER OF GINO BRITO
(GINO BRITO COLLECTION)

PAUL LORTIE WAS THE LEADER OF THE LORTIE FAMILY (RICHARD Z. SIROIS COLLECTION)

so I took out the 'n' and a 't,'" Brito says. Following his dad and grandfather, Gino Brito Jr. wrestled mainly for International Wrestling but he didn't have a lengthy career. "Maybe I made a mistake when I gave him my name, but I just wanted to help him," says his father. "He had a passion for wrestling, but not enough. When he stopped wrestling he didn't miss it." In 1983, Albert DiFruscia, Brito's nephew, slowly replaced Carpentier as an interviewer (both in English and in French) and became the local ring announcer for the promotion. He also worked as a commentator on CFCF 12. "I grew up in this business because of my grandfather Jack Britton. I started working for the office when I was 13 or 14 years old, selling programs and stuff. Becoming an interviewer was something that came up during a family dinner," he recalls. After International Wrestling closed, he became the local ring announcer for the WWF. "If I would not have had my own business at the time, I might have pushed to make it a career," says DiFruscia, now the owner of a car dealership.

THE LORTIES

Paul and Bob Lortie were two of the most influencial people in the very popular lightweight division in Montreal.

They started in the 1930s, but the brothers wouldn't stay in Montreal like most of the other lightweight wrestlers of their time. They travelled to Europe and wrestled in New York City as well. Jacques Rougeau Sr. told Greg Oliver that if Paul had started his career 20 years later, he would've been a big star. They were also the biggest promoters in Quebec aside from Quinn in the 1950s. Their nephews André, Paul (Ray) and Donald all became wrestlers. Donald Lortic was the most successful of them with a 14-year career. He wrestled under a mask as a part of The Medics tag team with Jose Gonzales.

THE VACHONS

A lot has been said about this wrestling family. But other than Maurice, Paul, Vivian and Luna, another member of the family embarked on a career in the wrestling world. Maurice's son, Mike, began wrestling in 1975 and would later briefly appear for International Wrestling. Other wrestlers who appeared under the name Vachon weren't related to the Vachon family. Stan, who teamed with Paul for a long time, wasn't a relative. Damien and Pierre, two independent wrestlers in the Vermont region, aren't Paul's sons. "They asked

LUNA WITH HER UNCLE MAURICE AND FATHER PAUL (PAUL VACHON COLLECTION)

to take my name," says Paul. However a famous former wrestler and promoter could be a member of the larger Vachon family. "One of Verne Gagne's aunts is originally from Lac Beauport (near Quebec City), and we also have an aunt who came from the same place. What's weird is that in the 1960s members from the Gagnes and the Vachons got married to each other very often," explains Paul. "Of all those millions you've made with the AWA, we should get a cut!" Maurice told Verne during one of Gagne's visits to the Montreal territory. It goes to show that the world of wrestling really is one big family.

THE ROUGEAUS

Like the Vachons', the story of the Rougeau family is very well known. But other members of this famous family shouldn't be left out of this history, starting with uncle Eddy Auger. "He was a very good wrestler, very credible," says Jacques Sr. about Auger, who was known in the U.S. as Pierre

JACQUES ROUGEAU SR. CAME OUT OF RETIREMENT TO TAG WITH HIS SONS (LINDA BOUCHER)

LaSalle. "Eddy Auger made a fortune in France — he was very popular," added Édouard Carpentier. There was also the brother of Raymond and Jacques, Armand Rougeau, who wrestled from 1982 to 1986. He was trained by his brother Raymond. "He made me think of my father as a wrestler. He was credible in the ring," remembers Raymond. "We spoke about bringing him to the WWF with us. He even had a match against Bob Orton at the Forum." But some problems with his back, neck and shoulder, from an earlier accident in his youth, made him retire at an early age.

Another sibling, Joanne, was a WWF promoter from 1995 to 2000 for Eastern Canada, from Ottawa to the Maritimes, including the Montreal territory. She gives credit to her brother for this job. "My brother Raymond ran his mouth!" she said, laughing. She was also married to Denis Gauthier. Their son, Denis Jr., is a former NHL player who now works for the RDS television network. A fourth generation of Rougeaus began wrestling in the 2000s when Jacques' sons laced up the boots. "As far as I'm concerned the Rougeau family is the wrestling family in Quebec," Jimmy Garvin says.

EDDY AUGER, THE FIRST GENERATION OF ROUGEAUS [ABOVE] (YAN O'CAIN COLLECTION) RAYMOND ROUGEAU AND BROTHER-IN-LAW DENIS GAUTHIER WERE ALL STAR'S TAG TEAM CHAMPIONS [BELOW] (TONY LANZA)

THE LEDUCS

The Leduc family has been veiled in secrecy for most Montrealers. Today people still think that Jos and Paul were real brothers. "So, as far as we are concerned, Jos was our uncle," remembers Kim Leduc, Paul's daughter. But Michel Pigeon and Léodard Mimeault both legally became Leducs. "My father changed his name legally after the birth of my second brother. I was born Leduc," says Kim. "But in the province when parents change their name, they can also change the names of their kids, as well, which explains why my brothers' family name is Leduc. Even Michel Pigeon changed his name legally, because his kids are named Leduc."

Paul's children got involved in the "family" business. After having been trained by Jacques Rougeau, Carl Leduc started working almost immediately for the WWF. "I didn't know how to wrestle then," affirms Leduc honestly today. Nonetheless he would work for the WWF for a year, wrestling mainly in towns in Quebec and the Maritimes. "I wrestled where Jos and my father were popular," he explains. The WWF even asked Jos to be my manager to help me start my career, but after one match they gave up on the idea." After wrestling Owen Hart in Quebec City Owen sent him to Calgary, to his father's famous dungeon. He took up the name Frank "The Freak" Einstein there. "I really learned how to wrestle in Calgary. Owen helped me a lot," he said. That was in 1997, the year where he was in contention for rookie of the year by the PWI. After an injury and a return to Calgary, where he wrestled with youngsters like Harry Smith, Teddy Hart and T.J. Wilson (Tyson Kidd), he went

ICEMAN, PAUL LEDUC'S SON, CARL, AND FRANK BLUES
AT THE NCW SUPERBOWL SHOW IN JOLIETTE

(BERTRAND HÉBERT)

to Toronto, where he helped train young wrestlers like Eric Young, now with TNA. "I'm the one who gave him the name," says Leduc, proudly. He continued to wrestle in Quebec afterward, getting involved in his family's promotion, the FLQ, but was never called back to WWE.

His sister Kim made her debut in the FLQ. She took up many roles in the promotion, both in the ring and backstage, before founding the first all-female wrestling company in Montreal. Their brother Yan, without being involved in ring action, was for a long time in charge of the technical aspects of FLQ shows. And what about their mother, Pierrette? "The person who was approached to wrestle against Vivian Vachon in the context of the Vachon/Leduc feud was my mom, but she never wanted to," Kim says. "Jos didn't want to involve our wives in the business," explains Paul. Mrs. Leduc would nonetheless be co-owner of the FLQ a couple of years later. Unfortunately Pierrette Brault died on February 28, 2011, at the age of 63.

THE MARTELS

Rick and Michel Vigneault wrestled under the name Martel, mainly because Vigneault isn't easy for Anglophones to say. "My brother was looking for a name and he liked the name of the Quebec country singer Marcel Martel," Rick says. But before the Vigneault brothers had the career they had, their mother's brother-in-law, Real Chouinard, wrestled for some time under the name Bob Casino. In 1960 he had wrestled against a young Bob Bedard, among others, who became Rene Goulet. In Ontario he teamed with his nephew Michel near the end of the decade. Their mother's brother, Aldrick Harvey, also wrestled without really making a name for himself.

Many years later another Martel made his debut in the business. It was Rick's nephew, Martin Lapointe. "I've never encouraged him to become a wrestler, until the rise of the cruiserweight in WCW," remembers Rick, mentioning the fact that Martin, under the alias Keven Martel, didn't have the weight and height that promoters once demanded. "I contacted someone who would help him go to Mexico and then to Japan, and with this experience, given the fact that he was a guy who looked credible, he could have joined the WWF or WCW," Rick says. Keven went to Mexico in July 1998, but after three weeks he missed his young son so much he decided to return.

RICK MARTEL'S NEPHEW, KEVEN, AND SUNNY WAR
CLOUD, WRESTLERS AND PROMOTERS IN QUEBEC CITY
(JOCELYN GAGNÉ)

Keven Martel finally had a local career, wrestling mainly for Jacques Rougeau's IW 2000 and Sunny War Cloud's CCW. "He had the talent to do it," Rick concludes. Finally, in spite of the many rumours otherwise, it should be noted that Frenchy Martin is not the brother of Rick and Michel. He was simply a friend of Michel who used the name Martel for business. Also in Puerto Rico another Martel made appearances. Daniel Martel was actually Michel's former partner in Calgary, Danny Babich.

THE MARSHALLS

Dick Marshall, born Léo Morneau on November 10, 1920, made a name for himself as a promoter in the '60s, '70s and '80s. After a short career as a wrestler, he took over Quebec City and the eastern part of the province, primarily for Grand Prix. When International Wrestling came onto the scene, his son Stan (Stanley Morneau) followed in his footsteps as promoter. "It was a family business. My grandfather's brothers René and Ray used to be referees; my sister and I also worked for our dad," said Stan's son Jimmy. Stan Marshall died of a kidney disease on May 13, 1999, at age 51. Although he's had major heart issues, Dick celebrated his 92nd birthday in 2012.

THE PROULX

The wrestling fans in Montreal know the Proulx family well. Everything started with Ludger Bossé, who wrestled under the name Tarzan Simard. His brother, Yvon, also wrestled, but he was primarily a manager. Then, with the help of Pat Girard at the Loisirs St-Jean-Baptiste, Simard decided to introduce his brother-in-law, Bertrand Proulx, to wrestling. Bertrand had a successful career. "He wrestled in Quebec, in the Maritimes and the U.S.A.," says his son Serge. In the Montreal territory he wrestled regularly against the McGuire brothers, the Caruso brothers and the Rougeau family, often teaming with André Proulx, who, however, wasn't related to the family. He retired around 1975. His two sons Ludger and Serge started their careers in 1981. Having both been trained by Pat Girard, Ludger was

LUDGER AND SERGE PROULX'S FATHER, BERTRAND, WITH ANDRÉ PROULX

(DENIS ARCHAMBAULT COLLECTION)

more successful than his brother at the beginning of his career, appearing regularly for International Wrestling. "He had wrestling in his blood and made Gino Brito and Rick Martel notice him," his brother remembers. During the 1980s he wrestled against Martel, Dino Bravo, Bret Hart and many others. "I started full time with the office when Rick Martel happened to know I was Bertrand's son. He was thankful because my father was one of the first to help him and to befriend him when he started his career in the Maritimes," recalls Ludger, who started his career on May 1, 1981. Serge, considered by many as one of the best wrestlers in Montreal over the past 15 years, made his debut in l'Épiphanie (40 minutes from Montreal) when he was 18. He also wrestled for International Wrestling in the mid-1980s, but really blossomed in the 1990s and early 2000s with ICW.

Serge's children also wrestled. Near the end of the 1980s, at the Loisirs, his adopted son Paul made his debut and later wrestled regularly with ICW. His son Francis first appeared in 1994, when he was just 14, and he still wrestles today. His daughter Francisca started in the mid-1990s, around the age of 15. Finally the daughter of Ludger's wife, Chrissy, also wrestled under the name Chrissy Proulx in the 2000s.

THE BIGGEST TRAGEDIES IN QUEBEC WRESTLING HISTORY

THE MURDER OF DINO BRAVO

It's unfortunately all too common — the wrestling heroes who stick around way too long because they either didn't prepare a life and career post-wrestling and the others who leave the world far too soon because of the lifestyle they led to succeed in wrestling. Some wrestlers, like The Iron Sheik, become caricatures, holding up fans for each and every dollar they can get. Others, like Eddie Guerrero and Owen Hart, leave us for a better world, becoming legends who are equally venerated by the fans and the other wrestlers. The circumstances of Dino Bravo's death are so absolutely unique they push the limits of understanding, even today. In hindsight there's now some perspective to bring to bear. But the 1993 murder of one of the last local wrestlers to have captured the imagination of the entire Montreal territory is still complex and an examination of the last moments of his life only scratch the surface of his story.

Throughout Adolfo "Dino Bravo" Bresciano's career there were lots of rumours about his relationship to organized crime. His dad's sister was married to the alleged leader of the Montreal mafia, making Vic Cotroni Dino Bravo's uncle. Cotroni himself had wrestled in the 1950s under the name Vic Vincent. But, in spite of the involvement of his nephew in the business in the 1980s, Cotroni never invested a cent in professional wrestling.

As for Dino Bravo, wrestling wasn't the only thing that put him in the headlines. In 1986 he was involved in a skirmish with a bus driver who took him to court. One year earlier Bravo, who was a big fan of hockey and especially the Canadiens, was escorted, along with a friend, out of the Montreal Forum by security guards after having verbally abused Michel

Bergeron, the coach of the Quebec Nordiques. In spite of the tussle the story ended without police intervention. "I met Bravo a couple of times before the event," remembers Michel Bergeron. "I thought he was just a big fan of the Canadiens and that he really hated the Nordiques, but I didn't think that he took it that seriously," he says, adding that he and Bravo never spoke to each other afterward. Ultimately Bravo was known to be quick-tempered.

In 1986 Bravo signed a lucrative contract with the WWF, which meant he would leave International Wrestling. The Montreal promotion would close down in less than a year later. "Dino was making a minimum of $300,000 a year with the WWF, in addition to bonuses, depending on the gate," explains Gino Brito. "The first year, he earned one million dollars. However he was not saving any of it. He had two or three cars, among which were a Mercedes, and also a house in Florida."

Then, after spending six years with the WWF, Bravo was forced to retire in May 1992. "He made a mistake here, as he thought they would keep him longer in New York. He wasn't important enough to be kept. His age caught up to him," Brito explains again, referring to the fact that Bravo was 43 when he left the WWF.

On March 10, 1993, less than one year after he retired from the ring, Adolfo Bresciano was assassinated in his luxurious house in Laval, Quebec. Bresciano's wife, Diane Rivest, had left the house with their six-year-old daughter around nine p.m. Upon her return, three hours later, she found the body of her husband on his favourite couch. Seventeen .22-calibre and .380 cartridge cases were found, but only seven bullets actually struck their target. The idea that there were possibly two gunmen was abandoned in following days, because the bullets found in the ceiling and one that went through the window indicated that the shooter used two weapons to make it harder for the police to understand the crime scene. From the very beginning of the investigation everyone agreed on the fact that Bresciano knew his murderer and let him in his house willingly. Indeed there was no trace of a struggle — Bresciano sat comfortably on his couch, probably watching the Canadiens that night. It was the third murder of its kind in the span of nine months in the luxurious Vimont neighbourhood. According to the police Bresciano knew the two previous victims, Robert Caverzan and Ghyslain Ranzo. La Presse mentioned that all three had close ties to the Italian

DINO BRAVO'S MURDER SHOCKED
THE WORLD OF WRESTLING (LINDA BOUCHER)

mafia. The Montreal media fought over Dino Bravo for one last time, as his shooting hit the headlines of the three major newspapers and the three French TV channels in Montreal.

But what would have made someone commit this crime? Following his murder Bravo's involvement in cigarette smuggling, a flourishing business in Quebec in the early 1990s, was revealed. "To keep the lifestyle he used to have he had to do something else," Brito explains. "Recently Bravo was seen in the south shore, not far away from the place where the Royal Canadian Mounted Police seized about $300,000 worth of cigarettes," reported Jean-Paul Charbonneau in *La Presse*, referring to an event that occurred on March 5, 1993. It seems that, for many, Bresciano's involvement in this field ceased to be a secret a long time ago. "Many people in wrestling confirmed his involvement in the smuggling of cigarettes. He operated at a relatively important level," adds Yves Chartrand of *Le Journal de Montréal*. The cigarette-smuggling hypothesis was long discussed, and most people still believe it to be behind his death today, but Bravo had all kinds of relationships. *La Presse* also reported that on the day following his death ". . . He also had acquaintances among the people of Italian origins arrested the previous week when the RCMP seized 477 kilos of cocaine smuggled into tomato cans in Montreal." The TQS television station also pointed to this, but the seizure-of-cocaine thesis would rapidly be abandoned in favour of the cigarette-smuggling one. We mustn't forget the fact that, in all likelihood, Bravo feared for his life.

"Judging from the information I have, Bresciano was involved in a fight the week before in Quebec City, and he told a close relative that a group of bikers may try to kill him," said famous Quebec crime journalist Claude Poirier on TQS in March 1993. In the same report Gino Brito agrees. "Now that it's happened, I've heard that he feared something might happen to him." Jean-Paul Charbonneau confirmed his colleague's statement in *La Presse*: "Other sources also say that he was involved in a violent fight at a restaurant in Quebec City, during a boxing show. He left before the police came." A couple of days later, as his friends and relatives gathered around Bravo for one last time at his funeral, speculation continued in the direction of cigarette smuggling. "If Bresciano made cigarette dealers lose half a million dollars, this would certainly be enough to explain the murder," reported Alain Bisson in *Le Journal de Montréal*. The *Allo Police* newspaper devoted two pages to a summary of the story immediately after the funeral, which journalist Georges-André Parent concluded by saying: "Was Dino a victim of the company he kept? Was he himself involved in a recent crime? Did he find himself stuck in a gang war? Could his murder be simply a personal vengeance and settling of scores? Everything is possible, but one thing is certain. This murder shocked a lot of people . . . and may lead to retaliation." When the journalist Parent referred to the implication of different gangs, he meant the bikers, the Mafia and the Native Americans, who, according to the newspapers at the time, were involved in the cigarette smuggling. Claude Poirier would say on TQS that the Bravo case was being transferred to the investigators of the provincial police. Since that time, nothing: no arrest, no new clue and no retaliation.

More than 17 years after his terrible death it has become much easier to remember the exploits of Dino Bravo the champion and one of the last wrestlers to have conquered the hearts of the fans in the Montreal territory than to try to understand the last days of Adolfo Bresciano. His daughter Claudia is now a young adult, but the spectre of her father, whom she unfortunately didn't have time to get to know well, is never too far. In May 2012, for the first time, she proudly accepted an homage in her father's name. Whether it's for his performances as a wrestler or because of his tragic destiny, the name Dino Bravo will remain forever engraved in the memories of Quebecers.

DECEMBER 24, 1985:
THE MONTREAL TERRITORY
LOSES THREE MAJOR PLAYERS

Probably the saddest event in the history of wrestling in the Montreal territory occurred on December 24, 1985. Wrestlers Pierre "Mad Dog" Lefebvre and Camille Tourville (Tarzan "The Boot" Tyler), as well as referee Adrien Desbois, died in a car accident that night in Laurentian Park.

After a show at the Georges-Vézina Arena in Chicoutimi, Lefebvre, Tyler and Desbois drove in the direction of Montreal. A snowstorm raged, and the road conditions weren't good. "It was Christmas Eve, and Tyler wanted so much to get back to Montreal," remembers Gino Brito. They took Desbois's car, but Lefebvre was driving, with Tyler sitting next to him and Desbois in the back seat. "I had wrestled against Lefebvre that night," Sunny War Cloud says about what would, unfortunately, be Lefebvre's last bout. "We talked about our plans for the next summer throughout the night," remembers Lefebvre's best friend, Raymond Rougeau. Having left just after his friend, he was travelling with his brother Jacques, Dino Bravo and Gino Brito, as they stopped at the well-known rest area, L'Etape, right in the middle of the park. "A guy who worked there told me that my friend Pierre Lefebvre had just left a couple of minutes earlier," he remembers. It was actually a little bit after the rest area, at 1:25 a.m., that Lefebvre lost control of his vehicle. When he skidded he changed lanes. A tanker was coming in the opposite direction. There was a head-on collision. The road, the 170, which crosses the park, is two lanes wide, one heading south and another heading north. The impact propelled the car into a ditch, and the three passengers died instantly.

Many people passed by the ditch after the accident. "When I saw the car in the ditch, I remember . . . I said that they certainly weren't alive. But, I didn't know that the passengers were Pierre, Adrien and Tarzan," remembers Rick Martel, who only heard about their death the following day from Stan Marshall. "We saw a tank truck in a jackknifed position on the lay-by. It had just happened . . . The police hadn't come yet. We said that he was lucky not to have fallen over in the ditch. But we hadn't seen the car . . . Otherwise I would've recognized it immediately," recalls Rougeau, who was told about the accident by a friend from Lac-Saint-Jean.

Later that night Frenchy Martin stopped at the same rest area. The guy at the pump told him about the accident.

"Hey, what happened to Pierre is very sad," he told him.

"How come you're sad for Pierre?"

"I'm talking about Pierre Lefebvre. My father pulled his car out of the ditch with a rope."

"I didn't get what the young man was talking about. I went in for a coffee. Some truck drivers were there, and one of them told me what happened," remembers Martin.

"The guys weren't lucky," he told me.

"What happened?" responded Martin.

THE TRAGIC LOSS OF TARZAN TYLER WAS A MAJOR BLOW TO A TERRITORY UNDER ATTACK

(BERTRAND HÉBERT COLLECTION)

"You don't know, Frenchy? The guys had an accident here a couple of hours ago."

Being originally from Saguenay, Robert Rancourt, Sunny War Cloud, remained in the region after the show. It was through the local radio that he heard the sad news. After having called the radio station to talk about the situation, War Cloud suddenly realized that there was another aspect to the tragedy. "I said to myself, 'Fuck, a referee was travelling with a wrestler.'" It must be remembered that in the 1980s the secrets of wrestling hadn't yet been revealed, and people thought that referees travelled either with each other or by themselves. "People reacted badly to this," remembers War Cloud. "They said that this wasn't normal, that wrestling must be fake." Former wrestler Serge Jodoin adds: "It was like giving proof."

The poor wrestlers probably took the truth of what caused the accident to the grave with them. Still it seems like everyone had their hypothesis.

Most people agree on the fact that alcohol probably wasn't a factor. Gilles "The Fish" Poisson, former wrestler and expert in coaching wrestlers, has an interesting hypothesis. "After a wrestling match you lose five to seven pounds. So, even if he drank a couple of beers, it wouldn't show. It would've taken many more to feel the effect." Did Pierre Lefebvre fall asleep while driving? "According to the investigators' report the truck driver said that Lefebvre didn't try to avoid him at all," notes Jodoin. However the most probable hypothesis is that the car simply skidded due to the road conditions. "The road conditions in the park during winter are just plain dangerous. It's so slippery, and you can't see a thing. Accidents are very common," says Rancourt. Being originally from Lac-Saint-Jean, Gilles Poisson, confirmed Rancourt's statement. "The park at this time of the year's very dangerous. Even those who live there skid. It's happened to me, too."

At the time the wrestlers who had to travel from city to city attempted to minimize the costs, and to do this four of them would often travel in the same car, when possible. As weird as this may seem, years after the accident many Quebec wrestlers have claimed to have been meant for the fourth spot in the car — it's as if every one of them felt blessed not to have been there. "I was supposed to come back with them, but I met one of my friends and I left a couple of hours later," Frenchy Martin remembers. "I was supposed to be with them. I didn't go because there was a death in my family. I was supposed to go with Adrien, Tarzan and Pierre. I was supposed to be the fourth man originally. When they left on the morning of the 23rd my grandfather died, so I cancelled," Serge Jodoin says. "The Hangman" Neil Guay is another possible occupant of the fourth empty seat: "I took time off to go see my in-laws in Matane for the holiday season. I always travelled with Tarzan. I could have been in the same car." Guay spoke to Tyler for the last time near the Quebec Bridge. "He told me that I was lucky as I was going to take some time off while they were booked to work in Chicoutimi."

Speaking in a quavering voice, Frenchy Martin said he "went to see the boys in the funeral parlour before going to wrestle in Ontario on Boxing Day, December 26." Rick Martel, who was one of the shareholders of International Wrestling at the time, succinctly sums up what everyone else was thinking: "This dealt us a major blow, because they were not only our friends, but they were also very important players for us."

CHRIS BENOIT

On June 25, 2007, the lifeless bodies of Chris Benoit, his wife, Nancy, and their son, Daniel, were found in their house in Fayetteville, Georgia. It was later revealed that Benoit murdered his wife and his son, before killing himself. Some hold that given Chris Benoit's notorious use of steroids, roid rage could be behind the two murders and the suicide. Others think that the number of head-butts that Benoit had performed throughout his career had damaged his brain, to the point of causing a kind of dementia that made him, in turn, commit such horrible acts. A

CHRIS BENOIT, THE ONLY WWE AND WCW
WORLD CHAMPION TO COME FROM QUEBEC
(SCOTT TEAL COLLECTION)

serious and scientific study was actually carried out to investigate the latter hypothesis. One mustn't, however, forget that Benoit used to take a considerable amount of antidepressants, as well. No one will ever know what took place in Chris Benoit's head that weekend, but everyone surely agrees that it was a horrific tragedy.

After these events his former employer, WWE, deleted him from all the video records and most of the written documents it has produced since. It has even edited some documents that were produced in the past. The Wrestling Observer Hall of Fame held a vote among its members to decide whether or not Benoit should be kept among the wrestlers who were inducted. In order to banish Benoit from the hall, a majority of 60 percent had to be reached; this majority wasn't obtained. The Quebec Wrestling Hall of Fame had taken Chris Benoit off the voting bulletins it sends to its members, but put him back in the 2012 bulletins, following a vote from its members.

All Canadian and American media covered the sad incidents of June 2007 in their headlines. It's far too easy to bury one's head in the sand and pretend as if this never happened. The objective here isn't to make either a hero or an example of Chris Benoit, but simply to state the facts. Consequently, in this book about the history of wrestling in Montreal and Montreal wrestlers, we can't ignore or negate Benoit's existence and wrestling career.

This is why we're including the following information.

Chris Benoit was born in LaSalle (now part of Montreal) on May 21, 1967, but left the province at the age of 12, when his family settled in Edmonton. In Alberta Benoit trained in the Hart Dungeon, under the supervision of Stu Hart. He started his career with Stampede in 1985. His role models at the time were Bret Hart and Dynamite Kid. In 1989 he went to wrestle in Japan for New Japan, where he was called both Pegasus Kid and Wild Pegasus. After a brief period where he worked for WCW in 1992 and 1993, he made his debut in ECW in 1994. After having accidentally injured Rocco Rock and Sabu, he was nicknamed The Crippler by Paul Heyman. This nickname would stick for the rest his career. He left ECW in 1995 because of problems with his work visa and went back to WCW the same year. He was part of, among others things, a version of the Four Horsemen, one of the most famous factions in professional wrestling. In 1999 he wrestled against Bret Hart in a match honouring Owen Hart. No longer able to deal with the backstage politics of WCW, Benoit let his bosses know he wanted to leave. In spite of the fact that WCW management gave him the world title when he defeated Sid Vicious on January 16, 2000, Benoit left the promotion with Dean Malenko, Eddy Guerrero and Perry Saturn.

On February 1, 2000, the four above-mentioned wrestlers, now called The Radicalz, made their WWF debut. Benoit finally got a major WWE push in 2004 when he won the Royal Rumble after having entered number one. This victory got him a championship match for the world title against Shawn Michaels and champion Triple H at Madison Square Garden during the main event of *WrestleMania XX*. The Canadian Crippler won the match with his submission hold, the Crippler Crossface, and the night ended with Benoit and his close friend Eddy Guerrero, both champions, celebrating in the ring. On May 31, 2004, at the Bell Centre in Montreal, Benoit and Edge lost their WWE tag team titles against Sylvain Grenier and Rob Conway. Very few people know that Chris Benoit was actually bilingual. "Chris Benoit was on the floor at one point and he spoke French to me," Sylvain Gernier remembers. In 2007 Benoit was transferred to ECW, then a division of WWE. His last match took place on June 19 against Elijah Burke (TNA's The Pope). He was supposed to win the ECW title five days later against CM Punk. During a 22-year career, the Rabid Wolverine would win many tournaments in Japan, the ECW, WCW and WWE tag team titles, the U.S. title, the Intercontinental title, the WCW and WWE world titles and would be recognized as one of the best in-ring technicians of his era. He has the distinction of being the only Quebecer to have wrestled a match that was given a five-star rating by *Wrestling Observer*.

THE DEATH OF MICHEL MARTEL

Between 1975 and 1978 Frenchy Martin and Michel Martel teamed in Puerto Rico for Carlos Colón's WWC. On June 30, in Ponce, Martel and Martin teamed with Jack Lafarb against Carlos Colón and the Invaders #1 and #2 (Jose Gonzales and Roberto Soto, respectively). After the match, as they were coming out of the shower, Martel started to feel unwell. "He told me that he felt so hot . . . that he thought he was dying," Martin relates. I asked him whether he was serious and he said yes, he thought he was really dying. So I offered to take him to the hospital, but he said that he was feeling better and that the uneasiness was over."

The two friends got into their car and headed in the direction of San Juan, which was more than an hour away. Michel felt the uneasiness return, and he thought he was going to vomit, but was unable to do so. As his state went from bad to worse, Frenchy decided to take him to the closest hospital. The doctors asked Frenchy to leave while they tried to save his friend. "When I returned, the doctor was on the phone, and I asked him about 'me amigo.' I don't remember exactly what he told me, but I understood that he died of a heart attack. But at the same time, this wasn't what I was hearing . . . My brain refused to make the connection," Frenchy Martin explains with a lot of sadness.

After receiving Martin's call Rick Martel went to Puerto Rico. "I didn't understand that what Frenchy tried to tell me was that my brother was dead," Rick remembers, thinking that he was involved in an accident or something. After spending 24 hours looking for Frenchy, Rick finally found him drinking, totally devastated by what had just happened. It was Hugo Savinovich, who was part of the Spanish commentators of WWE for a long

(JACKIE WIECZ COLLECTION)

**PUERTO RICO, HOME OF THE MERCENARIES.
MICHEL MARTEL AND FRENCHY MARTIN**

time, who was with Frenchy at the time. "I think that in Quebec City or Montreal he could've been saved," says Rick.

After the funeral in Quebec City, Frenchy returned to Puerto Rico. Even Rick would wrestle there. The promotion used the death of his brother in order to elevate Jose Gonzales on the card, making him Frenchy's rival. Rick understood the business. "We were right in a big program and we were drawing money, so, naturally, that's wrestling. In wrestling they take every opportunity they have to make a dollar," he said. "Gonzales, he just took the gravy out of it. He didn't push the boat; he just got on the boat when it was going. Bad luck happened, and that's what made him," Martin explained during an interview with *SLAM! Wrestling*. Ironically the same Jose Gonzales would stab Bruiser Brody to death in July 1988 in a locker room in Puerto Rico — even though he was acquitted by the court when it was "judged" to be an act of self-defence.

Born on October 4, 1943, Michel Vigneault became interested in professional wrestling after his uncles, Real Chouinard and Aldrick Harvey, talked to him about it. He started his career in Northern Ontario for Larry Kasaboski's territory in 1968. After wrestling for Johnny Rougeau's office he left for Calgary to work for Stu Hart's Stampede Wrestling. It was in Calgary that he brought Jean Gagne into the business, with whom Martel would have tremendous success as a tag team. After having worked in Mexico, the Maritimes and in Japan for the IWA, "Mad Dog" Martel found himself in Puerto Rico, where he and Martin would enjoy success in the tag team division under the name The Mercenaries, winning the tag team titles a couple of times.

Even though the Martel brothers weren't able to see each other often, they worked in the same territory just before the tragic event. "We spent a holiday, which lasted a couple of weeks, together back home in Quebec City, and we went to Atlanta travelling by car together. He wrestled some matches, and Ole Anderson liked him a lot. He wanted him to come and join me after Puerto Rico. It was obvious he was on the verge of making a breakthrough in the States," Rick remembers, thinking of the last moments he spent with his hero, confident and source of inspiration. "Michel was dynamic, and cutting interviews he just got it. He drank and ate wrestling all the time. A real student of the game."

MICHEL "LE PATRIOTE" VIGNEAULT

(GHISLAINE OUZILLEAU COLLECTION)

MICHEL VIGNEAULT WORKED FOR ALL STAR UNDER HIS REAL NAME

Even if his parents urged him to stop wrestling, Rick wanted to continue: "It was very difficult to go back on the road after the tragedy, but I found the strength to continue because of all the things he did to help launch my career."

LOUIE TILLET AND THE PITRE AFFAIR

Louie Tillet, a wrestler and booker in Florida and Alabama, probably had to present his most sincere and important promo 10 years before he ever stepped into a ring.

On January 9, 1953, his mother, Mrs. Marguerite Ruest-Pitre, was to be hanged for her role in a horrible crime that led to the death of 23 people in a plane crash in Sault-au-Cochon on September 9, 1949. Louie Tillet, whose real name is Maurice Michaud, and his half-brother, Jean-Guy Pitre, were respectively 19 and 10 when they sent a plea to authorities in an attempt to save their

(SCOTT TEAL COLLECTION)

LOUIE TILLET WAS ONE OF THE MOST BRILLANT BOOKERS IN THE HISTORY OF WRESTLING

mother. In the letter they write: "Sir, we don't know how, but do something to save our mother." They were not successful. Their mother would be the last woman ever executed in Canada.

Albert Guay, who wanted to get rid of his wife in order to cash in a $10,000 life insurance policy, asked the brother of Mrs. Ruest-Pitre, Genereux Ruest, a watchmaker, to make a bomb. He asked Mrs. Ruest-Pitre to put the bomb on the plane that his wife Rita Morel was to take. Although Mr. Ruest denied knowing anything about the reasons behind Guay's demand, and Mrs. Ruest-Pitre denied knowing the content of the parcel she carried, the two of them suffered the same fate as Guay. Since that day many people, having reconsidered the case, doubt that Mrs. Ruest-Pitre was guilty. Guay implicated her, they say, in order to buy time; but he was already dead when the Ruest-Pitre trial took place, so he was never to be confronted about his declarations. This story even inspired a very popular movie in Montreal in the 1980s. After the death of their mother, Michaud, who lived in Quebec City, decided to leave the province. It was under another name that he was to start his wrestling career a couple of years later.

Probably influenced by the French Angel, Maurice Tillet, a wrestler who was famous for a head that was disproportionate with the rest of his body and who was successful to a certain extent in the province in the 1940s and '50s, Michaud took up the name Louie Tillet. In 1960, after having made his debut, he won the Mid-Atlantic tag team titles with Gypsy Joe. "My brother sent him to Don Owen for the Portland territory," remembers Paul Vachon. He would wrestle against Nick Bockwinkel in a program for the promotion's title. Tillet would win many belts throughout his career, mainly in tag team. He was actually champion with two other Quebecers, Paul Vachon in Georgia and Tarzan Tyler in Florida. Although he worked all over the U.S., he was a regular in the territories of Texas, Atlanta, Tennessee, California and Florida. In 1963, in Texas, he would wrestle against Lou Thesz, the NWA champion. He even worked for the WWWF in 1973 and 1974, having had a match against Larry Zbyszko at Madison Square Garden.

Throughout his career he used many different ring names; he was also known as Flash Gordon, Joey, Joe Fargo and Masked Gladiator, but he was mainly known as "The King" Louie Tillet. His last good year as a wrestler was 1975, when he worked in Los Angeles. He won the Americas tag team titles with John Tolos against the Hollywood Blonds and the Americas title in singles competition against Les Thornton.

If Tillet was considered a journeyman wrestler, he was, on the other hand, famous for being an excellent booker, which led him to eventually be put in charge of many different territories. "Louie Tillet was one of the most brilliant men in the wrestling business. He took me under his wing. He thought me how to be a businessman in this business and how to put together matches, which helped me later on in my career with the WWE," says Gerald Brisco. From Knoxville to Los Angeles, via Florida and Alabama, he was in charge at one moment or another. "I worked for him in Tampa," remembers Paul Leduc. He also helped train Steve Keirn, who was part of the Fabulous Ones and currently manages the WWE development territory in Florida." He was also Ole Anderson's assistant in the early 1980s with Jim Crockett Promotions. While he was in charge of the Alabama territory in 1977, a young Terry Bollea, now known under the name Hulk Hogan, teamed with a young Ed Leslie (Brutus Beefcake) as Terry Leslie. He co-owned Sun Belt Wrestling in Jacksonville, Florida, in partnership with Don Curtis, also in the early 1980s.

Tillet, who had great rivalries with The Medics, Jose Lothario and Quebec wrestler Chin Lee, was famous for his Francophone character — even if most of his peers had to think that he came from France and not from the Montreal territory. The Pitre affair, one of the most documented and famous judicial stories in Canadian history, sent Tillet to America, where he'd earn a living as a wrestler for more than 25 years. The other side of the coin is that he is, without a shadow of a doubt, the Quebec wrestler whose real origins are the most mysterious to fans in the province.

THE GREAT VENUES OF THE MONTREAL TERRITORY

Many arenas and stadiums around the world are tied to professional wrestling. Madison Square Garden in New York is still recognized by many today as being the venue, but the Olympic Auditorium in Los Angeles, the Tokyo Dome in Japan, the Sportatorium in Dallas, as well as the ECW Arena in Philadelphia, all made indelible marks on the history of the business. Montreal isn't to be outdone.

THE MONTREAL FORUM

Often dubbed the Madison Square Garden of Montreal, the Montreal Forum began presenting wrestling shows in the early 1930s, but it wasn't until the late 1930s that Eddie Quinn and Yvon Robert began to fill the building. "The Forum was to become, for more than 20 years, the mecca of wrestling in North America," says journalist Claude Leduc. Robert, Moquin, Carpentier, Kowalski, Rougeau and Thesz would all thrill Forum crowds in their own way, so much so that even after the 1960s the Forum continued to be a favourite venue. Over the years the Forum would witness Paul Leduc's wedding, the exploits of Dino Bravo and Jacques Rougeau Jr.'s retirement match, as well as many WWF shows. It's recognized as one of the best wrestling venues of all time in North America. Built in 1924 and located at the corner of Ste-Catherine and Atwater, the venerable building is famous for being the home of the Montreal Canadiens until 1996 and of the Montreal Maroons from 1924 to 1938. It's also hosted numerous important boxing matches over the years and was the venue that housed the sensational performance of Nadia Comaneci at the 1976 Olympics.

SOHMER PARK

The first Montreal venue to become famous was actually Sohmer Park. Stars like Louis Cyr, Frank Gotch and Émile Maupas made it an important wrestling destination. Sohmer Park was located at the corner of Panet and Notre-Dame, behind the current Radio-Canada building. It was the biggest amusement park in North America before it burned down on March 24, 1919. The park, which opened on June 1, 1889, featured a hall that could accommodate 7,000 people.

THE VERDUN AUDITORIUM

The Verdun Auditorium is perhaps the most-booked venue in the history of the Montreal territory. It's located in Verdun, a town that merged with the city of Montreal in 2002. Since the early 1940s promoters like Lucien Riopel and Jack Ganson presented shows there in an attempt to compete with Eddie Quinn. Later Quinn himself would use the Auditorium when the Forum or other arenas were unavailable. In 1952 the Lortie brothers booked the building, and the first televised wrestling shows on Radio-Canada were broadcast from it. But it was really in the 1970s that the Auditorium came into its own, when Grand Prix presented its shows there every Tuesday evening. Given the fact that the MAC's jurisdiction didn't extend to Verdun, fans of wrestling in the metropolitan area could go there to watch women like Vivian Vachon in action. After Grand Prix, Celebrity Wrestling, Grand Circuit and other promoters continued to use the venue up until the early 1980s. International Wrestling later used it as a replacement venue when the Paul-Sauvé Arena was unavailable. Today Jacques Rougeau still presents shows there from time to time. Built in 1939, it seats about 5,000 for wrestling.

DELORIMIER STADIUM

Another favoured Eddie Quinn venue was Royals Stadium, better known as Delorimier Stadium. "In the summer the Forum was way too hot for the athletes and the fans, so Eddie Quinn presented one or two major programs per summer at Delorimier Stadium," Paul Leduc explains. Its first wrestling show was held on August 4, 1932. Delorimier Stadium ranks second, behind

MAGNIFICENT VIEW OF A WRESTLING SHOW AT THE JARRY PARK STADIUM (PAUL LEDUC COLLECTION)

only New York City's Madison Square Garden, for the number of times a venue has held the biggest wrestling crowd of any year. On a worldwide level the stadium is fourth, behind MSG, the Tokyo Dome and Chicago's Comiskey Park.

JARRY PARK STADIUM

Speaking of stadiums, one can't forget the role that Jarry Park Stadium played in the history of the Montreal territory: it held the two biggest crowds ever for a wrestling show in the province. Built in 1969 and situated in the Villeray neighbourhood for the arrival of the Montreal Expos in Major League Baseball, Jarry Park Stadium would be home to the Expos from 1969 to 1976, when the latter moved to Olympic Stadium. The stadium was subsequently renovated and since the late 1980s it has hosted the Montreal international tennis tournament. It's now called the Uniprix Stadium, and Jacques Rougeau brought wrestling back to the venue in 2002 with International Wrestling 2000 for a show that marked the return of Bret Hart to Montreal for the first time since Survivor Series 1997.

PAUL-SAUVÉ ARENA

In the mid-1960s All Star Wrestling started producing shows in a new building. "A fabulous sports palace, the Paul-Sauvé Arena," remembers Claude Leduc. This modern arena, situated in the Rosemont neighbourhood, was a part of professional wrestling for the next 20 years. "It was an arena that had 7,000 well-positioned seats," Leduc says. It was the favourite venue for All Star Wrestling in the 1960s and 1970s and also International Wrestling in the 1980s, when the two promotions presented shows on Monday nights. Built in 1960, the arena also served as a venue for junior hockey teams, and Johnny Rougeau's Laval National played there. In 1996 it was demolished to make way for condominiums.

MOLSON CENTRE/BELL CENTRE

The Bell Centre, called the Molson Centre when it first opened, has also presented important shows. Among these were the three WWE PPV events Montreal has hosted, not to mention the biggest indy crowd anyone can recall, the 12,000 who watched the International Wrestling 2000 show in 2001. All WWE TV that has come out of Montreal in the last decade was broadcast from there.

OLYMPIC STADIUM

The biggest venue in Montreal, Olympic Stadium, has never housed a wrestling show. But the Big O was in the running for a big event on three separate occasions. In 1986 talks started between International Wrestling and Olympic Stadium about presenting a match between Dino Bravo and Hulk Hogan. "With a championship match against Hulk Hogan, we could draw between 45,000 and 50,000 fans. We should get a scheduled date for the match on December 22 [1985]," said Bravo in an interview. Unfortunately, the match never took place. "What the stadium was asking was too much . . . The price of the stadium was way too high," remembers Rick Martel. Then the idea was resurrected in 1989. "As the rumour goes, the angle where Hogan was stretchered following a match against Bravo would have led to a *Saturday Night's Main Event* in Montreal. But, as rumours had it again at the time, the stadium and the Forum were too outdated for the shooting of such an event. No TV event was held here before the arrival of the Molson Centre, which seems to confirm the rumour," explains Patrick Lono. "We would've lost a lot of our credibility on the quality of the presentation of the show, because there would be lots of people who would've seen nothing of the matches. It was impossible to put giant screens in the right place at the time," confirms Guy Hauray, who was responsible for the feasibility report for the use of the stadium. "But Vince wasn't against the idea."

Gino Brito also remembers a discussion with McMahon: "When I was promoter for Vince in the early 1990s, he asked me to get information on the possibility of presenting a big show. I got back to him with the information, and his response was that he would prefer Toronto. In fact we'd have to pay the rental and a percentage to the sports commission. On top of that, we'd have to pay to the RIO, which is in charge of managing the stadium, a percentage of the gate and a percentage on the souvenirs sold. I remember that Vince told me that it would cost him $150,000 to $200,000 less to do it in Toronto."

The last time an Olympic Stadium show was considered was 1994. "After having retired, Jacques wanted to present a match between Bob Backlund and I at the Olympic Stadium, for the WWF title, with him as my manager," remembers Pierre-Carl Ouellet. "Jacques told me that I would become world champion, thanks to him being my manager. Jacques started the negotiations with the Olympic Stadium and with Vince," adds Ouellet. Rougeau was able to cut down the price of the location from $280,000 to $154,000. While he thought he could count on McMahon's support for the idea, it wasn't forthcoming. Indeed, according to Vince, it just wasn't the right time. "He didn't think we could fill a stadium and didn't want to take that risk," remembers Ouellet, who listened in on the phone conversation between Jacques and Vince. Always according to Ouellet, Rougeau told McMahon that wrestling was hot in town, to which Vince responded that wrestling wasn't hot, the WWF was. "Rougeau concluded the conversation, saying to McMahon: 'If I don't do it with you, I'm going to do it with Hulk!'" recalls Ouellet. Right after that call, Rougeau contacted Jimmy Hart and Hulk Hogan to talk about different scenarios. Ouellet versus Hogan, Jacques versus Hogan, Ouellet versus Savage or Hogan and Rougeau teaming were all denied, since WCW thought their telelvision was not strong enough to run such a large building. The whole thing ended in a legal dispute, since WCW had negotiated with Rougeau, whose contract was still valid until June 1995. During that time in Montreal, the fact that Rougeau had openly talked about returning to the ring was not well received by the media or the fans. In all fairness to McMahon, the date Rougeau had chosen was on Superbowl Sunday of 1995, not the best date to run such a big event.

In the future only something like *WrestleMania* would be able to fill Olympic Stadium. Unfortunately for wrestling fans the UFC is more likely to hold an event there, as local legend, welterweight champion Georges St-Pierre, could conceivably fill the building as a headliner.

THE HISTORY OF MONTREAL WRESTLING ON TV

Wrestling was first broadcast on Quebec TV in the fall of 1952 by Radio-Canada, live from the Verdun Auditorium on Tuesday evenings. "Paul and Bob Lortie . . . had the television," explains Gino Brito. In January 1953 wrestling moved to Wednesday evenings, when promoter Eddie Quinn took over the contract and had exclusive rights to all the matches held at the Forum and to the great star of the time, Yvon Robert. "Before the arrival of TV, Radio-Canada [which was also a radio broadcaster] broadcast wrestling matches on Friday evenings, but they emanated from Madison Square Garden in New York most of the time," remembers Paul Leduc. The emergence of TV was met by skepticism from some wrestling people. "Everyone, the experts, wrestlers, referees, were saying that Radio-Canada was going to kill the game," relates

MICHEL NORMANDIN WAS THE VOICE OF WRESTLING. YVON ROBERT WAS WRESTLING (PAUL LEDUC COLLECTION)

Paul Leduc in the *Saltimbanques du Ring*, fearing that people would prefer staying at home instead of going to arenas. Fears quickly dissipated. People quickly realized that wrestling was inexpensive to produce, had impressive ratings and that the attendance level of live shows actually increased because of the publicity. Wrestling became a popular, successful business. "Wednesday in front of the furniture stores, on the pavement, hundreds of people were watching TV . . . Wrestling was on. The whole province was empty," Maurice Vachon says in the *Saltimbanques du Ring*. Yvon Robert, the heel Killer Kowalski and the Flying Frenchman Édouard Carpentier were to become the first stars of the television era.

MICHEL NORMANDIN

"C'est la lutte ce soir!" ("It's wrestling tonight!") is how Michel Normandin started La Lutte on Wednesdays at nine p.m. "On Wednesday the program would stop right before the main event at the Forum in order to draw bigger and bigger crowds. Spectators in their homes were left with Yvon Robert about to wrestle against his opponent," explains Fernand Ste-Marie.

Although he was wrestling's first broadcaster, Normandin was no beginner. He was far from it, according to the archives of Radio-Canada. Normandin "was part of the first generation of sports commentators who worked for Radio-Canada." In 1936, about 16 years before the arrival of TV in the province, he was the first commentator for the Montreal Canadiens, and his program *Good Night Canada* was, to a certain extent, the predecessor of *Hockey Night in Canada*. His rhythmic flow and his ability to make almost anything interesting made him an ideal commentator. In fact he was also the voice of baseball's Montreal Royals for 13 years and he was the first TV commentator for both the Montreal Alouettes and competitive bowling.

Aside from his work as a commentator Normandin was also an advertising executive for the Dow Brewery, the sponsor of La Lutte, which is today part of the larger Molson brewery. For a long time he was a great ambassador for the sport, selling wrestling as a product that was as important as any other sport he presented.

It was definitely with Michel Normandin and television that wrestling was to know its first golden age in the Montreal territory. According to the archives of Radio-Canada, in the fall of 1955 La Lutte was ranked the seventh most popular program in Montreal. Between November 1957 and February 1958 a poll revealed that La Lutte was watched by an average of 1,495,000 people. To draw a comparison, at the same time hockey was watched by 2,117,000 and boxing by 1,664,000. Unfortunately Michel Normandin died of a heart attack on November 12, 1963, at just 50 years of age. In 2010 he was finally inducted

FRANK VALOIS ENJOYS A CONVERSATION WITH MICHEL NORMANDIN (TONY LANZA)

to the Quebec Wrestling Hall of Fame.

A few years before his death wrestling was losing some of its lustre, and in September 1960 Radio-Canada pulled the plug on *La Lutte*. Wrestling in Montreal was in decline until Johnny Rougeau started All Star Wrestling and began broadcasting *Sur le Matelas*.

SUR LE MATELAS

After Rougeau took over the territory, *Sur le Matelas* (the name belonged to channel 10) was hosted by Jean-Pierre Coallier, who had considerable experience in radio. But *Sur le Matelas* would only really take off when Jean-Jacques Fortin took over. Sometimes he was accompanied by Johnny Rougeau and at other times by Édouard Carpentier, who would make his first appearance on the program as an analyst. Fortin began in radio in 1949 in Roberval, and three years later he called games of hockey's Quebec Aces. After having returned to Lac-Saint-Jean Fortin appeared on the Montreal scene with CJMS, before making his debut at Tele-Metropole channel 10 in 1961. By the late 1960s Fortin was simply known as the Voice of Wrestling.

The program was a success for many years. In the 1970s, however, competition emerged.

GRAND PRIX WRESTLING

CFCF 12 filmed a colour pilot at the Maurice Richard arena, but Paul Vachon couldn't come to an agreement with them. He tried to impress channel

10 by showing the executives the pilot, but they were faithful to Johnny Rougeau, and he was thanked politely and then told, "No." Soon everything changed. On the recommendation of Jean Brisson, wrestling promoter and radio presenter in the Rimouski region, Vachon met Fernand Corbeil of the Télé 7 station in Sherbrooke. The people in charge offered to shoot three programs, once every three weeks, for $4,500. Grand Prix was on the edge of financial doom, but Vachon played the promoter who could afford this price. He imposed one condition, however, namely that a time slot be included in the station's schedule, because Corbeil's offer only covered the recording of the program, not its broadcast. Referring to the example of Verne Gagne's success with the AWA in Milwaukee, which broadcast his program on Sundays at 11 a.m., Vachon asked for this time slot. He was told that no one watched TV so early on Sunday mornings. "No one watches TV, because you're not even on the air," answered Paul Vachon.

The station decided to schedule a mass, which took place at 10:30 a.m., then presented Grand Prix Wrestling at 11 a.m. Jean Brisson was the commentator, and Édouard Carpentier was the analyst. It was then that Brisson would utter his famous, "See you next week, God willing" for the first time, a sentence that would be immortalized by Carpentier in the 1980s. The Télé 7 station studio was perfect for wrestling, with bleachers that could seat 200 spectators. "When Grand Prix Wrestling started on TV, two million viewers were tuning to wrestling every week," says Paul Leduc. The program would eventually be broadcast on eight stations covering the area between Ontario and the Maritimes. Once the process was set in motion the show snowballed. CFCF would soon come on board, but instead of simply dubbing the French version of the program, the station wanted to create a new program specifically targeting the Anglophone audience, recorded in the CFCF studios and presented by Jack Curran.

JACK CURRAN

Being part of the CFCF team since it started broadcasting in 1961, Curran, originally from New Brunswick, was considered as one of the best commentators of his day. "He was the best," Paul Leduc said in an interview with Greg Oliver of SLAM! Wrestling. It should be noted that Curran had considerable experience, having presented many programs for CFCF and the CBC, in addition to having performed in the theatre and voicing advertisements for the radio. He was even a publicist for the Dow Breweries, very much like Michel Normandin. In the same interview Paul Leduc sang the praises of Curran, saying that he and Ray Boucher "were almost as close, maybe better than J.R. and "The King" Lawler. They were really good commentators. For the interviews he was always asking the right questions." But Curran didn't only have Boucher, who was a sports commentator in the Ottawa region, as a partner, but also wrestler Luigi Mascera, Jack Britton and even the promoter of Grand Prix himself, Paul Vachon. He was famous for his good sense of humour and for helping Francophone wrestlers in their interviews. In the late 1970s, after Grand Prix closed down, he was a commentator for Superstars of Wrestling, presented by George Cannon. Curran died of cancer on July 10, 2003, in Ottawa. He was 71. Curran's work saw Grand Prix Wrestling awarded the title of best wrestling program in North America in 1972, an award given by the American magazine Wrestling. The English version of Grand Prix wasn't just broadcast in Montreal, but also in Ontario, the Maritimes, Vermont, upstate New York, New Hampshire and even Maine.

In 1977 the program Superstars of Wrestling, created by George Cannon and Milt Avruskin, made its appearance. First it was only presented on some Ontario networks like Global and Citytv, but the group eventually came to Montreal, specifically to Verdun. In addition to Montreal the shows, which were recorded in the CFCF studios, were broadcast throughout Canada and the world. In early 1984, Cannon sold his TV spot to the WWF and that's what was seen on CFCF 12 from that point forward. After the appearance of International Wrestling on the scene the group started losing momentum, and Avruskin wound up working as a commentator for International. Avruskin abruptly died in 2011. He was 64.

GUY HAURAY

In 1980 Édouard Carpentier was to introduce a businessman to the Varoussac Promotion, when Frank Valois and Gino Brito were trying to get a television contract. They also needed a partner who wasn't involved in wrestling

. . . That's when Guy Hauray became part of the deal. Born in St-Malo, France, Hauray was involved in martial arts and worked mainly as a coach/consultant for artists such as Cyndi Lauper. Hauray met Carpentier in 1977 at the first edition of the Montreal Film Festival during a night in honour of Alain Delon. "Frank Valois and Gino Brito were men of their word and good businessmen," recalls Guy Hauray, who no longer works in wrestling today. Only one meeting was enough for Hauray to start working with

GUY HAURAY AND EDOUARD CARPENTIER WERE KEY PLAYERS IN HELPING THE WWF SET FOOT IN MONTREAL

Varoussac. He worked for their first contract, with Télé 7, because it was part of the Pathonique network of five channels, all positioned strategically for the tours that Varoussac wanted to organize. Moreover it still owned the studio in which Grand Prix Wrestling was recorded.

SUPERSTARS OF WRESTLING (LES ÉTOILES DE LA LUTTE)

Cable TV would eventually allow fans in the territory to watch the NWA in Toronto on CJOH, with Maple Leaf Wrestling from the Toronto office and the WWF on channel 22, an ABC station. As for Superstars of Wrestling, they took the Grand Prix formula and recorded three programs every three weeks or so. Carpentier served as an analyst, a position with which he was very familiar, while Guy Hauray was in charge of the program. "Édouard Carpentier taught me how to be a TV commentator, and he was someone with whom it was such a pleasure to work," Hauray relates with real nostalgia. From 1980 to 1984 the time slot starting at 11 a.m. on Sundays belonged to them. "My brother and I would listen to the country music program at 10 a.m., right before wrestling, to make sure not to miss wrestling with Hauray and Carpentier," relates François Hébert. "We didn't go out in order not to miss the program — it was sacred." Some years later the same duo was to make their mark on the Francophone world at the worldwide level when the *Superstars of Wrestling* adventure on Télé 7 was to take a totally unexpected turn.

In 1983 promoter Denis Lauzon got a program on the Cogeco network on the CKTM and CKSH channels in Trois-Rivières and attempted to compete with Varoussac. As was the case for Télé 7, like all cable TV, these channels were available almost everywhere. However it was a fiasco. "We went to Rouyn-Noranda [eight hours away from Montreal], and there were only four people in the crowd," remembers Fernand Ste-Marie. The whole thing only lasted a couple of months, but the damage was done. Wrestling was popular on TV, and these stations wanted to have more wrestling. Varoussac had to take over. CFCF also wanted to broadcast local wrestling programs again, and that's why the new programs of the Trois-Rivières channel were translated into English and presented by Milt Avruskin. So in a couple of months viewers were to get three hours of wrestling, instead of one, per week. Getting this extra air time was to cause a disagreement between Varoussac and Guy Hauray. The latter remembers having been summoned to the office of International Wrestling's lawyer and not having been satisfied with the offer that was made in order to buy from him the rights that would allow the promotion to affiliate Télé 7 TV with the wrestling office. "I had total control over TV. I told them: 'Under these conditions, I'm gonna join the WWF.' They didn't believe me," Hauray explains. Overnight things changed. The fans of Montreal wrestling woke up one Sunday morning in December '84, tuned in and watched the *Superstars of Wrestling* — with wrestlers from the World Wrestling Federation — while the duo of Hauray and Carpentier still commentated. The enterprise register shows that Hauray and the WWF were in talks since October 1984. It was the Quebec version of Black Saturday.

International Wrestling went back to the Trois-Rivières and CFCF channels to compete with the WWF, which didn't record its programs in a studio. CFCF had previously changed the time slot for International Wrestling in March 1984, because it started broadcasting the WWF on Saturdays at noon. The war had started, and the last big Montreal promotion was fighting a

THE DYING DAYS OF INTERNATIONAL WRESTLING TV:
ALBERT DIFRUSCIA, BRUISER BRODY AND FLOYD CREATCHMAN (LINDA BOUCHER)

losing battle. "The TV channels were compelling us to improve the quality of our product, to make it like the WWF programs," explains Rick Martel. "It quickly became beyond our means." The promotion would actually have many different commentators, including Avruskin, Gino Brito, CFCF sports commentator Ron Francis and Floyd Creatchman. Since International Wrestling closed in 1987, no other wrestling promotion in Montreal has had a television contract with an important distributor.

After having joined the WWF Guy Hauray became Vince McMahon's right-hand man for Francophone TV. He was actually nominated vice president of the European operations. His company, Poly-Spec Tele Video, had the rights for the Francophone world and exported this product to Europe and Africa, recording the comments in the DGP studios in Laval. As far as Montreal was concerned wrestling was so popular that a second program was to be produced for Montreal on the sports cable channel TVSQ, the predecessor of RDS. An extra touch was to be added to the program through a number of segments like "Lutte Express," "Le Brunch du Rêve du Québec" and "Le Studio" with Frenchy Martin. In 1987 Stan Marshall presented the NWA in French on TQS. Leo Burke, the wrestler from the Maritimes and former booker of International Wrestling, was the analyst. "Stan Marshall called me and asked me to serve as a heel commentator," remembers Burke. "I had the right accent to make myself hated," he added. Raymonde Gagnier, a comedian from Quebec City, was the first woman to take part in a wrestling program in the province as the person who bridged the different segments. "It was really fun for us . . . but it only lasted one year. Leo Burke was very nice and as meek as a lamb! I used to sit on a stool much lower than his for him to appear taller," she recalls. "The NWA wanted to test the market with the ratings," Burke explains. But the NWA never wound up presenting shows in the province. André Belisle, who succeeded Hauray as commentator for International Wrestling, had to abandon his position when the Quebec Nordiques asked him to make a choice. According to the Nordiques it didn't look good for the voice of a National Hockey League team to present wrestling programs. Someone must've forgotten to pass on the message to Michel Normandin!

Periodically TSN presented the AWA and Stampede Wrestling to fans in the province, but the WWF would end up monopolizing everything. Even TVA got involved in wrestling again in 1988, more than 10 years after the end of *Sur le Matelas*, presenting the WWF on Saturdays at four p.m. The famous *Saturday Night's Main Event* was presented simultaneously on TVA three times, including the *Main Event* of February 5, 1988, where Andre the Giant won the belt away from Hulk Hogan in what is still considered the most-watched wrestling program in the history of American television. "I was with Vince, Dick Ebersol, 'Mean' Gene, Hulk and the Giant," Marc Blondin recalls, as the latter had joined the Francophone television team and participated in the events. "I was the only outsider." Involved with the CKOI radio station in the promotion of the WWF shows at the Forum, Marc Blondin started off as a ring announcer at the Forum. "I went to see Guy Hauray and told him: 'If you're looking for a ring announcer, I know a good one. Me!" he remembers, laughing. Guy Hauray says that he was a logical choice. "Marc was perfect for the interviews. He's short compared to the wrestlers and he had an excellent voice and was perfectly bilingual." From then on Blondin would be part of the commentators' team with Guy Hauray and Frenchy Martin.

Wrestling worked so well for TVA that the headlines in *Le Journal de Montréal* said TVA beat Radio-Canada, thanks to presenting a match between Hogan and Andre the Giant. The results of the BBM ratings even credit wrestling with the success of the programs that preceded and fol-

MARC BLONDIN INTERVIEWS ANDRE THE GIANT AND FRENCHY MARTIN IN FRANCE

(MARC BLONDIN COLLECTION)

lowed the WWF, as the latter drew an audience numbering 815,000 spectators, beating *Hockey Night in Canada*, which drew 807,000 that particular week. But what looked like a harmonious and promising relationship would quickly crumble. Vincent Gabriele, vice president of programming, left TVA. Unfortunately his successor wouldn't look at wrestling as favourably, especially when a school board accused TVA of promoting violence in the school's yard, a story that sparked a lot of discussion. As the WWF's agreement with TVA came to an end, neither party wanted to renew. Therefore WWF was broadcast on TQS in 1989.

In 1990 the WWF made its debut on RDS. Raymond Rougeau joined Guy Hauray behind the camera as the successor of Édouard Carpentier, who had been back for a while after a year-long suspension. Rougeau also put an end to Marc Blondin's WWF adventure. "In wrestling there's a hierarchy. Wrestlers come first, they precede non-wrestlers," says Marc Blondin, philosophically. Raymond conducted the interviews effectively and his status as a former wrestler would allow him to participate in the WWF Anglophone programs, as well. In 1994 Guy Hauray gave his notice; he didn't want to travel to record the programs in the Stamford studios, as the WWF was centralizing its TV operations. So Raymond Rougeau continued with a new partner, Jean Brassard. The latter was a French actor established in the U.S. who would be featured in many American television series after his work with the WWF, including *Sex and the City*, *The Sopranos* and *Law & Order*. Those who watched wrestling at the time certainly remember Brassard's sometimes questionable translations. In spite of the excellent work that Raymond Rougeau did, the duo would never succeed in captivating the Francophone audience, and the WWF would lose its contracts in France in the mid-1990s. The WWF mainly fell back on its English contracts on TSN to promote its shows in Montreal, and in 1998 the WWF would leave Francophone TV channels in Montreal for good.

In 1990 TSN presented the last version of Stampede Wrestling, starring Chris Benoit, Konnan, Davy Boy Smith, Owen Hart and Larry Cameron. Being a twin channel of TSN, RDS presented a shorter version translated into French with Olympic wrestler Renaud Coté as a commentator. In 1991, and for two more years, Marc Blondin made a return to wrestling beside the former star of International Wrestling, Richard Charland. This time they presented a 30-minute translated version of the *WCW Power Hour*. "We had good ratings. Richard and I went on tours together. We knew it from the people's reaction," says Blondin.

In the mid- and late 1990s, the Monday Night War raged between the WWF and the WCW. This was enough to make people interested in presenting wrestling again on Montreal television, this time on PPV. Raymond Rougeau and Jean Brassard presented the WWF PPVs on Indigo Channel and it was again broadcast in France. Being Ted Turner's personal coach, Guy Hauray was invited to create a European pilot for WCW, which he recorded with Édouard Carpentier. "I wasn't interested in confronting Vince — it was an uneasy deal for me. I actually refused to launch a wrestling promotion in France with Canal Plus, because I knew what competing with McMahon implies," holds Hauray. Marc Blondin then tried for a second run with WCW. "During one of his shows Jacques Rougeau told me: 'You have to call Sharon Sidello of WCW. She's looking for someone for international television,'" remembers Marc Blondin, who was Jacques's ring announcer.

As the program mainly targeted the international market, Blondin chose Michel Letourneur to help him. They represented WCW in the province when it was broadcast on RDS. Surprisingly the program only stopped airing a couple of months after the WWF bought WCW — the WWF clearly hadn't realized that the program was still on the air.

Marc Blondin wasn't at the end of the road yet. RDS asked him to be commentator for TNA in 2005, when a shortened version of *TNA Impact* was presented. Michel Letourneur, Pierre-Carl Ouellet and Sylvain Grenier succeeded one another by his side. It should also be noted that Jean-François Kelly, who presents the Quebec promotion news in a short segment on that broadcast, represents the only TV exposure Montreal indy wrestling has. The show gave Blondin the opportunity to be the local promoter for a TNA tour in Quebec in 2011. The program entered its seventh year in 2012 making Blondin second only to Carpentier as the longest running wrestling commentators in Montreal TV history.

CONCLUSION

THE LAST EMPERORS: DINO BRAVO, FRANK VALOIS AND GINO BRITO (LINDA BOUCHER)

QUEBEC, PROFESSIONAL WRESTLING 1867–1987

In Montreal, on June 23, 1987, at the age of 120, professional wrestling in the province of Quebec died.

Mourners of the deceased included its promoters, the late George Kennedy, Eddie Quinn, Johnny Rougeau, Bob Langevin and Frank Valois, as well as Paul Vachon and Gino Brito; its wrestlers, the late Eugene Tremblay,

Yvon Robert, Larry Moquin, Dino Bravo, Jos Leduc, Little Beaver and Sky Low Low, as well as Maurice Vachon, Jacques Rougeau Sr., Rick Martel, Jacques Rougeau Jr., Ronnie Garvin, Raymond Rougeau, Pat Patterson, Paul Leduc, Pierre-Carl Ouellet; and many other promoters, referees, managers, staff and wrestlers — as well as thousands of fans. The family will receive your condolences through its website, www.quebecwrestling.ca.

If this is only a spoof of a eulogy, Réjean Tremblay, then a journalist at *La Presse*, was the one who was asking the right question in the late 1980s, as the popularity of the WWF product was starting to decline: "But when Titan Sports squeezes the lemon to its last drop, what's going to happen?" The answer to this question — 20 years later — is disastrous. "We didn't like the WWF at first. We had a good thing going with International Wrestling. But in the end, we could not compete with such a big machine. So if you can't beat them, join them," Dino Bravo explained in 1989. "I should have closed down the office one year before, instead of wanting to defy Vince," adds Gino Brito.

The Montreal territory, which was, for a generation, one of the most important in the world, is barely interested in PPV events today. WWE itself has a hard time even generating publicity in Montreal. The absence of WWE on French TV for so many years is partly responsible, as is the fact that no one from Quebec is on the regular WWE roster right now. The lack of a bona fide current superstar of the Hogan, The Rock or Austin's stature is another reason for the state of affairs.

But Montreal will always be remembered as a beloved wrestling city.

"Montreal has been very important for me. At the time it was the best wrestling city in North America. The best wrestlers came in and fans were lucky like nowhere else," said Buddy Rogers in April 1983.

In 2012, JBL had similar words: "Montreal was always one of the best cities in the World. Unbelievable rabid sports fans. One place we liked in Canada was Montreal. Calgary had always a good crowd, Toronto was always pretty good, but Montreal was always really hot."

Even Gino Brito, who spent his whole life in this business and at one point lost every penny he owned, feels nostalgic about the state of pro wrestling in Montreal. "I'm 71 years old and I still miss wrestling every day," he says.

For a whole generation of wrestlers and fans, International Wrestling represented the last golden age of Montreal wrestling. "Wrestling in Quebec died 22 years ago," a magazine article published in *Dernière Heure* in 2010 argued. Hockey fans still remember 1995 and the departure of the Nordiques. Baseball fans still remember 2004 and the departure of the Expos. Fans of the Montreal territory will always remember 1987 as the year they lost wrestling.

From Michel Normandin to Marc Blondin, through Jean-Jacques Fortin, Édouard Carpentier and Raymond Rougeau, the end of a wrestling match was always synonymous with the famous and universal "One, two and three." But we can't finish a book on the history of Montreal wrestling with a simple pinfall.

Doris Lussier, a well-known comedian in Montreal, said upon the death of his friend Johnny Rougeau that "The death of a man is not the end of a mortal being, but, rather, the beginning of an immortal one." Professional wrestling in Montreal, through its mad dogs, midgets and screw jobs, had a complete and full life of more than a century. Even if it breathes less and less, it still tries to get a second chance at life. But, for so many people, wrestling in Montreal simply died, and if this is really its destiny we hope this book will be the beginning of its immortality.

Pat Laprade
Bertrand Hébert
February 2013

First of all, here is the list of the 46 members of the selection committee:

Al Campbell, promoter

André Rousseau, journalist

André Smith, wrestler

Armand Rougeau, wrestler

Bertrand Hébert, historian

Claude Leduc, Internet journalist

Claude Provost, promoter

Claude Tousignant,
    Internet journalist

Deepak Massand, manager

Denis Archambault, journalist

Dick Beyer, wrestler

Gino Brito Jr., wrestler

Éric Salottolo, promoter

Frank Blues, wrestler

Gino Brito Sr., wrestler

Greg Oliver, journalist

Guy Émond, journalist

Guy Laprade, fan

Jacques Comptois, wrestler

Jacques Rougeau Sr., wrestler

Jean-François Kelly, columnist

Jean-Paul Sarault, journalist

Joël Racine, booker

Louis Laurence, wrestler

Luc Charbonneau, fan

LuFisto, wrestler

Marc Blondin, presenter

Maxime Lanciault, wrestler

Michael Ryan, publicist

Nelson Veilleux, wrestler

Nicolas Brouillette, wrestler

Patric Laprade, historian

Patrick Lono, booker

Paul Leduc, wrestler

Paul Vachon, wrestler

Philippe Leclair, booker

Pierre-Carl Ouellet, wrestler

Raymond Rougeau, wrestler

Réjean Désaulniers, promoter

Sunny War Cloud, wrestler

Serge Jodoin, wrestler

Serge Proulx, wrestler

Serge Rochon, wrestler

Steve Charette, wrestler

Vance Nevada, historian

Yves Leroux, journalist

In 2008, each person sent a list of their best 25 wrestlers of all time. Only wrestlers born in the province were eligible. Then a grading system was created, giving a number of points to each position. The first position was worth 30 points; the second, 27; the third, 24; the fourth 21; the fifth,

20; the sixth, 19; and so on and so forth. The 25th position didn't receive any points, and all the wrestlers who weren't on the list of a committee member lost one point. Some positions were highly contested, as 48 points separated the sixth and ninth positions, and only nine points separated the 25th and 28th positions. Don't forget that this ranking represents what the 46 people who participated in it think is the reality. Had another 46 people done the same exercise, the results would have been different. You'll agree with some of the choices and disagree with others; this is absolutely normal. No ranking, no matter what the field may be, is unanimous. However it's very representative of the Quebec wrestlers who distinguished themselves throughout the years. On the right side of the name, you will find the number of points accumulated by the wrestler in question. So, without further ado, here are the best 25 Quebec wrestlers of all time.

1	Yvon Robert	1,191	14	Michel "Justice" Dubois	362
2	Maurice "Mad Dog" Vachon	1,036	15	Hans Schmidt	335
			16	Tarzan "La Bottine" Tyler	332
3	Rick Martel	908	17	Pierre-Carl Ouellet	329
4	Johnny Rougeau	889	18	Bob "Legs" Langevin	306
5	Dino Bravo	721	19	Larry Moquin	289
6	Pat Patterson	647	20	Pierre "Mad Dog" Lefebvre	257
7	Jos Leduc	616			
8	Jacques Rougeau Sr.	611	21	Frenchy Martin	216
9	Raymond Rougeau	599	22	Sky Low Low	208
10	Jacques Rougeau Jr.	561	23	Paul Leduc	171
11	Gino Brito Sr.	511	24	Stan Stasiak	150
12	Ronnie Garvin	489	25	Paul "The Butcher" Vachon	113
13	Little Beaver	483			

Yvon Robert reigns supreme for the first position with 29 votes. Rick Martel comes second with six votes, followed by Mad Dog Vachon with three votes. Six other wrestlers received a vote for the first position. Finally, as a bonus, here are the next 10 wrestlers, from position 26 to position 35. Note the only female presence in this ranking.

YVON ROBERT, WITHOUT A DOUBT THE GREATEST OF ALL TIME! (SCOTT TEAL COLLECTION)

THE BEST QUEBEC-BORN TAG TEAMS OF ALL TIME

"The wrestling tag team championship is the prerogative of Rudy and Emil Dusek, who, in addition to having gotten this titles last night at the Forum, have treated about 12,000 spectators to an impressive rendition of Brotherly Act. After a short match that necessitated three falls, Nebraska's tough athletes scored a victory over Yvon Robert and Larry Moquin in the first performance of tag team wrestling organized at the Forum."

These lines were written by Horace Lavigne in the April 26, 1945, edition of La Patrie, summing up the very first tag team match at the Montreal Forum. Even if tag team wrestling in Montreal started on November 18, 1937, in a show at the Maisonneuve Market presented by Sylvio Samson, the Forum hadn't yet witnessed this novelty. It's not surprising to find the Dusek brothers there, a team that went around the world, as well as the two most popular wrestlers at the time, Yvon Robert and his protégé, Larry Moquin, on the other side.

Tag team matches were to be subsequently always popular in the Montreal territory. One of the reasons behind this popularity is certainly the quality of the teams who worked on the Quebec scene over the years. Indeed the biggest feud in the history of the province pits two teams of Quebec wrestlers against each other, the Vachon brothers and the Leduc brothers. But which was the best team made up solely of Quebec wrestlers? The Vachons? The Leducs? The Rougeaus?

We've asked 12 people to come up with their own ranking of the 10 best teams. The ranking scoring system is very similar to the one used for the best 25 wrestlers of all time. Bearing in mind the purpose of the exercise, Quebec wrestlers who teamed with a partner from outside the province weren't eligible.

Here are the members of the committee:
Nicolas Brouillette (booker), Gary Howard (historian), Greg Oliver (journalist), Luc Charbonneau (fan), Pat Laprade (historian), François Poirier

(wrestler), Steve Charette (promoter), Patrick Lono (booker), Michael Ryan (publicist), Bertrand Hébert (historian), Vance Nevada (historian) and Claude Tousignant (Internet journalist).

1 Jacques and Raymond Rougeau
2 Maurice "Mad Dog" and Paul "The Butcher" Vachon
3 The Quebecers: Jacques Rougeau and Pierre-Carl Ouellet
4 Jos and Paul Leduc
5 Pierre Lefebvre and Michel Dubois/Pat Patterson/Frenchy Martin
6 Ronnie and Terry Garvin
7 Gino Brito and Dino Bravo
8 Frenchy Martin and Michel Martel
9 Kevin Steen and El Generico
10 Dino Bravo and Rick Martel

Following the vote for this ranking, in which Lefebvre was ranked separately with his partners, he ranked sixth, eighth and 11th. Given the peculiarity of the situation, the three teams were brought together to facilitate the ranking with, of course, Lefebvre as a common denominator. Surprised at the Steen and El Generico ranking? You mustn't be. Even if Kevin Steen and El Generico were part of the indy era of wrestling in Montreal and even if they had never performed in the WWE or TNA, they definitely secured a spot in the ranking by being one of the best tag teams in the world over the past few years.

Danno O'Mahoney	Montreal, QC	03-07-36

O'Mahoney beats Ed Don George on July 30, 1935, in Boston, MA, and wins the American Wrestling Association world title. On July 3, 1936, the Montreal Athletic Commission recognizes him as its first champion.

Yvon Robert	Montreal, QC	16-07-36
Vic Christie	Toronto, ON	03-03-38
Masked Marvel (Ted "King Kong" Cox)	Toronto, ON	09-06-38
Yvon Robert (2)	Montreal, QC	14-09-38
Cy Williams	Montreal, QC	19-12-38
Vacant	Montreal, QC	10-08-39

Williams loses his title as the Montreal Athletic Commission didn't hear from him upon the restart of the wrestling shows.

Ernie Dusek	Montreal, QC	10-08-39

Dusek defeats Danno O'Mahoney in the main event of the tournament on August 8, 1939.

Yvon Robert (3)	Montreal, QC	03-10-39
Joe Cox	Montreal, QC	27-02-40
Maurice Tillet	Montreal, QC	22-05-40

Leo Numa beats Cox in Quebec City on May 20, 1939, following the latter's disqualification, but the title change isn't recognized by the Montreal Athletic Commission, which claims that the Quebec City Athletic Commission didn't consult them prior to taking the decision.

Leo Numa	Montreal, QC	28-05-40

The Montreal Athletic Commission finally recognizes the decision taken by the Quebec City Commission, after having received an official report from the latter.

Lou Thesz	Montreal, QC	12-06-40

Yvon Robert (4)	Montreal, QC	23-10-40
Lou Thesz (2)	Montreal, QC	16-07-41
Yvon Robert (5)	Montreal, QC	17-09-41
Bill Longson	Montreal, QC	19-08-42
Yvon Robert (6)	Montreal, QC	12-05-43
Bobby Managoff	Montreal, QC	07-10-42

Managoff beats Robert on November 27, 1942, in Houston, Texas, and wins the NWA title, but the Montreal Athletic Commission, as well as the AWA, recognizes the switch on this date, saying that the match was bona fide for the world championship.

Yvon Robert (7)	Montreal, QC	15-09-43
Sandor Szabo	Boston, MA	22-03-44
Yvon Robert (8)	Montreal, QC	14-06-44
Frank Sexton	Montreal, QC	19-07-44
Yvon Robert (9)	Montreal, QC	23-08-44
Gino Garibaldi	Montreal, QC	01-11-44
Yvon Robert (10)	Montreal, QC	23-11-44
Joe Savoldi	Montreal, QC	04-07-45
Bobby Managoff (2)	Montreal, QC	12-09-45
Lou Thesz (3)	Montreal, QC	11-09-46
Bobby Managoff (3)	Ottawa, ON	20-02-47
Lou Thesz (4)	Montreal, QC	16-04-47
Yvon Robert (11)	Montreal, QC	26-11-47
Billy Watson	Ottawa, ON	21-04-49
Yvon Robert (12)	Montreal, QC	22-06-49
Bobby Managoff (4)	Montreal, QC	01-02-50
Yukon Eric	Montreal, QC	15-02-50
Bobby Managoff (5)	Montreal, QC	08-11-50
Buddy Rogers	Montreal, QC	09-05-51
Yvon Robert (13)	Montreal, QC	13-07-51
Vacant	Montreal, QC	14-01-52

Yvon Robert undergoes kidney surgery.

Killer Kowalski	Montreal, QC	02-04-52

Beats Bobby Managoff.

Verne Gagne	Montreal, QC	25-02-53
Killer Kowalski (2)	Montreal, QC	06-05-53
Yvon Robert (14)	Montreal, QC	15-07-53
Killer Kowalski (3)	Montreal, QC	19-08-53
Antonino Rocca	Montreal, QC	12-05-54
Killer Kowalski (4)	Montreal, QC	19-05-54
Pat O'Connor	Montreal, QC	21-07-54
Killer Kowalski (5)	Montreal, QC	10-11-54
Pat O'Connor (2)	Montreal, QC	09-03-55
Don Leo Jonathan	Montreal, QC	08-06-55
Yvon Robert (15)	Montreal, QC	17-08-55
Don Leo Jonathan (2)	Montreal, QC	24-08-55
Killer Kowalski (6)	Montreal, QC	14-12-55
Wilbur Snyder	Montreal, QC	14-03-56
Killer Kowalski (7)	Montreal, QC	04-04-56
Yvon Robert (16)	Quebec City, QC	13-04-56
Killer Kowalski (8)	Montreal, QC	30-05-56
Édouard Carpentier	Montreal, QC	15-08-56
Killer Kowalski (9)	Montreal, QC	26-09-56
Lou Thesz (5)	Montreal, QC	31-10-56
Killer Kowalski (10)	Montreal, QC	07-11-56
Édouard Carpentier (2)	Montreal, QC	08-05-57
Gene Kiniski	Montreal, QC	12-06-57
Killer Kowalski (11)	Montreal, QC	17-07-57
Buddy Rogers (2)	Montreal, QC	16-09-59
Killer Kowalski (12)	Montreal, QC	02-12-59
Buddy Rogers (3)	Montreal, QC	13-01-60
Killer Kowalski (13)	Montreal, QC	08-06-60
Édouard Carpentier (3)	Montreal, QC	21-09-60
Hans Schmidt	Montreal, QC	20-07-61
Johnny Rougeau	Ottawa, ON	07-11-61
Killer Kowalski (14)	Montreal, QC	23-07-62
Édouard Carpentier (4)	Montreal, QC	30-01-63
Vacant	Montreal, QC	30-09-65

THE MONTREAL CHAMPION BILL LONGSON WITH RAY STEELE IN THE DRESSING ROOMS AT THE FORUM

The Montreal Athletic Commission revokes the title from Carpentier as he didn't defend it in the previous year.

Hans Schmidt (2)	Montreal, QC	30-09-65

Defeats Sailor Thomas in a tournament final.

Johnny Rougeau (2)	Montreal, QC	18-11-65
Hans Schmidt (3)		66

Defeats Johnny Rougeau or the title is simply given to him, most probably on the first TV tapings, between January and June 1966.

Édouard Carpentier (5)	Quebec City, QC	07-06-66
Hans Schmidt (4)	Chicoutimi, QC	06-07-66
Édouard Carpentier (6)	Montreal, QC	03-10-66
Hans Schmidt (5)	Quebec City, QC	16-11-66
Mad Dog Vachon	Chicoutimi, QC	24-01-67
Johnny Rougeau (3)	Montreal, QC	05-06-67
Mad Dog Vachon (2)	Montreal, QC	14-08-67
Vacant	Montreal, QC	24-08-67

Vachon is injured due to a car accident in Quebec City.

The Sheik	Montreal, QC	23-10-67

Beats Gino Brito in a tournament final.

Édouard Carpentier (7)	Montreal, QC	06-11-67
Baron von Raschke	Montreal, QC	27-11-67
Johnny Rougeau (4)	Montreal, QC	05-02-68
Ivan Koloff	Quebec City, QC	23-05-69
Abdullah the Butcher	Montreal, QC	14-07-69
Jacques Rougeau	Montreal, QC	11-08-69
Abdullah the Butcher (2)	Montreal, QC	24-11-69
Johnny Rougeau (5)	Montreal, QC	30-03-70
Danny Lynch	Montreal, QC	19-10-70
Johnny Rougeau (6)	Montreal, QC	07-12-70
Jos Leduc	Montreal, QC	26-04-71
Mr. X/Tarzan Zorra	Montreal, QC	21-06-71
Abdullah the Butcher (3)	Montreal, QC	30-08-71
Carlos Rocha	Montreal, QC	27-12-71
The Sheik (2)	Montreal, QC	15-05-72
Jacques Rougeau (2)	Montreal, QC	17-07-72
Johnny Valentine	Montreal, QC	27-11-72
Vacant	Montreal, QC	08-01-73

Valentine doesn't show up for the title defence against Jacques Rougeau, and the title is declared vacant.

Jacques Rougeau (3)	Montreal, QC	08-01-73

The title is given to Rougeau.

Vacant	Montreal, QC	12-02-73

	The title is declared vacant following a no-contest between Rougeau and Waldo Von Erich.	
Jacques Rougeau (4)	Montreal, QC	19-02-73
	Rougeau beats Von Erich.	
Dick Taylor	Montreal, QC	07-05-73
Jacques Rougeau (5)	Montreal, QC	30-07-73
	Taylor doesn't show up, and the title is given to Rougeau.	
Michel Dubois	Montreal, QC	24-09-73
The Sheik (3)	Montreal, QC	03-12-73
Vacant	Montreal, QC	28-01-74
	The Montreal Athletic Commission revokes The Sheik's title.	
Tiger Jeet Singh	Montreal, QC	04-03-74
	Beats Jacques Rougeau.	
Vacant	Montreal, QC	18-07-74
	Singh doesn't show up to defend his title on July 15, 1974, against Mad Dog Vachon.	
Abdullah the Butcher (4)	Montreal, QC	22-07-74
	Beats Tarzan Tyler in a tournament final.	
Jacques Rougeau (6)	Montreal, QC	11-09-74
Tarzan Tyler	Montreal, QC	04-11-74
Jacques Rougeau (7)	Montreal, QC	13-01-75
Tarzan Tyler (2)	Montreal, QC	31-03-75
Johnny Rougeau (7)	Montreal, QC	03-09-75
Stan Stasiak	Montreal, QC	27-10-75
Jacques Rougeau (8)	Montreal, QC	01-12-75
Serge Dumont	Montreal, QC	08-03-76
Billy Two Rivers	Verdun, QC	03-08-76
Sailor White	Montreal, QC	11-10-76
Carlos Rocha (2)	Montreal, QC	29-11-76
Johnny Valiant	Montreal, QC	01-07-77
	The title is given to Valiant by the management. It is announced that Valiant beat Rocha in a match that took place in Winnipeg, MB, but, in fact, it was a phantom switch as Rocha didn't come back to defend the title.	

Dominic Denucci	Montreal, QC	04-07-77
Waldo Von Erich	Montreal, QC	26-09-77
Vacant	Montreal, QC	10-10-77

The Montreal Athletic Commission revokes Von Erich's title.

Spiros Arion	Montreal, QC	07-11-77

Beats Waldo Von Erich.

Tarzan Tyler (3)	Montreal, QC	12-01-78

The title is given to Tyler by the management. It is announced that Tyler beat Arion in a match in Hamilton, ON, but, in fact, it was a phantom switch as Arion didn't come back to defend his title.

Gino Brito	Montreal, QC	27-02-78
Tarzan Tyler (4)	Verdun, QC	26-09-78
Gino Brito (2)	Montreal, QC	05-02-79
Michel Dubois (2)	Montreal, QC	30-04-79
Vacant	Montreal, QC	14-05-79

Dubois doesn't show up to defend his title against Raymond Rougeau. The title is declared vacant.

Édouard Carpentier (8)	Montreal, QC	03-09-79

Beats Michel Dubois.

Pierre Lefebvre	Montreal, QC	11-08-80
Édouard Carpentier (9)	Montreal, QC	18-08-80

Carpentier refuses the title because Andre the Giant helped him.

Vacant	Montreal, QC	18-08-80

Promoter Frank Valois declares the title vacant.

Pierre Lefebvre (2)	Montreal, QC	01-09-80

Beats Carpentier.

Rick Martel	Montreal, QC	03-11-80
Michel Dubois (3)	Montreal, QC	12-01-81

Martel doesn't show up for the match, and the title is given to Dubois.

Dino Bravo	Montreal, QC	16-03-81
Vacant	Montreal, QC	26-07-82

Bravo is suspended because of having hit referee Yvon Robert Jr. in his match against Abdullah the Butcher at the Montreal Forum.

Billy Robinson	Montreal, QC	16-08-82
	Beats Rick Martel in a tournament final.	
Dino Bravo (2)	Montreal, QC	07-03-83
King Tonga	Hull, QC	09-10-84
Dino Bravo (3)	Montreal, QC	11-02-85
Vacant	Montreal, QC	11-02-85
	Bravo refuses the title because he won by disqualification.	
Dino Bravo (4)	Hull, QC	28-05-85
	Defeats King Tonga in a cage match.	
The Great Samu	Montreal, QC	30-06-86
Vacant	Montreal, QC	27-10-86
	Samu doesn't show up to defend his title.	
David Schultz	Montreal, QC	27-10-86
	Beats "Big" John.	
Vacant	Montreal, QC	29-12-86
	Schultz leaves the promotion.	
Abdullah the Butcher (5)	Montreal, QC	15-02-87
	Defeats Hercules Ayala.	
Promotion closes	Montreal, QC	30-06-87
	With the closing down of International Wrestling, the title would never be recognized again.	

THE HISTORY OF THE MONTREAL WOMEN'S TITLE

Kacey Diamond   Montreal, QC   10-11-06

Beats Stefany Sinclair, Sweet Cherrie and Julie Red Fuxxx in a tournament final.

Stefany Sinclair   Montreal, QC   16-03-07

La Parfaite Caroline   Montreal, QC   09-11-07

Vacant   Montreal, QC   12-09-08

Caroline got injured.

LuFisto   Montreal, QC   12-09-08

Beats Kacey Diamond.

Vacant   Montreal, QC   09-02-09

The ALF promotion closes down.

MsChif   Montreal, QC   05-09-09

SHIMMER champion is recognized by the NCW Femmes Fatales promotion.

Madison Eagles   Berwyn, IL   11-04-10

Vacant   Montreal, QC   05-06-10

NCW Femmes Fatales starts a tournament to crown its first champion.

LuFisto (2)   Montreal, QC   23-10-10

Beats Portia Perez in a tournament final.

Kalamity   Montreal, QC   08-10-11

In 2004 the very first Quebec Wrestling Hall of Fame was created in the province, paying tribute to the artists who excelled in entertaining Quebecers and offered awesome performances. Relying on a selection committee which consists of former professional wrestlers and journalists, as well as people who know the history of Quebec wrestling very well, this committee has to vote on new wrestlers to be inducted into the hall each year in two categories, namely Quebec-born wrestlers and wrestlers born abroad, commonly referred to as non-Quebecers. Here is the list of the wrestlers who were inducted into the Hall of Fame over the last seven years.

2004

Dino Bravo	Jacques Rougeau Sr.	Paul Leduc
Rick Martel	Jacques Rougeau Jr.	Gino Brito
Yvon Robert	Johnny Rougeau	Tarzan Tyler
Eddy Creatchman	Raymond Rougeau	Little Beaver
Mad Dog Vachon	Ronnie Garvin	
Pat Patterson	Jos Leduc	

2005

Abdullah the Butcher	Édouard Carpentier	Jean Ferré

2006

Bob Langevin	Don Leo Jonathan	Killer Kowalski
Hans Schmidt		

2007

Michel Dubois

Paul Vachon

Frenchy Martin

Pierre Lefebvre

Buddy Rogers

Lou Thesz

2008

Sky Low Low

2009

Eddie Quinn

Hulk Hogan

Vivian Vachon

Pat Girard

2010

Michel Normandin

Frank Valois

Ivan Koloff

2011

Larry Moquin

The Sheik

QUEBEC STATISTICS

Here is a table listing the 50 biggest crowds in the history of Quebec wrestling. The wrestlers listed below are those who main-evented the show in question or who were the draw behind that crowd.

DATE	ATTEND.	WRESTLER[S]	WRESTLER[S]	CITY	VENUE	PROMOTION
07/14/73	29,127	Killer Kowalski	Mad Dog Vachon	Montreal	Jarry Park Stadium	GP
07/17/72	26,237	Johnny Rougeau	Abdullah the Butcher	Montreal	Jarry Park Stadium	AS
07/18/56	23,227	Édouard Carpentier	Argentina Rocca	Montreal	Delorimier Stadium	QUINN
07/17/57	21,851	Killer Kowalski	Gene Kiniski	Montreal	Delorimier Stadium	QUINN
08/18/86	21,700	Hulk Hogan	Don Muraco	Montreal	Montreal Forum	WWF
08/18/54	21,616	Pat O'Connor	Yvon Robert	Montreal	Delorimier Stadium	QUINN
08/26/85	21,500	Jacques & Raymond Rougeau	Ronnie & Jimmy Garvin	Montreal	Montreal Forum	WWF/IW
08/15/56	21,454	Édouard Carpentier	Killer Kowalski	Montreal	Delorimier Stadium	QUINN
11/11/68	20,890	Johnny Rougeau	Ivan Koloff	Montreal	Montreal Forum	AS
07/20/61	20,743	Édouard Carpentier	Hans Schmidt	Montreal	Delorimier Stadium	QUINN
11/09/97	20,593	Bret Hart	Shawn Michaels	Montreal	Molson Centre	WWF
08/14/50	20,461	Yvon Robert	Yukon Eric	Montreal	Delorimier Stadium	QUINN

08/02/72	20,347	Don Leo Jonathan	Jean Ferré	Montreal	Montreal Forum	GP
07/15/53	20,341	Yvon Robert	Killer Kowalski	Montreal	Delorimier Stadium	QUINN
01/09/87	20,302	Randy Savage	Ricky Steamboat	Montreal	Montreal Forum	WWF
08/08/56	20,139	Édouard Carpentier	Killer Kowalski	Montreal	Delorimier Stadium	QUINN
08/07/57	20,000	Killer Kowalski	Édouard Carpentier	Montreal	Delorimier Stadium	QUINN
07/30/73	20,000	Jacques Rougeau	Dick Taylor	Montreal	Montreal Forum	AS
08/26/58	19,548	Killer Kowalski	Claude Dassary	Montreal	Delorimier Stadium	QUINN
12/23/84	19,500	Dino Bravo	King Tonga	Montreal	Montreal Forum	IW
02/06/87	19,202	Randy Savage	Ricky Steamboat	Montreal	Montreal Forum	WWF
02/27/87	19,000	Hulk Hogan	Kamala	Montreal	Montreal Forum	WWF
10/14/85	18,997	Dino Bravo & King Tonga	Greg Valentine & Brutus Beefcake	Montreal	Montreal Forum	WWF/IW
08/17/55	18,972	Yvon Robert	Don Leo Jonathan	Montreal	Delorimier Stadium	QUINN
07/25/83	18,394	Raymond & Jacques Rougeau	Pierre Lefebvre & Pat Patterson	Montreal	Montreal Forum	IW
02/08/88	18,373	Hogan, Savage, Steamboat	Hart Foundation, Honky Tonk Man	Montreal	Montreal Forum	WWF
07/14/58	18,327	Killer Kowalski & Don Leo Jonathan	Ben & Mike Sharpe	Montreal	Delorimier Stadium	QUINN

08/19/53	18,223	Killer Kowalski	Yvon Robert	Montreal	Delorimier Stadium	QUINN
02/12/74	18,184	Don Leo Jonathan	Jacques Rougeau Sr.	Montreal	Montreal Forum	AS/GP
11/29/61	18,000	Antonino Rocca	Great Togo	Montreal	Montreal Forum	QUINN
03/14/88	18,000	Hulk Hogan & Bam Bam Bigelow	Andre the Giant and Ted DiBiase	Montreal	Montreal Forum	WWF
11/15/85	17,822	Andre the Giant	King Kong Bundy	Montreal	Montreal Forum	WWF/IW
07/29/85	17,502	Jacques & Raymond Rougeau	Ronnie & Jimmy Garvin	Montreal	Montreal Forum	IW
04/22/68	17,348	Johnny Rougeau	Ivan Koloff	Montreal	Montreal Forum	AS
03/10/89	17,340	Dino Bravo	Hulk Hogan	Montreal	Montreal Forum	WWF
02/24/86	17,300	Tito Santana	Randy Savage	Montreal	Montreal Forum	WWF
04/11/97	17,023	Jacques Rougeau Jr.	Hulk Hogan	Montreal	Molson Centre	ROUGEAU
08/14/72	17,008	Maurice & Paul Vachon	Jos & Paul Leduc	Quebec City	Colisée de Québec	GP
02/17/69	17,000	Johnny Rougeau	Abdullah the Butcher	Montreal	Montreal Forum	AS
10/21/94	16,843	Jacques Rougeau Jr.	Pierre-Carl Ouellet	Montreal	Montreal Forum	WWF
01/20/54	16,703	Killer Kowalski	Argentina Rocca	Montreal	Montreal Forum	QUINN
11/29/71	16,577	Abdullah the Butcher	Carlos Rocha	Montreal	Montreal Forum	AS
04/11/83	16,500	Jean Ferré	Ken Patera	Montreal	Montreal Forum	IW
01/04/88	16,308	Randy Savage	Honky Tonk Man	Montreal	Montreal Forum	WWF
06/24/85	16,271	Dino Bravo & King Tonga	Road Warriors	Montreal	Montreal Forum	IW

07/18/50	16,192	Yvon Robert	Yukon Eric	Montreal	Delorimier Stadium	QUINN
05/31/72	16,164	Jean Ferré	Don Leo Jonathan	Montreal	Montreal Forum	GP
01/14/53	16,042	Killer Kowalski	Yukon Eric	Montreal	Montreal Forum	QUINN
09/29/69	16,000	Jacques Rougeau	Ivan Koloff	Montreal	Montreal Forum	AS
09/21/83	16,000	Dino Bravo	Rick Martel	Quebec City	Colisée de Québec	IW

NORTH AMERICAN AND WORLDWIDE STATISTICS

Since 1900, if we take the biggest crowd recorded each year and check where the show was held, here are the statistics about the best wrestling cities.

NORTH AMERICAN

CITY	COUNTRY	#
New York City	U.S.	34
Montreal	Canada	15
Chicago	U.S.	10
Boston	U.S.	6
Los Angeles	U.S.	6
St. Louis	U.S.	6
Philly	U.S.	4
Toronto	Canada	4
Atlanta	U.S.	3
Kansas City	U.S.	3

WORLDWIDE

CITY	COUNTRY	#
New York City	U.S.	19
Tokyo	Japan	11
Mexico City	Mexico	9
Montreal	Canada	9
Chicago	U.S.	8
St. Louis	U.S.	5
Boston	U.S.	4
Athens	Greece	3
Kansas City	U.S.	3
Philadelphia	U.S.	3
Toronto	Canada	3

SELECTED SOURCES

Berthelet, Pierre. *Yvon Robert Le Lion du Canada Français*. Montreal: Editions Trustar, 1999.

Boesh, Paul. *Hey, Boy! Where'd You Get Them Ears?* Houston: Minuteman Press Southwest, 2002.

Brisco, Jack and William Murdoch. *Brisco*. Newton: Culture House Books, 2003.

Capouya, John. *Gorgeous George: The Outrageous Bad-Boy Wrestler Who Created American Pop Culture*. New York: HarperCollins, 2008.

Copeland, Adam. *Adam Copeland on Edge*. New York: Pocket Books, 2004.

Dillon, James J., Scott Teal and Phillip Varriale. *Wrestlers Are Like Seagulls: From McMahon to McMahon*. Hendersonville: Crowbar Press, 2005.

Duncan, Royal and Gary Will. *Wrestling Title Histories, Fourth Edition*. Waterloo: Archeus Communication, 2000.

Flair, Ric, Keith Elliot Greenberg and Mark Madden. *To Be the Man*. New York: Pocket Books, 2004.

Foley, Mick. *Have a Nice Day! A Tale of Blood and Sweatsocks*. New York: HarperCollins, 1999.

Funk, Terry and Scott E. Williams. *More than Just Hardcore*. Champaign: Sports Publishing L.L.C., 2005.

Giroux, Lionel and Jean Côté. *Un nain dans l'arène de la vie Little Beaver*. Montréal: Editions Québécor, 1979.

Griffin, Marcus. *Fall Guys: The Barnums of Bounce*. Reilly & Lee, 1937.

Hamilton, Joe and Scott Teal. *Assassin: The Man Behind the Mask*. Hendersonville: Crowbar Press, 2006.

Hart, Bret. *My Real Life in the Cartoon World of Wrestling*. Toronto: Random House Canada, 2007.

Hart, Gary and Phillip Varriale. *My Life in Wrestling with a Little Help From My Friends*. New York: Gean Publishing, 2009.

Heenan, Bobby and Steve Anderson. *Bobby the Brain: Wrestling's Bad Boy Tells All*. Chicago: Triumph Books, 2002.

Hogan, Hulk and Micheal Jan Friedman. *Hollywood Hulk Hogan*. New York: Pocket Books, 2002.

Hornbaker, Tim. *National Wrestling Alliance: The Untold Story of the Monopoly That Strangled Pro Wrestling*. Toronto: ECW Press, 2007.

Jericho, Chris and Peter Thomas Fornatale. *Undisputed: How to Become the World Champion in 1,372 Easy Steps*. New York: Grand Central Publishing, 2011.

Johnson, Dwayne and Joe Layden. *The Rock Says ...* New York: Harper Collins, 2000.

Koloff, Ivan and Scott Teal. *Is That Wrestling Fake? The Bear Facts*. Hendersonville: Crowbar Press, 2007.

Krugman, Michael. *Andre the Giant: A Legendary Life*. New York: Pocket Books, 2009.

Lévesque, Réjean and Kathy Paradis. *Hommage aux célèbres frères Baillargeon*. Cap-Saint-Ignace: Plume d'oie, 1997.

Lévesque, René. *Attendez que je me rappelle*. Montréal: Québec Amérique, 1986.

McCoy, Heath. *Pain and Passion: The History of Stampede Wrestling*. Toronto: CanWest Books, 2005.

Michaels, Shawn and Aaron Feigenbaum. *Heartbreak and Triumph: The Shawn Michaels Story*. New York: Pocket Books, 2005.

Molinaro, John F., Jeff Mareck and Dave Meltzer. *Top 100 Pro Wrestlers of All Time*. Toronto: Winding Stair Press, 2002.

Mysterio, Rey and Jeremy Roberts. *Behind the Mask*. New York: Pocket Books, 2009.

Ohl, Paul. *Louis Cyr: Une Épopée Légendaire*. Outremont: Libre Expression, 2004.

Oliver, Greg and Steven Johnson. *Pro Wrestling Hall of Fame: The Heels*. Toronto, ECW Press, 2007.

Oliver, Greg and Steven Johnson. *Pro Wrestling Hall of Fame: The Tag Teams*. Toronto, ECW Press, 2005.

Oliver, Greg. *Pro Wrestling Hall of Fame: The Canadians*. Toronto: ECW Press, 2003.

Piper, Roddy and Robert Picarello. *In the Pit with Piper*. New York: Berkley Boulevard Book, 2002.

Rhodes, Dusty and Howard Brody. *Reflections of an American Dream*. Champaign: Sports Publishing L.L.C., 2005.

Rougeau, Jean. *Johnny Rougeau*. Montréal: Éditions Québécor, 1982.

Santana, Tito and Tom Caiazzo. *Tales from the Ring*. Champaign: Sports Publishing L.L.C., 2008.

Sarrault, Jean-Paul. *Fais-le Saigner*. Montréal: Editions Logiques, 1993.

Sullivan, Kevin. *The WWE Championship: A Look Back at the Rich History of the WWE Championship*. New York: World Wrestling Entertainment, 2010.

Thesz, Lou and Kit Bauman. *Hooker: An Authentic Wrestler's Adventures Inside the Bizarre World of Professional Wrestling*. Norfolk: Lou Thesz, 1995.

Vachon, Maurice and Louis Chantigny. *Une vie de chien dans un monde de fous*. Montréal: Guérin Littérature, 1988.

Vachon, Paul. *The Rise and Fall of Grand Prix Wrestling*. Laval: Impressions Prioritaire, 2009.

ClubWWI.com
http://www.clubwwi.com/
SLAM! Wrestling
http://slam.canoe.ca/Slam/Wrestling/home.html
Kayfabe Memories
http://www.kayfabememories.com/
Online World of Wrestling
http://www.onlineworldofwrestling.com/
Gary Will website
http://www.garywill.com/wrestling/
Internet Wrestling Classics
http://www.wrestlingclassics.com/
Wrestling Title Histories
http://www.wrestling-titles.com/
History of WWE
http://www.thehistoryofwwe.com/
Wrestling Observer
http://www.f4wonline.com/
Mid-Atlantic Gateway
http://www.midatlanticgateway.com/
Maple Leaf Wrestling website
http://mapleleafwrestling.4t.com/canadianpage.html
The Dan Gable International Wrestling Institute and Museum
http://www.wrestlingmuseum.org/